School of American Research
Advanced Seminar Series

DOUGLAS W. SCHWARTZ, GENERAL EDITOR

SCHOOL OF AMERICAN RESEARCH
ADVANCED SEMINAR SERIES

The Origins of Maya Civilization

Advanced Seminars are made possible
by a gift in recognition of

Philip L. Shultz

for his efforts on behalf of
the School of American Research

THE ORIGINS OF MAYA CIVILIZATION

EDITED BY
RICHARD E. W. ADAMS

A SCHOOL OF AMERICAN RESEARCH BOOK

UNIVERSITY OF NEW MEXICO PRESS • Albuquerque

Library of Congress Cataloging in Publication Data

Main entry under title:

The Origins of Maya civilization.

    (School of American Research advanced seminar series)
"Seminar sponsored and supported by the School of
American Research held October 14-18, 1974, in Santa Fe."
    "A School of American Research book."
    Bibliography: p. 425.
    Includes index.
    1. Mayas—Antiquities—Congresses.   2. Indians of
Mexico—Antiquities—Congresses.   3. Indians of Central
America—Antiquities—Congresses.   4. Mexico—
Antiquities—Congresses.   5. Central America—Antiquities
—Congresses.   I. Adams, Richard E. W., 1931–
II. Santa Fe, N.M. School of American Research.
III. Series: Santa Fe, N.M. School of American
Research. Advanced seminar series.
F1435.075   972   76-57537
ISBN 0-8263-0441-9

To the memory of our esteemed colleague
J. Eric S. Thompson
(1898–1975)

Foreword

"The transition from Formative to Classic was surely gradual—a flowering after orderly growth, not a new crop." These words were written in 1954 by J. Eric S. Thompson, that great scholar of all things Mayan, and it is to him that this volume is dedicated. Yet the contrast between his conception of the rise of the Maya, really a begging of the question, and the systematic examination, analysis, and model building expressed in this volume is but one reflection of the progress of archaeology over the past quarter of a century.

In the history of Maya studies, it was first enough simply to discover and report the great temples and works of art. Then the challenge was one of placing these and other material obtained through excavation in a historical framework. Thompson's own important work, *The Rise and Fall of Maya Civilization,* had this descriptive and chronological orientation. He was concerned with the results of the rise and the fall, not the processes that led to them. Only in the past decade have the accumulation of sufficient data and the stimulus of new research orientations made it possible to move in another conceptual direction—toward examining the causes and dynamics of these changes.

The 1974 seminar reported in this volume represented an attempt to explain the appearance of Maya civilization. An introductory paper by Richard E. W. Adams and T. Patrick Culbert systematically approaches this problem, reviewing the past explanations and intellectual history of Maya studies and outlining several key questions. The next six chapters present data on the rise of Maya civilization in specific areas: Tikal (T. Patrick Culbert), Belize (Norman Hammond), Rio Bec (Richard E. W. Adams), the Northern Plains and Central Yucatan (Joseph W. Ball), the Pasión Valley (Gordon R. Willey), and the Northwest Zone (Robert L. Rands). Possible relationships and influences from outside the Maya area are then examined from the perspectives of Olmec (Michael D. Coe) and Mixe-Zoque (Gareth W. Lowe), and Jacinto Quirarte considers early Mayan art styles as a clue to Maya origins. In Part 4 of the volume, processes and models are the focus of discussions by William T. Sanders (emphasizing environmental considerations), Robert McC. Netting (looking at subsistence through the ethnographic analogy of the Nigerian Ibo), David L. Webster (stressing the role of warfare), and William L. Rathje (focusing on trade and Tikal).

For the book's concluding chapter Gordon Willey reviewed papers, transcripts of seminar discussions, and subsequent correspondence concerning revisions. On the basis of these he here examines and synthesizes, by period, the historical data and external influences bearing on the rise of the Maya; summarizes and interrelates the processes and models postulated earlier in the book; and finally presents an "overarching model" that attempts a consensus of seminar conclusions. The result is a quantum leap from Thompson's "flowering" image to an overview of the multitudinous elements, ranked in order of their importance, that contributed to the rise of this civilization, as well as an awareness of the gaps remaining in our understanding of Maya origins.

Douglas W. Schwartz

School of American Research

Preface

The origins of Maya civilization was the theme of an advanced seminar sponsored and supported by the School of American Research held October 14–18, 1974, in Santa Fe. Participation was wider than the group of eleven scholars who eventually attended. Those who actually came to Santa Fe were Richard E. W. Adams (Anthropology, The University of Texas at San Antonio); Joseph W. Ball (Department of Anthropology, San Diego State University); Michael D. Coe (Department of Anthropology, Yale University); T. Patrick Culbert (Department of Anthropology, University of Arizona); Gareth W. Lowe (New World Archaeological Foundation); Robert McC.Netting (Department of Anthropology, University of Arizona); Jacinto Quirarte (Fine Arts, The University of Texas at San Antonio); Robert L. Rands (Department of Anthropology, Southern Illinois University); William L. Rathje (Department of Anthropology, University of Arizona); William T. Sanders (Department of Anthropology, Pennsylvania State University); and Gordon R. Willey (Department of Anthropology, Harvard University). Papers were also provided by Norman Hammond (Centre of Latin American Studies, Cambridge University) and David L. Webster (Department of Anthropology, Pennsylvania State University). Demitri Shimkin was a reader of all of the papers prepared for the conference and his closely reasoned commentary and suggestions formed a valuable contribution and stimulus to the conference. We only regret that he could not attend.

As it developed, then, fifteen papers were prepared and circulated along with Shimkin's comments before the seminar met. T. Patrick Culbert, Gordon R. Willey, and I worked as an informal organization committee, and Willey served as moderator of the seminar as he had at the previous conference on the collapse of Maya civilization (Culbert 1973a).

A master chronology chart was needed for the final report, and Joseph W. Ball accepted the additional task of preparing it.

Willey, as moderator, each day summarized the data and debate of the preceding day's meetings. These summaries, Adams's complete notes, and limited transcriptions of part of the conference tapes were circulated to all of the conferees afterward as an aid to revision of papers. These undigested notes are not published herein. Willey assumed the task of preparing the summary paper on the major discussions and conclusions of the conference.

In the intellectual history of Maya studies, it is clear that the origins of Maya civilization have never been quite as fascinating to scholars as the collapse of that exotic florescence. For whatever reasons (and they probably have to do with the great amounts of recent research into the Preclassic elsewhere in Mesoamerica), it seemed to many that enough data had accumulated by the early 1970s to make a conference on the origins question worthwhile. Therefore, when Douglas Schwartz suggested the possibility in 1972, a number of us were cautiously enthusiastic. The situation was somewhat similar to that in 1970 when a lot of new data had been accumulated on the collapse by recent major projects. However, given the more intractable nature of the Preclassic data, and the relative lack of applicable theoretical formulations, I, for one, felt somewhat less confident of the outcome of a conference.

I believe that the seminar was quite successful, although it did not solve the questions of the origins. The reader will have to judge for himself how close we came to our objectives of defining the problem and applying the data, testing theoretical formulations, and attempting to develop a reconciling model that could act both as an explanatory device and as a guide to future research. These were our goals.

We are most grateful to Douglas Schwartz and his excellent staff for creating the congenial atmosphere within which the conference took place. All of us will especially and fondly recall Mrs. Ella Schroeder and the cheerful home she made for us during our brief stay. Mrs. Schwartz was equally hospitable and helpful. Miss Joy Willett, our excellent typist, prepared most of the manuscript in final copy. The University of Texas at San Antonio provided vast quantities of xeroxing and secretarial services, for which we are grateful.

As this manuscript goes to press, word comes to us of the death of our colleague and friend, J. Eric S. Thompson, at the age of 76. All of us have been stimulated and encouraged to a greater or lesser degree by this great scholar. We dedicate this volume to his memory.

Richard E. W. Adams

Contents

PART 1

Background

1

The Origins of Civilization in the Maya Lowlands

RICHARD E.W. ADAMS

The University of Texas at San Antonio

T. PATRICK CULBERT

University of Arizona

INTRODUCTION

The ultimate aim of this volume is the development of a model that may explain the appearance of Maya civilization. We will be examining the transformation of a variant of Mesoamerican Late Preclassic culture into a highly developed and complex form defined as civilization. To lay the groundwork for the chapters that follow, a working definition of civilization is sketched below, followed by a working definition of Maya culture before and after the transformation. The volume will also survey the regional varieties of Late Preclassic culture, the varieties of transformational processes, and the resultant variations of civilization.

This introductory chapter, written to provide a common base for the chapters that follow, deals pragmatically with definitional problems. It includes an interpretational definition of Maya Classic culture, sets geographical and areal limits, and offers a historical review of thinking on the subject. A short section examines the nature of the data that bear on the problem. Current and past theoretical explanations of the origins of Maya civilization are discussed in a longer section. The chapter ends with a list of problems considered by the contributors, both in their papers and in discussions at the 1974 seminar.

DEFINITIONS

Civilization, as we see it, consists of a highly integrated and elaborated sociopolitical structure which includes all the material and functional features of urban life. The famous ten criteria of V. Gordon Childe (1950) certainly constitute a definition of civilization, although the lack of one or more of the formal criteria does not necessarily drop the culture from the civilized category.[1] We may begin with a functional definition of civilization as urban (including the Maya ceremonial centers as urban centers). Without, at this point, getting into the extremely complex matters treated so well by R. McC. Adams (1966), Service (1970), and others, we can state that the Maya in the Central Zone seem to have reached the threshold of such civilized life by about the time of Christ. Certainly by A.D. 250 civilization is well under way.

A Definition of Maya Lowland Civilization

The specific defining features of Maya Lowland civilization are:
1. Material and archaeological:
a. Monumental architecture made of cut-stone masonry, held together by lime mortar, covered by stucco, and incorporating rooms that use the corbeled arch in roofing.
b. An art style defined by specific conventions of perspective, iconography, and thematic messages. Perspective is mainly flat and two-dimensional, although regional and Late Classic variations show experimentation with three-dimensional ideas, expressed in foreshortening and other techniques.

4

c. Expression of the art style mainly through bas-relief sculpture, mural painting, polychrome and surface-modified ceramics, modeled stucco decoration of architecture, and jewelers' products such as carved jades, Fabergé-style composite productions, carved bones, and antlers. There is indirect evidence of illustrated books and wood carvings in the same style.

d. A writing and calendrical system which varied through time and space, expressed together with and apart from the art style, and in all the forms in which that style is expressed.

e. Sumptuous and elaborate burials for a minority of the population.

f. The combination of all of these features into functional, highly patterned urban centers. The courtyard group, the basic unit, consists of buildings of various types facing inward on an enclosed, paved space. The majority of Maya centers are made up of physically linked and functionally complementary courtyard groups. The art style decorates the buildings and is also expressed on sculptured stone shafts, which are often found in the courtyards. The writing and calendrical systems are expressed in their most intense forms in the centers.

g. The features noted above are all to be found contemporaneously, either singly or in combination, in the interstices between the centers in the remains of small houses and small-scale formal structures. The most intense expressions of all of the above-noted features, however, occur only in the largest centers.

2. Functional and inferential:

a. A pyramidal social structure centered on or headed by a hereditary elite and including a number of craft and occupational specialties, which were probably stratified. Many of the most complex specialties were designed to serve the needs of the upper class.

b. Expressions of elite status and relative social status through material remains.

    (1) Temples as kinship unit–ritual centers.

    (2) Temples as burial sites for apotheosized ancestors.

    (3) Palaces as administrative quarters, elite residences, and communal storage facilities.

    (4) Ball courts as foci for an elite-centered game of ritual and social consequence.

c. The residence, in at least some centers, of urban-density populations; for example, Tikal and its estimated 40,000 people.

d. The achievement of high-density, permanent rural populations at least in the Late Classic and probably in the Early Classic by means of labor-intensive farming, irrigation, *bajo* drainage, and water storage techniques. Management of these techniques and of the populations was a function of the elite class.

e. A political structure based on the control of a region by a large center and its subordinate and smaller centers, through elite kinship and marriage arrangements. These regions are estimated at between 6,000 and 15,000 square kilometers in size. Political linkage of regions was achieved by the same means or by warfare.

Many of these functional and inferential features are those defined by Service for the pristine state.

Geographic and Areal Focus of the Conference

According to the best evidence now available, the Maya Lowlands can be divided into several geographical-cultural zones. These are graphically represented in Figure 1.1 (after Culbert 1973a:Fig. 1). Fittingly, there are 13 zones, grouped into Northern and Southern Lowlands. The line between these groups seems to have shifted in the course of time. An alternative grouping is that proposed by J. E. S. Thompson (1945), who divided the lowlands into Northern, Intermediate, and Southern areas. R. E. W. Adams prefers this arrangement because of his work in the Rio Bec Zone. As will be detailed in Chapter 4, below, strong affiliation first with the south and later with the north characterizes Rio Bec–Chenes prehistory; therefore the Rio Bec Zone does seem to be an intermediate one between the polarities of Maya Lowland culture. Figures 1.2 and 1.3 represent the lowlands in terms of sites and correlate the Preclassic and Early Classic phases in the lowlands.

The expertise represented in this volume is heavily weighted toward the Southern Lowlands. Chapters on the Rio Bec and East Coast zones are included, but the important unpublished Northern Plains material was only indirectly controlled by J. W. Ball, who had examined the excavated material but had not dug it up. We hope that the processual model we have developed will also account for events and patterns in the Northern Plains, but an additional caveat of caution is necessary until the publication of the Dzibilchaltun work.

The earliest known appearances of civilization in the lowlands are in the Central, Pasión, and Rio Bec zones, These are our major geographical focus, but perspectives, processual insights, analogies, and information from all the other zones and from non-Maya areas are utilized and considered.

An Intellectual History of the Problem

One of the most titillating and attractive aspects of Maya prehistory has always been the fact that Mayan civilization was apparently indigenous to the tropical forest, developed without significant contact with the Old World or even with many of the Mesoamerican civilizations. Although this view has been modified by recent work, the Maya are still most often conceived as an isolate. This and other conceptions stem from the intellectual development of Maya archaeology. We can divide the history of Maya archaeology into four periods—the Early Explorer Period, the Great Explorer Period, the Carnegie Period, and the Multiinstitutional Period—each characterized by certain common viewpoints on Maya origins and development.

The Early Explorer Period (1787–1839). Very early visitors to the ruins of Palenque, such as Guillermo Dupaix and Jean Frédéric Waldeck, espoused theories of Old World origins for the builders, invoking Egyptians, Chaldeans, and the Seven Lost Tribes as the carriers of civilization. This approach grew out of the tradition of looking for Old World origins according to Biblical sources, begun in the sixteenth century by such otherwise sound scholars as Sahagún and Durán. The eighteenth-century Scotch historian William Robertson propagated this theoretical bias and denigrated the cultural achievements of American Indians. In the nineteenth century Augustus Le Plongeon brought the Maya in from Atlantis. The diffusionist tradition continued into the twentieth century with Grafton Elliot Smith, who proposed and attempted to prove Egyptian origins for the Maya. The latest proponent of a non–New World origin of Maya civilization is Erich von Däniken, whose extraterrestrial origins theory is unfortunately accepted, or seriously considered, by many who ought to know better.

All of these theories might be regarded as manifestations of an implicit racism in that they assume that the native Americans were not

7

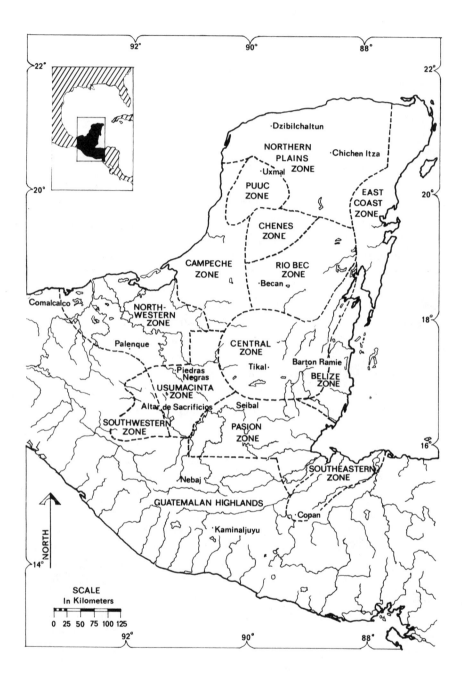

FIGURE 1.1. The Maya Lowlands: archaeological zones

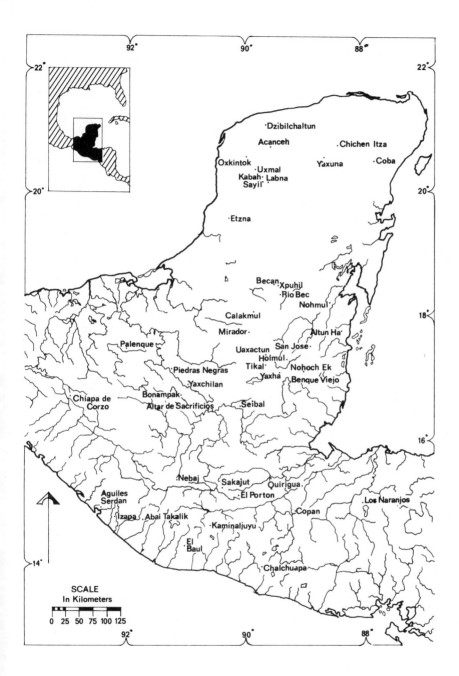

FIGURE 1.2.   The Maya Lowlands: sites (modified from Culbert 1973a:Fig. 2)

Christian Calendar 11.16.0.0.0 Correlation	Major Periods	Pacific Coast	San Lorenzo Tenochtitlan	Chontalpa	Palenque	Trinidad	Chiapa de Corzo	Chalchuapa
A.D. 650	LATE CLASSIC			Pre-Jonuta				Payu
		Loros			Otolum	Taxinchan	Maravillas	
550								
450	EARLY CLASSIC	Kato		hiatus	Motiepa	Kaxabyuc	Laguna	Xocco
350		Jaritos					Jiquipilas Istmo	
250					Picota			Vec
150	PROTOCLASSIC	Izapa	hiatus				Horcones	
50		Hato						Caynac (late)
B.C. 50				Castañeda		Chacibcan	Guanacaste	
150	LATE PRECLASSIC	Guillén/ Crucero						Caynac (early)
250								
350		Frontera/ Conchas 2		Franco	Pre-Picota	Xot	Francesca	Chul
450			Palangana					
550		Escalón					Escalera	Kal
650	MIDDLE PRECLASSIC		hiatus	Puente	?	Chiuaan		
750		Duende/ Conchas 1					Dili	Colos
850			Nacaste					
950		Jocotal	San Lorenzo B	Palacios				
1050		Cuadros	San Lorenzo A			Pre-Chiuaan		Tok
1150				Molina			Cotorra	
1250	EARLY PRECLASSIC	?	Chicharras			?		
1350			Bajío					
1450		Ocos	Ojochi					
1550		Barra						
1650								

FIGURE 1.3. Correlation chart for Preclassic and Early Classic phases in the Maya Lowlands

Seibal	Altar de Sacrificios	Barton Ramie	Tikal	Uaxactun	Nohmul	Becan	Dzibilnocac	Dzibilchaltun	Caribbean Coast
	Pasión				Waterbank			Copo 1	
	Chixoy	Tiger Run	Ik	Tepeu 1	Santana	Bejuco	IV		Vacío
hiatus	Verémos				Nuevo	Sabucan		Piim	
	−Ayn−−	Hermitage	Manik	Tzakol		*hiatus*			Salitre
Junco						Chacsik		*hiatus*	
	Salinas	Floral Park	Cimi		Freshwater		III		
		Mount Hope	Cauac					Xculul	Nizuc
Cantutse	Plancha			Chicanel	Colos	−Pakluum−	II		
		Barton Creek	Chuen					Komchen	Ciénega
Escoba	San Félix	Jenney Creek	Tzec	Mamom	López	Acachen	I	Nabanche	
			Eb		Swasey				
Real	Xe				↓				
					?				

capable of developing a native civilization. An exception can be found in the work of Colonel Juan Galindo, probably the first person to express in print the theory that the ancestors of American Indians built such great cities as Copan. There is no indication, however, that his articles had any influence on the few others who were interested.

The Great Explorer Period (1839–1924). John Lloyd Stephens set the theoretical tone for the period and for the discipline in his carefully argued interpretation of Maya ruins as native American. He considered speculation on the growth of Maya culture premature. Désiré Charnay's essays into Maya studies were tinctured by his vastly greater experience in central Mexico and his knowledge of the Toltecs. He saw Toltec influence everywhere, including in the Maya Lowlands. Charnay accepted Aztec myths about the Toltecs as great culture givers and thus saw everything through Aztec-colored glasses.

Alfred P. Maudslay was a careful and meticulous worker in the tradition of Stephens who went no further than his data allowed. His major interest was in gathering more information with which to outline the major features of Maya civilization.

Teobert Maler was also principally descriptive in his efforts, all the while lamenting the degenerate state into which the benighted descendants of the great builders of the past had fallen. Maler and Maudslay both made implicit assumptions of Maya cultural autonomy.

The Carnegie Period (1924–57). This period saw the growth of a diversity of opinion about Maya origins and the development of Maya civilization. There is a clear continuity between the diverse and unintegrated morass of present-day opinion and the ideas of the preeminent scholars of the last generation. More sophistication, more manipulation of more data, and more theoretical analogues set today's theorists apart from those of the Carnegie era. By and large, however, present theories are not new but are rather variations on the Carnegie set of themes.

Alfred M. Tozzer's major interest seems to have been in fully developed Maya civilization. Preeminent as he was in the field, and influential as he was to so many Mayanists, Tozzer limited his comments on the origins of Maya civilization to a general and often implicit espousal of Herbert Spinden's archaic hypothesis (see, for example, Tozzer 1957:9–10).

Samuel K. Lothrop and George C. Vaillant exercised great influence in the 1930s and 1940s with their Q-Complex theory, a synthesis of traits that seemed early and out of place in Central American cultures, including that of the Maya. Lothrop and Vaillant combined them into a complex which, they suggested, might represent a significant set of elements in the substratum from which Maya civilization developed. Essentially they argued for a partial donation from an ancient Central American culture located in El Salvador, Honduras, and maybe Nicaragua. The modern theoretical counterpart to this formulation is the Protoclassic theory advanced by Robert Wauchope, Gordon R. Willey, James C. Gifford, Richard E. W. Adams, and others, which explains origins of part of Maya civilization as partly and ultimately deriving from non-Maya Central America. It is interesting that the Protoclassic Floral Park ceramic sphere includes Holmul I material which was instrumental in stimulating Vaillant to suggest the Q-Complex. Vaillant also concluded that Maya culture had been highly regionalized and that no one zone had been an origin area for highly decorated ceramics or for any other aspect of hieratic culture. In short, he argued for an interaction model. His discovery of archaic-style figurines at Uaxactun and his familiarity with highland Mexican archaic led him to accept Spinden's postulation of highland and common archaic strata for all Mesoamerican civilizations including the Lowland Maya. (See especially Merwin and Vaillant 1932:64, 96.)

Early in his career, Sylvanus G. Morley was interested in the Q-Complex theory and also entertained the idea of donation of calendrics and writing from the Veracruz coastal plain area, the zone later designated as Olmec. Late in his career, during the 1940s, Morley shifted toward a more chauvinist position, rejecting the idea of outside donations of writing and calendrics, which he saw as the major Maya accomplishments. In his last synthesis of Maya history, *The Ancient Maya* (1946), he emphasized the uniqueness and isolation of Maya high culture. Morley argues in that book for an origin area of calendrics and writing in the zone of oldest monuments, around Uaxactun and Tikal, the Central Zone.

Oliver G. Ricketson, original as always, thought that Maya culture must have been developed by a combination of factors. One was the donation of sophisticated features from non-Maya areas; another was indigenous development. Ricketson also emphasized the role of climatic (or what we would now call ecological) stimulus in the cultural evolution of the Maya. Ricketson expressed these ideas most clearly in the introduction to his great report on Uaxactun (Ricketson and Ricketson 1937). His ideas anticipate some of the "interaction" theorists.

In a characteristically measured and thoughtful essay (1950), A. V. Kidder outlined his thinking on the origins of Maya civilization. He thought that the origins of agriculture were tied up with the origins of civilization and that cultivated plants were unlikely to have been developed in the Maya Lowlands. He was also impressed with the sophistication and complexity of the so-called archaic cultures and thought that many features of the Classic Period were actually earlier in date; he saw development of the already acquired culture as the major culture process of the Classic Period. On the other hand, Kidder, like Morley, thought that the key features of writing and calendrics were inventions of the Lowland Maya. However, Kidder did not discard the possibility that the "spark was . . . struck in some hitherto unsuspected region" (Kidder 1950:7). No doubt he was impressed by early material that his work in Highland Guatemala had revealed.

· J. Eric S. Thompson, in his last consideration of the origins of Maya civilization (1966), adjusted his thinking to some of the most recent data. Thompson believed that certain widespread traits—such as color-direction symbolism—in American Indian culture, that of the Maya included, ultimately derive from Asia. The mechanism he suggested was a steady diffusion through continual migration of new groups from Northeast Asia. Another base for the development of Maya civilization was that of the widespread Mesoamerican formative cultures, which shared certain features. Thompson held that hieroglyphic writing and sculpture were probably donated from outside—perhaps from Veracruz and the general Trans-Isthmian area including the Izapa Zone. Although he argued that the specific forms of Maya culture and their development were essentially autochthonous, he remarked that he always felt that the Maya were stimulated by and interacted with other cultures in Mesoamerica. In this he carried on the tradition begun by Ricketson and Vaillant.

It is interesting that both Kidder and Thompson shifted their positions from those they had espoused in 1940 in their essays in the

Tozzer volume *The Maya and Their Neighbors* (Hays et al. 1940). In that book both authors seriously considered the possibility that many of the distinguishing features of Maya civilization had come from outside, specifically from the Guatemalan Highlands. This theoretical tradition has been maintained in most recent times by Robert Sharer and David Sedat (Sedat and Sharer 1972).

At this point, we pass into the present generation of Mesoamericanists (the Multiinstitutional Period). It seems appropriate here to shift from a historical format to one analytically oriented toward theory, but first we shall briefly review the data.

THE DATA BASE

A realistic appraisal of the events and processes associated with the emergence of Maya civilization was clearly impossible as long as Mayanists operated on the premise that the traits of Maya Classic culture emerged almost overnight at the time of the first dated inscriptions. It has now been demonstrated beyond doubt that monumental architecture, complex ceremonialism, and evidences of class-structured society antedate the beginning of the Classic Period by a number of centuries. It is easy to forget, however, that these evidences of Preclassic social complexity in the Maya Lowlands have almost all been discovered within the last twenty years.

The existence of pottery-making residents of the Maya Lowlands well before the start of the Classic has long been recognized. Ceramic complexes of the Mamom or Chicanel horizons were identified and described at Copan, San José, Benque Viejo, and Uaxactun. But with the exception of those found at Uaxactun, the Preclassic remains were confined to pottery, fragments of floor or architecture, and very simple burials and caches that gave little hint of cultural complexity.

As they did in so many areas, the Carnegie excavations at Uaxactun established new landmarks in the appreciation of Maya Preclassic accomplishments. The most spectacular discovery was the remarkably preserved E-VII sub (Ricketson and Ricketson 1937), but substantial indications of early architecture were also uncovered by excavations in the A Group (A. L. Smith 1950). These results established the development of ceremonialism and monumental architecture before

Classic times, and interrelationships of the early Maya with other areas of Mesoamerica were suggested by those who saw Olmec influence in the masks of E-VII sub.

The first major Maya Lowlands project after World War II, the Barton Ramie Project (Willey et al. 1965), further broadened the data base for the Preclassic Maya. Although only small structures were encountered at the site, the data did provide additional Preclassic ceramic complexes, the earliest of considerable antiquity, and demonstrated the presence of substantial early populations. The interpretation of the Floral Park complex as the result of a site unit intrusion shed new light on events during the Protoclassic and helped explain the characteristics of the previously discovered ceramics of Holmul I (Merwin and Vaillant 1932).

In succeeding years, projects at Altar de Sacrificios, Tikal, and Seibal undertook the large-scale exposure that had been lacking in earlier excavations and further amplified knowledge of the growth of social complexity in the Preclassic Maya Lowlands. The Tikal North Acropolis excavations (W. R. Coe 1965b) revealed a long series of sophisticated Preclassic structures, as well as tomb burials that gave indication of differential distribution of wealth and far-flung trade contacts. Other, less extensive excavations showed the extent of Chicanel horizon pottery and architecture, particularly in the central portions of the site.

The discovery of the earliest known Maya Lowland pottery complex at the Pasión River sites of Altar de Sacrificios and Seibal indicated long Preclassic developments for both sites. Both showed strong standard Mamom and Chicanel ceramic traditions. Altar de Sacrificios pottery and architecture also showed a transition into the Early Classic through a Protoclassic. The Seibal sequence, in contrast, underwent extreme impoverishment or even a hiatus by the onset of the Early Classic Period.

The Rio Bec sites of Becan, Chicanna, and Xpujil have produced a long regional ceramic and architectural sequence beginning in Mamom and continuing through a Chicanel-sphere tradition of ceramics. Early and sophisticated architecture and the construction of a moat at the end of the Preclassic distinguish the early culture history of this area. An easy transition directly from Chicanel to Early Classic was found. The possibility of intensive agriculture in the Early Classic Period has important cultural evolutionary implications.

EXPLANATIONS OF THE MAYA RISE

That the Lowland Maya achieved a level of sociocultural complexity worthy to be termed civilization is undeniable. But the fact that they did so has proved to be a theoretical embarrassment for many anthropologists, and no single explanation for the rise of Maya civilization has gained consensus approval. The most frequently used general works on the Maya are strangely silent about the causes behind Maya civilization. Both Morley (1946) and Thompson (1966) make strong cases for the *in situ* development of Maya civilization, but neither deals with the reasons for that development. Michael Coe (1966) allows a greater role for introduced elements in Maya Lowland civilization but also fails to attack directly the question of causation.

Beyond the lack of explanation in standard references on the Maya, what of the universal theories that attempt to explain the rise of all civilizations? Many such theories are ecologically based, seeking causes in the arid or semiarid environments occupied by the majority of early civilizations. By and large these arid-zone theories are beclouded when transposed to the steamy surroundings of a tropical rain forest. The inapplicability, at least in direct form, of such models as Wittfogel's (1957) irrigation hypothesis and Carneiro's (1970) environmental circumscription is obvious. Sanders and Price's (1968) symbiotic model, based upon close juxtaposition of widely differing ecozones, seems equally unlikely for the Maya Lowlands.

Two ecologically based theories do merit examination in more detail. Flannery et al. (1967) suggest that the origin of social stratification in ancient Oaxaca is related to the existence of microzones of differing productivity. In their view, the best farming land was occupied first, and, as population rose, expansion into less attractive areas followed. The groups controlling the best land commanded a higher percentage of the society's resources and had the potential for developing into an elite class. This explanation has been expanded to account for the rise of social differentiation among the Olmec but has not been seriously considered for the Maya. The frequently mentioned homogeneity of the Maya Lowlands would seem to militate against the occurrence of the process, but this homogeneity is relative and exists on a macroscale; we know almost nothing about microzonation in the area. Until microecological studies of the Maya Lowlands have been made, the possibility of considerable local variation in productivity that might affect resource distribution should not be ruled out.

Recently, Puleston and Puleston (1971) have devised a new ecological explanation aimed specifically at the rise of Maya Lowland civilization. They believe that the initial occupation of the lowlands was confined largely to riverine environments, where a combination of river and agricultural resources provided an excellent diet and facilitated subsistence adaptation. Establishment of substantial populations away from the rivers was not possible before the development of a new subsistence adaptation heavily dependent upon the use of the ramon tree. In nonriverine areas, furthermore, drinking water was scarce. This problem was alleviated by the construction of reservoirs, a solution requiring the organization of large-scale labor forces. The Pulestons, in short, suggest that the impetus for Maya civilization came from a combination of large settlements made possible by ramon cultivation and the necessity of supplying direction to large labor crews.

The failure of most traditional ecological explanations to account for the rise of Maya civilization is one of the reasons behind a set of theories that seek the origin of Maya cultural complexity in outright diffusion or in influences thrust upon the Maya by contact with highly organized systems from more salubrious environments. The most forthrightly diffusionary model is Meggers's (1954) attempt to explain Maya civilization as a transplant from some other region. Made obsolete by the discovery of long Preclassic sequences at Lowland sites, Meggers's theory is now largely used as a diffusionary straw man. Other theorists who fail to see local reasons for cultural complexity in the Maya Lowlands turn to models in which the Maya reformulate their society in response to some external stimulus.

Wittfogel has historical primacy among the external-stimulus theorists. In *Oriental Despotism* (1957), he examines the case of Maya civilization at some length, although most of his data are drawn from ethnohistorical sources concerning the Contact Period and Postclassic Maya of Yucatan. He finds Maya society a good fit for his despotic model in that it exhibited strong state control accompanied by a weak development of private landholding and lack of a separate religious establishment. Wittfogel does not deal specifically with the reasons for the development of the Maya despotic system, but in a general statement he attributes most such developments in nonhydraulic areas either to direct conquest or to diffusion from areas in which true hydraulic states were already established.

Sanders and Price (1968) propose a two-stage model for the development of civilization in Mesoamerica. The first stage involves the rise of chiefdoms. Sanders and Price attribute the beginning of social differentiation, the feature that distinguishes chiefdoms from tribes, to a combination of population increase, the food surplus inherent in an agricultural technology, and economic cooperation and competition based upon the differing productive potentials of varying ecozones. Although they do not discuss the rise of chiefdoms in the Maya area explicitly, their treatment of the Olmec suggests that they consider the relatively high demographic potential of slash-and-burn agriculture in rain forest zones to be the principal stimulus to social differentiation in the lowland areas of Mesoamerica.

Sanders and Price attribute the transformation of chiefdoms into states to a second set of causal factors. Like Wittfogel, they emphasize the adoption of hydraulic agriculture as a major cause, to which they add the growth of complex exchange systems fostered by ecological variability. Since these factors are not operative in the Maya Lowlands, they resort to an external-stimulus explanation of what they consider to be state-level society in the Maya Late Classic. In their scheme, interaction between the Maya and Teotihuacan that may have included colonies of Teotihuacan traders resident at Maya sites stimulated a trend among the Maya toward increased urbanism and social stratification.

In dealing with external stimulus theories about the rise of Maya civilization, we must include Webb's interesting suggestions (1973) about a mechanism whereby secondary states might be generated by trade contacts between already existent states and chiefdoms. Although Webb himself does not apply the idea to the Maya because of his belief that the Maya never rose above the level of an advanced chiefdom, the scheme is potentially applicable for anyone who feels that the Maya did reach statehood and, in fact, would supply a specific mechanism to explain the results that Sanders and Price feel occurred. Webb proposes that the establishment of trade contacts between a state and a chiefdom could provide an influx of wealth sufficient to "overflow" the channels that normally serve as leveling mechanisms in chiefdoms. Thus the excess wealth could provide the resources necessary to establish a kingly base of power and the corps of personal retainers a leader needs in order to move beyond the kin-controlled mechanisms of the chiefdom.

From the theories that attempt to explain Maya civilization as a result of external contact, we may turn to a set of theories that seek the impetus for Maya development in demographic factors—a set that may be expected to grow in number under the increasing impact of Boserup's (1965) suggestion that population be treated as an independent variable. Sanders and Price's (1968) explanation for the origin of chiefdoms is, of course, a demographic explanation, as is, in part, the suggestion of Flannery et al. (1967) about the relationship between microzones and the origin of social stratification. Similarly, since Carneiro's theme of environmental circumscription (1970) is not applicable in large, environmentally homogeneous areas, he raises the possibility of social circumscription, an essentially demographic concept, to account for Maya civilization. In social circumscription, population pressure in the central part of a homogeneous area has the same effect as environmental circumscription and leads to competition for land, war and conquest, and social stratification.

In recent years there has also been an increased emphasis upon trade as an important factor in the growth of cultural complexity. Parsons and Price (1971) propose that organizational complexity generally grows out of the need to secure scarce resources. Both they and Sanders and Price (1968), however, believe that trade mechanisms are much more important in the ecologically diverse highlands than in the lowlands. Independently, Rathje (1971, 1973) has proposed a trade mechanism to account specifically for the rise of civilization in the resource-deficient lowlands. Starting from the assumption that commodities from outside the lowlands were necessary to the Maya and Olmec lifestyles, he posits the need for a high level of organization in the core areas of the lowlands to procure these commodities.

Finally, a number of anthropologists have focused upon the importance of ideology and religion in the rise of civilizations. Willey (1962) stresses the role of shared ideology in facilitating the communication necessary to cultural development, and has reemphasized the point specifically for Maya civilization (1971b). Webb (1973) believes that the Classic Maya were an advanced theocratic chiefdom who maintained their large ceremonial centers largely through the pleasures that the populace obtained by participation in the cult. Without coercive power and dependent upon the believability of the religious system, Maya Classic culture remained vulnerable in the extreme and lacked the ability to compete with better-organized state systems elsewhere.

The seminar faced basic questions about the nature as well as the origin of Maya civilized society. A number of important theoretical issues are involved, some of them already clearly defined and hotly contested in the literature.

From the neoevolutionary viewpoint, the question of whether the Classic Maya ever reached a state level of sociocultural integration is unresolved. Erasmus (1968) and Webb (1973) both argue that Maya Classic development terminated at the level of the chiefdom; Willey (1971a) joins them, although in less explicitly evolutionary terms, by doubting that an incipient Maya trend to urbanism and the state was ever completed. Sanders and Price (1968), on the other hand, suggest that by Late Classic times the Maya had come very close to and perhaps had reached the state level.

Another debate centers around the degree of urbanism present in the Maya Lowlands. Best exemplified by the controversy between Sanders (Sanders and Price 1968; Sanders 1973) and Haviland (1969, 1970) about the urban nature of Tikal, the polar viewpoints would seem to be (a) that Maya ceremonial centers integrated a large enough population to be called urban, and (b) that there are both urban and nonurban civilizations and that the Maya are a prime example of the latter type. The idea that the Maya were a nonurban civilization has a number of explicit champions and has gained a clear consensus, but other questions have been raised in the process. Most of the nonurbanists take cognizance of the fact that Maya sites do not fit the model of vacant ceremonial centers much better than they fit a fully urban concept. The use of such terms as *functional city, semiurban,* and *quasi-urban* for the Maya clearly points to the need for more precise formulations of kinds or degrees of nonurbanism.

Many of the abovementioned considerations of the rise of Maya Classicism are based explicitly upon the model of Maya society that has been traditionally accepted for several generations. If, as Culbert (1973a:x) and Willey and Shimkin (1973:473–74) suggest, a new model of that society is crystallizing, we must rethink all of these older views to see whether they may not be based upon implicit assumptions that are no longer valid.

Finally, more abstract epistemological questions may intrude upon our work, since we must consider not only our primary problems but also the approaches and methods most applicable to their solutions. Both Flannery (1972a) and R. E. W. Adams (1973a) have contrasted single-cause and multicausal explanations, and there has undoubtedly been a trend to formulate more complex sets of interrelationships in considerations of the origin and development of cultural phenomena.

PROBLEMS FOR CONSIDERATION

Certain features and aspects of the thematic focus of the conference concerned us all. We chose to list those we thought most significant in the form of questions or problems.

1. *Problem:* The source and mechanism of arrival and spread of original populations.

Comment: Space-time distribution patterns in both the Maya area and the surrounding areas will certainly give clues.

2. *Problem:* The cultural statuses of the original populations.

Comment: Note that the first two problems assume that there was more than one migration or colonization, and that origin areas are probably distinct. This assumption can be questioned, but if it is accepted, a logical extension is to define the varying cultural conditions of those populations.

3. *Problem:* The rate of population growth in the Preclassic.

Comment: Again, the problem is one of sampling of regional growths. The theoretical issue is that of a choice among a number of possible population growth models and analogues derived from ethnohistory, ethnology, history, and demography.

4. *Problem:* The appearance of signs of social complexity. (A specific definition of Classic Period complexity is given in the second section of this paper ["Definitions"]).

Comment: Elicitation of formal time-space patterns and of the inferential and circumstantially definable features are both desirable here. For example, when does craft specialization appear? What distinctions can be made among those specialties found at various classes of sites? Are certain regions specialized in certain products or crafts?

5. *Problem:* Is there useful differentiation to be made between

"folk culture" and elite culture? If so, when does this distinction occur in any given region?

Comment: This relates to the general problem of definition of Maya civilization and urbanism. In other words, is what we talk about as the defining aspects of civilization actually an elite-directed and focused subculture? If so, what was the nature of its relationships with the "folk culture"?

6. *Problem:* Were there differential rates of growth of social complexity among centers?

Comment: Related to, but not the same as, problem 4.

7. *Problem:* Relationships of early Maya social groups with exterior societies. Included under the rubric of relationships are the mechanisms of migration, diffusion, trade, and conflict.

8. *Problem:* The nature of Late Preclassic societies in the Maya Lowlands.

Comment: Regional diversity is again assumed.

9. *Problem:* The nature and meaning of the Protoclassic phenomenon.

10. *Problem:* Does the Preclassic-Classic boundary suggest significant transformation?

11. *Problem:* The nature of the discontinuities between Early and Late Classic Period cultures. The transformational implications and the inferential structure of Early Classic culture.

NOTE

1. Childe's ten defining criteria (1950) for urban life were as follows (our paraphrasing):

1. Cities were larger and had denser population than preceding settlements.

2. Cities had occupationally specialized classes and were more varied in composition and function than any village.

3. Cities were supported by a tax or tithe paid to a divine king or an imaginary deity resident in the center.

4. Truly monumental architecture was concentrated in the cities.

5. Ruling classes, civil servants, military leaders, and other specialists were supported by a productive surplus.

6. Writing and numerical accounting systems were devised to account for the surplus.

7. Such recording systems led to further elaboration for use in exact and predictive sciences and eventually to the creation of calendars.

8. Artistic specialists arose and gave art new directions, eventuating in the development of artistic canons.

9. Importation of raw materials was paid for by a further part of the social surplus.

10. Social organization became largely based on residence rather than exclusively on kinship, and in return for the security of such an arrangement, craftsmen accepted a lower social status. Ideological solidarity developed to cement allegiances to the urban centers.

PART 2

Maya Lowland Data Bases and Their Coordination

Early Maya Development at Tikal, Guatemala

T. PATRICK CULBERT

University of Arizona

INTRODUCTION

The Central Zone of the Maya Lowlands in the northern part of the Department of the Peten, Guatemala, was one of the first regions in the area to reach a complex level of cultural development. Tikal, a preeminent site of the zone during the Classic Period peak of Maya culture, seems to have been equally important during the Preclassic. Consequently, a review of information about the development of Tikal is an important step in attacking the question of the rise of Lowland Maya civilization.

The massive, extended research program of the Tikal Project (sponsored by the University Museum, University of Pennsylvania) has provided an almost unparalleled data base. Questions concerning the early development of Tikal were recognized to be of critical concern at the start of the Tikal Project (Shook 1958:5–6), and the scope and length of excavation permitted exposures of deeply buried Preclassic levels that have been matched at few other sites. At the same

27

time, summarizing Preclassic data for Tikal is a far less satisfying task than dealing with late levels of occupation, for most early remains, even after fourteen years of excavation, still lie hidden and unsampled under massive levels of later construction. The total site pattern that can be suggested with some security for the Late Classic and Terminal Classic periods (see Culbert 1973c) is unattainable for the very early periods that must be our concern in this volume.

CHRONOLOGY

The Preclassic Period at Tikal includes five ceramic complexes: Eb (which consists of early and late facets), Tzec, Chuen, Cauac, and Cimi (see Fig. 2.1). Eb is a member of the Mamom ceramic horizon

FIGURE 2.1. Tikal ceramic complexes

Dates	Complex		Horizon	
		Late Facet		
	Manik	**Middle Facet**	Tzakol	
		Early Facet		
AD 150-250 ± 50	Cimi		Chicanel	Floral Park
100BC-AD150 ± 50	Cauac		Chicanel	
250BC-100BC ± 50	Chuen		Chicanel	
500-250 BC ± 100	Tzec		Chicanel	
700-500 BC (± 100)	Eb	**Late Facet**	Mamom	
		Early Facet		

(Willey, Culbert, and Adams 1967), while Tzec is transitional between the Mamom and Chicanel horizons. The assignment of Tzec to a status transitional between horizons represents a change in my original assessment (Willey, Culbert, and Adams 1967:294) that was made for technical ceramic reasons and does not affect the content or temporal position of the complex. The Chuen and Cauac complexes are fully within the Chicanel ceramic horizon and sphere, while Cimi, although still Chicanel in ceramic content, dates to the time at which the Salinas–Floral Park ceramic sphere had arisen in other parts of the Southern Lowlands. Since our concerns in this volume extend into the Early Classic Period, it should be noted that the Tikal Early Classic includes only the Manik ceramic complex, divided into three temporal facets.

The absolute dates for the Tikal ceramic complexes presented in Figure 2.1 are largely derived from W. R. Coe (1965a, 1965b). I have added a tentative starting date for the Eb complex and chosen specific dates in cases where Coe suggests a range. The starting date of 700 B.C. for the Eb complex is based upon sheer guesswork, since the only radiocarbon date available for the complex is 588 ± 53 B.C. for an Early Facet Eb sample. The only date for the Tzec complex (456 ± 47 B.C.) is from a stratigraphic level in the early part of the Tzec sequence. The rest of the absolute dates are based upon the long series of radiocarbon samples from the North Acropolis excavations (see W. R. Coe 1965b for specifics on some dates). To avoid the very complicated discussion that would be necessary to consider the radiocarbon results in detail, I might simply note that most of the dates are consistent in general terms, but that there is enough variation between dates and the stratigraphic sequence to suggest that it is impossible to attain greater precision than the estimated + and − figures appended to absolute dates in Figure 2.1. We have not as yet correlated absolute dates with the facets of the Manik complex, so no absolute date entries are made for these subdivisions.

Completion of the analysis of Tikal Preclassic ceramic complexes permits a more precise alignment of the Tikal and Uaxactun sequences than that given in Willey, Culbert, and Adams (1967). The ceramic contents of comparable complexes are almost identical at the two sites, but the Uaxactun samples seem to be truncated at both the early and the late ends of the Preclassic sequence. The majority of the Uaxactun Mamom sample is quite late, for it includes types and shapes that are essentially identical to Tikal Tzec-complex material, and frequencies of Mamom vessel shapes from Uaxactun seriate nicely into the Tikal seriation pattern at a point somewhat later than the Tikal Tzec samples. The Uaxactun Mamom complex, however, includes some earlier material, for there are many correspondences between Mamom and Late Facet Eb, and a few pieces from the lowest level in Pit E-4 at Uaxactun (R. E. Smith 1955:14) that probably relate to Early Facet Eb. Figure 2.2 is a graphic representation of the relations between Uaxactun Mamom and Tikal Eb and Tzec. The Chicanel complex at Uaxactun combines the Tikal Chuen and Cauac complexes. Nothing in the Uaxactun samples, however, indicates the presence of the elements that are characteristic of Tikal Cimi, and it would appear that the Terminal Preclassic Period is missing from the Uaxactun collections, as R. E. Smith suggested (1955:22).

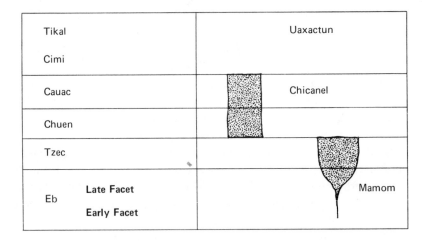

FIGURE 2.2.   Tikal and Uaxactun Preclassic complexes

DEMOGRAPHIC ASPECTS

The size and distribution of Preclassic population is a crucial question in understanding the development of Maya Lowland civilization, especially since several papers in this volume suggest that Late Preclassic crowding and consequent warfare was a stimulus for culture change. As in other time periods and other archaeological areas, the distribution of ceramic samples is the most readily available clue to Maya Preclassic demography. Yet the use of ceramic samples as a key to occupation involves more serious biases for these early phases than does similar use for late periods. Preclassic remains are frequently deeply buried under later construction and relatively easy to miss, especially when testing of an area is superficial. Early samples have also been subject to the maximum possibility of disturbance by prehistoric cultural practices, as well as to the vagaries of postabandonment natural processes.

In spite of these problems, it is still necessary to infer occupation from artifact samples if we are not to give up altogether the question of Preclassic demography. For Tikal, a rapid review of ceramic evaluations provides a list of 267 separate locations that were tested by excavation. The archaeological operations ranged from test pitting to exhaustive excavation, while the locations sampled varied between the area of a single test pit and the area of a total large group. Preclassic ceramics were noted as absent, present in small quantities, or present in substantial quantities.

The data (presented in Table 2.1) indicate that 128 (48 percent) of the 267 locations at Tikal produced at least some ceramic remains dating to the Preclassic Period.

TABLE 2.1

OCCURRENCE OF PRECLASSIC CERAMICS AT TIKAL

	No Preclassic Ceramics	*Some Preclassic Ceramics*	*Abundant Preclassic Ceramics*
Large Architectural Groups	24	22	15
Medium-Size Architectural Groups	22	23	3
Small-Size Architectural Groups	40	25	8
Vacant Terrain (no visible architecture)	4	8	6
Samples Not Attributable to Specific Groups	19	14	4

About 60 percent of excavations in groups of large-to-medium-size architecture produced Preclassic material, while only 40 percent of small mound structures and only 49 percent of excavations not definitely assignable to groups of specific size provided samples of this date. It is interesting that 14 of 18 tests (78 percent) in vacant areas where there were no surface indications of architecture yielded Preclassic remains. This may suggest either that Preclassic occupation was distributed in areas little used in later times or that later activity in other locations had systematically tended to destroy evidence of Preclassic occupation.

Many of the aforementioned occurrences of Preclassic material consisted of no more than one or two sherds mixed into later collections. Substantial amounts of Preclassic material were much less common. Only 36 of the 128 instances in which Preclassic ceramics were noted provided amounts classified as substantial. In other words, only 13 percent of all the Tikal localities tested provided enough Preclassic ceramics to make it seem certain that actual occupation areas had been encountered. Fry's (1969) ceramic testing project in the Tikal peripheries provided similar results, for he encountered Preclassic ceramics in only 14 of 102 test pits (13 percent). Even if we take into account the potential inaccuracies to which this rapid compilation of Tikal data is subject, the results from Tikal do seem to differ considerably from those at such sites as Becan and those in Yucatan, where substantial amounts of Late Preclassic material are reported to occur with the same frequency as Late Classic material (see Chapter 5, below).

The data considered above have treated the Preclassic Period as a single undifferentiated unit. This procedure was necessary to allow use of many samples for which identification of specific complexes proved impossible. The cases that permitted identification by complex are summarized in Table 2.2. It is clear that from the time of the very

TABLE 2.2.
OCCURRENCE OF PRECLASSIC CERAMICS
AT TIKAL BY COMPLEX

	Samples with Some Ceramics	Samples with Abundant Ceramics
Cimi	8	7
Cauac	16	9
Chuen	7	15
Tzec	4	5
Eb	rare	3

scanty Eb-complex remains there was a gradual growth in Tikal population through the start of Chuen times. The frequency of occurrences of the Chuen, Cauac, and Cimi complexes remains relatively stable. The slight decline of Cimi occurrences is more likely due to differential ease of recognition of the complex than to actual population change.

The Early Classic Manik ceramic complex showed a notable increase in the frequency of occurrence of both small and substantial ceramic samples, and hence inferentially an increase in population density. I have not attempted to count Manik occurrences for all Tikal operations, but a 10 percent sample suggests that Manik ceramics occur nearly twice as frequently as Preclassic ceramics. The data from Fry's (1969) peripheral area tests are even more striking, for 88 percent of his test pits showed at least some Manik complex sherds, an increase of more than 600 percent over the Preclassic occurrences. Separation of the Manik complex into facets depended upon such minor nuances that most evaluations could not be assigned to a specific facet. The Central Tikal data on samples studied quantitatively suggest that Early Facet Manik population remained low, probably at no more than Late Preclassic levels, and that the rapid rise of population occurred with the Middle Facet samples. Again, the data from Tikal indicate a situation markedly different from that in several sites in less central parts of the Maya Lowlands, where Early Classic remains were drastically reduced in quantity from those of the Late Preclassic. The Tikal population curve, in contrast, seems to have followed a general upward trend, interrupted only by occasional periods of relative stability.

THE CERAMIC SAMPLES

Since information about the amount and quality of ceramics is important in evaluating the accuracy of inferences made from ceramic analysis, it is necessary to review briefly the nature of Preclassic and Early Classic ceramic samples obtained at Tikal. In the following discussion, the samples referred to are the large and relatively homogeneous collections upon which the ceramic sequence is based.

The Eb complex is represented at Tikal by three samples, two of Early Facet Eb and one of the Late Facet. The two Early Facet samples came, respectively, from a pit in bedrock underlying all construction phases in the North Acropolis and from a chultun one and one-half kilometers east of the site center. The Late Facet Eb sample was obtained in tunneling Structure 5C-54, where it constituted the fill inside a wall that underlay the final structure. The single Tzec sample came from a small platform about one kilometer east of the Great Plaza. Although scattered Tzec sherds were not uncommon in early levels in the North Acropolis, no pure Tzec samples were encountered there.

The Eb and Tzec samples are not stratigraphically related to each other, and their arrangement in a sequence rests upon seriational arguments. A gradual change between the Tzec and Chuen complexes can be stratigraphically demonstrated in the deep midden that produced the Tzec sample, making this transition one of the most thoroughly understood in the Tikal sequence.

Beginning with the Chuen complex, the frequency of ceramic samples increases greatly. Nine separate locations produced pure Chuen complex samples, some in very large quantity. Five of these locations were near the site center underlying major Classic Period construction; the other four were in outlying parts of the site, widely scattered and well away from the site center.

The deep cut through the North Acropolis, which provides the stratigraphic basis for the remainder of the Preclassic sequence, deserves special consideration (see W. R. Coe 1965b for details). Physical stratigraphy in the location was excellent, and Preclassic sherd samples very large. Since most of the material represents intentional filling operations, frequently associated with destruction of earlier structures, "upwelling" of early material into later levels is commonplace. This process tends to blur frequency changes and the end points in the production cycle of ceramic elements. The complete sealing of levels, on the other hand, has produced an excellent and very precise series of points of introduction of new elements, since there is no mechanism by which downward mixing of late artifacts could have occurred. The lowest five floors of the North Acropolis sequence sealed pure Chuen-complex deposits including four sequent samples large enough for quantitative analysis.

The association of Chuen sherds with monumental architecture is unmistakable. The best evidence comes from the North Acropolis excavations, but several other fragmentary associations occur in the central area of the site. One of the Chuen samples from the outlying sections is associated with a construction of house-platform type.

Cauac-complex samples were obtained in quantity from four locations within Tikal. Two of these samples were from the North Acropolis–Terrace–Plaza area, including good samples from three sequent floors in the North Acropolis series. The other two samples came from remote areas of the site and were not associated with architectural features.

Cimi-complex samples were also obtained from four locations. One was a very large sample sealed by the fifth through seventh floors from the top of the North Acropolis sequence. The other three locations were from small-mound sectors of the site, but none was associated with architecture of Cimi date. The only stratigraphy within the Cauac and Cimi samples was that from the North Acropolis, but the other isolated collections seriated well with the North Acropolis data.

The Early, Middle, and Late facets of the Manik complex produced 3, 17, and 11 ceramic samples respectively. Although the Early Facet Manik material is genuinely scarce at Tikal, I do not consider the variation between the number of Middle Facet and Late Facet samples to be significant since the lengths of time that the facets persisted is not clear and the division into facets demanded many close decisions in cases which could have been classified as either Middle or Late. Samples from all Manik facets included both elite and residential contexts.

CERAMIC CHANGE AND EXTERNAL INFLUENCE

The strength and direction of external influences upon ceramic development is one measure of broader and more important kinds of cultural contacts. Such evidence is particularly crucial in relation to questions of the origin of Maya Lowland populations and the period of Protoclassic external impact that may relate to the start of the Peten Classic Period.

I presume that the source of the Eb ceramic complex is external to Tikal, and consider it likely that its bearers were actual immigrants to the region. Regrettably I am unable to pinpoint any area to which the ceramics of Early Facet Eb bear resemblances strong enough to suggest a genetic relationship. Neither the Xe complex from the Pasión sites nor the Early Jenney Creek complex from Barton Ramie is much like Early Eb, and it seems unlikely that either could be an Eb progenitor. Possible connections to known Preclassic complexes outside the Peten are even more remote. This lack of close relationships between early ceramic complexes in the Southern Maya Lowlands seems to me to be a strong argument for multiple migrations into the region from different source areas. One would expect immigration from a single source followed by expansion into an unoccupied area to produce a pattern of initial close similarities followed by increasing divergence. Exactly the opposite is the case in Maya Lowland Preclassic ceramic development. On the other hand, if one postulates multiple origins for the earliest lowland inhabitants, it seems surprising that none of the earliest complexes—with the possible exception of Jenney Creek (Sharer and Gifford 1970)—show convincing ties with known areas outside the Maya Lowlands.

Beginning with Late Facet Eb and continuing through the Cauac complex, Tikal ceramics show increasingly strong similarities to other Peten complexes. This pattern is part of the general trend of convergence in the Maya Lowlands that culminated in the monolithic ceramic homogeneity of the Chicanel sphere (Willey, Culbert, and Adams 1967). The source of the convergence must lie in increasing communication, probably fostered by trade and interaction spheres that operated throughout the Maya Lowlands. It would not surprise me to find that the process may have involved actual population movements from the Central Zone toward peripheral lowland areas.

Actual trade pieces and signs of outside influence also increase at Tikal during the time in question. Mars Orange Ware first appears at Tikal in Late Facet Eb samples and continues in Tzec. Also in the Tzec complex, the resist-painted Ahchab Red-on-Buff bears a resemblance to "Cloudy Usulutan" in both appearance and technique of decoration. By the time of the Cauac complex, trade pieces include Brown-Black Ware from the Guatemalan Highlands and Usulutan Ware from Salvador-Honduras. Contact with the Usulutan tradition stimulated the development of local types that imitated the multiple-line decoration of Usulutan but without using a resist technique.

The Cimi complex is differentiated from Cauac by a new cluster of Usulutan-related traits that again stimulate imitation by local potters.

"Black-Splotch Usulutan," which features a very liquid black paint used over red-on-orange; a few pieces of Mojara Polychrome; and several features of vessel shape, including mammiform feet, were introduced at Tikal at this time. Their ultimate origin is southeast of the Maya Lowlands. These are also all elements that characterize the Floral Park sphere in other parts of the Maya Lowlands. At Tikal, however, the new types and elements are simply additions to a continuing and little-changed local tradition. If the new Floral Park influences are associated with actual immigrations at Barton Ramie and Altar de Sacrificios, the situation at Tikal would seem to be different—more parallel to strong trade contacts with sources offering ceramic innovations. We should note, however, that there were no Cimi tombs that included offerings at Tikal, so it is impossible to say whether the extraneous influence would have been more marked in elite contexts.

By far the strongest external relationships of Tikal ceramics are to the Usulutan Ware pottery of Salvador-Honduras. The relationships are of considerable time depth, particularly if the Tzec-complex Ahchab Red-on-Buff derives eventually from cloudy Usulutan; they seem to be continuous; and they provide ample and undeniable evidence of both trade pieces and stylistic input. On the other hand, relationships with the Guatemalan Highlands are far less noticeable, consisting largely of isolated trade pieces in elaborate burials. The direction of Tikal external relationships does not seem to be a function of complementary resource zones; although the Salvador-Honduras Zone contains some highland areas and resources, it is basically a lowland area that does not differ greatly from the Maya Lowlands. I feel that the relationships would better be understood in terms of political or ethnic factors, probably involving whatever population inhabited the Copan-Quirigua area during this period.

The ceramic transition between the Preclassic and Early Classic complexes at Tikal is striking. It involves few new traits, for most Early Classic elements were present in scattered occurrences or in prototypical forms during the Late Preclassic. As examples, polychrome designs very like those of early Manik occurred during the Cimi complex in Mojara Polychome; a few sherds in Cimi deposits are indistinguishable from Aguila Orange; some Late Preclassic flanged bowls have a sharp z angle, while others approach the basal flange.

Yet with the first Manik deposits, the total change is radical. The standard features of the Preclassic disappear rapidly; things that had been very rare are suddenly dominant. Both shapes and types combine already-known elements in new ways that are absolutely distinctive. Most of the features that come to prominence in the Early Classic are related to Floral Park innovations. Teotihuacan influence is also present very early, for cylindrical tripods are already included in Early Facet Manik.

All of the evidence points to a drastic and probably rather sudden recombination of elements at the start of the Manik complex. It is hard to avoid the conclusion that such a radical transformation in a basic manufacturing industry must have been associated with general cultural changes of some magnitude. Yet I cannot posit the kind of "site unit intrusion" that has been used to account for similar ceramic changes at other sites, for Tikal was surely too large and too densely populated at the end of the Late Preclassic to have been subjected to a process of population replacement. The size of the Tikal population, however, would not preclude the possibility of a major change in site leadership or even minor population input into the elite level of society.

ARCHITECTURE

The excavations at Tikal have demonstrated both the sophistication and the magnitude of Preclassic architectural endeavors in the Maya Lowlands. The most detailed information comes from the massive section through the North Acropolis already reported by W. R. Coe (1965b). Coe's work showed that fifteen of the twenty North Acropolis floors, nine of the ten meters of construction underneath the final floor, and six of the eight reconstructions of the North Terrace all dated to the Preclassic.

The earliest solid evidence for cut-stone masonry and the use of lime plaster at Tikal occurs in association with Chuen ceramics in Structures 5D-Sub 14-3d, -2d, and -1st, which immediately overlay bedrock in the North Acropolis. The structures had been demolished by later activity at the locus, but the fragments that remained suggested that they had been larger and more formal than would be expected for simple residences. The remaining levels of the North Acropolis Preclassic sequence demonstrate rapidly increasing scope of construction and the appearance of most features of "Classic" Maya architecture well before the first levels that contained Early Classic ceramics. The apron molding was present in Chuen times; corbeled vaulting—at least for tombs—appeared by Cauac. A pattern of two or more pyramidal substructures flanking a "courtyard" was established by Cauac times, while the final center line of the North Acropolis and associated placement of structures came into existence during the time when Cimi ceramics were still in vogue.

There are clear indications, though far less exposure, of major Preclassic architecture in other areas near the center of Tikal. The most striking evidence is Structure 5C-54, an immense four-stairwayed pyramid 80 meters on a side and more than 20 meters high. Tunneling suggests that the final form of 5C-54 is of Late Preclassic date, and, although the surface is badly destroyed, the stairways seem to have been flanked by huge masks in a manner reminiscent of some of the Preclassic structures in the North Acropolis. In addition, the tunnel entering Structure 5C-54 from the east encountered an earlier wall and an extensive deposit of pure Late Facet Eb material not far from the outer surface. The wall and fill may well be the remains of a substantial structure of Late Eb or Tzec date, but the evidence is too fragmentary to permit solid conclusions.

One hundred meters east of Structure 5C-54, the "Seven Temples Plaza" was raised more than four meters in a massive filling operation in Cauac times, and stubs of buildings located underneath the fill suggest a development around the plaza that probably dates to Chuen times. Several standing structures in this same area of Tikal seem to be of very early Early Classic style, suggesting that this entire sector of the site may have been a focus of early ceremonial development that matched or even exceeded that known from the North Acropolis.

In summary, the architectural evidence demonstrates that formal, probably ceremonial, construction at Tikal began no later than the Chuen complex, and that by Cauac times the site was a ceremonial center of considerable magnitude. Basic patterns that were to mark the Classic form of the North Acropolis were present in association with the Cimi complex, and the great majority of traditional architectural forms were established two to three centuries before the beginning of the Early Classic.

TRADE

The products that characterized both the domestic and elite trade networks of the Classic Period were present very early in the Tikal sequence. Obsidian and quartzite were both present in Early Facet Eb samples and continuous at Tikal thereafter. Data on relative quantities of these materials are not available at present, so no analysis of the volume of trade involved can be attempted. It should be noted, however, that the quantity of material from the earliest complexes is so small that the mere presence of imported materials is suggestive of general availability. Certainly any hypothesis suggesting that trade in sumptuary goods preceded that in domestic goods is refuted by the Tikal data.

The exotics that are associated with the ceremonial-mortuary complex are attested by Chuen times. Shell and stingray spines from the coasts, jade and greenstone probably from the Guatemalan Highlands, and imported pottery from El Salvador and the Guatemalan Highlands all appear in Late Preclassic tombs and are indicative of trade in the same high-value imports that marked the Classic Period. To specify that the mechanisms of procurement or distribution of goods were the same in Preclassic Tikal as they were later would be to go far beyond the data, but the sources and uses of exotic materials seem to have been similar in the two periods.

STATUS DIFFERENTIATION

Although few archaeologists would disagree that the developments in Late Preclassic Tikal must have been associated with some form of status differentiation, the data that bear upon the question are neither abundant nor profound. The architectural complexity cited previously leads to the traditional archaeological inference of a controlling and directing class. Burials from the North Acropolis beginning in Chuen times were undeniably formal in tomb placement and construction and rich in contents, and the presence of shrines apparently used for continuing ceremonial rites on top of important tombs is suggestive of high status (W. R. Coe 1965b). But our knowledge of total burial practices for this time period is very fragmentary, and there are few "lower-class" burials that can be juxtaposed against the presumably elite burials of which we have fuller knowledge.

The fragmentary paintings on the walls of the Burial 166 tomb chamber and on the shrine that surmounted Burial 167—both features of Cauac date—are probably the strongest available evidence of status differentiation (W. R. Coe 1965b). The paintings show many of the features of dress and accoutrement that were associated with high status in Classic times. Even though it cannot be demonstrated that the figures portrayed were men rather than gods, the symbolism shown must have existed in the real world before it could be attributed to either gods or men.

Any attempt to comment knowledgably about the kind and mechanisms of status differentiation in Preclassic Tikal must rest upon theory rather than fact. The range of variation and size of samples available is too limited to test such precise and specific ideas.

DISCUSSION

To contribute to an understanding of the rise of Maya civilization, the Tikal data must be considered within the broader frameworks of the entire Maya Lowlands and of Mesoamerica in general. Comparison indicates that in many ways Tikal is simply a case in point—one example of general Maya Lowland patterns. In other ways, Tikal contrasts with other lowland sites in a manner that may suggest either regional differences or factors unique to the site itself. In summary, the following features of Tikal and Maya Lowlands Central Zone development seem noteworthy to me now that I have had the chance to interact with other participants at the Santa Fe seminar:

1. Tikal, like the rest of the Maya Lowlands, was occupied by sedentary ceramic-using populations very late in relation to most other areas in Mesoamerica. Although I have no ready explanation for the retarded initial settlement of the Maya Lowlands, I do not believe that it can be attributed to an inability to adapt to agriculture under rain-forest conditions. Neighboring rain-forest cultures on both the Gulf and Pacific coasts developed early, and although the

coastal zones offered riverine and marine resources lacking in the Maya Lowlands, I doubt that they presented a major contrast for agricultural adaptation.

2. Occupancy of the Central Zone of the Maya Lowlands does not seem to me to have lagged far behind that of the riverine zones that have the earliest ceramic complexes. I suspect that there were populations using Eb pottery at both Tikal and Uaxactun within a century or so after Xe-phase occupations on the Pasión. This reflects my opinion that rain-forest agriculture presented no serious problems for early inhabitants of the area, and contrasts with the Pulestons' (1971) conclusion that moving from the riverine zone into the central area of the lowlands constituted a major challenge.

3. The early inhabitants of the Maya Lowlands found themselves in an enviable position in regard to subsistence potential. Agricultural productivity must have been unusually high during the time when large tracts of virgin rain forest were still available, and circumstances seem to have been propitious for rapid growth and expansion of population. The situation probably led to a system dominated by deviation-amplifying mechanisms with all the implications spelled out by Rathje (Chapter 14, below).

4. Accepting the assumption that the early ceramic-using populations of the Maya Lowlands were immigrants from neighboring areas, these populations must have been already familiar with social differentiation and formal ceremonialism in their source area(s). The immediate appearance of items imported from outside the lowlands indicates that the early inhabitants received logistic support from or at least maintained contacts with the outside world.

5. Formal architecture and social differentiation are present at Tikal by the time of the Chuen complex, but there are hints that they may, in fact, have started as early as the Eb complex. In the Maya Lowlands as a whole, there is little solid evidence for class-differentiated society before the Late Preclassic, but exposures of earlier periods are very small at most sites, and I am not certain that Mayanists are not preconditioned to expect (and find) a "simple farming village" stage of cultural development.

6. By the Late Preclassic Chicanel horizon, most sites for which there is detailed information demonstrate both ceremonial architecture and social differentiation. Present evidence suggests that Tikal had a greater concentration of major architecture at this time than most

other sites in the Southern Lowlands, but this impression may well be a result of the fact that Tikal excavations have been so extensive. On the other hand, population at both Tikal and Uaxactun was less dense than that reported for several sites in less central locations. If future work confirms the suggestion that the Maya Central Zone is characterized by large Preclassic centers but relatively low population density, the evidence will fit poorly with the theories that suggest that social complexity in the Maya Lowlands was stimulated by overpopulation and warfare.

7. Toward the end of the Preclassic, the Southern Maya Lowlands felt a strong influence that had its origin somewhere outside of the lowlands to the southeast. The impact was strongest in the area covered by the Floral Park ceramic sphere. In the Central Zone, the influence was more remote, and previous populations seem to have continued and prospered. I do not feel, however, that the Tikal data are complete enough to reject the possibility of changes in the leadership or elite structure of the Central Zone sites.

8. The Protoclassic impact, whatever its nature, had a profound influence upon the subsequent development of Maya culture, and was a major impetus in the recrystallization that marked the start of the Early Classic. I believe that far more than changes in ceramic styles were involved, but the direction of change seems to have been positive rather than disruptive. Although localized warfare or population replacement may have occurred at some sites, there was no halt in Maya development as there was at the time of the Early Classic hiatus. Consequently, any political or population intrusions from outside the lowlands must have left intact much of the local infrastructure.

9. Teotihuacan influence may have entered the Maya Lowlands at about this time. Again, the influence was positive and led to increased prosperity of lowland sites. Both Floral Park and Teotihuacan stimuli may have had the effect of integrating the Maya Lowlands more firmly into general Mesoamerican spheres of communication and economic interchange, probably to the mutual benefit of all concerned.

(1897, 1900, 1905, 1911, 1914–16, 1918, 1927, 1938, 1939, 1943; Gann and Gann 1939), who between 1896 and 1936 recorded much material that would otherwise have been lost, and excavated at Santa Rita (where in 1896 he discovered the famous Late Postclassic frescoes in Mixteca-Puebla style), Louisville, Nohmul, and other sites in northern Belize. Analysis of his often fragmentary reports (Hammond 1973: 6–18) shows that he had gathered evidence of Chicanel, Floral Park, Tzakol, Tepeu, and Late Postclassic occupation. Haberland (1958) suggested the presence of Mamom at Louisville on the basis of sherds from the fill of a circular platform with inset stair, and a notable focus of Floral Park activity at Nohmul was documented by Anderson and Cook (1944) in the recovery of some thirty vessels from three chambers in the large outlying pyramid Structure 277;[2] these are discussed further below. In 1962 Bullard (1965) carried out the first stratigraphic excavation in the region at San Estevan, a medium-sized major ceremonial center[3] on the New River. His investigation of Structures I and II, two temple-pyramids at the southern end of the main group, elucidated a sequence beginning in the Late Preclassic with the Vásquez Chicanel ceramic complex, which had Mamom traits that Bullard chose to interpret as archaizing, followed by a Tzakol florescence and Tepeu decline, leading to abandonment by Tepeu 2; archaizing ceramics with basal-flanged bowl persisted, according to Bullard, into the Late Classic. Bullard's assessment of Late Classic decline was challenged by E. L. Green (1973) on the basis of test pitting in Corozal District, but her excavation of test pits through Gann's backdirt heaps (Schmidt, personal communication 1971) and her confusion of map grid squares with latitude and longitude (Green 1973:290) do not engender confidence in the reported results, which are in any case not site specific. Green's elephantine regression analysis yielded the mouselike truism that Maya sites are located near water and arable land (a point made succinctly by Wright et al. 1959).

There was, therefore, little recent or reliable information about the archaeology of northern Belize when the Corozal Project began work in 1973, and the immediate objectives included the construction of a regional ceramic chronology and the location of sufficient sites to indicate the probable ancient relationship among settlement, landscape, and resources. Within this necessary framework we intended to investigate in particular the Preclassic-Classic transition. We knew from the work of Gann and Bullard that the region had been settled before and during the transition and that it contained at least four sites with Floral Park ceramics: San Estevan, Santa Rita, Nohmul, and an unnamed site near the mouths of the Hondo and New rivers found by Gann (Gann and Gann 1939) which yielded three "mushroom" vessels probably of Hongo Composite type, a "chocolate pot," and a mammiform tetrapodal dish, among other finds. Gann had found a number of Protoclassic vessels at Nohmul, and there was also the large group reported by Anderson and Cook (1944) from Structure 277 (apparently Gann and Gann's Mound 10), where a monumental stucco mask 0.90 m in height was reported on the antepenultimate phase of construction.

Northern Belize, therefore, seemed a good place to examine the Preclassic-Classic transition and the role of the Protoclassic. It also lay across the valleys of the Hondo and New rivers, two major water routes from the Central Zone to the Caribbean, and might therefore reveal evidence of contact between the coast and the interior. Such evidence might document external stimuli of commercial, colonial, or migratory nature from the Maya Highland Zone or from central Mexico, factors which have been adduced as influences in the crystallization of Classic Maya civilization. The presence of the two major Protoclassic sites of Holmul and Nohmul on the Hondo, together with Barton Ramie on the Belize River and Altar de Sacrificios on the Pasión indicated that the riverine environment—as opposed to the interior or subsurface drainage of the "core" as defined by Rathje (1971)—might have had some significance in whatever development was reflected archaeologically by the Floral Park ceramic complex.

Since we began work in 1973, several other teams have begun independent research within the area of our excavation and survey concession. The University of the Americas is excavating at El Pozito (Fig. 3.1: Site 19), close to its southern limits, under the direction of Mary B. Neivens; David Freidel of Southern Methodist University is working at Cerros (Fig. 3.1: Site 20); Raymond V. Sidrys of the University of California, Los Angeles, carried out a season of test excavation in Corozal District in 1974; Alfred Siemens of the University of British Columbia and Dennis Puleston of the University of Minnesota carried out surveys of ridged-field complexes in the Hondo River Valley from 1973 through 1975. Bruce Dahlin of this group is concentrating on the archaeology of Albion Island, which lies between two branches of the Hondo. Some of the information in this chapter is based on personal communication from these colleagues, who are in varying degrees sharing their results with our project.

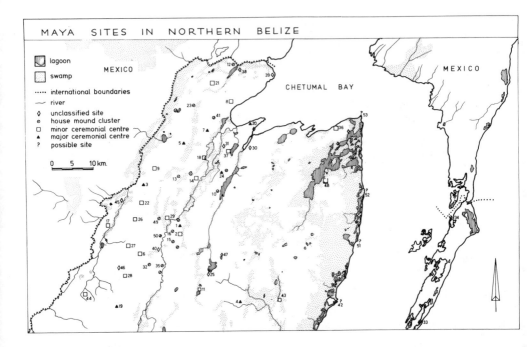

FIGURE 3.1. Archaeological sites in northern Belize, classified on Bullard's three-level hierarchy.

The area of our permit from the Government of Belize[4] comprised some thirty-five hundred square kilometers covering the whole Corozal District and the northern part of the Orange Walk District of modern Belize. Within this area our field program consisted of: (1) the accurate location of as many sites as possible, the detailed mapping of selected examples, the delineation of environmental zones, and the establishment of the relationship of settlement to environment; (2) extensive testing and intensive structural excavation to provide a chronological yardstick for the study of changing site distribution and utilization. Site location was carried out on foot, in motor vehicles and helicopters, and by examination of stereo aerial photographs (available satellite photographs had too much cloud cover to be useful). At present some fifty to sixty sites have been recorded, ranging in area from under one hectare to over twenty-four square kilometers; a similar range and density of sites is reported by Harrison (1975) for the adjacent region of southern Quintana Roo.

A hierarchy of site types with nine levels and the potential for adding several more has been proposed, and at least one site at each level has been mapped (Hammond 1975b). The levels suggested are: single mound; *plazuela* group; informal settlement cluster; formal settlement cluster; small minor ceremonial center; large minor ceremonial center; small major ceremonial center; medium major ceremonial center; large or regional ceremonial center. The classification, based on a synthesis of structure number, size, size differentiation, morphological diversity, and coherence of spatial organization, considers only surface features, that is, the final construction phase of each site. Insufficient excavation has been carried out to indicate whether any of these types are of restricted chronological significance, but the discovery by David Freidel (personal communication 1975) that the major structures at the medium major ceremonial center of Cerros apparently date from Late Preclassic times, with little subsequent construction or occupation, is a warning against regarding the regional settlement pattern as a reflection of Late Classic site utilization and demographic density.

The topographic structure of northern Belize has been characterized as a series of parallel limestone ridges running north-northeast, divided by fault troughs containing rivers, swamps, and lagoons, and decreasing in elevation and definition from west to east (Hammond 1974a: Fig. 2). Fourteen environmental zones have been isolated on the basis of topography, soil, and vegetation (Hammond 1973: 2–6). Most of the sites located so far are clustered on the higher ridges in the western part of the region or are adjacent to river, lagoon, or coast; more detailed analysis of site location in terms of specific soil type, climax plant community, and microlocal topography is in progress. The three sites that can be placed on the ninth (highest) level of the regional site hierarchy as regional ceremonial centers, Aventura, Nohmul, and El Pozito, all lie on the crest of the westernmost ridge—Aventura on its eastern arm, with the lower-order center of Louisville on the far side of a belt of swamp to the west—and the politically important spacings are clearly those along the ridge, namely, Aventura to Nohmul (19 km), Nohmul to El Pozito (28 km), and El Pozito to Lamanai (24 km).

(Lamanai, or Indian Church, currently being excavated by David M. Pendergast of the Royal Ontario Museum, lies on the eastern margin of this ridge, on the New River Lagoon, beyond the southern limits of our survey area.)

The eye of faith can discern the outlines of a Christaller central-place landscape with lower-order ceremonial centers spaced around these major sites, but the pattern cannot be substantiated without considerable further work to the west in the southernmost part of Quintana Roo. Among the several sites there that are relevant to the archaeology of the Hondo River Valley, perhaps the most important is Ucum, apparently a medium major ceremonial center, which stands on the bluffs above the confluence of the Hondo and Ucum rivers, controlling the eastern end of the historically attested trade route across central Yucatan to the Puuc (Roys 1943:52). Again, the simpler techniques of locational analysis can be used to define theoretical territories around sites. The Thiessen polygon for San Estevan (Fig. 3.1: Site 1), measured against all adjacent major ceremonial centers, has an area of some 324 sq km, while a circular territory based on the mean distance to adjacent major centers has an area of 276 sq km; we might suggest that, given coeval and coequal function of all sites used in the analysis, the ceremonial center of San Estevan controlled a territory of 300 ± 25 sq km. On a smaller scale the technique of site catchment analysis (Vita-Finzi and Higgs 1970) is useful in defining the range of resources economically exploitable from a home base, and the cumulative results of nearly sixty such analyses (upon which I am currently at work) should bring out any regularities in the pattern.

The Corozal Project has so far carried out excavations at eight sites and collected surface material from many others, at some of which Raymond Sidrys has also carried out test excavations. The overall results suggest that occupation of northern Belize began in very early Middle Preclassic times or even toward the end of the Early Preclassic (using the chronological dividing line of 1000 B.C.). The earliest ceramic complex, the Swasey, is so far known only from one site, Cuello (Fig. 3.1: Site 6), where the project's excavations in 1975[5] found it stratigraphically preceding the López Mamom complex. One radiocarbon date for an early López level at Cuello has so far been processed: 1020 ± 160 b.c. (Q-1476), calibrating on the MASCA formula to 1020–1500 B.C. This is the earliest radiocarbon date so far reported for the Maya Lowlands (see Fig. 3.2), more than three centuries earlier than the date for the Xe complex at Seibal (UCLA-1437) of 660 ± 75 b.c., which calibrates to around 900 B.C., and marginally earlier than the date of 975 ± 340 b.c. (LJ-505) for Formative I under Structure 605 at Dzibilchaltun. The Dzibilchaltun date, although accepted by E. Wyllys Andrews IV, was at variance with another Formative I sample from the same structure, which gave a date of 180 ± 200 b.c.; the mean of these two dates, around 580 b.c., seems to be that accepted by Andrews V (1974) at present for formative I (now Nabanche). Although it is exciting to play chronological leapfrog, one radiocarbon date does not make a chronology, and until further determinations for the Cuello sequence are available, Q-1476 should be treated with suitable caution.

At present we are able to say little about Swasey-complex ceramics, on which analysis has not begun, except to remark some resemblance to Xe but no great similarity to either early Eb or early Jenney Creek. The López Mamom ceramic complex (see Fig. 3.3) fits well into the overall Mamom sphere as defined by Willey, Culbert, and Adams (1967) and Ball (Chapter 5, below) and has so far been found at five sites, Cuello, Nohmul, Colha, San Estevan, and Louisville (accepting Haberland's [1958] attribution for this last). Outside the region this sparse presence is found also at Altun Ha to the south and Becan to the west.

The succeeding Cocos Chicanel ceramic complex has been found at 17 sites, including all those of subsequent ceremonial-center status that have been sampled. It is of characteristic Chicanel appearance, dominated by the Sierra ceramic group. (We should note, however, that subtle variants even between sites in northern Belize indicate that among the ceramics of this region there is less uniformity than seems to be claimed for other parts of the Chicanel sphere. This may be of some relevance given the diversity of the succeeding Floral Park sphere.) Cocos has a late facet, more or less equivalent to late Cantutse at Seibal, in which vessels made from a standard Chicanel waxy fabric exhibit such features as ring bases, Z angles, and incurving-sided bowls with vertical neck, basal ridge, and possibly basal flange. Among the more notable Cocos vessels are a grotesque humanoid effigy vessel from Kichpanha, 14 flaring-sided bowls with pale resist decoration from the foundation cache of Structure 138 at Nohmul, and 4 vessels included in the foundation cache of Structure 110 at Nohmul. These 4 comprised 2 flaring-sided red bowls, a similar black bowl, and a deep black bowl for which the flaring-sided black one acted as a

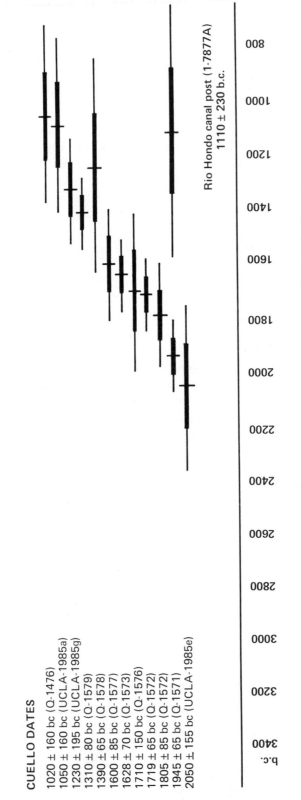

FIGURE 3.2. Radiocarbon dates for the Early Formative Swasey phase at Cuello, northern Belize. An Early Formative date of 1250±110 B.C. (Q-1575) for Jenney Creek levels at Barton Ramie, collected 1976, is not included. Swasey ceramic-complex pottery, dated to 2000-1000 B.C. in radiocarbon years, 2600-1250 B.C. in calendar years, has also been found at the sites of Nohmul, San Estevan, El Pozito and Santa Rita in northern Belize and at Becan, Campeche, and suggests widespread lowland occupation before 1000 B.C. The earliest radiocarbon dates for the Pasión Valley are of 660±75 B.C. from Seibal and 745±185 B.C. from Altar de Sacrificios. No radiocarbon dates from Peten are known of before 600 B.C.

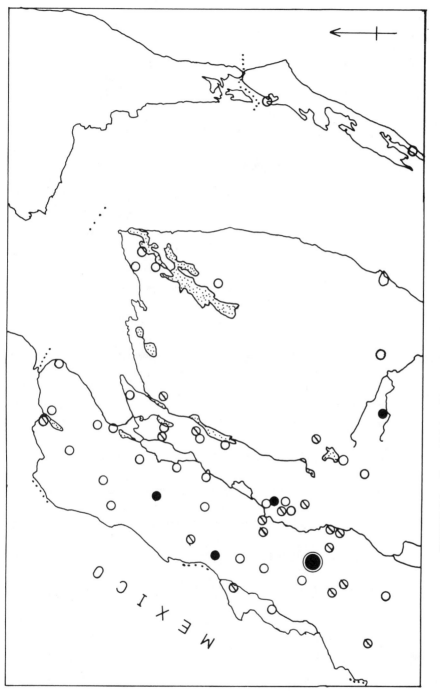

FIGURE 3.3. Sites with López Mamom occupation in northern Belize (solid discs); site with pre-Mamom Swasey occupation (solid disc with ring); sites for which no chronological data are available (open barred discs).

cover. Among the contents of the two black vessels were four small jade "bib-head" pendants (all probably made from the same block, and certainly from the same source, as determined by X-ray fluorescence and neutron activation analysis) and two scalloped earflares; the pendants differed clearly enough to represent four distinct iconographic personalities. The same four personalities recur on a similar set of heads recovered in 1975 from a Late Preclassic cache at Cerros (Freidel, personal communication) which also included a larger mask in a more sophisticated version of the same style, expressing the concept of life/death duality, and a pair of earflares; in this case the four small heads were laid out orthogonally toward the cardinal points of the compass, with the larger mask at the center. It may be that we have in both caches representations of the gods of the four world directions or the four quarters of the Maya conceptual universe (Barthel 1968). These same four iconographic personalities may also appear on the Pomona jade earflare (Kidder and Ekholm 1951), which is of terminal Preclassic date, being associated with a number of Chicanel vessels and also two tetrapodal mammiform bowls. We have, at the very least, evidence of a structured pattern of cache deposition, associated with the construction of nondomestic buildings and involving ceramics, jade, and some sort of quadripartite conception. The known distribution of "bib-head" pendants up the East Coast north from Nohmul to Tancah and in Yucatan at Chichen Itza (Proskouriakoff 1974), Ake, and Ticul suggests that this concept may have a wider spread and also that at this date jade may have been traded up the Motagua River–Caribbean Coast route suggested (Hammond 1972) for obsidian in the Classic Period.

The Freshwater Floral Park ceramic complex, which is morphologically but apparently not chronologically separable from the late Cocos facet, brings in mammiform supports and polychrome painting, together with increased gloss finish which is still burnish, rather than gloss-slip. The unslipped component consists of jars and possibly bowls, the jars with outcurving or flared necks and bolstered rims, the body and neck with herringbone striation right up to the rim. The monochrome slipped wares are predominantly orange and light red, with some cream, perhaps falling into the lighter end of the orange range, and a little greenish-buff. A "proto-orange" ranges from buff to light orange, with fire clouding frequent and an easily eroded slip. A glossy light red-orange continues into the Early Classic Nuevo Tzakol ceramic complex, and features rare scribed arc ornament. A moldy red has a loose, porous, friable paste, orange-red in color and dullish in surface with much crackling. A Red-on-Orange is close to Guacamallo Red-on-Orange at Altar de Sacrificios, and there is an orange polychrome decorated in red and black. Forms include a jar with low vertical neck and direct rim; incurving-sided bowl with vertical neck, similar to the basic form of Chiquibul Modeled at Barton Ramie; ring bases and Z-angle bowls; mammiform supports and rounded Z angles on waxy red fabric; basal-break bowls with flaring sides and mammiform supports; flaring-sided bowls with mammiform supports; some medial-angle bowls with (missing) tetrapodal supports and others with vertical neck. Some Cocos types are found associated with Freshwater levels; the degree of contemporaneity, rather than mixing due to later disturbance, is not yet clear, but Cocos material is certainly found redeposited with Classic and Postclassic ceramics elsewhere.

Floral Park–sphere ceramics are known from six sites (Fig. 3.4). One, near the mouths of the Hondo and New rivers, is not locatable (Gann and Gann 1939: Plate 10); the others are San Estevan (fragments of two vessels; Bullard 1965: Fig. 12k), Santa Rita (two vessels; Gann 1918), Aventura and Chan Chen (unspecified; R. Sidrys, personal communication 1975), and Nohmul (Gann 1911; Gann and Gann 1939; Anderson and Cook 1944; Hammond 1973, 1974a). The Nohmul material includes both a complete ceramic complex, the Freshwater Floral Park complex (Pring 1974)—including unslipped, monochrome, and polychrome types recovered in the 1973–74 excavations in several parts of the site—and a large collection of complete vessels including 13 tetrapodal bowls with mammiform supports. Most of these vessels come from three looted chambers in Structure 277, and their precise associations have been lost, as have several of the vessels, both at the time of discovery and later. They can, however, be seriated into the stratigraphic sequence established by Merwin at Holmul. At Nohmul the Freshwater Floral Park ceramic complex is associated with substantial building activity in several parts of the site at some distance from the ceremonial precinct, and Freshwater ceramics are also present in quantity in the earliest levels of the suggested "port facility" on the banks of the Hondo River. A large and organized population is suggested. At most of the sites occupied in the Cocos phase, however, particularly those where there is continuity from the Late Preclassic into the Early Classic, Freshwater ceramics

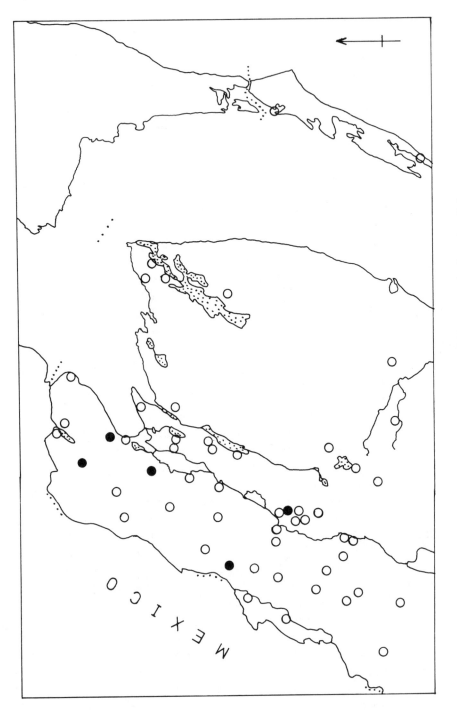

FIGURE 3.4. Sites with Freshwater–Floral Park occupation in northern Belize.

are lacking. Their absence suggests that there cannot have been a regional Protoclassic phase as a distinct unit of time; rather, the Freshwater complex must have been in use at Nohmul, and perhaps a few other sites, while Chicanel-sphere ceramics continued to be made and used elsewhere in the region, and perhaps in parts of Nohmul itself. It may well be that the stratification reflected by this complex is not one of chronological succession or geographical distribution, but of social differentiation. (A similar hypothesis could explain why, in the Terminal Classic on the Pasión, Jimba ceramics are restricted in spatial distribution to Group A at Altar de Sacrificios but occur mixed with Bayal pottery in trash deposits both there and at Seibal. In effect this sort of hypothesis reconciles R. E. W. Adams's [1971, 1973b] notion of separateness with J. A. Sabloff's [1973, 1975] evidence of contemporaneity.)

Ceramics of the Nuevo Tzakol complex are known from 19 sites, of which 15 also yielded Cocos Chicanel material. Of the other 4 sites, 3 seem first to have been occupied in the Early Classic, and 1, Kichpanha (Fig. 3.1: Site 11), seems to have been abandoned after the Preclassic until the Late Classic, when it may well have been a satellite settlement of the great chert-tool factory at Colha (Fig. 3.1: Site 4). At sites with both Late Preclassic and Early Classic material there has been no reported evidence of a hiatus in occupation such as would be compatible with a separate Protoclassic time period. The Nuevo ceramic complex falls completely within the Tzakol ceramic sphere, with a degree of regionalization yet to be determined.

Although the Late Classic is beyond the scope of this volume, we might note that evidence from that period documents a reorientation in ceramic style from the Peten to northern Yucatan, including the inception of a local slateware tradition, that supports Ball's (1974a) hypothesis of increasing northern influence in the Southern Lowlands. The total excavation of Structure 139 at Nohmul (Hammond 1974a, 1975a) revealed a Late Classic masonry podium with Terminal Classic graves (one containing a red-on-cream barrel-shaped pedestal vase and a resist-decorated slateware plate; see Hammond 1974a: Plate XXIIIb), superimposed on which was a stonewalled building of apparent Late Postclassic architecture. There was evidence of continuity of occupation, suggesting that the Terminal Classic in northern Belize extended into what is formally the Early Postclassic (supported by Sidrys's recovery of Plumbate and Fine Orange sherds from several sites in Corozal District [personal communication 1975]) and that the region lies close to the northeastern limits of the Classic demographic collapse, with elite activity in the ceremonial centers ceasing but occupation and trade continuing at a reasonable level of organization. A caveat must be entered, however: Late Postclassic ceramics were surprisingly rare in the construction levels of the stonewalled Building Z of Structure 139, consisting of one Tulum Red sherd, and were absent from the corresponding levels of the architecturally identical Structure 141, which faces it across the patio. The quantity of Late Postclassic material is more compatible with short occupation (D. C. Pring, personal communication 1975). The buildings are similar to that reported by Eaton (1976) in his Operation 21 D east of Becan, dating to the Late Classic Chintok phase of A.D. 730–830. If the Nohmul buildings were of this date, the continuity of occupation from the level with Terminal Classic graves would be commonplace, though nonetheless suggesting north Yucatecan influence, and the persistence of organized life through the collapse period not proven.

The northern orientation of culture persists into the Late Postclassic proper. Tulum Red and buff censer wares have been found in northern Belize at 29 sites, many of which show evidence of minor but organized ritual activity in the construction of small slab-faced platforms on or against presumably abandoned Classic ceremonial center structures and the deposition of large quantities of effigy *incensario* fragments. Occupation, where its magnitude can be measured, seems to be light, except perhaps at Santa Rita, where Gann (1900, 1918) found Late Postclassic ceramics in virtually every mound he excavated, and where elite activities including fresco painting were clearly carried out. At this period northern Belize is a noted cacao-growing area, historically part of the polity of Chetumal (Roys 1943:52, 54; 1957) and archaeologically a southern extension of the East Coast Zone. It is tempting to see Santa Rita, on its old, defensible sea cliff, as the southernmost of the epigonal Maya coastal nuclei, similar to Tancah rather than Tulum.

The overall sequence from northern Belize suggests uninterrupted occupation from at least the early Middle Preclassic, and possibly from a date prior to 1000 b.c.,[6] down to the Late Postclassic and the Spanish conquest; the colonial sequence has not yet been investigated, although to the south, at Lamanai, Pendergast is obtaining significant results. Although the striking increase in site occupancy from Mamom (5) to

Chicanel (17) may be just an artifact of sampling, it matches well with the situation reported by other contributors to this volume. The similar number of Chicanel and Tzakol occupations and their presence on most of the same sites argue against an intermediate Protoclassic Period when only Floral Park ceramics were in use and only 5 sites occupied, and the evidence from Nohmul suggests that the Freshwater Floral Park complex is contemporary with the Late Preclassic and substantially derives from the Cocos Chicanel complex. This outline of the culture sequence in northern Belize may now be subsumed in a general discussion of some of the problems facing the seminar.

PROBLEMS

We shall address three sequential and cumulative problems of process: (1) the origins of settlement in the lowlands; (2) the origins of complex society there; and (3) the origins of civilization *sensu stricto*. The latter two processes need to be considered separately because several areas of the New World, particularly northwestern South America, evolved complex societies without attaining formal civilization, but in doing so acquired some of the characteristics seen by Adams and Culbert (Chapter 1, above) as defining Classic Maya civilization.

The Origins of Settlement

The earliest indications of human occupation of the Maya Lowlands are not archaeological but botanical. Wiseman (1975) infers human interference with the vegetation in the northern Peten around 4000 B.C. from changes in the pollen sequence detectable in a core from Lake Eckixil by the use of principal-components analysis. His dating is based on a sedimentation rate derived by comparison with the sedimentation rate in Laguna de Petenxil a short distance away (Cowgill et al. 1966). At Petenxil the "*Zea* intrusion," with fragments of burnt corn stalk, has a radiocarbon date of 2100 b.c., calibrated to 2400 B.C. A sedimentation rate of 0.70 cm per year is proposed for Eckixil, and on this basis a weedy disturbance in the pollen spectrum at 450 cm is dated to about 4000 B.C. Wiseman suggests that following this initial intrusion of man into the lowlands an economy based on manioc, camote, and other root crops supported the population, with maize seed-crop agriculture coming in, presumably from the highlands, in the latter part of the third millennium B.C.

At present there is no archaeological evidence to support Wiseman's proposal, although this does not affect the value of his data. Apart from the evidence of glottochronology, the next suggestion of human occupation in the lowlands comes from northern Belize, where a radiocarbon date of 1020 ± 160 b.c., calibrated to 1020–1500 B.C., comes from an early Middle Preclassic burial at the site of Cuello (which is, perhaps coincidentally, close to Puleston's [1974] claimed early aceramic site of Richmond Hill). Further determinations on the levels stratigraphically earlier than the burial, associated with the pre-Mamom Swasey ceramic complex, are awaited.[7] Other radiocarbon dates for the Maya Preclassic include one of 975 ± 340 b.c. from Dzibilchaltun's Nabanche Mamom complex and another for the same context of 180 ± 200 b.c., their mean being 580 b.c.; 660 ± 75 b.c. for the Real Xe complex at Seibal; 558 ± 53 b.c. for early facet Eb complex and 456 ± 47 b.c. for early Tzec at Tikal; 320 ± 80 b.c., and 250 ± 90 b.c. for Late Preclassic, presumably Komchen, at Dzibilchaltun. With the exception of LJ-505 and LJ-508 for Dzibilchaltun, considered separately, these dates fall into correct stratigraphic order until we come to the most recently determined, Q-1476 from Cuello, which extends a Mamom-type Middle Preclassic back to and beyond the formal limits of that period, falling between and, in its 1-sigma range, overlapping two recent dates for Cuadros-Jocotal and Conchas from Salinas La Blanca on the Pacific Coast (UM-101/2). The recently excavated material from El Portón and Sakajut in Verapaz (Sedat and Sharer 1972) is claimed to be of late Early Preclassic date, and it seems reasonable to suggest that at about 1200 ± 100 B.C. one or more influxes of population moved north and/or east into the lowlands, bringing with them the first ceramic tradition for the area.

There are two opinions as to the origins of such an influx, which may be characterized as the "highland" and "lowland" positions. The former, advanced by the late James Gifford and subsequently by Sharer and Sedat, sees Lowland Maya origins in the highlands of El Salvador and Guatemala, based on similarities between the ceramics of Chalchuapa and Barton Ramie. The theory suggests a presumably water-borne Motagua River–Caribbean Coast–Belize River route as the entry into the Central Zone, and a movement, again presumably water-borne, from the Alta Verapaz down the Chixoy and Pasión into the Pasión Zone. Ceramic affinities between the Xe Complex on the Pasión and early levels at El Portón and Sakajut, together with at least indirect contact in the acquisition of obsidian, show that the latter hypothesis is tenable, but one wonders why emigrants from Chalchuapa should have traveled as far upcoast and upriver as Barton Ramie rather than using the southeastern flanks of the Maya Mountains. If we accept these links then we implicitly accept the existence of canoe transport at this date, and the potential for bulk commodity movement via canoe may have been a factor in the processes of settlement and highland-lowland contact. (If we accept Ocos-Chorrera links, of course, long-distance voyages would be a commonplace by 1200 B.C. in any case.)

The "lowland" position advanced by Joesink-Mandeville, Michael Coe, and others proposes penetration up the Usumacinta Basin and the west coast of Yucatan from the Gulf Coast farther west, where Olmec culture was rising to its apogee at San Lorenzo. There is an attractive parsimony about this model, which does not involve a change of environment. The Usumacinta Basin, like the Grijalva Trench, is an embayment of the peripheral coastal lowlands (the importance of the lowlands was emphasized by Parsons [1969]). These lowlands present a broad range of terrestrial, semiterrestrial, and aquatic resources for exploitation within a small geographical compass (M. D. Coe and Flannery 1964), and a move inland along the rivers would preserve much of this diversity, particularly the protein and transport potential, water availability, alluvial levee soils, and the richly varied plant communities of the river margins. At a site such as Seibal the fertile black soil on the limestone would replace the alluvium of the coastal plain, and Seibal, at present the earliest known site in the Western Lowlands, is ideally situated on high, well-drained, well-aired, and potentially defensible limestone bluff, yet with the resources of river, lagoon, and *bajo* within easy reach. Altar de Sacrificios is similarly, if less spectacularly, placed to exploit a wide range of local resources, and it is this tactical position rather than the strategic one envisaged by Willey and Smith (1969:8) that probably governed the location of the original settlement. Barton Ramie again exploits river, alluvium, and terrace and is only a few kilometers from limestone hill soils, while Cuello lies on the crest of a broad and fertile limestone ridge with the perennial New River and its damp bottomlands only five kilometers away.

When settlement moved back from the rivers into the hinterland, this range of resource zones was diminished, as Puleston and Puleston (1971, 1974) note, but not to the uniformity so often assumed. The rolling topography of the limestone hill country provides a fair range of ecological niches—defined by degree of slope, aspect, prevailing wind, insolation, and drainage—each of which has distinct characteristics including subtle gradations of climax vegetation, soil texture, and responsiveness to agriculture. The limestone upland niche complex is itself intercut by lower-level niches including *bajo* and seasonal water sources, and both the upper- and lower-level niches were modified by the later Maya inhabitants to increase their potential and/or counter the deleterious effects of human activity. Dennis Puleston's notable contribution has been to point up the potential of ramon *(Brosimum alicastrum)* as a staple, but I am not convinced that its intensive exploitation in the Middle Preclassic was, as he argues, the critical factor in opening up the hinterland. I feel rather that ramon attained its greatest importance much later, in the Late Classic, when it could have extended the carrying capacity of the Central Zone as other resources became stretched—that it was a "critical" resource as defined by Wilkinson (1974) rather than a basic one. Ramon was probably utilized in the Preclassic, along with anything else edible, but its reputation as a famine food among the Maya is more convincing than Puleston's desire, as it were, to have it for every meal.

Movement away from the rivers would automatically create a two-level hierarchy of site locations—good and better—so the beginnings of a complex settlement pattern may already be present in the Middle Preclassic. Regionalized Mamom ceramics have been shown by Ball (Chapter 5, below) to extend into northern Yucatan, but the southern part of the Mamom sphere remains firm through the succeeding Chicanel, Tzakol, and Tepeu spheres. By the Late Classic the area contains the largest number of most closely packed major ceremonial centers in the Southern Lowlands (Hammond 1974b:323). This primary region of uniform culture encompasses much of Rathje's (1971) "core," and its clear suitability for settlement accords ill with the postulated absence of advantage which is the *primum mobile* of his model for the rise of Classic civilization.

The major problem at the moment seems to be establishing which of several competing pre-Mamom complexes was ancestral to this first pan-lowland sphere. Culbert (Chapter 2, above) remarks that neither Xe nor Jenney Creek is a likely progenitor for the Early Eb material at Tikal, and although the later north Belizean material is close to Tzec at Tikal, there is again no apparent close relationship between Swasey and early López, and Eb. Culbert sees this diversity as evidence for multiple migrations into the Maya Lowlands from different source areas. In considering the rapid spread of the Preclassic, Adams (Chapter 4) and Ball (Chapter 5) invoke the parallel of the Neolithic Danubian I culture in prehistoric Europe. It might be worth noting that many of the marked differences between Danubian culture and the immediately ancestral Starčevo-Körös groups in the Balkans are directly ascribable to the crossing of the ecological frontier between Mediterranean and Temperate Europe; different resources differently exploited produce cultural differences. It may be that our failure to find precise antecedents for the first Lowland Maya settlers is due to a similar transmutation across the highland-lowland ecotone.

The Origins of Complex Society

The consensus of this volume is that a complex society existed in the Southern and at least part of the Northern Lowlands by the Late Preclassic. The evidence comes from the excavations at Tikal, Altar de Sacrificios, Uaxactun, Becan, Dzibilchaltun, and other sites where monumental public architecture implies the existence of (1) a labor force living outside but owing allegiance to the ceremonial center, (2) specialist artisans, and (3) some administrative organization to plan, construct, and use these community buildings. Trading contacts including jade sources—probably in the Motagua and possibly in other parts of the Guatemalan Highlands—indicate the inception of sumptuary as well as consumption trade and probably used the same trade routes and distribution mechanism that had served for obsidian since Xe times. Jade and obsidian were both low-bulk items, but the consumer and the purpose of consumption differed.

The presence of bark beaters by the Late Preclassic suggests the making of writing surfaces[8] and hence the use of writing to record sacred or secular matters. Records of an administered redistributive and external trading system based in the ceremonial center might, for example, be kept in written form (a parallel would be the Linear A and B tablets of Minoan Crete). Such a trading system implies differential production of commodities in varying ecological niches within the region of control; central control of such commodities equals maximum access to them. Stratification of society in terms of differential access to at least nonperishable resources, insofar as these are used as grave goods, begins to be archaeologically detectable by this period.

Such social strata would seem to have included at least: (1) overall direction responsible for strategic planning; (2) executive bureaucracy responsible for tactical fulfillment in terms of resource procurement, quantity assessment, and infrastructure support; and (3) labor force charged with practical fulfillment of executive decisions, perhaps further divided into skilled artisan and unskilled laborer levels.

All this socioeconomic information is discernible from the archaeological evidence, which, in the consensus of the contributors to this volume, also indicates an increase in population and in uniformity of material culture in the Late Preclassic. In northern Belize, according to present knowledge, this increase is expressed as a 350-percent rise in site unit occupations over the Mamom level; every investigated site of subsequent major ceremonial center status and many of minor center status were occupied by this time. The settlement of all favorable, as opposed to usable, locations suggests a population at optimum density, and the noted uniformity of Chicanel culture, particularly in ceramics, over the whole sphere indicates a high degree of interaction between sites, perhaps at the level of a noncoercive but numinously sanctioned ritual overlordship. The inception of sumptuary trade, presumably between the topmost levels of local hierarchies if not by directed specialists, may be a facet of or a stimulus to such interaction. Public monumental architecture suggests the beginning of ceremonial underpinning for the elite and the numinous sanctions they controlled. It also indicates that certain sites were beginning to function as the repositories of communal effort and loyalty for certain regions—site territories containing populations whose loyalty above the kin level was directed toward a common focus. What R. E. W. Adams (Chapter 4, below) characterizes as "ancestor worship" may be rather a ratification of territorial possession by appeal to the past.

Although we now acknowledge the existence of complex society in the lowlands in Late Preclassic times, it is perhaps surprising that we should only recently have done so. The existence of monumental public architecture and sculpture in the adjacent Olmec region has been known for several decades, and in the late 1960s communal architecture of the late second millennium B.C. was found in Oaxaca (Flannery 1970). Olmec ceremonial centers are now known to occur east into the Grijalva Trench (see Lowe, Chapter 9 below). There is in fact no a priori reason why the earliest Lowland Maya settlements, if and when we find them, should not prove to have architectural and, inferentially, social differentiation. Willey (Chapter 6, below) notes "modest public architecture" at Altar de Sacrificios in the late San Felix Mamom phase, and some jade is known from the lowlands by this date; Willey admits the possibility of a Xe ceremonial center at Seibal. It may be that our relatively small exposures of and samples from Middle Preclassic levels have led to a failure to realize that the increasing complexity of Maya society which we now accept for the Late Preclassic may have begun more than half a millennium earlier.[9]

The Emergence of Civilization

If population density and site spacing were optimal by the Late Preclassic, any increase in density would produce the basis for competition. The more favored locations—those with both ample resources and the sanction of antiquity—were natural central places in the cultural landscape, already evolving into the regional capitals of the Classic. Competition had been implicit in the Mamom riverine-hinterland site distribution, but increased pressure on overall resources would make it explicit. As Netting notes (Chapter 12, below), rapid cultural intensification and elaboration coincide with increasing population density and land scarcity; the effort needed by newly founded sites to compete with advantaged neighbors could have resulted in greater internal organization and cohesion and more effective competition. Some such process may lie behind the rise of Tikal and other centers in Rathje's "core."

We may gain insight into the results of competition by examining two advantaged Late Preclassic sites in northern Belize that failed to attain or maintain higher-order status in the Classic Period. Kichpanha (Fig. 3.1: Site 11) seems to be a minor ceremonial center with a small pyramid and a large platform structure in the Late Preclassic; thereafter it consists of nothing more than a cluster of *plazuela* groups on the terrace above the lagoon. The site lies more or less where the territories (as defined by Thiessen polygons) of the Classic major ceremonial centers of Colha, El Pozito, and San Estevan meet (Fig. 3.1: Sites 4, 19, 1). Kichpanha may have been unable to carve out a realm for itself in the face of their competition. For this model to be convincing, however, we need evidence of a stronger Early Classic presence at Colha than we have so far. An alternative model could be a move of the minor ceremonial locus eastward from Kichpanha to Colha in the face of competition from the two stronger centers. The case of Cerros (Fig. 3.1: Site 20), on a peninsula in Corozal Bay, is a curious one. Until the 1975 excavations by David Freidel this medium major ceremonial center, with two substantial pyramids, was blithely assumed to be of Classic date; so far, however, the excavations have produced evidence of major construction in the Late Preclassic, including a Chicanel cache only a meter or so down in one of the pyramids, with a little Early Classic refurbishment and then apparent abandonment until the Late Postclassic, when the site was used as a pilgrimage center. Whether Cerros was shut out by the development of the major center at Aventura some ten kilometers to the west or became cut off from its hinterland to the south by the rise of other sites we do not yet know, but as with the Early Classic decline of Seibal such a geopolitical model seems the only alternative to depopulation by natural agency as a feasible explanation for the underutilization of such an advantaged site. The construction of the ditch and rampart at Becan at the same period is another expression of competitive process (Webster: Chapter 13, below; R. E. W. Adams: Chapter 4, below), but Becan survived the pressure.

Competition existed not only between human communities but between each community and its environment. Greater-than-optimal population density would force a group to extract the maximum support from its territory. This process of intensification, discussed by many of the contributors to this volume, can perhaps be codified in six dimensions: horizontal, vertical, temporal, specific, microlocal, and manual. Some of these are more quickly and easily adopted than others, but most operate simultaneously, so that any model for intensification of resource extraction must be a multidimensional one.

Horizontal intensification is perhaps the most obvious course, but some methods of apparently horizontal intensification, such as the conquest of new territory or the exploitation of previously unused potentially arable areas, are really *extensive* methods of increasing resource input. Horizontal intensification involves putting more productive units into the same area, shortening journey-to-work time by locating the residence amidst the land its occupants farm. The farmsteads reported by Eaton (1976), closely scattered across the landscape, are examples of this phenomenon. Even the largest of them is hardly more than the residence of a single family—and this possibly nuclear rather than extended, if allowance is made among the structures for storage and cooking facilities. The small walled enclosures attached to the houses are interpreted as work and storage areas, but they could equally well have been used as turkey pens.

Vertical intensification increases the amount of exploitable land within the region of control by bringing into production environmental zones hitherto unused because of their altitude, steepness, or wetness. Previously unproductive niches are adapted to become gently sloping, well-drained, stable arable land. Thin soils that erode once their forest cover has been removed can be trapped by hill terraces such as those reported by Turner (1974) in central Yucatan and by various authors in the Cayo District on the northern flanks of the Maya Mountains in Belize. At the same time the angle of slope of the land surface is reduced, providing what is effectively well-drained artificial alluvium (Turner 1974: Fig 3). Wet land on river or swamp margins can be turned into two productive niches, drained land and open water, by the construction of raised fields (Fig. 3.5), known widely in the Americas (Denevan 1970) and specifically in the Maya Lowlands in the Candelaria Basin (Siemens and Puleston 1972), the area roughly between Becan (Turner 1974; Harrison 1975) and Lake Bacalar and south from there along the Hondo and New rivers in northern Belize. The construction and use of raised fields in northern Belize seems to begin in the Late Preclassic and peak in the Early Classic; Dahlin (1974) suggests a diminution in their use on the basis of site unit occupancy in the Albion Island area after Tzakol 2, but given the continued florescence at both El Pozito and Nohmul, the two regional major ceremonial centers in the vicinity, local population movement asymmetrically sampled (Dahlin's suggestion is made on the basis of four test pits) seems an equally likely explanation. The site exploitation territory of Nohmul clearly included a substantial number of such fields, constructed where the shallow limestone ridge ran down under the heavy clays of the Hondo and New river valleys and immediately

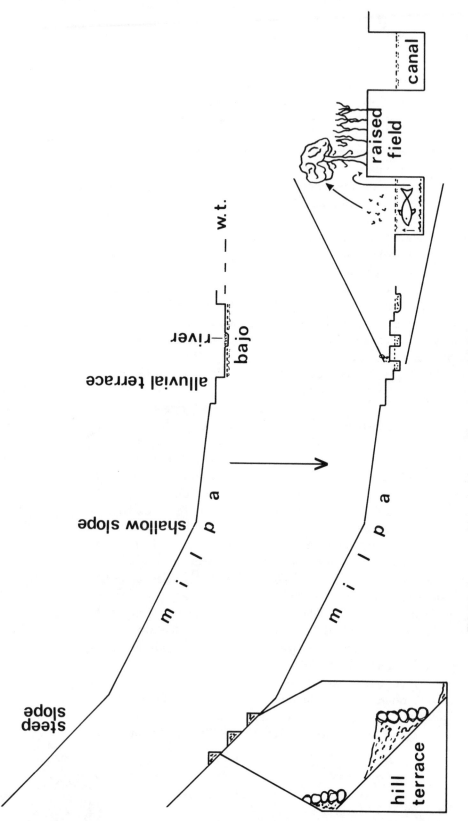

FIGURE 3.5. Vertical intensification of agriculture by the creation of artificial environmental niches, hill terraces, and raised fields.

accessible from the adjacent milpa land. The fields are in fact a logical extension of the milpa, as the canals between are extensions of the river or lagoon that they border. The fields, enriched by silt cleaned from the canals, would be perennially fertile like chinampas; they were undoubtedly used for growing maize (D. Puleston, personal communication 1974), probably for root crops, and in my opinion for cacao. The canals could be used for trapping or farming fish (Thompson 1974) and shellfish such as *juté* (*Pachychilus pyramidalis* Mor.) as a dependable protein source. The juxtaposition of the two niches would be advantageous both for easy access—to the fields by canoe for moving bulk produce and to the fishponds on foot—and because of the interaction of the denizens of the two niches; Dahlin (personal communication 1974) points out that cacao is pollinated by water-breeding midges, the eggs of which in the canals would form a source of fish food. The canals are relatively shallow, and the engraved bone from Burial 116 at Tikal which shows three Chacs fishing from a canoe in shallow water using a creel may illustrate the exploitation of such a controlled fish population. It is perhaps significant that the structure beside the Hondo River at Nohmul which has been interpreted as a port facility (Hammond 1974a:186)—a broad flat mound with a single substructure on the landward side, easily accessible to the river yet above flood level—yielded a large number of notched clay pellets, often dubbed "net sinkers." The open surface could have been used for stacking merchandise or for drying fish, for shipment upriver into Peten or for local storage. It may be significant that its construction took place at the end of the Late Preclassic (the plentiful associated Freshwater Floral Park ceramics hint at elite residence and control of the facility) and that by the Terminal Classic it was being used as a cemetery; thus its effective period of use as a port, if that is what it is, coincided with that of the construction and use of the raised-field complexes in the Hondo River Valley.

Temporal intensification, which increases resource extraction in a given period of time, may involve shortening the agricultural cycle or packing in more labor by manual intensification. It now seems accepted that the present extensive long-fallow milpa system could be compressed somewhat without irreversible damage to the soil, and in parts of the lowlands a much shorter cycle could have been the natural state of things. The data presented by Culbert, Magers, and Spencer (1974) are interesting in view of the ring of Classic major ceremonial centers positioned advantageously around the edge of the Maya Mountains massif; they include Ixkun, Caracol, Poptun, and perhaps Pusilha and Lubaantun on the southeastern slope, although there the rainfall is much higher.

Specific intensification means increasing the number of species cropped (see Netting, Chapter 12, below). It may extend into silviculture and increased systematic gathering of wild foods, both plant and animal. Vertical intensification aids this by providing contrasting niches in which complementary species will flourish, while a shorter cycle (temporal intensification) may mean that successive crops of different plants can be grown on the same land in the same year.

Microlocal intensification consists of increasing the number of species grown simultaneously on the same spot by layering—vegetative tubers and rhizomes underground, cucurbits on the surface, corn growing up with beans twined around it, and scattered trees selectively preserved when the land was cleared. A special case of this type is the dooryard garden (see Netting, Chapter 12, below), where small-bulk flavorings, delicacies, and decorations are grown within easy access to the kitchen in the highly fertile and humic soil resulting from recycling of domestic refuse.

Manual intensification, which is perhaps necessary for almost all of the other kinds of intensification, means putting more man-hours per hectare per year. The absolute yield increases as a result, although the yield per man-hour declines for dry farming; it may be that some other forms of intensification, such as the construction of raised fields, were a conscious attempt to counter this decline.

The ways in which these different kinds of intensification were combined must have varied across the lowlands with the local climate, topography, and degree of population pressure, but we can agree that many or all of them were used, and that the present low-pressure extensive milpa system lies at one end of a long continuum of possible types of land use in the Maya Lowlands.

Given (1) that such intensification did occur, (2) that a variety of intensification requiring organized mass labor, namely, the construction of the raised fields, was brought into play in the Late Preclassic, a time when a truly complex society is clearly present, and (3) that the appearance of Floral Park ceramics and inscribed monuments at the same time presages the emergence of the full panoply of Classic civilization, what connection, if any, is there between these coincident phenomena? The common factor, I believe, is that they are all a heightening of existing activity, rather than original events. Classic society may have been more stratified than that of the Late Preclassic, and more codified within a class and dynastic system, but what we call "Classic civilization" is simply the increased expression of this system in public architecture and monuments, sumptuary manufacture, and conspicuous funereal consumption, visible results of increasing central control over growing populations and the resultant ability to support nonprimary producers with the managed surplus of the rest.

The innovative ceramics of the Floral Park sphere are an aspect of this increased sumptuary manufacture, a form of "economic extensification" (Netting, Chapter 12, below) which is more or less restricted to pottery. The Floral Park sphere represents the first real differentiation between everyday and special purpose vessels: in the Late Preclassic the same ceramic types appear in graves, caches, and middens, whereas the bulk of the Floral Park types (but by no means all) come from burials and caches. This differentiation comes some time after that of architecture into public and private sectors, and the social/occupational differentiation implied by it, and is also later than the initial use of sumptuary goods to mark differential status in death, although this differentiation becomes more marked at the time of the Floral Park manifestations. Presumably the function of these innovative ceramics was similarly to mark status by the rarity, novelty, and increased energy input represented in such features as mammiform supports and experimental polychrome ornament. The iconographic sources of Protoclassic ceramic traits seem to be geographically distant and locationally diverse, but their combination and their effect were present only in a restricted area of the Southern Lowlands. A full Floral Park sphere ceramic complex is found at only a few sites—Nohmul, Barton Ramie, Altar de Sacrificios, and, by inference, Holmul—in an area embracing the upper basins of the Hondo and Belize rivers and the lower Pasión. In the same area, elements of the Floral Park sphere are present at such sites as Tikal, but there they clearly form part of the indigenous Terminal Preclassic ceramic complex. Beyond this central area of occurrence vessels of the most prominent Floral Park types—tetrapodal polychrome dishes with mammiform supports—are found to the limits of the Southern Lowlands. Their present northern limit of distribution runs from Xulha on Lake Bacalar to Dzibilnocac and Edzna in the Chenes region; a westward limit is reached at Aguacatal on the Laguna de Terminos and an eastward one at Pomona in the Stann Creek Valley of central Belize, where the Floral Park vessels are associated with a number of Chicanel types (Kidder and Ekholm 1951). The archaeologically attested southern limit seems to run from Altar de Sacrificios via Seibal to Poptun (Shook and Smith 1950), although a looted vessel photographed in Chichicastenango, El Quiché, was said to come from the north of that department, around the upper Lacantun or Chixoy (Hammond, field notes 1975), and certainly El Quiche seems a likely center of origin for some Floral Park modes.

The central area of Floral Park complex distribution formed the heart of the preceding Mamom and Chicanel spheres and later of the Tzakol and Tepeu spheres which mark the heartland of the full Classic. At many sites within this area the transition from Chicanel to Tzakol suggests neither population intrusion or hiatus, and much of the ceramic inventory shows impressive continuity from Mamom through to Tepeu. The occurrence of Floral Park is not necessarily covariant with other forms of cultural elaboration in the Late Preclassic, for example at Uaxactun. The crucial role of Floral Park ceramics is in initiating the astounding Maya polychrome tradition, and in diversifying the ceramic inventory, but whether this demands even a small influx of fresh population is a topic worthy of some consideration.

It is a commonplace that the most striking Floral Park mode, the swollen mammiform support, appears first in the highlands, from Oaxaca to Central America, and has a distribution extending into northwestern South America; it formed a prominent feature of Lothrop's mother culture and of the Q-complex that he and Vaillant adumbrated in papers at the 1927 American Anthropological Association meetings. The other two main modes, polychrome decoration and Usulutan, may be related to one another in that the Late Preclassic importation of true Usulutan (probably by the same means as jade and obsidian), may have stimulated the development of polychrome decoration out of a predominantly monochrome ceramic tradition. The increasing complexity of lowland ceramics may have stimulated the emergence of full-time local specialists in throwing pottery (if they did not exist already) and decorating it. Throwing and decorating, in other words, may have been separate skills, as they were in Classical Greece, where both potter and painter signed their work. As in Greece, too, there may have been a consonant rise in the status of ceramics as a sumptuary product. While most of the innovative and highly desirable vessels would gravitate toward elite possession and disposal, reinforcing the status value of ceramics, a proportion would pass to other elites in diplomatic-commercial contacts, and some vessels—carved jades, for example—would trickle lower down the social pyramid.

The appearance of Floral Park ceramics can be seen, therefore, as one aspect of cultural elaboration, an archaeological reflection of increasing central control and increasing interaction both with neighboring centers with whom there was a competitive relationship to be assuaged by alliance or warfare, and with distant regions with whom mutually beneficial exchange occurred directly or indirectly. The artificial environment of the raised-field systems can similarly be seen as a response to increasing central control; it served to maintain the population, minimize disruption in the control system, and provide resources to fund external contacts. Trigger (1974) notes that the political subsystem in a society is concerned with (1) foreign relations, (2) defense against external attack, (3) internal order, and (4) organization of complex activities relating to the general welfare of the society; 1–3 may serve to avoid disruption so that 4 may be executed, but 4 will in itself be by definition partly homeostatic. The construction and operation of an artificial environment comes under both 3 and 4, requiring and also stimulating the provision of a disciplined labor force working by a definite plan. Such a force would stabilize the society both by absorbing the surplus energy of a growing population, which might otherwise prove disruptive to the system during a period of competition for stretched resources, and by creating additional resources to inject more stability into the system. The direction of such a labor force by a regional center would act as a deviation-amplifying mechanism, the "backwash" of Rathje's anisotropic model (Chapter 14, below). By controlling a disciplined labor force, the center would increase its power, productivity, resource control, and ascendancy over the rest of the realm; it would control potentially centrifugal forces while simultaneously harnessing these resources to support functions 1 and 2, the maintenance and improvement of the position of the center and its realm vis-à-vis its neighbors and more distant contacts.

This use of energy in the "common" cause is paralleled by the construction of massive public buildings in the ceremonial center, which, like the artificial environmental zone, can be interpreted as work-making projects not unlike WPA projects in the Great Depression. At an earlier date the manufacture, transport, and destruction of Olmec giant sculpture and the burial of Massive Offerings may have served a similar purpose. In the case of architecture and sculpture the benefit is mainly psychological, but the absorption of energy has a stabilizing and friction-reducing effect because effort and recompense are ordained from above and sanctioned by the numinous. The aggrandizement of the ceremonial center increases the stake each individual has in the system and focuses loyalty in a centripetal manner. Thus the amplitude of the site hierarchy within the realm of a single major center increases, like social distance, with the complexity, energy input, and value of sumptuary goods and their possession.

The increased exploitable territory created by public-works projects such as terracing and raised-field construction could be used both for basic subsistence and for sumptuary products, inessential but desirable, such as cacao. More cacao could be produced in the purlieus of, for example, Nohmul, than could easily be consumed there by a population unlikely to have exceeded 10,000 (particularly if cacao was already a desirable product to which access was restricted by rubric), and there would probably be a surplus for disposal elsewhere. Dahlin (1974) suggests that the capacity to produce more of a substance than the local population can absorb is itself an indication of interregional trade otherwise archaeologically undetectable, and this would seem a reasonable proposition. Export could have been to non-cacao-growing portions of the lowlands, but the presence in Late Preclassic northern Belize of substantial jade items indicates that desirable scarce goods were being brought from at least as far away as the middle Motagua Valley—some 400 kilometers as the crow flies—and suggests that distribution may have extended further, even to the highlands. It is even possible that the provision of highland raw material such as obsidian and jade stimulated the production of cacao on an organized basis and that the Lowland centers then became dependent on the external highland market. The movement of lowland culture into the Verapaz region reflected by Chama ceramics, among other evidences, may have been an attempt to retain control of the highlands in the face of some threat to this vital outlet, removal of which would threaten the stability of the lowland realms themselves.

The presence of Teotihuacan artifacts, and apparently at least one Teotihuacano of high enough status to be ritually knowledgable, at the small major ceremonial center of Altun Ha at the close of the Preclassic (Pendergast 1971), the discovery of other green Pachuca obsidians of characteristic Miccaotli form in the Early Classic Chacsik phase at Becan (Rovner 1974), and the occurrence of green obsidian blades at a similar date at Dzibilchaltun all attest to a Teotihuacan interest in the Maya Lowlands from the Late Preclassic onward. Sanders and Price (1968) and Parsons and Price (1971:183–84) suggest that Teotihuacan may have seen Kaminaljuyu as a center from which to control the acquisition of cacao from Xoconusco, and the Teotihuacan interest in the Maya Lowlands may have been similarly inspired. If Parsons (1969:160) is correct in his assertion that cacao emerged as a currency as well as a ritually important product early in the Classic, then the combination of a suitable locale in the Hondo and Belize river basins with the presence of an already-complex society throughout the Chicanel sphere, which included those areas, could have led to the rapid emergence of large-scale centrally controlled cacao cultivation as the essential catalyst beginning the chain reaction (or "multiplier effect") that produced the dynastically ruled, bureaucratically administered, and artistically inspired phenomenon of Classic Maya civilization.

NOTES

1. The work has been carried out under a permit from the government of Belize and has been financed by major grants from the Trustees of the British Museum and the Research Committee of the British Academy. Additional support has come from the Crowther-Beynon Fund of the Cambridge University Museum of Archaeology and Ethnology. From 1973 to 1975 I held a research fellowship at Fitzwilliam College, Cambridge, and from 1972 to 1975 I held a postdoctoral research fellowship endowed by the Leverhulme Trust Fund at the Centre of Latin American Studies at the University of Cambridge, where the Project was provided with office accommodation and secretarial facilities; additional facilities were provided by the Faculty of History and are gratefully acknowledged. In Belize enormous logistic support was provided by Belize Sugar Industries Ltd., a subsidiary of Tate & Lyle Ltd., who also contributed generously to the production of the Project's 1974–75 Interim Report. Excavations at Nohmul were on BSI land; at Colha excavations were on the property of John and Herbert Masson and their family, who provided enthusiastic cooperation and

hospitality. Support and hospitality were also given by successive commanders of British Forces in Belize and members of the Officers' Mess at Airport Camp. Industrial sponsorship in the provision of services and equipment came from the Harrison Line, Rank Pullin Controls Ltd., Rabone Chesterman Ltd., BXL Ltd., and Nig Banda Ltd. The personal assistance of Miss Elizabeth Carmichael; Mr. William Fagg, C.M.G.; the late Sir Eric Thompson, K.B.E., F.B.A.; Professor D. C. M. Platt; Professor Brian Van Arkadie; Mr. Frank Curtis, O.B.E.; Mr. F. F. "Polo" Orio, Jr., M.B.E.; Colonel John Shipster, O.B.E., and Mrs. Shipster; Colonel J. I Fraser-Orr, M.B.E., M.C., and Mrs. Fraser-Orr; Colonel D. R. Green, M.C.; Mr. Joseph O. Palacio; Miss Felicity Mordaunt; and all those who worked with the Project in the field are most gratefully acknowledged. Ceramic data in this paper derive from the work of D. C. Pring.

2. Nohmul structures are numbered in accordance with the 1973 survey by the Corozal Project (Hammond 1973).

3. Site designations are in terms of the nine-level hierarchy defined in Hammond (1975b).

4. The permit was issued in 1973–74 by the Hon. A. A. Hunter and in 1975 by the Hon. Santiago Perdomo, in both cases after consultation with the Archaeological Commissioner, Mr. Joseph O. Palacio.

5. Carried out by Mr. D. C. Pring; the radiocarbon determination was kindly provided by Dr. V. R. Switsur of the Cambridge University Radiocarbon Laboratory.

6. Puleston (1974) suggests that the aceramic site at Richmond Hill may be of Early Man date.

7. Determinations are currently being carried out at UCLA by Dr. Rainer Berger and at Cambridge by Dr. V. R. Switsur. Four further Cambridge dates (Q-1571-4) range from 1630 to 1950 b.c. and three from UCLA range from 1050 to 2000 b.c. A span of 2000–1000 b.c., 2500–1250 B.C., is suggested for the Early Preclassic Swasey phase. A date of 1250 ± 205 b.c. (Q-1575) is also available for the Jenney Creek phase at Barton Ramie. It should be noted that the arguments presented on pages 50–51 and 60–61 are now of historical interest only. These new dates indicate sedentary occupation by people with a developed ceramic technology before 2000 b.c./2500 B.C. Data from the 1976 excavations include possible human use of the site by 3200 b.c./4000 B.C.

8. Willey (personal communication 1974) suggests that the bark beaters may have been used for making bark cloth garments, but the presence of an apparent sherd spindle whorl in a Plancha Chicanel context at Altar de Sacrificios and of others in Floral Park context at Barton Ramie suggests that the alternative of spun thread and woven textiles was available.

9. Subsequent (1975–76) evidence from Cuello suggests that this is in fact the case, with small-scale public architecture dating back to the Early Preclassic, c. 1700 b.c./2100 B.C.

4

Rio Bec Archaeology and The Rise of Maya Civilization

RICHARD E. W. ADAMS

The University of Texas at San Antonio

INTRODUCTION

In this chapter I will attempt to set up a data-oriented framework and then present information from the Rio Bec region that is pertinent to the origins of Maya civilization. I will then suggest an interpretative synthesis of the regional sequence. The final section of the chapter deals with the theoretical implications of general and specific patterns of Maya civilization and explores various processual explanations.

My data are drawn from two separate but related projects carried out from 1969 to 1973 in the vicinity of the sites of Becan, Chicanna, and Xpujil (Fig. 4.1) in what Thompson (1943) has called the Intermediate Area.[1] Fieldwork in both projects was funded by the National Geographic Society. From 1969 to 1971 the Middle American Research Institute sponsored the work with E. W. Andrews IV as project director. I acted as field director at the site of Becan; Jack Eaton was field director at Chicanna. Summary papers based on that work have recently been published (R. E. W. Adams 1974), as well as a number of

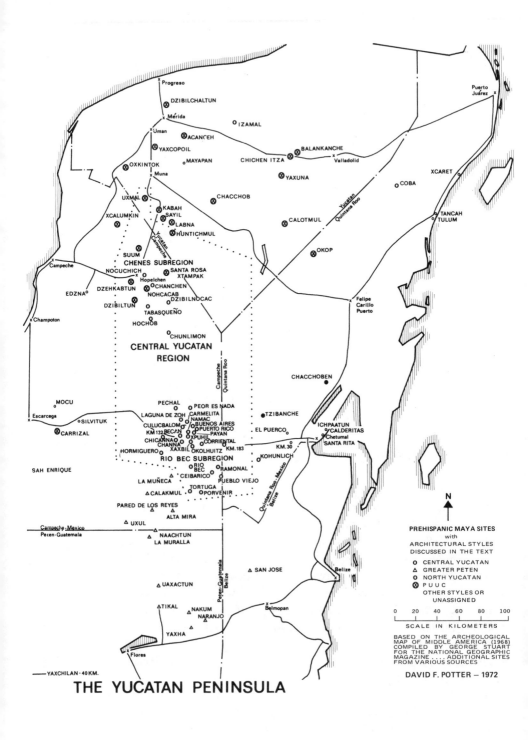

FIGURE 4.1.   Map of the central Yucatan area

preliminary statements. In 1972 and 1973, a group from the University of Wisconsin, Madison, and myself from The University of Texas at San Antonio formed the Rio Bec Ecological Project, whose purpose was to gather data on soils, climatic patterns, ancient farming patterns, and some specific archaeological problems. I was project director and James Stoltman and, later, Jack Eaton acted as field directors. Four doctoral dissertations deriving from the projects have been completed and three (Ball 1973; Potter 1973; Webster 1972) are being revised for eventual publication in the MARI series; Turner's will appear elsewhere. Turner has published a paper on ancient intensive agriculture (1974) and Eaton's on the prehistoric farmsteads in the region is in press (1976). Other papers and articles are in preparation. Preliminary and summary reports were furnished monthly to Monumentos Prehispánicos of the Mexican Instituto Nacional de Antropología e Historia under terms of our permit.

BACKGROUND

In dealing with the rise of Maya civilization we are grappling with something more difficult to define than the phenomenon of its collapse. The conference on the collapse (Culbert 1973a) defined Maya culture and its disappearance on the basis of what happened to certain key features: polychrome pottery, corbeled vaulted stone architecture of both temple and palace forms, hieroglyphic writing and stelae, and the art style. These features, however, are found at first only in a few lowland regions; their most intense expression and extensive distribution are to some extent functions of time and of the events of the Late Classic. Furthermore, the establishment of the systemically related features of Maya culture may be very different from its Late Classic and Postclassic reformulation and trans-formations. The initial appearance of complex culture in the Maya Lowlands is a specific part of the larger phenomenon of successive florescences; there were at least four florescences in the lowlands. Although the later ones are not directly within the scope of the conference, by examining the various cultural peaks in Maya prehistory we may gain some comparative insights that will help us in dealing with the main problem. These florescences seem to show a certain regularity of pattern.

The first peak on the curve of Maya prehistory begins in the late Preclassic or Protoclassic. Certainly by A.D. 250 most sites suggest the presence of the sociopolitical structure, the ceremonialism, and most of the material expressions that mark civilized Maya life. The quantum jump made at this time is discussed at length below. It is interesting that the first period is the longest. It apparently lasts about three hundred years, some fifty years longer than subsequent periods. About A.D. 534 (9.5.0.0.0.) an inscriptional hiatus occurs which is also reflected in the ceramic sequences at certain sites. This hiatus marks the end of the first period. Following an eighty-to-one-hundred-year break, Late Classic culture appears in most areas. This second period lasts from two hundred to two hundred fifty years in its regional expressions (A.D. 650–850). A catastrophic collapse follows in the Southern and Intermediate Lowlands. A kind of delayed Late Classic starts later and continues in the Puuc and Northern Plains of Yucatan for two hundred years, until ca. A.D. 1000. There follows the third major florescence, the Maya-Toltec period at Chichen, which, according to the chronicles, lasted about two hundred years (A.D. 987–1187). The final florescence is that of the Mayapan episode, lasting about two hundred fifty years (A.D. 1194–1441, or 247 years). The point to be noted here is that there seems to have been a certain regularity of florescence and duration in Maya culture history. There are, however, important qualitative distinctions to be made among these periods; these will be examined in the final section of the chapter.

The Preclassic Becan Sequence

The evidence from the sites of Becan and Chicanna is heavily ceramic and architectural. There are few inscriptions in the area and no readable texts at either site. Some settlement pattern survey has been done but the results are available only in very preliminary form (P. Thomas 1974).

The regional ceramic sequence begins with a Mamom ceramic sphere complex, the Acachen, 600–300 B.C. (See Fig. 1.3). According to J. W. Ball (1973:333a–i) it is closely related to the geographically adjacent Mamom complexes to the north and south, but has its own regionalized flavor. Early-facet Acachen relates especially to the early Mamom (Pit E-4, stratum 1) material at Uaxactun. Acachen becomes more divergent from Mamon-Mamom in its late facet. Achiotes, Joventud, Chunhinta, and Pital groups are all shared as are flaring-sided plates and cuspidor bowls. No resist decoration is known in Acachen, however. The Dzibilchaltun Nabanche complex (formerly the Zacnicte and early Chacah) is likewise close enough to be included in the Mamom ceramic sphere according to Ball (1973:333e). Achiotes, Sapote, and Joventud groups all occur in Nabanche's inventory as well as in Acachen. Regionalisms separate Nabanche and Acachen to about the same degree as they do Acachen and Uaxactun's Mamon. These comparative statements are somewhat in contradiction to those previously made by E. W. Andrews IV (Willey, Culbert, and Adams 1967), but are based on more detailed work and comparative study by Ball and E. W. Andrews V.

Pakluum complex follows smoothly out of Acachen and is a member of the Chicanel ceramic sphere. Dates on Pakluum are estimated as 300 B.C. to A.D. 250 (550 years). Three facets subdivide the phase (see Fig. 1.3). Rather extraordinarily close linkages between Uaxactun Chicanel complex and Pakluum are pointed out by Ball (1973:333i and passim). So close are the types, forms, and decorative modes that it is said that the Uaxactun illustrations could serve as well for much of Pakluum, but there are a few significant differences. Sherd tempering is absent at Becan. The dominant Sierra Red Group constitutes 60 percent of the slipped wares and 35 percent of the Pakluum complex as a whole, much more than in Chicanel complex at Uaxactun. According to Ball (1973:271), "Standard Chicanel Sphere forms such as everted-rim dishes and medial-ridged dishes predominate."

All Protoclassic-stage pottery is missing in Pakluum, nor does it appear in the next complex in the Rio Bec Zone. No Holmul Orange Ware, Usulutan related types, mammiform feet, or early (Ixcanrio et al.) polychromes show up in the Becan Zone. In this respect, Becan is like Tikal and Uaxactun, showing a continuity of Preclassic pottery tradition, but with significant material changes in architectural and other material categories, and, by inference, in the sociopolitical area. Pakluum complex can be subdivided into three facets, but Ball has not yet published the characteristics on which this division depends.

Nearly all presently known Preclassic architecture at Becan relates to the last two facets of the Pakluum ceramic phase, that is between 50 B.C. and A.D. 250. Our work indicates that Rio Bec Preclassic architectural development was extensive and even extraordinary in at least one aspect. According to Ball and Potter's calculations (1974), there are over 500 square meters of plaster paving at Becan dating from Pakluum. Several hundred square meters are at nearby Chicanna, the only Preclassic architectural remains yet known from that site's Preclassic occupation. Associated with these pavements are several formal buildings in which:

1. Building materials consist of dry-laid block limestone masonry, which usually forms a face over loosely packed, dry-laid, rubble fill. Thin, well-smoothed plaster was used to finish off structures.

2. Forms consist of (a) simple platforms, both rectangular and round (at least eight known); (b) pyramidal bases supporting simple platforms (one large structure [IV-sub] 10 m high); (c) superstructures with walls partly of stone and presumably perishable roofs (Str. XXVII).

3. Formal details include (a) inset stairways; (b) rounded corners on platforms; (c) thatched roofs; (d) superstructures with stone walls up to 1 meter high; (e) red painted surfaces on buildings and platforms; and (f) plaster pavements associated with buildings.

Of the eight platforms, at least five are parts of *plazuela* groups outside the main Becan site. They seem to be rural residential groups of the common house-ruin-cluster type defined by Bullard (1960:Fig. 2a–bb) and found all over the Maya Lowlands. Less certain because of insufficient excavation is the nature of the two platforms found under the Becan Ball Court (Str. XI). These may also be residential group platforms, but the fact that both are larger than usual and rest on a sequence of two preceding plaster floors argues that their function was something more. Their location within what was already a ceremonial center adds weight to this interpretation. On the other hand, the badly preserved remains of round and polychrome painted platforms were found by Taschek in a *plazuela* group.

On the edge of the dry ditch fortification at Becan and preceding its construction is Structure XXVII (Figs. 4.2, 4.3), a small but fairly elaborate platform with a frontal inset stairway flanked by banquettes. It affords about 23 square meters of space and is only about a meter high. Dry-laid stone walls a meter in height rise from the edge of the platform; the rest of the superstructure was probably perishable. The plan is that of a single room, open on one side. The whole building was plastered and painted red. Like the ball court platforms, XXVII rested upon extensive pavement.

FIGURE 4.2.   Becan Structure XXVII, Pakluum-Chicanel in date

The largest Preclassic building at Becan is Structure IV-sub. Only the top of this 10-meter-high platform is known, since it was detected by excavation through the floor of the elevated patio at the top of the latest phase of Structure IV (Figs. 4.4 and 4.5). A three-tiered platform rests on a lower platform, the nature of which has not been determined. Inset stairway, masonry techniques, and other characteristics fit Structure IV-sub into the general Preclassic architectural trends at Becan. The space on the top platform, ca. 50 square meters, is much larger than that available on Structure XXVII (ca. 23 square meters). Again, there are indications that a partial masonry wall formed a single room surmounted by perishable materials and a thatched roof.

An extraordinary feature of Preclassic Becan is its dry fortification ditch, which Webster and Ball believe to have been constructed either in late-facet Pakluum or Early Chacsik, the first of the Classic phases. The ditch (Fig. 4.6), first described by Ruppert and Denison (1943),

FIGURE 4.3.   Reconstruction drawing of Becan Structure XXVII

has been exhaustively described and analyzed by Webster (1972, 1974). About two kilometers in circumference, encircling the highest ground in the vicinity, it is reinforced in its protective function by the fact that Becan is edged around 250 degrees of its 360-degree circumference by marshy *bajo*. The site of Becan thus enclosed constitutes an area of about 19 hectares (46 acres). A parapet runs along the entire interior of the ditch except where broken for entrances across seven causeways. Webster calculates that "the *average* vertical obstacle presented to attackers would have been 11.3 m. or about 37 feet. (During construction of the ditch, Pakluum phase Str. XXVII was covered by spoil, thus preserving it.) Quite probably the embankment was additionally strengthened by a wooden palisade, although no traces of one have survived" (1974:125). The fortifications have parallels to those at Tikal, but are much more formidable, being at present the largest known from the Maya Lowlands. In comparison, the Mayapan and Tulum walls are insignificant.

FIGURE 4.4.   Becan Structure IV-sub, Pakluum-Chicanel in date

For our purposes, the importance of the Becan ditch lies in the manpower invested in it and the sociopolitical implications. Webster estimates that about 350,000 man-days would have been required to excavate the ditch and pile up the 80,000 cubic meters of embankment. Webster's doctoral thesis (1972) and his chapter (13) in this volume set forth his arguments regarding the evolutionary role of militarism in the rise of Maya civilization. These ideas are considered below.

Early Classic and the Hiatus at Becan

Ceramic sampling from test pits and structural excavations for other purposes indicate that Becan probably has substantial Early Classic architectural remains. While only one Early Classic building has been

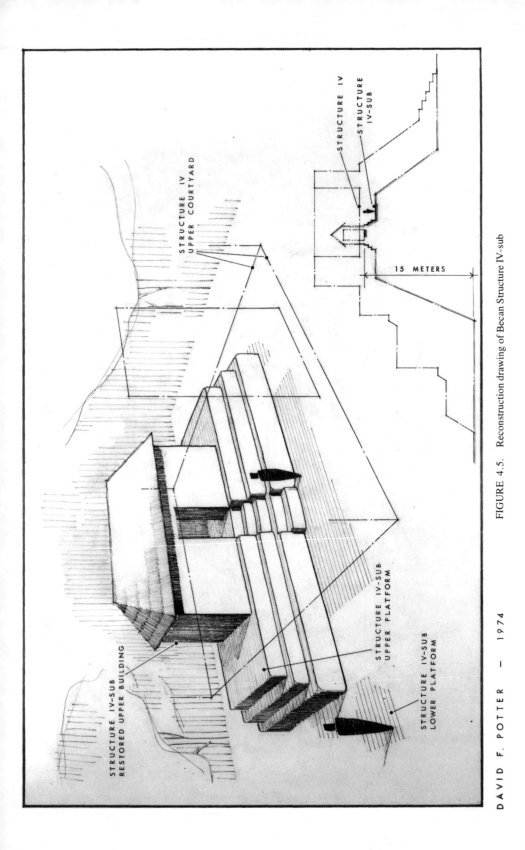

STRUCTURE IV
UPPER COURTYARD

STRUCTURE IV-SUB
RESTORED UPPER BUILDING

STRUCTURE IV-SUB
UPPER PLATFORM

STRUCTURE IV-SUB
LOWER PLATFORM

STRUCTURE IV

STRUCTURE
IV-SUB

15 METERS

DAVID F. POTTER — 1974

FIGURE 4.5.   Reconstruction drawing of Becan Structure IV-sub

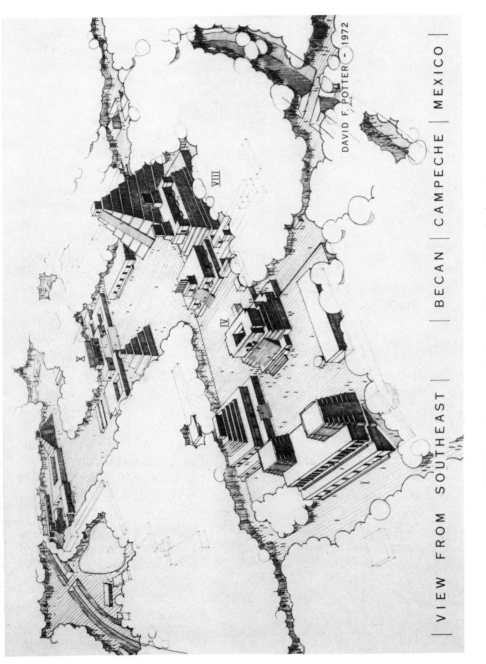

| VIEW FROM SOUTHEAST | BECAN | CAMPECHE | MEXICO |

DAVID F. POTTER — 1972

FIGURE 4.6. Reconstruction drawing of Becan and its Preclassic moat

excavated, adjacent excavations in the moat and small structures indicate that the entire very large B-XIII complex at Becan may be Early Classic. Aside from this possibility, however, most of the structural activity at Becan seems to be Late Classic. As noted above, the Late Classic Chenes-style palace, Structure IV, directly overlies the large Pakluum structure within it, with no apparent intervening construction phases. This suggests that the Preclassic architecture of the zone continued to be used extensively in the Early Classic period. We can be certain that the moat was kept in repair during the Chacsik phase, as it completely lacks Chacsik trash deposits.

Two ceramic complexes and phases represent the period A.D. 250–600. Chacsik is the earliest and the longest. It is a regionalized Tzakol ceramic sphere complex with linkages to both the north and south. Peten-style fine wares such as Dos Arroyos Orange Polychrome show up, and trickle-decorated wares clearly tied to northern ceramic traditions also occur. The distribution of Chacsik is both puzzling and significant. All Chacsik material found to date occurs exclusively within the fortified area at Becan.

Sabucan complex constitutes the period typologically equivalent to Tzakol 2–3 at Uaxactun. It is during this time that Becan ceramics drop the northern influence and become "Petenized," according to Ball (1973:381). It is also during this period that Teotihuacan formal elements appear in the form of tripod cylinder vases and apron lids. The extraordinary cache of a cylinder tripod, a large hollow figurine, and ten solid figurines, all of Teotihuacan style except for the decoration on the vessel, dates from Sabucan. We should note that the structure (Becan Str. XIV) within which it was found may have had *talud-tablero* features. Ball points out that the ten figurines represent groups of deities and warriors familiar from Teotihuacan figurines (1974b). Irwin Rovner found green obsidian from the Mexican state of Hidalgo in Chacsik deposits (1974). Together with the surrounding defense works, these data suggest that the already extant fortress of Becan may have been taken over by a Teotihuacan-allied elite, or that the elite of Becan allied themselves to the great central Mexican city. A third possibility is that the Teotihuacanos shut themselves up in a redoubt built with corvée labor. Consistent finds of fragments of human bone throughout Sabucan deposits reinforce the impression of violent events.

After an apparently inconsequential and inactive phase at Chicanna corresponding to Chacsik Early Classic, late-facet Chacsik sees the resumption of formal architectural construction. Group A plaza is floored at this time, and Structure XI-sub is built. Considering the small, relatively focused amount of excavation at Chicanna, these data suggest that late-facet Chacsik was a significant period at that center (Eaton 1972, 1974).

Rio Bec Regional Late Classic Civilization

Beginning with the Bejuco ceramic complex (A.D. 600–730) and ending with Chintok (A.D. 730–830), the Rio Bec area undergoes the most significant cultural florescence of its entire history. It is during this period that what Potter has defined as the Central Yucatecan Style (formerly Chenes–Rio Bec) is developed and expressed in amazing numbers of fine structures and centers. A general population rise is associated with this architectural florescence, as evidenced by the work of Turner (1974), P. Thomas (1974), and Eaton (1976). Turner estimates the population density, based on ceramically controlled samples of households and farmsteads, as ca. 168 persons per square kilometer. Thomas, using raw housemound data, estimates at least 900 persons per square kilometer. This figure, however, is discredited by Thomas's statement that the estimate "does not differentiate by period of occupation and cannot be taken as other than an indication of potential population density" (1974:145). Eaton and Taschek's excavations indicate on a small-sample basis that the population density of the Late and Terminal Classic periods was at least congruent with the standard estimates (see Willey et al. 1965) and at least within the limits of Ursula Cowgill's estimates (1961). Further, Turner's work indicates that this population was sustained by intensive agriculture based on terracing, check damming, swamp drainage, and raised fields. Most of the population at this time lived in elaborate farmsteads as defined by Eaton's work (1976). Bejuco times were apparently secure, since the moat was used not for defense but for a trash dump.

Both Bejuco and Chintok complexes increasingly regionalized away from Peten norms (Ball 1973:347). Although Ball puts Bejuco into the Tepeu ceramic sphere, it is much more closely aligned with the areas to the east and west than those to the south or north. Chintok complex, an even more regionalized body of ceramics, has also been established as the type complex of a new ceramic sphere. Ball notes that Chintok fine wares drop out almost entirely at the time of architectural excellence. It is during the final part of Chintok that the collapse of Rio Bec Late Classic culture occurs.

Terminal Classic and Postclassic

Xcocom complex (A.D. 830–1050) represents the immediate postcollapse period in the Rio Bec Zone. No major architectural construction is known from this period, although the civic buildings were occupied. Occupation is of the "squatter" sort, with garbage and trash piling up in palace and temple rooms, implying social dissolution. There is a possible Puuc-style building phase at Chicanna, but if it existed, it was short-lived. By the beginning of Xcocom, then, most of the Rio Bec civic centers have lost their functions as elite-class cultural foci, and population activities in the interstices are as important as those in the monumental areas.

Ball distinguishes two facets in Xcocom. The Early facet (A.D. 830–950) includes the horizon markers of Altar and Balancan Fine Orange groups. Ball has recently argued that the appearance of these markers is also an indicator of the presence in the Rio Bec area of Putun Maya, who are thought to have moved north from Tabasco and into the peninsula proper at about this time (Ball 1974b:88). Late-facet Xcocom (A.D. 950–1050) is characterized by smaller samples and weaker distribution, indicating a decrease in population. Many of the Bejuco and Chintok period farmsteads were abandoned during this period, and a reversion to slash-and-burn agriculture may have taken place. The major horizon marker to appear in Late Xcocom is Tohil Plumbate. However, Ixpop Polychrome and Paxcaman Red are completely lacking, indicating expiration of Xcocom before those horizon markers come into currency.

The considerable continuity between Chintok and Xcocom, especially in the unslipped groups, indicates some population continuity. There are changes, but many are within the traditions. Pixtun Trickle-on-Gray is an example of modulation in the northern trickle-decoration tradition already present at Becan. However,

Xcocom represents a massive introduction of new fine wares to the region, which may well mean that an elite-class intrusion from the north took place at this time.

SEQUENCE SUMMARY AND DISCUSSION OF BASIC QUESTIONS

Preclassic Buildup

The Becan-Chicanna-Xpujil region was first occupied by slash-and-burn farmers using Mamom-style pottery by about 550 B.C. Slow population growth and the establishment and expansion of small civic centers seem to have been the important processual events. Chicanel pottery is characteristic of the end of this period of numerical and spatial expansion. The sources of the earliest populations are not easily discernible from the Rio Bec evidence, which indicates close relationships to practically all surrounding and contemporary ceramic complexes during both Middle and Late Preclassic times. We can probably infer that the Rio Bec Zone was colonized long after the initial populations had penetrated the Maya Lowlands and lost their distinctiveness, both passage of time and expansion through space resulting in continued homogeneity of cultural traditions. The Danubian I and II expansions in Europe are probably analogous to the Maya case. In both instances, there is a remarkable uniformity of culture over a vast area due to the use of shifting agricultural systems and expanding populations. As populations expanded numerically, they expanded spatially. Growth was rapid enough to maintain similarities in basic patterns over a vast area.

The rate of population growth during the Rio Bec Preclassic can only be guessed at with the data now in hand. During the period from ca. 550 B.C. to about A.D. 1 it seems to have been slow and gradual. About the time of Christ, population growth seems to spurt. It reaches a plateau about A.D. 200 which is maintained until about A.D. 300, when it declines sharply. In any case, it is our impression that the landscape prior to A.D. 300 is filled to the capacity of slash-and-burn agriculture to supply subsistence.

Indications of sophisticated social complexity are few until about A.D. 50, midway through the Pakluum phase, when formal architecture begins to appear in the form of small, one-room buildings of masonry walls and perishable materials scattered about the countryside in small paved areas. This was apparently the case in rural areas as well as in the future locations of ceremonial centers. Again there are no definite data, but the larger Pakluum structure found within Becan Structure IV may be later than the simple platform and may thus represent a more complex stage of development associated with the much more extensive pavements. The implications are that basic patterns of social complexity and stratification are laid down during this period. No direct evidence from the Rio Bec Zone permits us to infer that ancestor worship, either as a general pattern or as a royal culture, is an important institution at this time. However, lineage distinction and ancestor worship seem to develop at this period in the Tikal-Uaxactun area and along the Pasión River. Craft specialization in architecture may appear now, with at least part-time artisans acting as masons, plasterers, and other construction specialists. As in the Late Classic, the techniques and styles of the rural architecture reflect the same standards as the civic architecture in room width, platform shape and size, and other details. This congruity indicates that the persons living in the rural interstices were the same as those building the civic centers and thus hints at part-time rather than full-time specialization. It is noteworthy that ceramics of the Late Preclassic (Late and Terminal Pakluum) do not show the experimentation and implied craft specialization that are present in Late Chicanel–sphere ceramics of other lowland areas, for example in the Late Plancha phase at Altar de Sacrificios.

If there is a useful distinction to be made between folk and elite culture, it is not readily apparent by A.D. 50 but certainly exists by A.D. 250. In other words, this is the first shift point in the Becan sequence.

As nearly as we can detect, there is a complete absence of the Protoclassic phenomenon, so important in the rise of the Classic at certain sites. If the Protoclassic development operated as a factor in the evolution of Rio Bec civilization, it was by indirect means and without material manifestations. This is somewhat puzzling considering the geographic proximity of the Becan-Chicanna Zone to the Northern Belize area, where Protoclassic is apparently so strong. However, if the Protoclassic is a regional cultural phenomenon carried by militarism and/or elite-class intrusion into other parts of the Maya Lowlands, then it would understandably be resisted and its material manifestations rejected in areas out of its control. Certainly, Late Preclassic Becan was in conflict with some such group, and its fortifications may have been built to resist just that sort of an intrusion.

The immediately succeeding period, the Chacsik phase, seems to have been a difficult period for the Rio Bec centers, with Becan somewhat isolated, judging by the restriction of the ceramics to the fortified zone. The Sabucan phase may have seen a resolution of the conflicts that had lasted from Terminal Pakluum through Chacsik. The fortification ditch fell into disuse sometime during the period, the ceramics reflecting strong ties to the Peten traditions, and significant Teotihuacan linkages were present. Architectural activity revived.

The late Classic florescence of the Becan-Chicanna-Xpujil Zone may or may not reflect a general florescence for the entire Rio Bec area. Survey data indicate a general florescence at least as far south as Calakmul, but we have no good data on what happened to the south of the zone where we have excavated. To the north, the Chenes site of Dzibilnocac seems to burgeon at about the same time (Nelson 1973). This is the second significant processual shift point that we see in the culture history. By A.D. 600 (Bejuco phase), there is definitely a quantum jump in population (Turner 1974). The subsistence system is now based on intensive agriculture, reflected in terracing, check dams, increased water-storage facilities, and *bajo* utilization based on drainage and raised field techniques. We are inclined to explain this response in terms of Boserup's theory. The increase in number and complexity of sites implies that we are in the presence of fully developed Maya Late Classic culture, with all the sociopolitical features that the term denotes. A sociopolitical collapse occurs about A.D. 750, followed shortly by northern elite intrusions. Population declines after A.D. 950 and perhaps before.

A Processual Survey of Maya Prehistory

The following account owes a great deal to David Webster, J. W. Ball, and some of my other colleagues in the Rio Bec work. Because Webster's chapter in this volume (Chap. 13) is especially important, I shall summarize its relevant points here. According to Webster's argument, differential ecology led to differential population densities in the Preclassic Maya Lowlands. Those areas with highest densities found themselves led to militaristic expansion or faced with the need to resist aggression from other groups. Either path led to greater sociopolitical complexity. Warfare, in Webster's view, was the short-term solution giving rise to the social mechanisms that allowed long-term solutions, ultimately intensive agriculture and the managerial apparatus it demanded.

Early militarism provided a managerial motivation for the rise of a Maya elite which also served as the focus for group identification, internal social management, and redistributive functions. Ceremonial centers defined the local community, served as economic redistribution centers, and functioned as political-administrative centers. The latter function included military leadership and organization. An important point is that the centers were related to resolution of conflict as well as to organizing for its practice. The first Maya elite may have been professional warriors who gave a defensive-offensive edge to communities struggling to maintain themselves in a world of diminishing resources.

I would comment that the shock effect of militarism in new technical forms is usually ephemeral and lasts only until a parallel sociopolitical unit matches formal and technical military advances. At that point either a steady state is reached, or a new round of technological innovation is set off and the cycle is repeated. Mesoamericans generally and the Maya especially seem not to have invested heavily in technological matters after the basic initial innovations of the Preclassic had been made. Investment took the form of labor-intensive use of extant technology. Occasionally a more efficient use of technology through more sophisticated social organization gave one group the edge.

However, the importance of intense and even violent competition is not without permanent, or at least short-term, beneficial effects, usually in terms of social organizational shift points. The effects also seem to be irreversible; at least they were not reversed in Maya culture. That is, the systemic structure, once constructed, was not modifiable in a simplifying direction except under catastrophic conditions. This tendency, in turn, led to the bimodal or quatrimodal curve of Maya cultural development.

Only the first rise on the curve concerns us immediately, but it is instructive to look at the whole course of development, as it may give us some insights into the nature of the initial rise. Chronologically, the first rise of civilization was at the end of the long period called the Preclassic. This first period of systemic success is the Early Classic. In those parts of the Maya Lowlands in which such development took place (nearly all of the lowlands) a hiatus occurs, either at the end of the Preclassic or the end of the Early Preclassic. Late Classic Maya culture follows in many areas, although some Early Classic sites were apparently abandoned or quiescent and static. Late Classic florescence is followed by a catastrophic collapse in the Southern Lowlands and the intermediate zone, including the Rio Bec and Chenes areas. The florescence is a prolongation or delayed Late Classic in the Puuc region and Northern Plains area generally. A third florescence is confined to the Northern Plains and represents a Maya-Toltec hybrid culture centered on a colonial Mexican capital at Chichen Itza. This regionalized variant is as vigorous as the Puuc and Late Classic variants, but is much more spatially restricted. The end of Maya-Toltec culture is not well understood, but the culture seems to have come to a violent halt, judging by the accounts in native chronicles. Mayapan and the renaissance of Maya culture of a more traditional type is the fourth florescence, but a weaker one than the three preceding. Again, the period ends with a violent and sudden disaster, this time well documented in the chronicles. A final period of Maya prehistory is a short (ninety-year), confused episode, important because it may represent a buildup of Maya culture toward another florescence.

Several features of these cycles of buildup, collapse, and recovery are noteworthy. One is the apparent similarity of duration of florescences. The qualification is necessary because the transition from Preclassic to Early Classic is so little known at most sites. Given this caveat, however, all florescences seem to have lasted about two to three hundred years: the first florescence endured for perhaps as much as three hundred years; the Late Classic florescence after the hiatus lasted about two hundred fifty years; the Chichen Maya–Toltec episode and the final Mayapan period lasted some two hundred years each.

Qualitatively, however, there is a significant difference between the florescences. The first two periods represent quantum jumps in social organization and in population. The second two periods are something like the cyclical renewals and reformulations of Middle Eastern cultures as suggested by Kroeber (1944). Steward's (1955) periods of conquest and collapse also describe these last two periods.

At this point, then, we can pass to a higher level of generalization and attempt to frame some general statements of interaction and relationships which are both explanatory and hypothetical. Building on Webster's suggested stages (Chapter 13, below), I feel that Maya prehistory can be divided into five processual episodes.

Stage 1. Stimulus: Population growth in an empty landscape. *Response:* Emigration and spread through space. In the Maya case, this covers the Middle Period and part of the Late Preclassic, and the technological referent is slash-and-burn and garden agriculture.

Stage 2. Stimulus: Population growth in a landscape occupied by maximum numbers of people subsisting on slash-and-burn and garden agriculture. *Response:* Conflict–social organizational feedback syndrome. This development of a classic warfare and leadership pattern, à la Webster, applies to the Late Preclassic and Early Classic Maya. The development of large water-storage facilities as a practical development gives the elite another means of social control, as suggested by Carneiro's formulation of resource circumscription (1970).

Stage 3. Stimulus: Population growth in a landscape overcrowded for slash-and-burn agriculture even supplemented with imports, gardening, and orchards. *Response:* Involution of systems in the following forms: (1) intensive agriculture with formal, massive works, and (2) development and expansion of a managerial elite immediately below the aristocratic elite. For the Maya, this is the Late Classic period of the Southern Lowlands and the Rio Bec–Chenes areas. The Puuc seems to have had a delayed Late Classic which outlasted that in the other areas.

Stage 4. Stimulus: Military intrusion of foreign cultural forms into a fairly homogeneous cultural area and establishment of a permanent colonial capital controlling a large area. *Response:* A reworking of previously established forms and reorganization of social organization into less aristocratic forms. The Maya-Toltec period is the period being generalized upon; the capital was at Chichen. It is possible that the delayed Late Classic florescence in the Puuc is also partly stimulated by Mexican influence, although more indirect, as suggested by J. W. Ball. Note also the brief and somewhat Mexican-flavored hybrid florescence at Seibal and perhaps at Motul de San José during the Terminal Classic Period in the Southern Lowlands.

Stage 5. Stimulus: Withdrawal and/or absorption of the foreign influences and the political and military apparatuses supporting them. *Response:* The revival of more nativistic forms of culture, albeit still in a hybrid form. The Maya period from which this stage is derived is that of the Mayapan episode.

The qualitative differences between the various florescences is underlined by framing them in the processual stages outlined above. Admittedly interpretive, the stages are also synthetic of data on hand. Turning back to the immediate problem, that of the initial rise of Maya civilization, one can see that several characteristics set it apart from the other florescences. For one thing, population was less dense than in stages 3, 4, and 5. Relative to what went before, however, population reached something of a threshold, leading, if one accepts Webster, to military conflict and hence to greater sociopolitical complexity. It is also possible that the last ninety years of Maya prehistory, from the fall of Mayapan to the arrival of the Spaniards, may have seen a reversion to about the population density of the Late Preclassic and to conflict of about the same kind.

Another kind of distinction for the Late Preclassic is the probable lack of the intensive forms of agriculture that were present later. On the other hand, the gardening and orchard tending practiced at this time may have been more intensive than what went before.

To attempt to summarize the differences between the first two and the last two florescences even more succinctly, we might take a slightly different stance. If the first two florescences established the systemic nature of Maya civilization, then the last two were products of a striking characteristic of complex cultures, namely, self-perpetuation through reformulation.

The Formal Qualities of Maya Culture

Even if one accepts all the processual arguments set forth to explain the rise of Maya civilization, they still leave unexplained the formal qualities of that culture. One may despair and say that this is a paleopsychological problem, which, in part, it is. However, behavioral responses to social systems are available from the ethnographic and historical literatures, and one can make tentative statements on those bases. No single analogy from ethnographic literature can be adequate for such a statement. Since we are dealing with a processual (i.e., temporal) situation, sequential analogues are required for a convincing case. Conversations with Thomas C. Greaves have contributed heavily to the following construction.

Prestige-conferring systems of symbols are invariably conservative. The reason is, of course, that the more the symbols become reified and elaborated the more communicative the functions they perform. The Maya may have begun with a system of meritoriously selected leaders in a Middle Preclassic village context. It is well known, however, that in traditional, village-centered societies, the leaders' kin have an edge in succeeding to leadership roles. That is, leadership almost invariably becomes kin-unit associated. Prestige of lineage aids in competition for office. The Big Man phenomenon of Oceania is an example of this process. Many may aspire to be Big Men in Melanesia, but only a few actually make it, and they tend to be those who have former Big Men among their older kin. Such a situation can explain the later Maya ancestor-worship emphasis. However, it does not explain the formal qualities that Maya civilization assumed. The explanation of that question, I believe, lies in the interplay between the nature of Preclassic leadership and the changing role of Maya leadership in the Late Preclassic and Early Classic. If Webster's and my own schemata are correct, then the leadership during the Late Preclassic and Early Classic was under pressure to become military leadership, at least in part. Under such pressure, the old symbols are usually not discarded, but are often reinforced. For example, Main Line Philadelphians are still very much oriented toward traditional family mansions and many activities which are more consonant with rural estates than with urban living. Many still engage in fox hunting and the social activities surrounding it, although relatively few personally cultivate the lands over which the hunt is run. Most of the Main Line families are engaged in business, but the traditional symbolism of social prestige has survived and even become more important to social status. Another, perhaps closer analogy, can be derived from the behavior of present-day Latin American elites. These groups tend to invest money made in commerce or government in landed estates, the prestige symbol of the old aristocracies. Such landed estates, especially where agrarian reform has taken place, are often financial losers, which is remarkable since those investing in them have made their money by astute financial activities. As Greaves points out, "Clearly the estates are symbols" (personal communication).

Maya leadership in the Preclassic almost certainly was kinship oriented and reinforced by ancestor worship. Proper and increasingly elaborate burial was traditional through the Late Preclassic; small thatched roof temples were erected over burial platforms as at Altar de Sacrificios (Burial 105, Str. B-III, Plancha phase). Eventually these became stone and mortar temples, and the burial chambers became tombs (e.g., Tikal Burial 85). At this point, the shift point into Early Classic, the argument is that the leadership roles were changing—becoming more military and more managerial in addition to dealing with conflict resolution and the like. Large-scale water storage was probably begun during this period of transition. Management of such created resources would have been a new role. Leadership had either to adopt the new functions or relinquish the offices. Reinforcement of traditional forms of prestige activities, in this case ancestor worship, also meant elaboration of the burial monuments. This is offered as an explanation of one of many of the formal qualities of Maya civilization. If one accepts this argument, then it may also be postulated that the elite desired to live in close proximity to their ancestors and their monuments. The building of sumptuous housing and offices for an exalted social class is a functionally related step. In accounting for two classes of buildings, temples and palaces, one accounts for probably 95 percent of Maya monumental architecture. The stela cult is seen as an elaboration of the ancestor and lineage glorification idea. It may well have been adopted and adapted from the Izapan cultures, but it was functionally very appropriate to the classic Maya, who carried it and much else of their cultural inheritance to new levels of complexity.

NOTE

1. Nearly all illustrations accompanying this paper are derived from my colleagues' work on the Rio Bec projects. Many of these will illustrate the final reports of Ball, Potter, and Webster. My thanks to these colleagues and to the National Geographic Society for access to this material.

5

The Rise of the Northern Maya Chiefdoms:
A Socioprocessual Analysis

JOSEPH W. BALL

San Diego State University

The primary purpose of this chapter is to discuss the culture-historical and sociopolitical processes which I believe culminated in the formation of the first chiefdoms among the Maya of the Northern Plains and Central Yucatan regions.[1] I have chosen to examine this particular aspect of the development of Classic-stage Maya culture because I believe that fundamental to any understanding of the civilization materially reflected by the spectacular archaeological remains is an explanation of the sociopolitical factors which permittted its emergence and shared in its existence. Two recently proposed theories of the origin of Classic Maya civilization (Puleston and Puleston 1971; Rathje 1971) bear out the primacy of this question. Each, although presented as a theory of the origin of civilization, is, in fact, a hypothesis of the development of complex sociopolitical organization among the Preclassic Lowland Maya.

The theory of sociocultural evolution here developed is specific to the Northern Plains and Central Yucatan regions. Possibly it is capable of fractional or substantial extension to others; however, it is equally probable that the events and processes which led to the appearances of chiefdoms in ecological zones as diverse as the Pasión drainage, the Belize Valley, the north central Peten, or the Campeche Plains differed to some degree. My personal belief is that the processual models here espoused, with appropriate zonal modifications, are substantially extendable to most of the Lowland Maya area.

The treatment of the Northern Lowlands here presented is somewhat uneven, reflecting the spottiness both of the available information and of my own familiarity with it.[2]

THE MIDDLE PRECLASSIC BACKGROUND: THE PIONEER STAGE

The Archaeological Record

In the dry northwestern corner of the peninsula, small settlements of early agriculturalists were present by the close of the seventh century B.C. in the vicinities of year-round water sources such as the cenotes at Chichen Itza, Yaxuna, Mani, Chacchob, Ake, Soblonke (Caucel), and Ucu. Excavation of one such settlement in the neighborhood of Cenote Xlacah on the Dzibilchaltun site revealed that it

> consisted of apsidal houses with mud and loose stone walls and roofs of perishable material. The walls . . . were stuccoed at the base. The houses resembled modern native construction, but were rounder and equipped with a single door rather than the present pair. In front of these houses and facing south was a low platform with stucco-covered packed mud and stone walls. No sign of a superstructure remained. (Andrews IV 1965a:29, Fig. 2a)

A century or two later, the settlement had taken on a somewhat more permanent look:

> The platform was considerably enlarged, the stucco this time covering crude block-masonry walls. There were at least four houses, of the same shape as those of Period I but made with true masonry walls of almost unworked blocks, usually presenting a relatively even fracture at the wall surface. The roofs were of perishable material. One of the structures, built off the edge of the platform and reached by a sloping stairway, was probably a sweat house, containing channels for conveying water to a sunken zone

with a massive hearth formed of thickly nested potsherds. (Andrews IV 1965a:29, Figs. 2b, 3)

Similar small communities were scattered throughout the entire Lowland Maya area. Excavations have revealed their presence at Xtampak, Dzibilnocac, and Edzna in northern Campeche; Becan and Xpujil in southeastern Campeche; and Tiradero in northwestern Tabasco. The widespread remains of Middle Preclassic settlements in the Southern, Eastern, and Western Lowlands are well known.

Middle Preclassic pottery complexes from Becan, Edzna, Dzibilchaltun, and other Northern Lowland sites share a set of vessel forms, surface finishes, and decorative treatments among themselves and with the contemporary complexes of the Southern Lowlands which permits their inclusion within the Mamom ceramic sphere. This set of shared characteristics gives Mamom-sphere complexes a superficial homogeneity which poorly conceals a considerable degree of interzonal heterogeneity. The general impression produced by them is one of strongly emphasized local development within a vaguely defined areal tradition. The complexes of the Central Yucatan region's southern zone, the Rio Bec, are typified by the Acachen Mamom complex of Becan.

Acachen includes storage jars of both unslipped-plain and unslipped-striated types. The Añejo Variety of Sapote Striated is characterized by unpatterned, light, fine-line brushing or scratching and a very friable paste. Achiotes Unslipped occurs via the same wide-mouthed, high-necked, thin-walled jar forms characteristic of Sapote Striated: Añejo Variety with the important addition of strap handles to the Achiotes Unslipped vessels—a mode which they share with some Joventud Red and Chunhinta Black jars.

Acachen's slipped wares are dominated by three groups: (1) the monochrome red Joventud; (2) the monochrome black Chunhinta; (3) the dichrome red-on-cream Muxanal. Of these, the Joventud group is by far the most important, occurring in high frequencies during both of the two postulated facets of the complex. Early-facet Joventud Red pieces tend to have brighter, less waxy-appearing, and flakier slips than late-facet examples, which tend to possess deeper, more highly polished slips, very closely related to those of Late Preclassic Sierra Red.

The dichrome Muxanal group is of surprisingly great importance.

Apparently absent during Acachen's early facet, it accounts for between 4 and 14 percent of the complex's late-facet deposits. Its status as a majority type at Becan is unique among known Mamom-horizon complexes.

The monochrome black Chunhinta group is very important in Acachen's early facet but considerably reduced in frequency by late-facet times. Both plain and incised types of the cream Pital group occur with extreme rarity.

Acachen is characterized by a tremendous variety of decorative techniques involving surface manipulation executed via a relatively small number of vessel forms. No occurrence of the double-line break was noted. Cuspidor and flaring-sided plate forms predominate among Joventud-group types. Restricted-orifice bowls occur in all groups but are most common in the Chunhinta; thin-walled *tecomates,* on the other hand, are relatively rare and are restricted to the Joventud group. Flat-bottomed dishes with outsloping-to-flaring sides and rounded or beveled lips are diagnostic for the Muxanal group but also occasionally occur in the Joventud and Chunhinta. Jar forms are common to the Achiotes, Sapote, Joventud, and Chunhinta groups, with strap handles occurring on at least some Achiotes, Joventud, and Chunhinta examples. A restricted-neck, bolstered-rim bottle form identical to that reported by Brainerd (1958:24, 48, Fig. 30c4–8) from sub-Chicanel deposits at Mani, Yucatan, occurs in both the Joventud and Chunhinta groups.

No Mars Orange Ware, red-on-buff, or resist-decorated types occur at Becan.

Turning to the lowlands' northern extreme, the Nabanche Mamom complex of Dzibilchaltun (the ceramic assemblage associated with the small hamlets described above) is representative of those found at several Northern Plains sites.

Nabanche's dominant ceramic types pertain to the Achiotes, Sapote, Joventud, and Chunhinta groups. In the unslipped wares category, there are distinctive, well-developed local varieties of Achiotes Unslipped and Sapote Striated. The latter shows close rim-form ties to Acachen's Añejo Variety. Nabanche's monochrome red Joventud group includes oval-section-spouted jars, gadrooned jars, and thin-walled *tecomates* virtually identical to Acachen Joventud counterparts. Preslip groove incision is a popular decorative mode in both complexes. The gray-to-buff mottled Capaz Variety of Chunhinta Black occurs in both Nabanche and early Acachen, in both cases appearing via thickened-rim, restricted-orifice bowls pertaining to a preslip, groove-incised type (Deprecio Incised). Muxanal Red-on-cream is present at both sites and, although the representative forms differ widely, slip characteristics and motif designs are remarkably consistent between the two. Pital Cream is present in minority status; however, Dzibilchaltun's Pital is not the mottled, Blotchy Variety of the Rio Bec and Pasión zones but a true clear monochrome.

Regionalisms separate the Becan and Dzibilchaltun material at both the varietal and group levels. A red-on-black dichrome occurs which is totally unrepresented in the Becan material. Apart from Muxanal, Nabanche contains a highly variegable tan, buff, or cream-slipped group which encompasses such varied types as red-on-buff (positive-painted); black and buff; and red-on-black and buff (positive-painted). Nothing similar is known to be present in Acachen. Resist orange-on-buff, absent from the Rio Bec collections, is well represented at Dzibilchaltun. Cuspidor-shaped bowls are rare at the latter site, as is the chamfered-wall mode. Although Acachen and Nabanche share the vertically oriented, oval-section spout mode (Andrews IV 1968:Fig. 4a,c), the Mani-style, bolstered-rim bottle is unrepresented in the Dzibilchaltun collections even though present in high frequency only 85 kilometers south-southeast at Mani. The overall impression conveyed by comparison of the two complexes is one of probable similar origin followed by individualized, reciprocally isolated developments.

Extensions of Nabanche-like pottery are indicated as far east as Yaxuna and Chichen Itza by occurrences of the Sapote, Joventud, and Chunhinta groups. To the south, Mamom-sphere pottery has also been reported from Mani, Chacchob, Sacalum, Kabah, Sayil, Holactun, Santa Rosa Xtampak, and Dzibilnocac (Brainerd 1958; Folan 1972; Nelson 1973; type collections, INAH 1974:personal observation).

Taken as a zone, these sites have yielded representatives of the Sapote, Joventud, Chunhinta, and Muxanal groups. Their combined form repertoire includes flaring-sided plates with beveled lips; thin-walled *tecomates;* cuspidor-shaped bowls; gadrooned jars; jars with oval-section spouts; and the Mani-style bolstered-rim bottle form. This last mode appears to be restricted to a zone extending from the Mani-Chacchob-Sacalum district southward to the Becan-Xpujil locality. Generally speaking, the technological and stylistic attributes of the known Mamom-horizon pottery occurring between the Becan and Dzibilchaltun localities suggest the existence of a smooth ceramic continuum along the north-south axis of the peninsula during Middle Preclassic times. At least three ceramic zones are probably present along this continuum: (1) one encompassing the Becan locality and extending northward an indeterminate distance into the Chenes subregion; (2) one encompassing the Puuc Hills and extending northward as far as the Mani-Chacchob-Sacalum neighborhood; (3) one encompassing the Northern Plains between Ucu in the far northwest and Chichen Itza in the east. Acachen and Nabanche represent the extremes of this continuum, and this relationship is well reflected in the similarities and differences between the two complexes.

Ultimately, Mamom-sphere pottery can be derived from early Middle Preclassic assemblages restricted in distribution to the Pasion, Usumacinta, and Belize drainages. The presence of such pottery at the sites discussed above indicates that before 500 B.C. outward expansion from the southern riverine localities had already served to populate most of the Lowland Maya area.

Socioprocessual Discussion

A key to the nature and origins of late Middle Preclassic Maya social organization well may lie in the many-within-one character of the Mamom ceramic sphere. If it is assumed that each recognizably distinct complex within the sphere represents a discrete, functionally intrarelated community of some magnitude (minimally defined by the common production and/or utilization of the same ceramic assemblage), then the sphere as a whole can be described as a significantly larger, more dispersed, more loosely intrarelated interaction group—one encompassing considerably more internal variance, but still functionally intrarelated. Such a description strikingly suggests Sahlins's (1968:20) characterization of the segmentary tribe as an example of "extreme decentralization, to the extent that the burden of culture is carried in small, local, autonomous groups while higher levels of organization develop little coherence, poor definition, and minimum function." I suggest that the Mamom ceramic sphere represents an archaeologically observable, material reflection of the segmentary tribal level of social organization, and this is how I would characterize the sociopolitical condition of the Maya of the Northern Plains and Central Yucatan regions between the seventh and third centuries B.C.

If the above characterization is correct, then a genetic as well as functional link should exist among those communities encompassed by the sphere. Such a bond is, in fact, historically present and archaeologically visible in the common origin of Mamom-sphere complexes in the Xe ceramic sphere. The Mamom complexes of the Central Yucatan and Northern Plains zones represent divergent developments out of the areally restricted, typologically homogeneous Xe sphere of the Pasión drainage.

The nature, origins, culture history, and processual significance of the riverine communities are discussed elsewhere in this volume. What is of crucial importance to this discussion is that between 1000 B.C. and 700 B.C., as sedentary farming-fishing-collecting communities gradually filled the southern riverine niches, the forests and bush of the Central Yucatan and Northern Plains regions remained uninhabited. There is not so much as a suggestion of occupation prior to the late Middle Preclassic in the archaeological record of this area.

In the seventh century B.C., demographic pressures within the riverine niches apparently became sufficient to produce outward expansion away from the riverbanks and into the tropical forests of the interior.

Assuming that the riverine-restricted, homogeneous complexes of the Xe sphere represent material reflections of sedentary, riparian, levee farming-fishing-collecting communities and that the latter constituted an egalitarian tribal group, then the developmental process resulting in the appearance of Mamom-sphere complexes should be explainable as a function of the historical, demographic, and/or social processes which caused or enabled that group to spread away from the river and into the open forests of the Southern and Northern Lowlands. As noted above, I believe that by the seventh century B.C. the number and size of southern riverine settlements were such as to overburden this choice ecological zone and bring about intercommunity territorial competition and the withdrawal of some groups into the uncontested lands of the interior. The social organizational consequences of such expansion probably are reconstructable on the basis of Sahlins's observation that expansion in an open environment may well be accompanied by segmentation, the normal process of tribal growth and spread. But in the absence of competition small segments tend to become discrete and autonomous, linked together primarily through mechanical solidarity. These circumstances, in other words, favor fission but select against complementary opposition or fusion, and long-term occupation will eventually fix this structure, make it comparatively inflexible. (1961:342)

I suggest that the fission-multiplication, spread, and diversification which characterize the Xe-Mamom developmental process directly reflect a social developmental process such as that described by Sahlins. The fact that the developed Mamom sphere suggests a material reflection of segmentary tribalism adds further weight to this argument.

Puleston and Puleston (1971:336–37) suggest that this step was accompanied by a "transition from a livelihood based on riverine agriculture and fishing to one . . . emphasizing the procurement of food by hunting and gathering in a forest modified by silviculture." While I agree that a change in subsistence mode necessarily accompanied expansion away from the riverine niche, I do not believe that diverse resource exploitation constituted the primary replacement mode. Rather I believe the shift to have been from a system of intensive river-levee cultivation and fishing to one of extensive (swidden) forest cultivation and supplementary collecting. Were the Pulestons' model correct, then the archaeological record should show a gradual outward spread into immediately adjacent lands coupled with early (seventh through fifth century B.C.) population concentration and organization and the contemporaneous appearance of sociopolitical-ceremonial centers. It does not. The record shows that not only Tiradero, Becan, and Xpujil but even Ake, Chichen Itza, and other far northern localities were the sites of small village communities *by the sixth century B.C.* Not only was the spread of such communities extensive, but it occurred rapidly enough to result in the remarkable homogeneity of vessel forms, slips, and decorative treatments referred to above. Moreover, the Pulestons (1971:335) themselves point out that

without the frequently flooded river levees, a relatively permanent form of cultivation had to be given up for the comparatively inefficient slash-and-burn method if maize was to continue as the principal crop. Such a shift with its consequent increase in the requirement for labor and accompanying decrease in productivity could have resulted in little more than widely dispersed and meager hamlets, such as occur in the region today, were it not for the presence of another vital resource, the ramon.

It is precisely such "widely dispersed and meager hamlets" that typify the late Middle through early Late Preclassic communities of the Central Yucatan and Northern Plains zones.

In sum, the widespread but thin distribution, apparent speed thereof, meagerness of material culture, and homogeneity of ceramic tradition combine to suggest shifting cultivation as the subsistence basis of the pioneer settlers of the Northern Lowlands and the mechanism responsible for their dispersal. I thus would agree with R. E. W. Adams's (1971:155) suggestion that the outward spread of Mamom-sphere pottery reflects the movements of peoples reliant upon an extensive system of agriculture, the rapidity and extent of their dispersal being directly analogous to that of the Danubian slash-and-burn farmers of fifth millennium B.C. Europe (Piggott 1965:50-51). Returning to my primary concern, the sociopolitical condition of the Middle Preclassic pioneers, important additional confirmation is added to the arguments presented above by Sahlins's observation that

> the main run of forest agriculturalists . . . tend to be organized as simple segmentary tribes. For this mode of adaptation [swidden agriculture] commonly maximizes local cleavages at the expense of regional organization. Capitalizing the tribal infrastructure, it lends itself to a decentralized system of autonomous communities rather than a pyramidal chiefdom.
>
> Swidden agriculture has a centrifugal effect on the distribution of settlements, and a population dispersed through tropical forest is not well-situated for political unification. (1968:31)

To sum up, by the sixth century B.C. the Central Yucatan and Northern Plains regions were already inhabited by semi to fully sedentary slash-and-burn agriculturalists with a segmentary tribal level of sociopolitical organization. I would further suggest that a pioneer situation obtained in which unoccupied land was still available in sufficient quantity and community groups were still small enough to enable each community group to carry on the expansive, swidden type of farming and still maintain not only its individual political autonomy and territorial integrity but a sufficient degree of isolation to foster semiindependent cultural development as well. This pattern was to remain generally true for the regions in question for some three to five centuries.

External contacts and trade, even extralowland trade, were important during this phase in supplying a number of material necessities. At Becan, obsidian blades of necessarily foreign origin are present in Acachen deposits of fourth or fifth century B.C. date. The earliest Dzibilchaltun communities, on the other hand, have produced no confirmed evidence for the presence of exotic products or raw materials amidst their extensive remains (I. Rovner and J. Taschek 1974:personal communications). W. L. Rathje (1971) has noted that such items as igneous rock metates and manos, obsidian cutting implements, and salt necessarily were imported into the interior regions of the Southern Maya Lowlands. On the basis of his assumption that each of these commodities constituted an indispensable part of the Lowland Maya subsistence complex, Rathje goes on to

> hypothesize that given the preconditions of environment, subsistence base, technology, and the existence of basic resources not located in the lowlands, complex socio-political organization in the rain forests of Mesoamerica developed originally in response to the need for consistent procurement, importation, and distribution of non-local basic resources useful to every household. (1971:278)

I believe that there is good reason to question the inference that extraregional trade among tribesmen—even for genuinely necessary resources—is invariably a sufficient condition to sociopolitical development. Sahlins points out that

> it is . . . common for tribesmen to develop regular trade with outsiders . . . . tribes often set their border along some ecological seam . . . and establish within their respective zones unique patterns of adaptation. As producers of complementary goods, settlements of different tribes may then enter into strategic exchange: a crucial flow of materials penetrates the cultural boundaries. . . . the evidence of ethnography and archaeology suggests that inter-tribal division of labor and trade are commonplace, possibly because the adaptations of the simpler tribes tend to be narrow and ecologically specific. (1968:22–23)

Now it is undoubtedly true that commerce between tribal-level societies and others at a more advanced stage of development can lead and has led to sociopolitical evolution (for a comprehensive discussion and bibliography of trade as a mechanism in the formation of secondary states and chiefdoms, see Webb 1973:370, 375–78). However, I believe (with Webb) that trade-stimulated sociopolitical evolution results primarily from the infusion of superabundant wealth into a tribal economy, not from any necessity on a tribe's part to organize or maintain trade. Moreover, I suggest that such politically developmental commerce is most likely to be initiated and maintained in the interests of the organizationally more advanced participant system, not the less developed one. Thus a state, such as Teotihuacan, might conceivably channel enormous amounts of wealth into the economy of a chiefdom or tribe in exchange for some item necessary or desirable to itself. It is difficult to imagine, however, a way in which a chiefdom or tribe lacking such a commodity could conjoin a state to enter into or maintain such a pattern of reciprocity.

That the Northern Lowlands did possess at least one resource, salt, of sufficient interest to bring about repeated intrusions by outsiders is evident from their later Classic and Postclassic history (Ball 1974a; Ball and Eaton 1972:774). The existence of that resource means that at least one precondition to the operation of the trade mechanism was present. Temporal and historical factors, however, conjoined to prohibit its inception.

In considering the evolution of Lowland Maya culture, it is important to keep in mind that the transition from egalitarian tribal communities to ranked chiefdoms probably was under way by the late fourth century B.C. in some cases and had clearly taken place in most by the second century A.D. Such a span—let us say 350 B.C. to A.D. 150—would seem to have been too late to have been directly influenced by contacts with the civilization of the Olmec chiefdoms and too early to have resulted from intervention by the rising Teotihuacan state. Commercial contacts with the chiefdoms and tribes of Highland Guatemala do not seem likely to have produced an economic supersaturation of sufficient magnitude to result in sociopolitical change.

It thus seems unlikely that trade was *the* effective mechanism in the development of the earliest Lowland Maya chiefdoms.

Returning to Rathje's hypothesis of primary sociopolitical evolution through trade, I suggest that there is good reason to question the basic premise of his argument. Metates and manos might have been necessary components of the maize-oriented subsistence complex; their igneous composition was not. Tabulations from several Northern Plains and Central Yucatan sites indicate that, in fact, locally available raw materials (cherts and fine-grained and even coarse-grained limestones) served to satisfy consumer demands. To exemplify this, let us examine the metate and mano counts for the most thoroughly investigated site in each of those regions.

At Mayapan, in the Northern Plains, recovery totals of 745 metates and 54 manos have been recorded (Proskouriakoff 1962:322). Ninety-seven percent of the metates and eighty-five percent of the manos are of local origin. The respective remainders of three percent and fifteen percent are of imported igneous rock.

To date, the Becan locality has produced only 47 metates and 33 manos. Forty-two (89 percent) of the former and twenty-six (79 percent) of the latter are of local limestone.

The enormous volume of chert percussion blades and flakes in Becan deposits argues against a heavy dependence on imported obsidian for cutting implements (I. Rovner 1973:personal communication).

Finally, salt is indeed a necessary human requirement; however, it is one resource that probably is more abundant in the Lowland Maya area than anywhere else in Mesoamerica.

In sum, consideration of the actual archaeological record suggests that the role of trade as a prime mover in the emergence of Classic Maya civilization is in need of some serious reassessment.

THE LATE PRECLASSIC: PREDATORY TRIBES AND CONQUEST CHIEFDOMS

The Central Yucatan Archaeological Record: 350 B.C.–50 B.C.

Between the fourth and first centuries B.C., communities grew and multiplied until they filled virtually every corner of the Maya Lowlands. It is a rare test pit anywhere in Campeche or Yucatan that fails to produce cultural remains of that date. Vestiges of Late

Preclassic settlement are not only widespread; they are also quite densely distributed in terms of both spatial continuity and depositional thickness. Growing permanence of settlement is suggested by the increased frequency of plastered plaza floors and stuccoed masonry platforms over that of the preceding period.

Local ceramic assemblages of the Late Preclassic Chicanel sphere are remarkably alike in vessel forms, surface finishes, and decorative treatments from the northeastern tip of Yucatan to the southern edge of the Peten. The relative intensity of this similarity is significantly greater than that existing among the complexes of the Mamom sphere. Whereas the latter is characterized by extensive local diversity within an apparent areal similitude, Chicanel seems to represent genuine areal homogeneity locally differentiated by minor variations. The Pakluum Chicanel complex of Becan typifies Late Preclassic assemblages throughout the central Yucatan region.

Pakluum does not contain an unslipped-plain storage jar type. Its Sapote Striated:Rastro Variety appears via both wide-mouthed, low-necked jars and thickened-rim, restricted-orifice bowls. The fine-line striation is deeper and sharper than was the case on Añejo Variety jars and frequently occurs in "herringbone" patterns.

The red Sierra group dominates Pakluum's slipped wares, accounting for 55 to 60 percent of its slipped pottery and about 35 to 40 percent of the complex as a whole. Standard Chicanel forms such as flat-bottomed, flaring-sided dishes with wide-everted or everted-thickened rims; medial-flanged dishes; and medial-ridged dishes predominate in this and the other slipped groups. Polvero Black is well represented via jar forms but relatively uncommon otherwise; Flor Cream is virtually absent; Repasto Black-on-red is present in low frequency.

Secondary manipulative decoration is uncommon in Pakluum. Chamfering, zoned incision, zoned punctation, and reed impression, all present in Acachen, lose popularity and disappear. Prefired, preslip groove-incision, common in Acachen, is virtually absent from Pakluum, occurring only rarely via the Sierra group's Laguna Verde Incised. Hongo Composite, a red-slipped and unslipped, fingernail-impressed type, occurs with some frequency and is believed to make its first appearance during early-facet Pakluum (ca. 300 B.C.–50 B.C.). The distinctive "mushroom stand" form of Hongo Composite has a long history in the Pasión drainage, appearing during late San Felix and persisting through Plancha and into Salinas. It also occurs at Guanacaste, Chiapas, during the roughly coeval Guanacaste phase.

Zapatista Trickle-on-cream brown and Ciego Composite (red-slipped and unslipped-striated) are important types believed to appear during late-facet Pakluum (ca. 50 B.C.–A.D. 150). Both have close typological counterparts in Dzibilchaltun's Xculul complex and are believed to have emerged in the Rio Bec as a result of stimulus diffusion from the north.

Essentially identical pottery is spread across southern Quintana Roo and Campeche from the Bajía de Chetumal to the Laguna de Terminos (R. Fry 1974:personal communication; type collections, INAH 1974: personal observation). Moving northward through the Central Yucatan region, material indistinguishable from that of Becan has been recovered from Santa Rosa Xtampak and Dzibilnocac. Examining the Paklum collections in Merida recently, D. Forsyth (1974:personal communication) commented that much of the monochrome red pottery of the Edzna II complex could easily be lost among the Pakluum even on the basis of paste appearance (macroscopic). The same is true of several collections that I have recently examined from a series of sites on the peninsula's west, north, and east coasts between Aguacatal, Campeche, and Tancah, Quintana Roo. On the Northern Plains, a somewhat more complicated picture holds true.

The Northern Plains Archaeological Record:
350 B.C.–50 B.C.

Over the last fifty years, an enormous body of complex, at times confusing information has been accumulated and published concerning the nature and distribution of Preclassic ceramics in the northernmost Maya Lowlands. Publication of the final report on the important Dzibilchaltun sequence should clear away much of the present confusion. Until such time, a good deal of this discussion must be considered preliminary, based as it is on my familiarity with the early ceramics of several other Northern Plains sites and a passing firsthand acquaintance with the Komchen- and Xculul-complex pottery of Dzibilchaltun.

Northern Plains pottery of the late fourth through second centuries

B.C. seems to represent a predominantly localized developmental continuum out of Nabanche Mamom. It is characterized by polished, monochrome slips which differ from those of the Middle Preclassic; however, I am here hesitant to classify these as Paso Caballo Waxy (the Chicanel-sphere slipped ware) because of what I presently consider to be several important distinctions in slip character, form repertoire, and decorative treatment. Rather, I believe the slipped pottery of the Komchen phase to constitute a distinct regional slipped ware derived, but distinct, from Flores Waxy and contemporary with but distinct from Paso Caballo Waxy. This same span of time witnessed a sharp reduction in the form repertoire of Northern Plains pottery from that of the preceding period; however, given the region's relative provincialism through the phase, an impressive set of innovations was introduced. Probably the most interesting and important of these was the controlled trickle painting technique. At Mani, an arbitrary stratigraphic level of mixed Middle through Late Preclassic composition included, together with thin-walled *tecomates,* chamfered bowls, and flaring-sided red-on-black plates (Brainerd 1958:Figs. 17e, 31d16, el5), an assortment of late Nabanche-Komchen downturned-everted-rim dishes bearing controlled trickle paint (Brainerd 1958:Figs. 31c21–22,37,40). The latter occurred on what ordinarily would have been a reddish buff type. A similarly treated Komchen-complex dish from Dzibilchaltun (type collections, INAH 1973:personal observation) further supports an early appearance for trickle painting. Although apparently not destined to gain true importance anywhere until somewhat later in the Preclassic, trickle painting was eventually to become the most consistently popular decorative mode in the Northern Lowlands throughout the Classic and Postclassic periods (R. E. Smith 1971:62). The idea seems to have entered the Rio Bec subregion during the late facet of Pakluum, that is, at about the time of its popularity increase north of the Puuc Hills. Another important Northern Plains innovation of the late fourth through second centuries B.C. was the combination of surface striation with slipping on large storage jars so as to produce preslip-striated vessels in monochrome red or black. The resultant composite jars seem to have supplanted the contrastively drab unslipped-striated ware for storage purposes throughout the Komchen phase. Preslip-striated vessels are known from Chichen Itza, Mayapan, Santa Cruz, Acanceh, Dzibilchaltun, Quinta Miraflores (Merida), Ucu, Mani, and Kabah.

acropolis 20 by 110 meters square . . . with courts and terraces on different levels reaching a height of more than 8 meters. (Andrews IV 1965a:51)

At about the same time, exotic sumptuary items—such as jade—made a plentiful appearance in the local archaeological record (J. Taschek 1974:personal communication).

All in all, the late fourth through second century span represented a major Preclassic cultural peak at Dzibilchaltun, one equal to if not surpassing anything else to appear on the Northern Plains for several centuries to come.

The Northern Plains Archaeological Record: 50 B.C.–A.D. 250

In the first century B.C., the Dzibilchaltun Maya appear to have entered into an era of cultural decline and collapse. The Xculul phase

was one of decadence and decreased population in the zone. No indications of formal architecture have been found. Structural remains are those of low platforms which served as foundations for perishable living structures. Pottery, scattered thinly over the zone, is characterized by distinct aesthetic and technological deterioration. (Andrews IV 1965a:51)

An apparent drop-off in sumptuary imports coincides with these other signs of cultural deterioration.

Although we lack stratigraphic confirmation, it is possible that Usil Red Ware (R. E. Smith 1971:30–31) had its inception during this interval. Via its constituent types of the red Xanaba group, this ware frequently parallels the contemporary Paso Caballo Waxy in form repertoire. Called Formative Flaky Redware by Brainerd (1958:49), it has surface characteristics closely matching those described by Andrews IV as typifying Xculul pottery. Compared to the polished, waxy finishes of Nabanche and Komchen,

[Xculul] slips become streaky and lose in adherence. Whereas Phase I and II slips were commonly crazed in firing, those of this phase tend to flake off. The normally hard sherd-tempered reddish pastes of I and II are largely replaced by softer, much coarser, gray paste tempered with black limestone. (Andrews IV 1965a:41)

It is important to remember, however, that not all of the Northern Plains pottery of the phase falls into this class. The first century B.C. also witnessed the introduction of true Paso Caballo Waxy Ware from the south. Between 100 B.C. and A.D. 250, two quite distinct ware traditions thus appear to have coexisted on the Northern Plains. Paso Caballo Waxy with its roots in the south and its general affinities to the earlier pottery of Nabanche and Komchen is aesthetically and technologically the finer of the two. Nevertheless, Usil Red Ware, despite its obvious status as a second-rate local imitation of the latter, seems to have successfully competed with and supplanted it. The situation is reminiscent of that at Barton Ramie where Vaquero Creek Red replaced Sierra Red during the Mount Hope phase (Willey et al. 1965:337–42).

The precise sequence of events with respect to the introduction of Paso Caballo Waxy Ware, the development of Usil Red Ware, and the supplantation of the former by the latter remains to be worked out. Form modes and contextual associations indicate that, although dominant, red Xanaba types still shared the scene with such Paso Caballo Waxy types as Sierra Red, Polvero Black, and Escobal Red-on-buff as late as the early third century A.D. Preslip-striated jars of Komchen ancestry also seem to have persisted this late, although Sapote Striated vessels were present as well. The importance of Usil Red Ware prior to A.D. 150 remains an open question. Quite possibly it appeared as early as the first century B.C. as a local successor to Komchen-phase polished ware and an inferior imitation of the newly introduced Paso Caballo Waxy. To date, however, I know of little certain evidence to prove its existence prior to the appearance of the Terminal Preclassic (A.D. 150–250) types with which it is generally associated and whose forms it so frequently assumes.

The Xculul Chicanel complex of Dzibilchaltun and contemporary assemblages of pottery from Soblonke, Quinta Miraflores, Mayapan, Dzab-na, Yaxuna, and Mani collectively have produced not only a general Chicanel-sphere-like assortment of forms and decorative treatments but such specific types and modes as Sapote Striated (apparently reintroduced), Sierra Red, Polvero Black, Flor Cream, Repasto Black-on-red, Laguna Verde Incised, everted-rim plates with hollow tetrapod supports, the "mushroom stand" form, and the grooved-hooked lip mode. The flow of goods and ideas was not entirely one-way. Ciego Composite, a red-slipped and unslipped-striated type, may have moved from the Northern Plains, where it is very popular during Xculul, to the Central Yucatan region, where it is far less common. The trickle decorative mode clearly moved from north to south but apparently no farther than the Rio Bec subregion. Interestingly, local adaptation of this mode involved not only simple replication but modification. On the Northern Plains, it is most frequently encountered as positive (reduced) streaking or negative (oxidized) staining on monochrome red or reddish buff pottery; at Becan, its predominant occurrence is via the cream to brownish buff Zapatista group. Conversely, sherds from Mani demonstrate that when Northern Plains potters adopted such Chicanel-sphere standards as Hongo Composite, they were unable to forego so favored a local treatment as oxidized trickle-on-red staining (Brainerd 1958:Figs. 17e1,18).

Despite its apparent aesthetic and technological shortcomings, Usil Red Ware was far from being the last gasp of a moribund ceramic tradition. To the contrary, it represented the first, admittedly equivocal, experiments with the more highly refined (and consequently thinner, more opaque, and flakier) slips of an incipient gloss ware tradition. By the close of the third century A.D., locally produced Usil Red and imported Peten Gloss Wares would constitute the bulk of slipped pottery in use on the Northern Plains. During the Terminal Preclassic, such types as Escobal Red-on-buff, Aguila Orange, and San Blas Red-on-orange were introduced directly from the south (probably via the west coast) together with form modes such as the grooved-hooked lip and the basal Z-angle dish. Northern Plains potters were quick to adopt and adapt these new ideas, adding several innovations of their own. Grooved-hooked lips appear on Xanaba Red dishes from Chichen Itza, Yaxuna, Acanceh, Dzibilchaltun, Quinta Miraflores, and Ake (see Brainerd 1958:Figs. 6b2, 17f26, 65c13). Plain and incised basal Z-angle dishes with streaky black or black-brown slips are present at several north coast sites. The slips appear to have been applied as secondary washes over vessels of red-on-buff type. True Escobal Red-on-buff also occurs via flaring-sided dish forms. Red-on-orange dishes, sometimes with prefired, postslip punctation, appear at several north coast and inland sites. The latter include Ucu, Dzibilchaltun, Merida, Ake, Acanceh, Dzab-na, Chichen Itza, and Balankanche (see Brainerd 1958:Figs. 6d1–2,g2;17g5; 63a1–2).

The most striking Northern Plains innovation of the Terminal Preclassic was Valladolid Incised-dichrome (R. E. Smith 1971:31–32), a red-on-orange, postslip-incised type possibly inspired by imported San Blas–group dishes. Restricted to wide-mouthed, high-necked jar forms, Valladolid Incised-dichrome is known from Chichen Itza, Balankanche, Yaxuna, Mayapan, Acanceh, Merida, and Kabah (Brainerd 1958:Figs. 6a2,5–7,6g1,3; 63a10–11). Contemporary short-necked jars seem to have had flaky red slips and unslipped-incised necks (Brainerd 1958:Fig. 6a1,4,19).

There is a single possible occurrence of Sarteneja Usulutan at Mani (Brainerd 1958:172, Fig. 31c6); however, I am aware of no instances of the Protoclassic Floral Park–sphere diagnostic Holmul Orange Ware on the Northern Plains.

The Xculul-phase collapse of Dzibilchaltun as an important demographic and civic center does not appear to have been symptomatic of a general Northern Plains condition. While the former locality was experiencing its first era of cultural decline and depopulation, other centers were apparently flourishing. At Quinta Miraflores, a small, now-demolished mound site located about four kilometers east of the present main plaza of Merida, E. M. Shook reported the remains of

> vertical and sloping terrace walls, lime-plastered stairways, and floors of four successive building stages. The structure in each stage apparently had been a rectangular platform, with steps on either the east or the west side, supporting a building of perishable material. There was no evidence of vaulted masonry buildings. Substructure walls were built of rough uncut stones, then surfaced with lime plaster. A collection of 900 potsherds. . . from this Quinta Miraflores mound belongs to the Preclassic period. (1955:290)

Nine kilometers north-northwest of Merida, the site of Soblonke was found to

> consist of 6 low mounds from 0.5 to 1.5 meters high and a larger structure 3.25 meters high. The last has . . . vertical and sloping structural walls built of rough, uncut stones and surfaced with lime plaster. The construction is of the same type as that at Quinta Miraflores and at Xcanatun [Dzibilchaltun] and again only Preclassic pottery comes from the mound fill and debris. (Shook 1955:291)

A single "Preclassic unit with rough, uncut masonry walls" also has been reported from Ucu (Shook 1955:292), while at Yaxuna Brainerd (1951:76) described an acropolis-type mound "about 60 by 130 meters" consisting of "a raised terrace with several buildings or substructures on it."

I have examined sherd collections from each of the above contexts and, with the exception of that from Ucu, have found them to suggest Xculul rather than earlier structural activity. The small platform at Ucu may have been of Middle Preclassic (Nabanche) date; however, it too was covered over by a larger, Terminal Preclassic (Xculul 2) structure.

Thus, the first century B.C. eclipse of Dzibilchaltun did not herald a period of overall deterioration on the Northern Plains. The Komchen-phase primacy of the former site gave way to the rise of several other centers of possibly equal impressiveness.

The Central Yucatan Archaeological Record: 50 B.C.–A.D. 250

Between the first century B.C. and the third century A.D., the Becan locality experienced a population upsurge, apparent settlement concentration—or at least nucleation—and public architectural undertakings of considerable magnitude (see R. E. W. Adams:Chapter 4, above). The peak of this development seems to have occurred between A.D. 150 and 250 when the great defensive system was constructed; the 46 acres enclosed by it were transformed into a nearly continuous expanse of plazas, platforms, and pyramidal structures; and an as yet indeterminate sector of the immediately surrounding countryside was given over to clusters of *plazuela*-like complexes, presumably of residential nature.

The ceramic traits associated with the early segment of this florescence have been described above. Following A.D. 150, the Pakluum pottery tradition persisted, but it was strongly colored by a number of important typological and form-mode additions. The known distribution of Holmul Orange Ware, however, suggests a trade and tradition network from which Becan was excluded despite its spread northward on both east and west flanks. Although they may be coincidental, I am inclined to believe that the contemporaneous influx of Protoclassic Floral Park–sphere elements into the Northern

Lowlands; their exclusion from the Becan locality; and the construction of the Becan fortress were causally interrelated.

By the mid third century A.D., Becan consisted of a strongly fortified concentration of public civil-religious and private residential architecture. The countryside surrounding this citadel held numerous structural complexes of residential and/or civil-religious nature. Local population seems to have reached a magnitude which would be approximated again only during mid-seventh- through early eighth-century Late Classic and ninth- through tenth-century Terminal Classic times. Local ceramics suggest the persistence of a Chicanel-like Preclassic tradition despite indications of contact with Protoclassic-sphere neighbors. The tradition is not devoid of its own incipient Classic components, however, and there is every reason to believe that terminal-facet Pakluum was developing into a Tzakol-like, Early Classic complex. The Becan locality did pass through the Protoclassic *period;* I do not believe it participated in a Protoclassic *stage*. Similarly, other than in a strictly chronological sense, there seems little rationale for labeling the Terminal Preclassic as Protoclassic on the Northern Plains.

Socioprocessual Discussion

The widespread, dense distribution of Chicanel-sphere ceramics and the essential typological uniformity present among even widely separated member complexes of that sphere suggest extensive interregional contacts at an intensive level. The fact that identities extend to coarse, locally produced domestic pottery and are not confined to mortuary, ceremonial, or other specialized categories argues against trade or socially enjoined exchange as the sole or primary mechanism of diffusion. Rather, it is suggestive of a culturally homogeneous population enjoying relatively continuous interaction within the lowland bounds. This, of course, need not imply either absolute ethnic uniformity or any sociopolitical unity; the tribal population involved could well have been fragmented into numerous, distinct, and sometimes mutually antagonistic groups. A shared cultural tradition, however, is implicit in the archaeological record. Genetically, the replacement of the regional diversity of the Mamom sphere by the areal homogeneity of Chicanel probably reflects the supplantation of the small, numerically few, and scattered communities of the Middle Preclassic by increasingly larger, more numerous, and more contiguous ones during the late fourth through second centuries B.C. Following the segmentation process of the seventh through early fourth centuries, it is unlikely that increasing contiguity necessarily brought about any intercommunity political harmony. The homogeneity of Chicanel implies a shared *cultural tradition,* no more.

Processually, the Mamom and Chicanel spheres represent two archaeologically visible segments of a spiraling interaction continuum of gradual population growth, community enlargement, and tribal segmentation. Repeated over three or four centuries, these processes, gradually at first and later more rapidly, easily could have filled the Maya Lowlands with land-hungry swidden agriculturalists. In essence, we see here a classic example of cultural adaptive radiation.

It is unlikely that the above sequence of events ensued without the accompaniment of intercommunity hostilities. Sahlins (1968:32) correctly notes that "continuous cultivation in secondary forest will not evoke any antithesis between sword and plowshare. On the contrary, cultivation may pass directly into intercommunity competition—over valuable land." The growing swidden agricultural community possesses a built-in need for increasingly more farmland. In even a slightly crowded environment, such need can generate intercommunity warfare, to be resolved by the defeat and displacement of one group and its withdrawal into other, as yet uncontested territory. The archaeologically inferred fact that such conflict must have occurred among member communities of the same tribal group should be in no way surprising. In discussing a model of warfare among swidden agriculturalists with population spread and territorial expansion as its functions, A. P. Vayda (1961:350–51) points out that it is characterized by "recurrent *intratribal* as well as extratribal hostilities" (italics mine). The social structure of many segmentary tribes is itself an adaptive response to the demands and opportunities of such intercommunity competition-expansion. Individual communities naturally defend their own territories; however, in cases where conflict occurs between two member communities of a larger descent group, noninvolved but lineally related "third party" communities may enter the dispute as temporary allies of their nearer kinsmen (Bohannan 1954; Sahlins 1961). In this way, maximum force is massed against those communities spatially most removed from and lineally most distantly related to those of the tribal "heartland." Territorial competition is thus displaced *outward,* and its impetus is toward the withdrawal-expansion of the most peripheral groups (Sahlins 1968:50–52). In this way, the swidden agricultural tribe expands to fill its environment.

The Northern Maya Lowlands of ca. 350 B.C. probably comprised a patchwork of differentially interrelated village communities of swidden agricultural tribesmen. Materially, at least, these communities shared a common cultural tradition. Almost certainly a number of social and ritual ties interlinked them as well. Political organization, however, most likely still stopped at the village level. Incessant territorial conflicts possibly gave rise to occasional alliances among more closely affined communities against more distantly related ones. These fragile pacts, however, were subject themselves to stresses and strains of the same origin as those crises which had brought them into being in the first place and probably rarely survived them. The overall situation is well summarized by Sahlins:

> The effects on intercommunity relations are complicated, but on the whole this self-centered concern for *lebensraum* probably encourages local solidarity at the expense of tribalism. Friendly understandings with certain nearby communities could prove useful, both to curb competition and promote alliance against other groups. Even so, beyond this minimal sphere of peaceable relations, itself not entirely secure from dissention, the community is often set apart by its own interests from a hostile world, which very likely includes fellow tribesmen. (1968:32)

The processual status described above persisted until the late fourth to early third century B.C. During the course of this interval it was critically upset by a previously negligible factor: the macrogeography of the Northern Lowlands.

Yucatan is a peninsula. Surrounded on three sides by water, it is a circumscribed environment, albeit on a grand scale. Despite the extent of the Northern Lowlands (roughly 141,500 sq km), it is quite conceivable that a slowly but steadily growing population reliant upon an extensive system of agriculture could fill it to its maximum carrying capacity over the course of several centuries. The virtually uninterrupted blanket of Late Preclassic remains suggests that by the first century B.C. such was in fact the case. It is unlikely that conditions were any better farther south. Demographic saturation of the available environment probably would not automatically have slowed the processes of population growth and expansion. Nor is there reason to believe that territorial competition would have been decreased to any degree by this situation; in fact, elimination of the withdrawal-expansion option for those defeated in territorial contests probably had the effect of exacerbating warfare. Defeated groups now faced a new problem: there remained nowhere to go.

In a series of papers, R. L. Carneiro (1961, 1970, 1974) has proposed a theory of sociopolitical evolution which argues that

> states [and, I believe, chiefdoms] first rose in areas of circumscribed agricultural land when increasing population pressure led to wars of conquest. In circumscribed environments, defeated peoples had nowhere to flee, and so were subject to incorporation into the political unit of the victor. The way in which militarily successful societies organized themselves to wage war and to administer conquered peoples and territory became the nucleus of state [and chiefdom] organization. (1974:180)

I believe that the archaeological record as presented and interpreted above indicates that by the Late Preclassic Period the Maya Lowlands in general and the northern regions thereof in particular were substantially and continuously occupied by a still-growing population of swidden agricultural tribesmen. The extent and density of this population was such as to bring about conditions of environmental circumscription on its peripheries (as in the case of those northern communities squeezed between their expanding neighbors to the south and the arid north coastal zone) and social circumscription at its center (as in the case of the communities of the central Peten). Given the archaeologically and geographically inferred preconditions of growing population, a swidden agricultural subsistence system, and a circumscribed environment, I propose that supravillage-level sociopolitical organization first appeared in the Northern Maya Lowlands in response to territorial competition and expansionist warfare among its inhabitants. A combination of offensive-defensive alliances, absorptions of defeated groups, and tighter internal sociopolitical organization could have given rise to a number of larger, more powerful village communities. In the face of persisting need to extend their territories farther, maintain their own holdings, and effectively organize composite populations of allied and absorbed villages, these gradually would have stabilized as true ranked societies or chiefdoms. I further suggest that if the above hypothesis is correct, the earliest evidence of supravillage-level sociopolitical organization should occur among communities in those regions where the effects of territorial circumscription, environmental and/or social, were most severely pronounced.

Following Carneiro (1970:737), I predict that the focus of greatest severity for social circumscription should occur at the geographic heart of the tribal range and therefore slightly south of the areal concentration of this chapter.

I suggest that communities on the perimeters of a tribal range bounded by expansion-prohibitive barriers of an ecological nature will begin to feel the effects of environmental circumscription earlier than those behind them. Moreover, the intensity of these effects seems likely to vary proportionately according to the ratio of a community's territorial limits formed by impassable natural barriers. The Northern Plains Zone, bounded on three sides by the Caribbean, the Gulf, and their adjacent littoral zones of salt marsh and mangrove swamp, clearly represents a region likely to experience the mobility-limiting effects of environmental circumscription quite early in its history.

Another factor deserving of consideration is the comparative agronomic potential among different regions of the tribal range. Clearly, the effects of any form of circumscription are likely to be felt sooner and more intensely in zones of relatively poor agronomic conditions since these are likely to necessitate a greater field:crop ratio and thus larger territorial requirements than those of more favorable conditions. If we assume that the general environmental conditions of the last five centuries more or less closely replicate those of the preceding two millennia, it is a relatively easy matter to select the Northern Lowlands' agronomically poorest region. The warm, semiarid Northern Plains Zone, of which Diego de Landa was moved to write in 1566, "Yucatan is the country with least earth I have seen, since all of it is one living rock and has wonderfully little earth" (Tozzer 1941:186), receives an annual average of less than 100 millimeters of rain (Vivo Escoto 1964:Fig. 10) to nourish its thin lateritic soils. The northwesternmost portion of this zone receives less than 500 millimeters of rain annually.

The potential effects of these conditions on per capita (and consequently per community) requirements of cultivable land are suggested by the following data. In 1960, the Central Yucatan and Campeche Plains regions produced roughly 9 percent more maize per unit of cultivated land than did the Northern Plains (about 753 as compared to 689 kilograms of maize per hectare). Beans and chile, two other native staples, were respectively 37 percent and 24 percent more productive in the regions south of the Puuc Hills than to their north. Root crops showed a similarly poor return in the north, the camote (sweet potato) yield per unit of cultivated land falling about 9 percent below that of the southern regions. Finally, while details on ramon nut production are not available, another important arboricultural product, the avocado, showed a staggering 104 percent higher return per unit of cultivated land in the comparison regions than on the Northern Plains.

The effect of such reduced productivity most probably would have been to bring proportionately larger amounts of land under cultivation in the far north than were necessary to feed an equivalent number of people farther south. Add to this the expansion-prohibitive barrier of the coastal salt marshes and the combined demographic pressures arising out of both local population growth and northward crowding from the south, and the Northern Plains emerges as the region most likely to experience first the pattern of intensified territorial warfare, alliances, conquests, and absorptions described above.

In terms of archaeological visibility, I suggest the following minimum criteria for the recognition of chiefdom-level sociopolitical organization: (1) evidence of social, political, religious, or other ranking among the sites of a region as reflected by differential sizes and the differential distribution, presence, and/or magnitude of monumental architecture among those sites; and (2) evidence of intracommunity personal or familial ranking as reflected by differential access to local and/or exotic sumptuary items and their differential distribution in functional contexts such as graves and middens.

Review of the overall archaeological record presented above discloses that the earliest known conjunctive appearance of these criteria north of the Peten was at the Dzibilchaltun site in the Northern Plains region. I suggest that the Komchen-phase florescence of Dzibilchaltun represented a direct, successful product of the consolidational-organizational demands of socioenvironmental circumscription among swidden agricultural tribesmen. The most recent presentation of Dzibilchaltun chronology (Ball and Andrews V 1975:Table 1) suggests that between 300 B.C. and 100 B.C. the site grew to be a large demographic and politico-religious center. It thus antedated the rise of Becan as a recognizable center by a good century or more and was roughly contemporary with or even slightly earlier than Cauac-phase Tikal.

As indicated earlier, there is some question as to whether or not the Komchen-phase ceramics of the Northern Plains should be included within the Chicanel sphere. A definitive statement on this must await publication of the final Formative ceramic sequence from Dzibilchaltun by the Middle American Research Institute. Whether Komchen pertains to Chicanel or is definitive of a contemporary Northern Plains ceramic sphere, there is no doubt that Komchen-like sherds are distributed widely and densely north of the Puuc Hills. Thus although fourth century B.C. events might have involved the establishment of a decided cultural division along the Puuc range, demographic conditions north of the dividing line were every bit as crowded as those to its south. The emergence of Komchen Dzibilchaltun as a major power might itself have been related to a possible halt of Chicanel-sphere expansion at the Puuc. If that chiefdom did emerge via the processes discussed above, it follows that its *minimum* sociopolitical aims would have included the checking of encroachments by outsiders on its own lands. Moreover, outward expansion by the chiefdom should have taken place to the maximum extent possible without endangering its own ability to maintain territorial integrity. I suggest that the possible ceramics-reflected line of cultural division along the Puuc reflects precisely such a situation.

On an areal basis, the potentials of the Puuc as a territorial boundary are obvious. Those controlling the heights of the inverted V-shaped range would have commanded the plains to their immediate north and south as well. It seems unlikely that "hostile" communities would have attempted to occupy land immediately in the shadow of this natural stronghold. Even within a warfare system based on village raids, ambushes, and personal combat, it would have been tactically naïve to establish a settlement beneath the hilltop holdings of one's enemies. In a bilaterally expansionistic situation, settlements immediately in the shadow of a potentially offensive tribal perimeter—such as the Puuc—seem more likely to pertain to the faction controlling the perimeter than to that outside it. In case of attack from farther out, it would be a simple matter to retreat to the defensive line. Hostile settlements, on the other hand, would expose themselves to a greater than normal risk of attack with little hope of retribution. In this light, it is significant that Komchen-like ceramics not only extend up to the Puuc from their northern side but occur as traces at Kabah and Sayil on the immediately adjacent southern plain as well.

Natural and cultural ecological conditions seem to have contributed to the development of supravillage-level sociopolitical organization on the Northern Plains at a time when conditions in the Central Yucatan forests still permitted demographic growth and expansion into as yet open areas. Emergence of one or more powerful centers in the far north by the third century B.C. meant that as Chicanel-sphere tribesmen expanded in that direction, they eventually came to encroach upon lands already claimed and held by the northern chiefdom(s). Following a hypothetically predictable series of clashes between peripheral villages of the chiefdom(s) and encroaching southern tribesmen, the chiefdoms may well have established a defensive territorial line along the natural barrier offered by the Puuc Hills. Given such a development, Komchen-related communities could be expected to appear on the plain to the Puuc's immediate south, as they apparently do.

South of the Puuc Hills, conditions continued much as before. Richer, deeper, rendzina soils and an annual rainfall of 1,000 to 2,000 millimeters more evenly spaced throughout the year produced substantially better agronomic conditions in the Central Yucatan region and presumably lowered the territorial requirements of its inhabitants. Nevertheless, unless population size was static or in a state of decline—conditions for which there are no supportive data—farmland requirements could have done nothing but increase over the centuries as long as the swidden system remained in vogue. By the first century B.C., demographic pressures were reaching a critical state south of the Puuc. The hypothetical social barrier formed by the Northern Plains chiefdom cut off further withdrawal-expansion in that direction. Flows of true Chicanel-sphere ceramics up both flanking coasts of the Northern Plains suggest a situation sufficiently desperate to force some groups to abandon a forest agricultural way of life for a coastal fisher-collector one. As had happened a century or more earlier to both north and south, circumscriptional factors—in this case predominantly of a social nature—were coming into play among the Central Yucatan communities.

There are at least some suggestions that the first century B.C. witnessed the initial concentration of sociopolitical importance at Becan (see R. E. W. Adams:Chap. 4, above), and it is possible that the rise of this center dates to that interval. When compared with the record for the late second to early third centuries A.D., however, the earlier remains appear relatively inconsequential. Certainly there is nothing to compare in magnitude with Komchen Dzibilchaltun or Cauac Tikal. One reason for the failure of the competitive pressures of the first century B.C. to produce a more impressive response in the Central Yucatan may lie in the opening of a "safety valve" on the region's northern perimeter, for it was at this juncture that Komchen Dzibilchaltun collapsed.

The causes behind the first century B.C. failure of this Northern Plains chiefdom must remain purely matters of conjecture. It seems unlikely, however, that it would have succumbed to the unorganized raids of the Central Yucatan tribesmen. To date, no evidence exists either for the presence of an opposing Central Yucatan chiefdom or for a violent end to the Northern Plains center. Processually, its breakdown may simply reflect the cyclic instability which typifies ethnographically known chiefdoms (Service 1962:151–52). Webb (1973:379) notes that "any expansion of the system to the point of linking disparate groups, of undertaking novel tasks (or even traditional tasks in amounts exceeding customary levels), or of requiring innovative policy-making causes the system to snap." Perhaps increasingly numerous and frequent raids out of the overcrowded south together with the coastal flanking movements of displaced southern tribesmen brought about a strain on the Komchen-phase chiefdom which culminated in its collapse. Another potential factor in the Xculul-phase decline could have been the occurrence of increasingly severe local nutritional and/or disease problems. Shimkin (1973) has pointed out that the importance of infectious diseases and malnutrition has probably been improperly minimized as a possible factor in the case of the Classic Maya collapse. His comments concerning the deleterious effects of increasing population densities and residential stabilities on health could equally well apply to the Komchen Dzibilchaltun center. Decline as a result of disease is at least a viable possibility and it offers the advantage of explaining the apparent first century B.C. population loss of the locality.

Whatever the cause of the chiefdom's collapse, it had the effect of removing the social barriers to further northern expansion out of the Central Yucatan region. In the first centuries B.C. and A.D., Chicanel-sphere ceramics and, inferentially, tribesmen spread around the Puuc and through the northern bush. Their intermixture with and gradual absorption into the indigenous population is probably reflected in the Xculul-phase ceramics situation as discussed above.

The opening up of the far northern territories seems to have lowered expansionistic pressures enough to reestablish a noncritical, competitive status quo throughout the Northern Lowlands. As noted above, a second powerful center may have developed at Yaxuna during this interval, but the data are inadequate to establish this with absolute certainty. Left to themselves, events probably would have repeated a similar sequence in time. A series of new, intrusive factors, however, was about to enter the picture.

Archaeological data presently available are inadequate to permit evaluation of whether the Floral Park–sphere elements now known from the Northern Lowlands reflect population intrusion or intergroup trade. This is a problem which merits further intensive investigation, particularly in those areas of southern Quintana Roo and northern Belize from which Floral Park traces are known and which lie adjacent to some of the stronger foci of the sphere, such as Holmul and Barton Ramie. I am inclined to believe that an actual movement of peoples into the northern regions did take place during the second century A.D. and that future research will bear this out. Taken together, I would interpret the Northern Lowland distribution of Floral Park–sphere elements, including their exclusion from the Becan locality, and the contemporaneous construction of the Becan defensive system as an archaeological example of Vayda's (1961:352) "second model of warfare and expansion among swidden agriculturalists: intratribal peace and mobility plus wars of territorial conquest against other tribes." The consolidational-organizational demands of territorial warfare in a crowded environment thus again would underlie the appearance of a Northern Lowland chiefdom. In this case, I suggest that terminal Pakluum Becan represented the fortified politico-religious center of a primarily defensive enclave chiefdom crystallized among the communities of the southern Central Yucatan region during a successful mobilization against foreign intrusions of the second century A.D. The apparent nucleation of terminal Pakluum residential complexes in the immediate vicinity of the stronghold might further reflect this situation.

The Becan chiefdom represented an essentially indigenous development despite the interplay of exotic elements in its genesis. It was neither overly isolationistic nor a cultural dead end, however, as is indicated by the large amounts of imported goods, borrowed ideas, and material innovations present among the archaeological remains of terminal Pakluum date. By the early third century A.D., the Pakluum Becan chiefdom was on the threshold of Classic-stage Maya culture (civilization). By A.D. 300, the latter was established in the Rio Bec Zone. Between these dates, however, a severe trauma seems to have affected the Becan chiefdom, dramatically reducing and dispersing its population and bringing an end to the impressive structural undertakings of the Terminal Preclassic era.[3]

NOTES

1. The Central Yucatan region is defined by Potter (1973) on the basis of a shared Late Classic architectural style (formerly subdivided into Rio Bec and Chenes). Geographically, it is roughly equivalent to the Rio Bec, Chenes, and Puuc zones as delineated by the Santa Fe conference on the collapse of Classic Maya civilization (Culbert 1973a: Fig. 1), although excluding the actual heights of the Puuc Hills. The Northern Plains Zone stands as defined by Culbert (1973a: Fig. 1). I would note that Potter prefers to see the Central Yucatan as a single homogeneous region in terms of architectural style and culture tradition, whereas I suspect that two culturally distinct regions (a southern Rio Bec and a northern Chenes) are discernible beneath the superficial unity of a shared architectural tradition.

2. All distributional and chronological ascriptions, evaluations, and comparisons not representing specific citations are based on my personal examinations of the relevant materials. These materials, which represent the efforts of numerous institutions and individuals over some four decades, are currently housed in the archaeological bodega of the Instituto Nacional de Antropología e Historia de México in Merida, Yucatan. I would like to express my gratitude to the Mexican authorities, especially Arq. Manero Peón and Arq. Norberto González, who have given me access to those collections. The bulk of this paper represents independent research carried out on my part between November 1973 and May 1974. I would like to thank Mr. and Mrs. Walter A. Ball and Dr. and Mrs. Richard F. Taschek for the generous financial assistance that made this research possible.

3. This is Part I of a two-part synthesis of the Northern Plains material. Part II treats the Early Classic material and will be published in Volume X of *Estudios de Cultura Maya*.

6

The Rise of Classic Maya Civilization: A Pasión Valley Perspective

GORDON R. WILLEY

Harvard University

INTRODUCTION

The Pasión Valley Zone (see Fig. 1.1) is a region of the Meso-american archaeological subarea known as the Maya Lowlands. It occupies the south-central and southwestern portion of the Gua-temalan Peten flatlands and, in this geographical position, is a part of what has been called the Southern Maya Lowlands, as distinct from the Northern, or Yucatecan, Maya Lowlands. The two largest ar-chaeological sites of this Pasión zone or region are Altar de Sacrificios (Willey and Smith 1969), at the confluence of the Pasión and Salinas rivers, in the southwest corner of the Department of Peten, and Seibal, some fifty kilometers to the east, at the great bend of the Pasión River (A. L. Smith and Willey 1969). This chapter is an attempt to view the rise of the Maya Classic civilization of the lowlands from the perspective of the archaeology of the Pasión Zone and, especially, from these two sites, from which most of our information on the prehistory of the region is derived.

It is my intent to develop this story of Maya civilizational growth in the Pasión Valley under four chronologically sequential headings. The first of these concerns the matter of origins: the spatial-temporal setting, the question of the ethnic derivation of the peoples involved, the probable sizes and settlement distributions of the populations, and the cultural status and general cultural affiliations of these societies. The second heading is that of the Preclassic Period configuration of development of Maya culture on the Pasión scene: the demographic trends through time, the matter of subsistence, and the inferences that are to be drawn from the archaeological record as to the rise in social and cultural complexity. The third topic takes up the crucial Preclassic-to-Classic transition: the nature of the changes and the factors of internally generated or externally stimulated processes that produced these changes leading to the rise of the Classic Maya civilization. The second and third sections compose the main part of the paper, treating as they do the rise and crystallization of the Maya Classic pattern. A shorter fourth section is devoted to the subsequent Classic Period configuration of development through time: the Early Classic culture, the Early-to-Late Classic changeover with its curious hiatus in cultural activities, and the Late Classic success and subsequent failure. While this discussion of the Classic carries us beyond the central theme of the "rise" of Maya civilization in the Southern Mesoamerican Lowlands, it is germane to our attempt to see the Maya civilizational growth phenomenon in the fullest perspective.

This full perspective leads us to a fifth and final section of the paper. While the main focus of attention throughout is the Maya Lowlands, some cognizance must be taken of various contemporary events in other parts of Mesoamerica. In noting these I have been led to offer some theoretical considerations about what I have called the "phenomena of centralization and decentralization" in the growth of Mesoamerican and other civilizations.

ORIGINS

Place and Time

In considering the origins of Maya culture in the lowlands we must widen our geographical frame of reference beyond the Pasión Valley and, indeed, beyond the Maya Lowlands. We must also go back in time to a point earlier than our earliest evidences of Pasión Valley or Maya Lowland occupation. The requisite setting is southern Mesoamerica, and the period is that of the beginnings of ceramics, economically significant agriculture, and settled village life. I am aware that these three things, functionally interrelated as they may be, were not necessarily contemporary in their southern Mesoamerican inceptions; nevertheless, it is probably safe to say that by about 2000 B.C. pottery making, farming, and sedentary communities were jointly established in a number of southern Mesoamerican regions. These would include the Chiapas-Guatemalan Pacific Coast, the southern Veracruz-Tabasco Lowlands, Oaxaca, and the Tehuacan Valley in Puebla. In a recent unpublished paper on southern Mesoamerican chronology, G. W. Lowe (1973a) has designated the period of 2000–1500 B.C. as Early Preclassic I, and he has identified the Chiapas-Guatemalan and Tabasco-Veracruz complexes of this period as pertaining to a Barra-Ocos pottery tradition. This early southern Mesoamerican pottery tradition is, almost certainly, ancestral to the oldest ceramics that have been found so far in the Maya Lowlands. The line of ceramic descent is followed through the Cuadros-Jocotal complexes (Joesink-Mandeville 1972), which would date to Lowe's Early Preclassic II Period (1500–1250 B.C.). Included would be such pre-Olmec or "incipient" Olmec phases as Bajío and Chicharras at San Lorenzo. These, in turn, are followed by the complexes that are associated with the Olmec stylistic horizon in the Early Preclassic III Period (1250–1000 B.C.). The Olmec horizon gave way to the epi-Olmec and related cultures of the early part of the Middle Preclassic Period, and the earliest pottery known from the Maya Lowlands dates to this time. It has been designated as the Xe ceramic sphere.

Pottery of the Xe sphere has been found at Altar de Sacrificios (R. E. W. Adams 1971) and at Seibal (Willey 1970; Willey et al. 1975) in the Pasión Valley region. The dates for these Xe-sphere complexes are ca. 800–600 B.C. The bearers and makers of this Xe pottery appear to have been the first settlers of the Peten Lowlands. Just where these first settlers came from is open to debate. It may have been from the old Olmec and epi-Olmec homeland on the Mexican Gulf Coast. Robert Rands (1974:personal communication) reports Xe-like pottery from the lower Usumacinta, suggesting one possible route of movement. On the other hand, an entry from the Guatemalan Highlands is suggested by the presence of such ceramic complexes as the Middle Preclassic Sakajut, in the Alta Verapaz, and El Portón, in the Baja Verapaz (Sedat and Sharer 1972; Sharer and Sedat 1973; Willey 1973:25–27). The situation is complicated by the fact that we are dealing with a widespread early ceramic sphere in which it is, as yet, difficult to discriminate fine-grained spatial and temporal differences.

Whether or not there were other ceramic-making peoples in the Maya Lowlands contemporaneous with the Xe-pottery-making groups of the Pasión Valley must be left as an open question for the time being. T. P. Culbert, in discussing the Tikal sequence (Chapter 2, above), is inclined to date the Eb phase at that site on a time level with Xe; however, he points to some typological differences between the two. In the Northern Lowlands, claims of contemporaneity between Xe and such phases as the Mani Cenote and the Nabanche have also been made (Joesink-Mandeville 1972), but other opinion would place these northern phases on a later Mamom sphere horizon (J. W. Ball, Chapter 5, above). In the light of these disagreements and doubts it is probably safest to hold open the possibility that the earliest ceramic traditions and peoples of the Maya Lowland heartland could have come from more than a single geographical source and could have entered the area by more than one route. At the same time, it seems most likely that even if this was the case the generic line of ceramic development for the earliest Peten pottery is the one which can be traced from Barra-Ocos through Cuadros-Jocotal and Olmec.

People

Ethnic Identity. Ethnic and linguistic identifications of prehistoric peoples are always risky, but as there are strong cultural continuities from the earliest Maya Lowland Middle Preclassic settlers to the later Classic Period Maya, with their Maya hieroglyphic texts, it seems probable that the Xe immigrants were Maya-speaking. Such an argument can be extended to maintain that the Olmec spoke a Mayan language. M. D. Coe made this suggestion a number of years ago (1962), and L. R. V. Joesink-Mandeville (1972) develops the idea further by specifying a southern Cholan and northern Yucatecan language branching from a common Olmec-Maya stock. While this is the kind of archaeologic-linguistic interpretation of which we can never be absolutely sure, it impresses me as the best of the various possibilities. Another possibility would be that the Olmec were of an ancestral Zoquean linguistic stock and that there was a linguistic disjunction in the line of ceramic development that we have been following in this historical reconstruction of the Maya Lowlands.

Demography. The settlement pattern of the Xe-phase occupation of the Pasión Valley was that of small village communities. At Altar de Sacrificios (Willey 1973:1–2, 22–23) Xe pottery and indications of small house occupation were found scattered over the area (about 1,100 by 400 m) of the swamp island location of that site. A concentration of such debris under Group B of those ruins suggests a cluster of at least four buildings around a little plaza, and four other house locations were discovered a few hundred meters from this Group B cluster. At Seibal (Willey et al. 1975) Xe sherds and household refuse were found in relatively circumscribed areas on the tops of the two highest hills of that site. From this limited evidence one would conclude that the populations of Altar de Sacrificios and Seibal would not be over 100 persons for each. Although there is no other recorded evidence of Xe-sphere settlement in the Pasión Valley, there are a great many small clusters of house-mound structures along the river between Altar and Seibal, and it is possible that some of these were occupied this early. But the present conclusion, from very limited evidence, is that the first settlers of the Pasión Valley were relatively few in number and lived in small, scattered villages.

Cultural Status

It can be assumed that the Xe peoples of the Pasión Valley were farmers. All contemporaneous Middle Preclassic peoples of southern Mesoamerica followed such a mode of subsistence, and in many regions adjacent to the Maya Lowlands agriculture had been known since the beginnings of the Early Preclassic Period. At Altar de Sacrificios jack beans *(Canavalia ensiformis)* were the only domesticate actually found in a Xe context; however, charred maize was associated with the immediately succeeding Mamom-sphere phase of the Middle Preclassic (Willey 1972:248). Farming was supplemented with forest hunting (deer, brocket, and other animals) and with riverine fishing.

All our evidence would indicate that the simple farming-hunting-fishing economy of the Xe communities was linked to a small-village-type social organization. Such villages probably were politically autonomous. Village politico-religious functions are suggested by modest architectural and artifactual finds. At Altar de Sacrificios, the principal concentration of Xe houses and refuse underlies the later Preclassic and Classic ceremonial structures, implying continuity of a sacred locus. The possibility that this was a modest ceremonial center is strengthened by the discovery of a possible pottery mushroom stand and a little red sandstone altar or table in Xe contexts at this spot (Willey 1973:22–24). At Seibal the ritual side of Xe life is attested by a cruciform cache of jade celts and an "ice-pick"-type bloodletter, the latter artifact being a typological link to the Olmec heritage (Willey et al. 1975). Yet it should be emphasized that the Xe scene did not include major ceremonial centers with constructions indicative of corporate labor direction under centralized authority. That kind of society, which was already known in other parts of southern Mesoamerica, had not yet come into being in the Pasión Valley, nor, as far as we know, in any other part of the Maya Lowlands at this early time.

Consonant with societal status are other aspects of Xe culture as we view it in the Pasión Valley. There are no burials indicative of exalted social or political position. Except for the few ritual items we have mentioned, there are no luxury goods and few exotics. Obsidian from the Guatemalan Highlands is present in Xe levels at both Altar de Sacrificios and Seibal, and igneous rocks for some (but not all) metates and manos are clues to extraregional contacts. But other than these items there is no evidence of long-distance trade, either in raw materials or in manufactured goods.

In reviewing Xe cultural status we should remember that the Maya Lowlands were at this time less advanced sociopolitically than were their neighbors and contemporaries of the Gulf Coast Lowlands, the Chiapas-Guatemalan Pacific Coast, or Oaxaca.

THE PRECLASSIC CONFIGURATION OF DEVELOPMENT

Demographic Trends

We can be sure, I believe, that populations in the Maya Lowlands showed a more or less steady growth throughout the Late Preclassic

Period. This observation is based on settlement-pattern data; while such data are difficult to translate into absolute population numbers, there can be little doubt that there was a relative increase in numbers of sites and numbers of individual residences over earlier times. The evidence with which I am most familiar—that from the Belize Valley (Willey et al. 1965:575–76) and the Pasión Valley (Willey 1973:23–24, 63–65; Willey et al. 1975)—supports this statement, as do settlement studies of other parts of the Maya Lowlands, for example, Tikal (see Haviland, 1965, 1966, 1970; W. R. Coe 1965a). Further reinforcement is offered by the known increase in the numbers of Late Preclassic, as opposed to Middle Preclassic, ceremonial centers for the area as a whole.

In the Pasión Valley, there was a small increase in the number of house sites occupied in the Altar de Sacrificios San Felix Mamom phase over the count for the Xe phase at that site, but this was followed by a dramatic increase of occupied house-mound locations in the Plancha Chicanel phase of the Late Preclassic Period. At Altar this house-mound-count sampling was limited to the swamp island of the ceremonial-center location and its immediate adjoining ground, so some question might be raised as to whether an overall regional population increase is indicated or only a concentration of formerly outlying settlements around the ceremonial-center nucleus. The Seibal data, however, which are drawn from a surveyed zone of approximately twenty-five square kilometers around that ceremonial center, confirm the population growth trend as absolute for the overall region. In the Seibal zone, Xe residences were confined, as indicated, to two small sections within what was later to become the precinct of the Classic ceremonial center; Escoba Mamom house locations were somewhat more numerous and more widely scattered, but those of the Late Preclassic Cantutse Chicanel phase were considerably more numerous and widely distributed (Willey et al. 1975).

Subsistence

Changes in subsistence practices during the Preclassic Period in the Pasión Valley region are difficult to document from the present record. One can only assume, given the demographic increase record for this period, that there was a commensurate overall increase in agricultural production. Given the ecological setting in this part of the Peten, I am inclined to think that such an increase was simply a geographically expansive one: more land was brought under cultivation with essentially the same food plants and cultivation techniques. I assume the key crops were maize and beans, although root-crop cultivation cannot be ruled out (Bronson 1966; see also Cowgill 1971). Judging from present-day conditions, it does not appear that the breadnut, or ramon nut, could have been an important subsistence item at either Altar or Seibal (see Puleston and Puleston 1971). Some kind of swidden fallowing system must have been the predominant practice in maize cultivation. It is possible that in certain Pasión Valley locations, such as some river bottomlands with seasonal flooding and silt deposition, this was a short-fallow system, more productive than one with long-fallow periods, but even this is uncertain. To the best of our knowledge there are no cultivation plots or ridges in the lowlands along the lower Pasión that resemble those described for the Candelaria region to the north (Puleston and Puleston 1971), nor are there any known ridgings or terracings on nearby higher terrain such as those recently reported from the Rio Bec country (Turner 1974).

The Rise of Social and Cultural Complexity

Settlement and Architecture. The terrain at Altar de Sacrificios precludes an urbanlike concentration of houses immediately surrounding the ceremonial center. As already noted, on the small swamp island on which the ceremonial center is located there was a steady increase in the number of house constructions, but this did not approach urban proportions at any time during the Preclassic Period or later. There may also have been an increase in house locations all along the lower Pasión drainage, as well as along the nearby course of the Salinas, during the Preclassic, and with river transportation Altar de Sacrificios may very well have had urban functions during this time. For Seibal, Gair Tourtellot's (1970) settlement pattern analyses are not yet complete; however, I think it is fair to say that a concentration of at least 1,000 to 2,000 persons was present in the Seibal center and its immediate peripheral zone in Late Preclassic times, and it is likely that the center drew upon the support of a good many more individuals from outlying districts.

The beginnings of modest public architecture at Altar de Sacrificios can be traced back to the latter half of the San Felix Mamom phase. At the close of that phase there was a five-meter-high earth platform in the Group B section of that site, and this and other clay platforms, which were arranged around a small rectangular plaza, had terrace features and were coated with crude masonry facings of lime-encrusted river shells (the best substitute for boulders in this stone-less setting). Such platform structures, it should be emphasized, represent substantially more labor than the outlying house mounds of the same phase and suggest corporate activity. In the succeeding Plancha Chicanel phase the four structures around Group B plaza were rebuilt several times so that the terminal Plancha-phase large pyramid attained a height of nine meters. This structure featured multiple terraces, basal moldings, stucco-laid shell masonry, and some red sandstone masonry. The latter building material was brought to the center from locations several kilometers distant (Willey 1973:63).

At Seibal we know that small stone and plaster constructions were made during the Mamom-sphere phase although we have no definite evidence of any as large as the late San Felix Mamom platforms at Altar de Sacrificios. In the succeeding Cantutse Chicanel phase large masonry and plaster constructions were erected. None of these were completely exposed or cleared by us, and most were found under later buildings of the Classic Period. We do know, however, that such features as terrace molding decorations were in use (Willey et al. 1975).

Art. There is nothing from either Altar or Seibal that would qualify as monumental art on the Mamom-sphere level. For Altar we have the fragment of a stucco architectural scroll element associated with late Chicanel pyramid construction.

Craft Goods, Burials, Caches. Mamom-sphere pottery at both Altar and Seibal is largely monochrome, with the better wares slipped in red, black, or white (cream). Lowe (1973a) has pointed out a notable change in these wares midway through the Mamom-sphere time period: the establishment in the latter half of the period of a greater uniformity or standardization of vessel forms and surface finish, especially in the waxy gloss of vessel surfaces. This move toward ceramic standardization, which continues in force throughout the succeeding Chicanel sphere, he sees as correlated with the first attempts at public ceremonial architecture—as noted, for instance, in our late San Felix Mamom constructions at Altar. Taken together, these changes suggest to him the wisdom of a downward revision of the Middle Preclassic–Late Preclassic time boundary for the lowlands as a whole. Such a revision would place early Mamom, lacking in special structures and characterized by less standardized ceramic concepts, at the end of the Middle Preclassic; late Mamom, with ceremonial center structures and pottery standardization, would come at the beginning of the Late Preclassic to be followed by Chicanel. The estimated dating on this, according to Lowe, would assign early Mamom to the 600–400 B.C. time slot and late Mamom to 400–200 B.C. The Seibal Preclassic pottery, does, I think, conform to Lowe's observations. Indeed, my impressions are that the entire Seibal ceramic run from Xe through Chicanel represents a rather gently graded continuum toward the standardization of the late Chicanel monochromes (see Sabloff 1975). R. E. W. Adams (1971:154), on the other hand, sees more of a break between Xe and Mamom at Altar de Sacrificios, a discontinuity which he is inclined to correlate with foreign introductions and even population migrations. The one thing all of us who are familiar with the Altar and Seibal pottery are agreed upon, however, is that there is no notable aesthetic elaboration until the very end of the Chicanel-sphere phases at both sites, when bichrome and trichrome types make a small appearance (R. E. W. Adams 1971:125–26; Sabloff 1975; Willey 1973:32). These types resemble those of the widespread late Late Classic Usulutan-ware horizon and look like local imitations of them.

Small, solid, handmade pottery figurines, which were present in Xe, are more numerous in the Mamom phases at both Altar and Seibal. These are always found in household contexts and never with burials or in any other special contexts. They disappear almost entirely in the succeeding Chicanel-sphere phases; this disappearance correlates negatively with the increased pottery vessel standardization and the beginnings and growth of hierarchic architecture.

In general, other implements and artifacts are relatively rare all through the Preclassic. Manos, metates, and chipped-stone choppers or celts are the most common, and these show little change in form through time. At Altar de Sacrificios a number of little sandstone tables or altars and other curious forms carved in this soft stone are found in the Mamom phase, especially in the Group B ceremonial-center context. These have not turned up at Seibal, though, and hence appear to be a localized peculiarity related to the availability of this particular red sandstone near Altar. Perhaps similar objects were made of wood at Seibal. Small stone ornaments—beads and pendants—are as early as the Mamom phase at Altar but more common in the Chicanel phase. These include jadeite specimens and indicate trade in this material at these times. Obsidian bladelets also continue in these, as well as in all later, phases. The pattern of occurrence of all such items at Seibal is the same.

At Altar de Sacrificios the San Felix Mamom burials were all simple interments, accompanied by a pottery vessel or two and sometimes a small stone ornament or a polished stone celt. The Plancha Chicanel burials were made in ceremonial-center buildings, as well as in outlying locations. Some of these ceremonial-center burials have certain status aspects, especially one of a man found in a sand-stone-covered crypt which was constructed like a crude corbeled vault (A. L. Smith 1972:261). Pottery vessels and occasional jadeite ornaments were found with the Plancha burials, although no grave of the phase could be described as richly furnished. At Seibal, although complete burial data have not been published, we can observe that the Mamom- and Chicanel-phase graves were furnished in a similar modest fashion.

At Altar the first votive caches were found in the Plancha Chicanel phase. These always consisted of pottery vessels, which sometimes contained jade beads or obsidian bladelets. Most occurred in ceremonial-center structures. This kind of votive ritualism was to become a strong theme in later Classic Maya culture. At Seibal, we have already mentioned a votive cache of the Xe phase. Another, but simpler, cache from Seibal dates from Mamom and two others from Chicanel.

Trade. There is a slight indication of increasing trade contacts during the span of the Preclassic. At both Altar de Sacrificios and Seibal, jadeite was added to obsidian as an import in the Late Preclassic. Exhausted obsidian cores are present at both sites, implying that the bladelets were made there. While there is no sure evidence, it is likely that jadeite beads and other simple jadeite ornaments were also manufactured in the Pasión Valley sites. Manufactured imports may be lacking altogether in the Pasión Valley Preclassic. One possible exception is the jade bloodletter found in the Xe cache at Seibal.

External Influences. How important were external influences in the growth of Preclassic society and culture in the Pasión Valley? This is a moot question. I have already discussed the question of the first settlement of the region, possibly from the Gulf Coast via the Usumacinta drainage, or possibly from nearby highlands. The latter interpretation, as noted, follows from some findings by Sedat and Sharer (1972) although Sharer and Gifford (1970) had broached the idea earlier on the basis of ceramic ties between Xe-sphere material and pottery types from Salvador. They suggest that these contacts may have continued on into Mamom times, and R. E. W. Adams (1971:154–55) goes even further with this latter point, suggesting a migration by peoples from the direction of Salvador as an element in the San Felix Mamom phase at Altar de Sacrificios. While I am willing to concede that the San Felix Mamom phase had contacts with the Guatemalan Highland–Salvador country, such as those stimulated through the obsidian trade, and that these could have kept highland and lowland potters in touch with each other at this time, I see no need to postulate an additional colonization of the Pasión Lowlands to explain the ceramic similarities.

Of greater interest in the interpretation of external influences at the close of the Plancha Chicanel phase at Altar de Sacrificios is the question of diffusion or migration. The question arises in connection with the Usulutan-like pottery found at Altar, but it also has a wider cultural reference, for these terminal Chicanel innovations are but the prelude to a number of culture changes that resulted in the eventual appearance of Classic Maya civilization. We shall return to this crucial transition shortly.

A Summary Integration of Inferences

The Pasión Valley. Preclassic social and cultural development in the Pasión Valley may be inferred as follows. Peoples of a village farming tradition, very probably linguistically and ethnically Maya, first settled in the valley sometime in the Middle Preclassic Period. They may have entered the region from the Gulf Coast–Usumacinta country or from somewhere in the Guatemalan-Salvadoran Highlands to the south. Their cultural affiliations, as revealed by their ceramics, are difficult to pinpoint precisely; however, we know that this ceramic and cultural heritage was in a line of development that can be traced in the

Barra-Ocos, Cuadros-Jocotal, and Olmec traditions. We must stress, though, that the early Xe-sphere farmers of the Pasión Valley operated on a much simpler sociopolitical level than some of these cultural ancestors.

During the Preclassic Period there was a steady, and probably gradually accelerating, population growth in the Pasión Valley. This demographic change was accompanied by settlement and architectural changes and innovations, especially by the construction of building platforms that marked ceremonial centers. Such platforms are known from the latter part of the Mamom sphere (ca. 400–300 B.C.), and their appearance may be taken to signal the Late Preclassic Period. By the close of the Preclassic Period, at about the beginning of the Christian era, ceremonial-center platforms and pyramids were of a size that implied corporate labor effort and centralized community organization. They also embodied architectural features and artistic embellishments that foreshadowed later Classic Maya accomplishments. In the Pasión Valley, however, the signs of monumental art were still few, and there were no indications of the Maya glyphic or calendrical achievements to come. There was little in the way of luxury manufactures, either of local origin or outside import. Trade with the highlands of Guatemala is indicated by the presence of obsidian, which is found throughout the Preclassic Period, and of small amounts of jadeite, which is largely confined to the Late Preclassic Period.

I am inclined to attribute the inferred sociopolitical changes, as attested in ceremonial-center building, to *in situ* population increases and the need for centralized governmental and religious authority. This is not to argue that Preclassic Pasión Valley society developed in a vacuum. The peoples there were undoubtedly aware of the ceremonial-center-cum-village pattern of life that probably already existed in the nearby highlands and that was developing in many other regions of the lowlands; nevertheless, I do not see the Late Preclassic ceremonial-center phenomena of the Pasión Valley as something that was imposed on these villagers from the outside by invading peoples. Rather, the demographic and social pressures were generated locally; the response was conditioned by a shared cultural heritage and concomitant development throughout the Maya Lowlands.

The Maya Lowlands at Large. Available evidence from all parts of the Maya Lowlands indicates the Preclassic Period, and particularly the Late Preclassic, to have been a time of population growth, of the establishment of many new sites, and of the proliferation, especially, of ceremonial centers. In other words, the course of development in the Pasión Valley for that time was in no way unique. It is possible, or even likely, that the origins of the Preclassic peoples for other lowland regions were not the same as those for the Pasión. Still, the nature of the subsequent development was very similar, and I think that the most likely immediate causes for this development were in territorial agricultural expansion and population increase.

While the advances of Late Preclassic culture in the Maya Lowlands were, in general, chronologically coordinate throughout, it is probable, and perhaps even demonstrable, that some region, or regions, were ahead of the others in cultural innovations. From what we know now it appears that the northeast Peten, or what Culbert (1973b) has called the Central Zone, was such a region. Tikal is the principal ceremonial center of this zone, and the cultural elaborations of its terminal Late Preclassic Cauac phase far outstrip those of the Pasión Valley and, perhaps, those of any other Maya Lowland region at that date. Thus I can conceive of the Central Zone and Tikal as the center for the diffusion of many of the cultural ideas of the Late Preclassic Period, and of Altar de Sacrificios and Seibal as having been influenced by such a center. But again I would argue that the demographic and social preconditions for the ready acceptance of this influence were already present and had been locally generated in the sites along the Pasión.

THE PROTOCLASSIC TRANSITION

Definitions

Chronological. The concept of a Protoclassic Period in the Maya Lowlands was developed to refer to those early centuries of the Christian era just prior to the earliest Initial Series dates. The exact dating of the period, as defined by archaeologists, has varied somewhat. The span of A.D. 0–300 is a reasonable approximation. In his recent chronological charts (1973a), Lowe has narrowed this to A.D. 100–250. In a developmental sense, the definition of the period, as the name implies, is one of transition from Preclassic to Classic.

Content. As is often the case in archaeological synthesis, there has been some confusion between time period and culture content for the

Protoclassic. A series of ceramic traits, usually found together as a complex, is identified in the archaeological literature with the Protoclassic (see Willey and Gifford 1961). These include a dish or bowl with mammiform tetrapodal supports, Usulutan or Usulutan-imitated painted styles, and polychrome decoration of an incipient Classic Maya sort. Such traits are found in a number of Maya sites in contexts immediately antedating the Classic Period levels. The Holmul I complex on the eastern edge of the Peten Central Zone (Merwin and Vaillant 1932) and the Floral Park phase at Barton Ramie in the Belize Zone (Willey et al. 1965) are examples. In general, this "Protoclassic ceramic complex" tends to be best represented on the eastern side of the Maya Lowlands although, as we shall see, it is present on the western side at Altar de Sacrificios. In some of the great sites of the Central Zone, however, it is lacking or only weakly present. The Uaxactun Matzanel phase (R. E. Smith 1955) is thus not much more than a token construct based on a few pottery specimens, and it is my understanding that the Holmul I–Floral Park kind of pottery is absent or nearly so at Tikal (see R. E. W. Adams 1971:158). But it is quite clear that Uaxactun and Tikal were vigorous entities during the Protoclassic Period—that they were, in fact, going through the important architectural, artistic, and intellectual transitions that led to the Classic.

These transitions include the innovation and development of corbeled-vault architecture, as at Tikal (see W. R. Coe 1965b), and of monumental artistic symbolism, as seen in the Protoclassic Period jaguar masks on Temple E-VII-sub at Uaxactun (Ricketson and Ricketson 1937). And as the upper limits of the Protoclassic Period are set by the earliest Initial Series stelae dates and texts, there can be little doubt that the Maya form of the Long Count calendar and the Classic style of Maya hieroglyphic writing were in the final stages of creation in these Central Zone sites at this time.

The Protoclassic in the Pasión Valley

In the Pasión Valley the Protoclassic is the first period in which developments at Altar de Sacrificios and Seibal diverge. While this was a time of great activity at the former, it was an era of population decline and semiabandonment at the latter.

Altar de Sacrificios. The Protoclassic phase at Altar is known as the Salinas. In the dating estimates given by R. E. W. Adams (1971:147–48) and justified by radiocarbon determinations and Maya Initial Series dates, the Salinas phase is placed between A.D. 150 and 450. This, of course, carries the time of the phase upward into what is generally considered the Early Classic Period. Adams based his extension of the time span upon the presence of Initial Series stelae at the foot of the Structure B-I pyramid, the earliest of which (Stela 10) had a Long Count date of 9.1.0.0.0. This is the earliest monument for the site as a whole and is translated to the Christian date of A.D. 455 in the 11.16.0.0.0 Correlation. From ceramic associations there can be little doubt that the final construction phase of the pyramid B-I, a sandstone block masonry covering of the earlier Preclassic structure, pertains to the Salinas phase. If we accept the conventional terminal dating of the Protoclassic (ca. A.D. 250–300) as the end of the Salinas phase, then something between 150 and 200 years must have elapsed between the completion of the Salinas sandstone masonry facing of the pyramid and the erection of the red sandstone stela with its date of 9.1.0.0.0 (A.D. 455). The alternative interpretation, which Adams preferred, and in which I concurred (Willey 1973:18–19), assumes that the stela dedication date and the completion of the Salinas construction phase of the pyramid were essentially contemporaneous. This interpretation carries with it the implication that the changeover from Protoclassic to full Classic was not exactly synchronous for all of the Maya Lowlands. In some regions, rather, the stela cult and the Classic institutions which it symbolized were not instigated until decades or even centuries after their inception in the Peten Central Zone. This, I think, is an important point and deserves serious examination. In this connection it is unfortunate that the dating of the outer structure of pyramid B-I at Altar de Sacrificios must remain somewhat equivocal.

To compress this discussion, let me review, however briefly, the other changes at Altar in the Salinas phase. Salinas pottery includes the traits of the "Protoclassic pottery complex" referred to above: vessels with mammiform tetrapodal supports, Usulutan or Usulutan-like ware in greater quantity than in the late Plancha phase, and vessels in an incipient Maya polychrome tradition. For the first time there is a real difference between what might be called "ordinary" and "luxury" ceramics. There is an increase in the amount of pottery and other goods found with some burials, and these "richer" burials are often accompanied by exotic items such as stingray spines or marine shell ornaments, indicative of status differentiations among individuals. A number of votive caches can be associated with the Salinas phase. A huge cache of pottery vessels was found beneath the red sandstone stairway of the outer structure of the B-I pyramid. Other caches contained exotic items, including marine products; and it is possible that some caches of 9 or 13 items, including eccentric flints or obsidians, date to Salinas times. These eccentrics are a very definite and distinctive Maya Classic feature. In the realm of monumental art, it is probable that a large sandstone altar (Censer Altar C) belongs to the Salinas phase. It was found in association with the red sandstone facade of Structure B-I and has been carved with a dragonlike face that is reminiscent of Late Preclassic Kaminaljuyu art and also of the stucco masks on the Temple E-VII-sub at Uaxactun (Graham 1972:85–86; Willey 1973:37, 66). The style of the carving is also suggestive of later Maya Classic monuments. We have here, then, a sculptural piece that can be considered a transitional form between Preclassic and Classic modes.

In sum, the Salinas phase at Altar de Sacrificios dates from what is generally considered the Protoclassic Period into the Early Classic Period. Ceramic content and affiliations link it to the styles of the Protoclassic. Its architecture, its monumental art, and many of its other traits either point toward or follow in the Classic manner. At the close of Salinas, with the introduction of the stela cult, the site is fully embraced in the Classic Maya world.

Seibal. At Seibal, Sabloff (1975) dates the late facet of the Cantutse phase (A.D. 0–275) to the Protoclassic Period. Having enjoyed an expansion in population and, probably, a ceremonial-center building boom in the earlier (300–0 B.C.) facet of the phase, the site began to undergo a shrinkage during the late facet. Ceramics are those recognized as a part of the Protoclassic tradition—Usulutan-imitation wares and vessels with mammiform tetrapodal supports—but these are more restricted in their site distribution than the earlier Cantutse styles. No notable building pertains to the late facet of the phase. In the succeeding Junco phase (A.D. 275 to about 500), which would parallel the most impressive building activities of the Salinas phase at Altar, Seibal is virtually abandoned.

The Nature and Significance of the Protoclassic in Wider Perspective

Both in the Pasión Valley and elsewhere throughout the Peten Lowlands the Protoclassic Period was a time of accelerated culture change. The direction of this change was toward the formalization of the trends seen in the preceding Late Preclassic Period. If the Preclassic, and especially the Late Preclassic, had been a time of growth—in population, sociopolitical complexity, arts and crafts, and religious elaboration—then I would characterize the brief Protoclassic as a time of consolidation and, probably, centralization. The burgeoning architectural developments of the Preclassic were literally capped with the more formalized and refined structures that were to set the patterns for the Classic. In ceramics there was a synthesis of the preexistent local Chicanel-sphere tradition with foreign influences, leading to the first polychrome productions of the new tradition. Locally made luxury goods appeared for the first time, and there was a variety of exotic products; such objects distinguished the graves of certain individuals but not others. The degree to which such evidence of status difference among individuals is indicative of social class distinctions is a moot point. In view of the fact that the practice of honoring certain personages—probably persons of royal lineage—by stela portraiture and accompanying hieroglyphic texts began immediately after the Protoclassic, I think it highly likely that a class structured society was coming into being during the Protoclassic.

Viewing the data from both Altar de Sacrificios and the wider Maya Lowlands, R. E. W. Adams (1971:155–58) and I (Willey 1973:38–39) have arrived at opposing interpretations concerning the importance of foreign influences and peoples as agents of the changes seen in the Protoclassic. Adams details the similarities between the styles and traits of what I have called here the "Protoclassic pottery complex" and various ceramic groups of Late Preclassic and Protoclassic date in the Guatemalan Highlands and Salvador. I do not think there is much doubt that these were the sources of the stimuli for Protoclassic ceramic innovations and changes in the lowlands. I do, however, doubt that these ceramic traits were brought by invading groups that effected a partial population replacement at sites such as Altar de Sacrificios and that these groups, as conquerors, turned the politically less sophisticated Lowland Maya from Preclassic to Classic ways.

150

A few pages back I argued that I thought it likely that the appearance of the stela cult was not a suddenly synchronous event throughout the lowlands but that these ideas spread somewhat more gradually from a single center. In my opinion the stela cult was generated in the Central Zone of the Peten, quite probably at Tikal, in the Protoclassic Period, and diffused from there at the end of that period in a conscious attempt at political control and centralization. Now while it is true that Maya Lowland Long Count calendrics, hieroglyphics, and stela art have prototypes in the Highland Guatemalan Kaminaljuyu and Chiapas Izapan cultures—and probably before that in an ancient Olmec heritage—it is also a recognized fact that the Maya Lowland rendering of these calendrics, glyphs, and art is in a distinctly local, Peten style. The earliest monuments in this style are found in the Central Zone, so the institution probably spread from there to other lowland regions. Although the Pasión Valley sites are geographically closer to the Guatemalan Highlands and to Kaminaljuyu than is the Central Zone, we have no evidence from the Pasión of an earlier development of the stela cult from highland prototypes. Indeed, the earliest stelae known from the lower Pasión, those dating from early in the ninth cycle and associated with the Structure B-I at Altar, are clearly derivative from the Tikal-Uaxactun area (Graham 1972:119).

THE CLASSIC CONFIGURATION OF DEVELOPMENT

The Early Classic

Early Classic ceremonial centers appear to be fewer in number than those of the Late Preclassic and, probably, the Protoclassic. This, I think, is a function of the sociopolitical changes that occurred during the Protoclassic, that is, the changes leading toward political centralization mentioned above. The causes behind this centralization are not clear; however, it is possible that they arose out of competition between Late Preclassic centers toward the close of that period. There are some indications that the Late Preclassic-to-Protoclassic may have been a time of troubles, at least in certain lowland regions. In this connection, the fortifications of the large center of Becan, in the Rio Bec region of Campeche, come to mind. According to David Webster (see Chapter 13, below), these structures, built toward the close of the Protoclassic, came about in response to war-fare and competition among centers that arose in the Late Preclassic. Closer to home, in the Pasión Valley, the decline and near-abandonment of Seibal at the end of the Late Preclassic and during the Protoclassic may have resulted from competition within the Pasión region in which Altar de Sacrificios may have been the more successful competitor.

This growing political centralization may have been stimulated by contacts with the distant Central Mexican metropolis of Teotihuacan. We know now that Teotihuacan-Maya trade relations began much earlier than previously supposed (Pendergast 1971), and in the hieroglyphic texts at Tikal there are indications that Teotihuacan personages were involved in the life of that city as early as the latter part of the eighth cycle (Proskouriakoff 1974:personal communication). Indeed, it is a hypothesis worth exploring further that, through its alliances with Teotihuacan, Tikal became the capital of an Early Classic political domain located in the Central Zone of the Peten and beyond, and that the "great period" of Teotihuacan influence at Tikal, ca. A.D. 450 to 550, marked the climax of this profitable alliance and of the Early Classic "empire" or state.

The possibility that the Peten sites of the Early Classic Period were members of a centralized "empire" or state should be considered in the light of overall Maya Classic Period development. Let us note that the earliest known Maya Initial Series monuments appear in the latter part of the eighth cycle. These all occur in sites in the northeastern Peten, in a relatively small geographical area within the Central Zone—at Uaxactun, Tikal, Uolantun, and Balakbal. This distribution and the size of these sites in relation to one another suggest an Early Classic polity dominated by and perhaps colonized from Tikal. In the next two and a half centuries the stela cult spread to other sites. By the end of the fifth katun of the ninth cycle (9.5.0.0.0 or A.D. 534), stelae were known from Xultun and Naachtun in the northeast Peten and, outside the Central Zone, at Altar de Sacrificios, Yaxchilan, Piedras Negras, and Copan. Although some of these sites were to rival Tikal in size and beauty in the Late Classic Period, they were definitely of lesser magnitude in the Early Classic, and they could well have been dominated by Tikal—culturally, economically, and politically—at that time.

The Hiatus and the Early-to-Late Classic Transition

Definition. The course of Lowland Classic development was interrupted shortly after 9.5.0.0.0, or A.D. 534. This interruption, which lasted until 9.8.0.0.0, or A.D. 593, a period of some forty to sixty years, is called the hiatus. It is marked by a notable decline in stela dedications and in major architectural construction. The hiatus phenomenon is particularly pronounced in the Central Zone heartland of the Early Classic sites, especially at Tikal and at Uaxactun. The dated stelae gap is also present at Altar de Sacrificios, Yaxchilan, and Piedras Negras. At Copan there are a few 9.6.0.0.0 and 9.7.0.0.0 katun dedications, in contrast to the numerous dated monuments of the centuries immediately before and after. Curiously, the only sites which initiate the stela cult during the hiatus period are those farthest from the Central Zone, on the peripheries of the southern Maya Lowlands—Pusilha in southern British Honduras, Tulum and Coba in the north, and Tonina and other sites in the distant central Chiapas highlands.

About halfway through the Classic Period, in short, Maya civilization of the lowlands underwent some trauma or reorientation. While sites were not completely abandoned, hierarchical activities were allowed to lag. After the hiatus, however, Maya civilization regained its balance, and went on to new achievements for another two centuries.

Causes and Significance. In another paper (Willey 1974) I posed the question of whether or not the hiatus phenomenon might have been a kind of unconscious "rehearsal" for the Terminal Classic collapse of the Maya civilization. Were similar pressures and types of events impinging upon the Maya at both these times in their history? I speculated that the withdrawal of Teotihuacan influence, and especially Teotihuacan trade connections, could have produced a short-term crisis. The timing of events seemed about right for this, and the idea was attractive, especially if the Early Classic domain had been a centralized one directed from Tikal, where Teotihuacan influences are so pronounced. I repeat this speculation now but with some modifications. While the Teotihuacan trade was undoubtedly important to the Early Classic Maya, and its severance a loss, a more general and overriding factor may have been that a centralized Maya Lowland state was simply becoming too large by the sixth century A.D.

to be effectively controlled from Tikal and the Central Zone. The hiatus may thus reflect a political and administrative breakdown that was especially severe in those sites of the Central, Pasión, and Usumacinta zones which were integral parts of such a state network. Sites geographically more remote from this central administration— those on the eastern, northern, and western peripheries—may have been spared the lapse because they had never become closely knit components of the system.

The Late Classic

Success and Florescence. The success and florescence of the Late Classic Period after 9.8.0.0.0, or A.D. 593, is measured by the revival of the Early Classic centers of the Central Zone; the renewed vigor of Altar de Sacrificios, Yaxchilan, Piedras Negras, and Copan; and the establishment of many new centers. Prosperity, as seen in the maintenance of these splendid cities and in overall population growth, lasted for two hundred years. During this time there was rivalry between regional centers and regional dynasties (Proskouriakoff 1963–64), and there were also alliances. Tikal's historic prestige undoubtedly remained very high, as Joyce Marcus's (1973) study of the distribution of emblem glyphs and of the "marrying out" of Tikal women attests. Still, I think it unlikely that Tikal ever again held the same controlling position in lowland political affairs that, following my hypothesis, it held in the Early Classic Period.

Decline and Failure. Toward the close of the eighth century A.D., Classic Maya civilization began to fail. This failure is seen in the same stela and architectural lapses that marked the faltering of the hiatus. This time, however, there was no recovery. By 10.3.0.0.0 (A.D. 889) the last dated monuments had been recorded. Within a few decades after that, most of the centers of the Southern Lowlands, as well as many of those farther to the north, had been abandoned. The external stresses and internal pressures combining to bring about this decline and failure have been discussed and debated at great length in a previous Maya symposium volume (Culbert 1973a), and we will not review or comment upon these here except to say that by the ninth century A.D. the fate of Classic Lowland Maya civilization had become bound up with trends and events of the wider Mesoamerican scene.

SOME OBSERVATIONS ON THE PHENOMENA OF CENTRALIZATION AND DECENTRALIZATION IN THE GROWTH OF MAYA CIVILIZATION

It is, I think, an almost universal condition in the growth of civilizations that their development proceeds in alternating phases of centralization and decentralization, of unification and regionalization. We see this kind of diachronic configuration in the ancient Near East and the Mediterranean and in China. In the New World we are familiar with it in Peru, where John Rowe (1960) has capitalized on it in his area chronology of Initial Period, Early Horizon (Chavín), Early Intermediate Period, Middle Horizon (Tiahuanaco-Huari), Late Intermediate Period, and Late Horizon (Inca). And in Mesoamerica we are aware of a comparable sequence outline: Olmec, derivative post-Olmec regionalism, the dominance of Teotihuacan, the subsequent Late Classic Period Balkanization, Toltec supremacy, post-Toltec fractionation, and the Aztec imperium. In making this observation I am not proposing some kind of misty determinism. The causal forces of such centralizations and decentralizations are obviously highly complex and diverse. Still, they lie within the realm of comprehensible human social and cultural behavior. Horizonal unification can be effected by military conquest, religious prose-lytization, the demands of trade, the thrust of technological thresh-olds, or stylistic diffusions that seem to be motivated by nothing more than aesthetic preferences. Its breakdown may have roots in the negation of any of these things. Each case must be examined and analyzed in its own terms and circumstances, although I think we may eventually draw parallels and analogies between different cases. In this frame of mind I think it might be worth our while to view the rise and growth, as well as the decline, of Maya civilization in a framework of these phenomena of centralization and decentralization.

At the earliest level of our Maya Lowland story the Xe and Mamom phases are geographically marginal derivatives of what had once been the interlinked Olmec world of southern Mesoamerica. These Middle Preclassic cultures are obviously not bound together with the same kind of ties—whether religious, political, or commercial—that characterized the former Olmec horizon. The Middle Preclassic Period is, in effect, an era of decentralization or noncentralization. The Late Preclassic Maya Lowland cultures continue in this pattern of regionalization, apparently with numerous growing and autonomous ceremonial centers or petty political capitals. At the end of the Late Preclassic Period, Lowland Maya society underwent important changes. As I have outlined, these consisted of a formalization and consolidation of the achievements of the Late Preclassic. I think the changes also involved centralization of political authority, and the most likely locus of that authority, in the Southern Lowlands at least, was what had been the greatest of the Late Preclassic sites, Tikal. The primary causes behind these changes are to be found *in situ* in the lowlands. They are the universalistic causes of population growth, agricultural expansion to new territories, the proliferation of politico-religious centers, the competition and conflict among these numerous centers for resources, and the need, arising from all of this, for centralized authority. That Teotihuacan statecraft played some part in this rise of Maya centralization seems very likely. Few cultures exist in a vacuum, and we know that the Maya did not. But this would have been an instance of the right stimuli reaching the right set of preconditions.

The Maya Early Classic state, then, was formulated at Tikal and its environs in the Central Zone. Its authority was symbolized by the stela cult, hieroglyphic writing, a unified calendar, and a powerful art style. Its social order was dichotomized into an aristocratic elite and a commoner-peasant class. These symbols and this way of life radiated out from the Central Zone to become the established pattern at the Late Preclassic ceremonial centers of other zones. On the wider Mesoamerican scene this kind of sociopolitical organism was fully consonant with the era of horizonal unification that had been established by the great Central Mexican power of Teotihuacan, and, insofar as we can tell from the archaeological record, the Early Classic Maya realm had made its successful adaptation to this Pax Teotihuacana.

Any such unification always includes the dialectical opposition of forces for breakdown, and these were at work in the Maya Lowlands. Blanton (1972) has discussed this process as it was involved in the collapse of Teotihuacan. There are, he maintains, limits to growth under any given system of organization. The Teotihuacan realm, according to Blanton's hypothesis, reached a point at which no single politico-religious capital—or, in economic terms, no single "extractive center"—could dominate and administer the whole. Breakdown and a return to a more regionally fragmented authority occurred for a period. For the Maya Lowland Early Classic I suspect that much the same thing happened. Quite probably, a weakening of Teotihuacan in the sixth century A.D. precipitated the crisis that is reflected in the hiatus of the latter half of the sixth century. In any event, the Early Classic Maya Lowland state dissolved.

The Maya recovered, however, and went on to an era of creativity in the Late Classic Period. The political failure—if such it was—caused a hesitation but no complete break in the Classic Maya tradition of art and intellectual life. The great lowland ceremonial centers continued; the main difference was that now there were more of them. The system was not destroyed, only decentralized. Tikal was no longer the only "supercity." Piedras Negras, Palenque, Yaxchilan, Naranjo, Calakmul, and Copan rivaled it in size and magnificence; besides these spectacular centers, there were a host of others. I would speculate that in the Late Classic there were several Southern Lowland states where previously there had been only one. These states, each with its capital and its satellite sites, coexisted in a system of rivalry, with wars, conquests, defeats, and shifting royal alliances. They also coexisted in a system of cooperation in cultural, intellectual, and probably commercial sharing. As one views it in this light, this Maya continuity of the Late Classic Period, after the crisis of the hiatus, was a remarkable and, in many ways, a unique achievement in Mesoamerica. The Late Classic Maya appear to have steered a middle course between regional fragmentation and imperial regimentation. This was no easy course, as attested by the stresses inherent in such a system (Willey and Shimkin 1973). It was an adaptation, however conscious or unconscious on their part, that lasted for two hundred years—no small feat. When eventually it failed it was because the Maya could not accommodate this adaptation to the new imperial policies that were being propagated in other parts of Mesoamerica.

The Rise of Classic Maya Civilization in the
Northwestern Zone: Isolation and Integration[1]

ROBERT L. RANDS

Southern Illinois University at Carbondale

In tracing the rise of civilization in the Northwestern Zone[2] from its Preclassic foundations to its Late Classic culmination, we find both differences from and similarities to developmental trends in other parts of the Southern Maya Lowlands. We will begin by summarizing these trends on the basis of present information, much of it as yet unpublished. More extended documentation and scrutiny of these trends appear in subsequent sections of the paper. Although falling in the Northwestern Zone (Fig. 1.1), the coastal site of Aguacatal, Campeche, is omitted from consideration, as its pottery has been described in detail by Matheny (1970). Late Classic developments in the Northwestern Zone are discussed primarily with regard to Palenque, where a viable state or kingdom appears to have been achieved.

CHRONOLOGICAL OVERVIEW

At the western extremity of the Northwestern Zone, in the environmentally favored region of the Chontalpa, extensive drainage canals, recently bulldozed as part of the "Plan Chontalpa," have exposed abundant ceramic deposits, thereby facilitating the recovery of early materials. Largely unpublished investigations in this region by E. B. Sisson have shown the existence of Early Preclassic ceramics with strong Olmec affiliations. The Chontalpa's relative proximity to the Olmec heartland, as well as the region's fertile alluvial soils, may help to explain the nature of his discoveries. Sisson considers it probable that Olmec ethnic groups are represented, a minor Maya penetration into the Chontalpa being indicated by the appearance of Waxy Wares in the Late Preclassic.

On the rich, recent alluvium of the Middle Usumacinta, significant occupations appear to have existed at least from the beginning of the Middle Preclassic Period. The Chiuaan ceramic complex of Trinidad, Tabasco, belongs to this horizon and has been reported on in preliminary form (Rands 1969). The adjacent site of Tierra Blanca is probably of at least comparable antiquity. Occupations of equivalent age, although on a much reduced scale, are suggested in the Low Sierras of Chiapas. Olmecoid and Xe-like features appear in the ceramics of this time, although information about other aspects of culture is largely lacking. The Middle Preclassic was a period of marked ceramic change well before the introduction of Waxy Wares. Considerable population growth during this period may be inferred.

By Late Preclassic times, ribbonlike extensions of cultures within the Chicanel sphere existed along the Usumacinta, still hugging the recent alluvium and adjacent bluffs. Earthen mounds were numerous; a number have been partially destroyed in obtaining road fill, revealing their ceramic contents. Heights up to six or eight meters are indicated, and it is possible, although not certain, that even larger earthworks along the river pertain to this period. Chicanel remains also occur in the Low Sierras of Chiapas, although they are less densely concentrated than those on the Middle Usumacinta. Additional Preclassic deposits are known at several sites along the foot of the Sierras. Somewhat surprisingly, however, in view of their relative abundance at nearby sites, Late Preclassic ceramics are sparse in excavations at Palenque. Even more rare in the Low Sierras are remains attributable to the Protoclassic Period, although at sites on the Usumacinta in the vicinity of Balancan, such as San José del Rio, Chacavita, and Tierra Blanca, Protoclassic horizon markers are better known.

In contrast to the firmly established Preclassic tradition in portions of the Northwestern Zone, few Northwestern sites show major Early Classic components. In part this is undoubtedly the result of inadequate sampling; it may also reflect a nucleation of the population into a smaller number of somewhat larger centers. However, these factors do not appear fully adequate as a general explanation of the feeble expressions of Early Classic culture in most of the sites with which I am familiar. Major architectural works dating from late in the Early Classic are known but only on a limited basis.[3] At Palenque, the plaza platform underlying the pyramid of the Conde (although not the temple-pyramid itself) is an Early Classic construction, dating from the Motiepa ceramic complex. Judging from the prevalence of Early Classic sherds in the construction fill of the small ball court at Palenque, this structure is also apparently of Motiepa date. A partially dismantled structure underlying Temple XVIII-A contains a tomb of comparable Early Classic date (Rands 1974). The crudeness of the associated pottery and an aesthetically uninspired mosaic mask of jade contrast with fine workmanship in jade earplugs and traces of sophisticated painting on the doorjambs of the tomb (Ruz Lhuillier 1961: Figs. 6, 9a–f; Pls. 46, 49). Sculptures which can be reliably assigned to the Early Classic period are unknown in the Northwestern Zone, yet recently deciphered texts suggest that the dynastic history of Palenque can probably be carried back prior to the fourth katun of Baktun 9, ca. A.D. 500, GMT (Lounsbury 1974). I suspect that one of the major exceptions to the marginal development of Early Classic culture in the Northwestern Zone may prove to be at Chinikiha, midway between Palenque and Piedras Negras, although no definite conclusion to this effect is warranted at the present time. On the Middle Usumacinta, where rich riverine resources favored environmental circumscription and the development of dense populations, population reduction on a significant scale may have taken place at the close of the Late Preclassic or Protoclassic periods. A similar hypothesis may be advanced for the somewhat less environmentally favored, less circumscribed occupations of the Low Sierras.

Much of the pottery of the Northwestern Zone attributable to the Early Classic Period is regionally distinctive, a far cry from that of the Tzakol ceramic sphere. At the beginning of the Early Classic Period of Palenque (Picota complex), distinctions from coeval cultures of the Peten were especially pronounced; red-slipped monochrome pottery, lacking either waxy or gloss finish, occurred frequently, whereas members of the Aguila Orange group were absent. The Early Classic Kaxabyuc complex of Trinidad was equally divergent. Later in the Early Classic (the Motiepa complex of Palenque), this situation changed somewhat, as Peten Gloss Ware was introduced in limited amounts. Additional cultural features, of a nonmaterial or perishable nature but important in the development of civilization, may have been introduced at the same time. Despite the peripheral location of the Northwestern Zone, Teotihuacan influences seem muted.

The Early Classic marginality of the Northwestern Zone relative to more highly developed centers in many other parts of the Maya Lowlands was followed by striking Late Classic attainments. Cultural florescence was especially pronounced at Palenque. For a time Palenque seems to have incorporated a number of other sites in the Low Sierras into its sphere of cultural and political influence. A time of rapid architectural and presumably sculptural innovation, this was the only phase at Palenque during which a strong polychrome ceramic tradition was established locally (Otolum complex). There are suggestions that toward the middle of the Late Classic period (Murcielagos complex), the sociocultural influence of Palenque was being directed in greater degree toward the Chiapas-Tabasco plains. Perhaps the zone of Palenque's influence in the Sierras was diminished in size or cohesiveness at this time. By the end of its elite occupation midway through the Balunte complex, Palenque may have been able to muster only a somewhat reduced labor force for major architectural undertakings. Though sculptural productivity decreased, it maintained a high artistic level, apparently until the effective abandonment of the site.

After the near hiatus, or stagnation, of the Early Classic, the Middle Usumacinta once again shows evidence of dense populations and cultural advancement, or so we may infer from the archaeological record as it is known at Trinidad and other sites in the Zapata-Balancan region. For a time (Taxinchan complex), the Classic Maya polychrome tradition flourished. The tradition appears, however, to have had only a tenuous hold. Although a decline in other aspects of culture need not necessarily be assumed, there was an exceptionally early replacement of the polychromes by fine paste monochrome pottery (early Naab complex). This technically excellent pottery appeared well before the Fine Gray–Fine Orange horizons, by which time most of the Middle

Usumacinta sites seem either to have been abandoned or reduced in size (Rands 1973a).

Toward the close of the Late Classic Period the environmentally marginal lands between the Usumacinta and the Low Sierras appear to have had a significant population for the first time. The region, referred to as the Intermediate Plains, may have been occupied by people from the Low Sierras. Ceramic affiliations, in any event, were far closer to Balunte of Palenque than to Naab or Jonuta materials of the Usumacinta Valley. The possibility of overpopulation in the Low Sierras, with the resultant displacement of people into less desirable land, must be considered (Rands 1973b). On the other hand, the abundant rainfall in the Low Sierras, which provides the potential for a system of double cropping, may have partially offset this critical drain on the carrying capacity of the Sierras. Susceptibility to centrifugal forces—which were always present to the extent that Maya agriculture was committed to a swidden system—may have been augmented by peculiarities of Late Classic sociocultural organization. If so, the "budding off," or rupturing, of communities may have taken place, with minority factions moving into low-population areas. Whatever the causes of the apparent Late Classic movement into the Plains, occupation there was ephemeral, for the region seems to have been abandoned prior to the spread of Fine Orange Ware from the closely adjacent floodplain of the Usumacinta. Under these conditions of close proximity, the failure to have located any examples of Fine Orange Ware from the Intermediate Plains is striking.

In the Chontalpa, at the far-westerly site of Comalcalco, the architectural style of Palenque was replicated in fired-brick architecture. In spite of the impressive Late Classic developments, however, evidence is lacking that a significant Maya polychrome tradition ever existed at the site.

PROBLEM AREAS

The overview of cultural developments in the Northwestern Zone through the Late Classic Period given above is intended to provide background for a more detailed presentation which will focus on Palenque. First, however, attention is directed toward several broader problem areas. Why, after the strong Middle and Late Preclassic developments, does the Early Classic appear weak, aberrant, marginal? Rathje's core–buffer zone hypothesis (1971, 1973) may be cited here, but it remains to be seen whether the Northwestern Zone was sufficiently integrated with the Central Zone to produce the type of interrelationships postulated in that hypothesis. Conceivably, such interrelationships may have existed on the widespread Chicanel horizon. Apparently a viable hypothesis should explain significant population reduction in the Northwestern Zone (though not in the Maya heartland) by the beginning of the Early Classic Period and at the same time provide a *raison d'être* for the cultural cleavage which for the most part existed between Usumacinta sites, such as Piedras Negras, and sites of the Northwestern Zone. Why did the cultural achievements of Tikal's Late Preclassic heritage accelerate while Palenque, building on a comparable Chicanel base, made relatively small progress during the Early Classic period, thus falling outside the major currents of the Classic Maya cultural tradition? Spectacular as they were, the Early Classic developments at Tikal seem in some respects easier to account for than those at Palenque, as the requisite sociocultural momentum appears to have been widely generated by terminal Preclassic/Protoclassic times. Such momentum may, of course, have resulted partly from non–Lowland Maya influences (for example, Izapa-Kaminaljuyu, Teotihuacan-Kaminaljuyu), which largely bypassed Palenque and the West.

Another problem concerns the rapid, spectacular rise of higher civilization, for example in Palenque, at the beginning of the Late Classic Period. To a degree, this was a general trend in the Southern Lowlands, where a number of major sites sprang up (or at least took on the outward trappings of elite Maya culture) at comparatively late dates. Nevertheless, many of these sites had participated in Lowland Classic culture on at least a lay level, as suggested by close correspondences to Tzakol ceramics.

In approaching these problems, it is necessary to consider logically distinct, though interrelated, phenomena. What factors enabled the Classic Maya tradition to move outward from the core area at this particular time? A reorganization of Peten Maya culture following the withdrawal of Teotihuacan influence and the subsequent hiatus (Willey 1974) may have been a causal factor. Because Mayas of the Western Lowlands had not participated as fully in a Teotihuacan sphere of influence, the cessation of such influence may not have resulted in equivalent cultural uprooting and disturbance. A hypothesis of heightened cultural growth in the West by default seems overly simplistic, however.

A different explanation would focus on population growth within the core area and subsequent expansion into the less densely occupied peripheral regions. However, unless differential factors in population growth in the different regions are isolated, this approach seems of limited utility as an explanatory device.

What factors facilitated not only the acceptance of Classic traits from the core area but their new expression in original, highly effective forms? Suggested approaches to the problem focus both on conditions within the core area and on innovations which took place on the peripheries. One such approach is somewhat difficult to reconcile with the conception (Borhegyi 1971) of Teotihuacan as a stimulating, innovative center for the introduction of exotic culture into the Peten. Rather, I see the so-called conservative nature of Peten culture—its adherence to old ways and mannerisms—as the critical factor. Some modifications may normally be expected in the diffusion process, and under given conditions the extent of the changes might increase. With slightly varying emphases, both Kroeber (1948) and Service (1960) have argued that formerly vigorous centers of innovation eventually tend toward sterility as new developments occur among peoples who are uncommitted to the old ways.

According to Kroeber, style patterns—a term used to include more than art styles— provide the opportunity for facility and skill to be acquired; traditions flourish as a result. Nevertheless,

> the process cannot go on mounting indefinitely, because it began with a limitation of choice, a selection among possibilities. Therefore every style is necessarily prelimited: it is an essential commitment to one manner, to the exclusion of others. . . . The range of its channeled skills will extend so far; beyond, they fail. Then we say that the style has exhausted itself, its characteristic pattern has broken down. . . . The style either loses its skill of touch and its products deteriorate; or it becomes frankly repetitive. . . . A pickup in quality will normally be possible only with a new start toward a new style. And the evolution of a new style is likely to be easier to outsiders or novices than to the group which has been reared in an old style. (Kroeber 1948:329)

In similar vein, Service has advanced a principle termed the Local

Discontinuity of Progress. This means that an "underdeveloped civilization has certain evolutionary potentials that an advanced one lacks." Thus, "Imperial Germany . . . became more efficient industrially than her predecessor, England, because of 'the merits of borrowing'. . . . England, conversely, was finally less efficient than Germany because of 'the penalty of taking the lead' . . . " (Service 1960: 99). As Plog (1973) points out, not all examples of this kind of change involve shifts to different evolutionary stages of development.

At the beginning of the Late Classic Period, patterns present in the core area since Protoclassic times had probably not reached the point of exhaustion and breakdown or suffered seriously from having taken the lead over more peripheral parts of the Maya Lowlands. (The hiatus might, however, be examined with these as well as other possible factors in mind.) As the arguments of Kroeber and Service suggest, however, changes might have taken place as the essentially conservative tradition of the Lowland Classic Maya was made increasingly available to outsiders, Maya who had as yet not participated fully in that tradition. A complimentary approach focuses on the marginally Classic background of the recipient societies. These groups, although sharing general features of Maya culture, may have retained old concepts in a less specialized form; moreover, they may have been exposed to a differing set of influences from non-Maya sources. An amalgam—the newly introduced Classic traits, stemming out of the core area, with locally diverging elements of culture—might have acted as a catalyst, resulting in a vigor and brilliance of expression greater than that previously attained by either donors or recipients. Diffusion of the recently reworked traits back into the core area could, in turn, have helped to revitalize the Classic tradition there.

The foregoing argument has much appeal. Nevertheless, the nuances of conservatism in the greater Peten and influences stemming out of Teotihuacan are yet to be effectively recognized, let alone put into a meaningful perspective. Might not the termination of close contacts with Teotihuacan have provided the opportunity for a resurgence of Lowland Maya culture in the core area, so that the Peten again became a center of elaboration, giving at least the appearance of taking new cultural directions?

This level of analysis is also limited by its failure to identify the new systemic relationships which were being worked out with adjacent sites when Palenque was emerging as one of the major Maya centers. New relationships must have arisen—directed in part by a growing administrative class—on political, ceremonial, and economic levels. According to Sanders and Price (1968), aspects of sociopolitical organization were derived from pristine Teotihuacan, enabling secondary states to emerge in the Peten. A partial replication of this process can probably be seen in Palenque's somewhat retarded rise to viable statehood.

The following hypothesis posits Tikal vis-à-vis Teotihuacan and Palenque vis-à-vis sites which may have included Tikal and other centers in the core area, Copan in the far Southeast, and Usumacinta sites such as Piedras Negras. In both cases, some concepts of dynastic rule and other aspects of central administrative organization may well have preceded the effective reworking of theocratic and managerial traits as they diffused into new cultural-ecological settings.

The acquisition of "full" civilization on the level of the secondary state would, therefore, be a three-stage process (the stages, of course, overlapping sufficiently to pose familiar chicken-and-egg problems of priority). The stages are: (1) local attainment of sufficiently complex culture to promote contacts and effective acquisition of traits from the donor culture (seen in the Motiepa complex of Palenque); (2) local copying (voluntary or otherwise) of state-supportive institutions of the donor culture (seen in early Otolum of Palenque); and (3) local reworking of and experimentation with the diffused and preexisting institutions, those forms which are more efficient in the new social-ecological setting tending to survive and flourish (seen in late Otolum and the beginning of the Murcielagos ceramic complex).

For a time, these more efficient forms would have a "momentum" of their own; they would be central to future sociocultural developments. The process described as stage 3 was accelerating in late Otolum and lasted at least for most of Murcielagos, extending with reduced vigor into early Balunte. Eventually, the viability of these forms would decline. In part, the decline may be described by terms such as inertia or exhaustion; however, external as well as internally induced developments may be involved. Although couched in somewhat different terms, with emphasis on the origins of higher civilization and the state, the hypothesis advanced here is quite compatible with those of Kroeber and of Service cited above.

PRECLASSIC OCCUPATION

Sisson's summary of the Chontalpa ceramic sequence (1970) recognizes two Early Preclassic phases, two or three from the Middle Preclassic, and one from the Late Preclassic. The earliest of these, the Molina, has close resemblances to the Bajío and Chicarras phases at San Lorenzo Tenochtitlan (ca. 1350–1150 B.C.). Relationships to the Cotorra, Cuadros-Jocotal, and San Lorenzo phases are found in the Chontalpa during Sisson's Palacios phase (ca. 1050–900 B.C.). Mounds may have been present at this time or may have appeared in the subsequent Puente phase (ca. 900–500 B.C.). The Franco phase (ca. 500–300 B.C.) and the Late Preclassic Casteneda phase follow, the latter being marked by the introduction of Waxy Wares. This brief summary indicates the existence of an extended occupation on the western border of the Maya area well before an effective settlement of the Southern Lowlands. This occupation must be taken into account in considering possible routes of entry into the Maya Lowlands. The Olmec presence on the borders of the Maya area underscores the problem of why the Maya Lowlands as a whole were so late in acquiring a significant population.

Tierra Blanca is located on the Usumacinta River in the Municipio of Balancan, Tabasco. The river has cut into the site, exposing Classic and Preclassic remains. The present remarks are based on surface collections and on materials in the Regional Museum of Balancan. Of special interest are ceramic figurine heads of a strongly Olmec style (Figs. 7.1a, 7.1b[4]; Berlin 1955:Fig. 1r). Preclassic potsherds sometimes relate to early levels at the closely adjacent site of Trinidad. However, present sampling indicates that the Late Preclassic is much better represented at Tierra Blanca than at Trinidad.

A short distance downstream from Tierra Blanca, Trinidad has revealed an extensive Middle Preclassic occupation, commencing with the Chiuaan ceramic complex (Rands 1969). An even earlier horizon may be indicated by a white-slip, thick-walled *tecomate* from the lowest excavation level. Smudged, thin-walled *tecomates* and restricted-orifice vessels are characteristic of Chiuaan, as well as flat-based, flaring-walled bowls. Decorative techniques emphasize incising (slanting parallel lines, cursive elements, and the double-line break); fluting and punctation also occur. Fragmentary Conchas-like figurines, widefaced and with grooved-and-punctate eyes, apparently

FIGURE 7.1. Preclassic figurines from the Palenque region. *a,b*, Tierra Blanca; *c,e*, Trinidad; *d, f, f*₁, Palenque

belong to the Chiuaan complex (Fig. 7.1c). Ceramic correspondences include Conchas I (M. D. Coe 1961), Xe (Willey 1970; R. E. W. Adams 1971), and especially Nacaste-phase pottery of San Lorenzo (M. D. Coe 1970). In view of these correspondences, it is striking to note the absence of everted-rim bowls from Chiuaan and subsequent materials—that is, until the much later introduction of Waxy Wares in the Chacibcan complex.

Abundantly represented, the Middle Preclassic Xot complex of Trinidad is characterized by lessened use of incising and other plastic techniques, with increased treatment of the surface by burnishing or applying a matte red slip. Stepped planes suggest chamfering. Although thin-walled *tecomates* continue in Xot deposits, a new shape repertory includes a flat-based bowl, rounding gently to an almost vertical wall, and a flaring-sided bowl with sublabial molding. A figurine head (Fig. 7.1d) apparently belonging to this complex more closely resembles Mamom than Conchas examples. Although occasional Mamom features are approximated in the pottery, these are on a modal level, and Xot appears, as a whole, to be more regionally isolated than was the preceding Chiuaan Complex. The absence of waxy finish and of everted rims from Xot materials underscores the distinctive nature of the pottery. Unless there was notable lag in the spread of these traits, Xot should in large part precede Mamom.

Toward the close of the Middle Preclassic sequence at Trinidad, on a horizon approximately coeval with Chiapa III, profound changes in local ceramic patterns were ushered in with the Chacibcan complex. In a preliminary account of the complex (Rands 1969), I suggested that it should be placed at the beginning of the Late Preclassic Period. However, an assessment that Chacibcan was somewhat earlier, dating from the Middle Preclassic, seems preferable. Waxy Ware, notable for its exceptionally high polish, appeared for the first time. That this pottery was of extraneous origin—trade ware—is indicated by the consistent presence of carbonate (limestone) temper, a material unavailable locally to dwellers of the alluvial Usumacinta bottomlands. In contrast, all other ceramic complexes of Trinidad—Preclassic, Classic, or Postclassic—are characterized by the presence of volcanic glass (ash or dust), either as temper or as a natural inclusion in the clay. Simultaneously with the Waxy Wares, the wide-everted rim made its initial appearance, in an ungrooved form. The Chacibcan complex is not well represented at Trinidad, and it appears that other Preclassic sites, such as Nueva Esperanza, overlapped in part with this occupation. Increasingly, ceramics of the region seem to have incorporated Lowland Maya diagnostics until distinctively Chicanel pottery was widely dispersed along the Usumacinta River.

Most thoroughly studied of the Late Preclassic pottery from the Middle Usumacinta is that excavated by Ferree at San José del Rio (personal communication). White paste pottery related to Xe and Chiuaan is present in small quantities at the site. The massive Xot complex of Trinidad is apparently unrepresented, although later Middle Preclassic pottery is known. Multicolored pottery—streaky black on red and orange; white, red, and orange with black trickles, blobs, and dots—exhibits a wide experimental range.

Chicanel-like materials, including Sierra Red, predominate at San José del Rio. Protoclassic remains include deep tetrapod (?) white-slipped bowls and occasional Usulutan-like red-on-white sherds.

As indicated earlier in this chapter, Preclassic pottery has been difficult to locate at Palenque. In part, no doubt, this is a sampling phenomenon: nothing has been undertaken comparable to the great trench through the North Acropolis at Tikal (W. R. Coe 1965b). Bedrock has been reached on many occasions at Palenque, although mostly as the result of test pits or limited architectural investigations. Even so, the paucity of Preclassic ceramics is notable. This is especially true in the major ceremonial precinct—the area, now cleared of forest growth, which has been the principal center of investigations since the days of Holmes, Maudslay, Stephens, and their predecessors and has been the focus of more recent programs of research by the Instituto Nacional de Antropología e Historia. To a lesser degree, this part of the site has also been the primary focus of my ceramic investigations. But Palenque is a large, compact site; its major architecture extends throughout an area perhaps five times as great as what has customarily come to be thought of as "Palenque." Sampling over most of the site is, therefore, inadequate. However, excavations in the extreme western part of the site have yielded Preclassic sherds that, in Palenque's terms, can only be described as abundant. Still farther to the west, in milpas beyond the zone of major architectural construction, surface reconnaissance has contributed significantly to the still limited amount of Preclassic material from in and around the site. Several pottery figurine heads in Olmec or Olmecoid style have been reported from Palenque. One, in the bodega of the Museo

Nacional de Antropología, Mexico (Fig. 7.1e), must be somewhat suspect, as the names of famous sites have a way of getting assigned to pieces of uncertain origin. The case for correct provenience is enhanced, however, by the presence of two somewhat similar figurine heads in the museum bodega at the site of Palenque. A ceramic specimen, corresponding to effigy rings of La Victoria, the Valley of Guatemala, and Tres Zapotes (M. D. Coe 1961:98,Fig. 42a) has been badly weathered, although facial proportions and treatment of the ear are consistent with the Olmec style (Fig. 7.1,f). In view of these considerations, the purported Palenque provenience of carved jade heads in typical Olmec style (heirlooms?) cannot be summarily dismissed. The occurrence at Palenque of a stubby, red-slipped Preclassic figurine leg is certain (Ruz Lhuillier 1973:Fig. 263a). It is strange, however, that with a single exception the typical Middle Preclassic grooved-and-punctate eye is, to the best of my knowledge, unknown from the site.

A few Palenque sherds apparently relate to a Middle Preclassic horizon (Rands 1974:Fig. 1,i-k). More common, however, is Chicanel-horizon pottery, including Sierra Red. As at nearby sites in the Low Sierras, polishing is pronounced; the term Waxy Ware is aptly descriptive, a fact of no little interest considering the badly weathered condition of most sherds from the region. In the slipped pottery, the Late Preclassic paste is normally brown with aplastics of volcanic ash, corresponding closely to materials of comparable date along the Middle Usumacinta. Jars, on the other hand, although sharing certain Usumacinta shapes, are more likely to be unslipped (possibly weathered) and carbonate tempered. Although sampling is inadequate to produce firm conclusions, the impression is strong that in relationships between the Low Sierras and the Middle Usumacinta during the Late Preclassic Period, people from the latter region were essentially the donors. The flanks of the Low Sierras seem to have participated somewhat marginally in the widespread Chicanel sphere. Yet at no other time do Palenque and its environs seem so fully to have shared a Maya ceramic tradition.

In summary, we can infer a horizon sloping from west to east, extending from San Lorenzo in Veracruz to the Chontalpa and Usumacinta. Certain sites away from the rivers, such as Palenque, seem also to be represented. Although many details are lacking, the general situation appears consistent with ideas advanced by the

Pulestons (1971) about preferential exploitation of riverine environments in the initial colonization of the Maya area.

EARLY CLASSIC OCCUPATION

In initial ceramic investigations at Palenque, Early Classic remains were almost as difficult to isolate as Preclassic pottery (Rands and Rands 1957), partly because our preconceptions of Early Classic ceramics of the region were based too closely on Tzakol cultural standards and partly because of the relative paucity of Early Classic remains in the site's major ceremonial precinct. Further fieldwork has provided data which permit the following reconstruction, still provisional in certain critical aspects, of Early Classic developments at Palenque.

The Picota ceramic complex, at the beginning of the Early Classic, differed to an extraordinary degree from Maya pottery outside the Northwestern Zone (Rands 1974:Figs. 3, 4). Resemblances were on a modal level only—occasional examples of the basal flange, somewhat more common occurrences of the ringstand base, and strange though relatively abundant slab feet. Low, solid, and often massive, the latter may have been a prototype of the well-known Teotihuacan form. Slab feet apparently occurred only on deep, outflaring bowls with widely everted rims. Ring-base vessels sometimes share the latter form but commonly have direct rims. Monochrome red pottery was characteristic, the matte slip lacking the distinguishing features of either Preclassic Waxy or Classic Gloss wares. Vertical grooving, alternating with ungrooved spaces, was the principal form of decoration. Red resist pottery and fine-line incising occurred, although rarely. Polychrome pottery and orange slip appear to have been totally absent. A surprisingly large amount of fine paste pottery was present for an Early Classic Maya ceramic complex.

As is well known, innovations that appeared first on the Protoclassic horizon provided the basis for a new ceramic orientation over most of the Southern Maya Lowlands. At Palenque, the problem of continuities or discontinuities between Late Preclassic and Early Classic developments is somewhat different because of the marked divergence of Picota from other Early Classic ceramics. To what extent, if at all, do the Picota materials reflect the retention of Chicanel traits, and, if sources other than the Chicanel and the Floral Park–Tzakol ceramic traditions seem to be indicated, where do these sources lie? At least partial disjunction of Picota and the earlier Chicanel-like pottery of the site is indicated by the absence from Picota of Waxy Ware and of volcanic-ash temper. Retention of Preclassic traits in modified form is suggested by the importance of monochrome red pottery and wide-everted-rim bowls. It appears unnecessary, however, to attribute continuity in these features specifically to the local Chicanel-like population whose cultural remains directly underlie Picota-complex materials. Had site-unit intrusion occurred, the ceramic features thereby introduced might have included Chicanel analogues derived ultimately from other Preclassic sources. It is important to understand the role of Chicanel in possible developments leading to civilization at Palenque, for on no other horizon were ceramic correspondences as close with most of the Southern Maya Lowlands. Within the Northwestern Zone, there are suggestions that certain elements of the Picota complex may have been of western derivation. Within a broader Mesoamerican framework, Picota ceramics appear marginal to developments among both the Peten Maya and known Mexican centers of Early Classic culture.

No examples of ceremonial architecture have as yet been identified on the Picota horizon. One would expect that this situation will change with adequate archaeological sampling. Even so, we can only suppose that elite-ceremonial activities were limited for an Early Classic site, an inference which is consistent with the marginal nature of Picota ceramics.

A number of Picota traits continued into the Motiepa ceramic complex (Rands 1974:Figs. 5, 6). The most striking characteristic of Motiepa was the introduction of Peten Gloss Ware, in which members of the Aguila (Orange) and Balanza (Black) ceramic groups were best represented. On techno-stylistic grounds, it is clear that much of the new pottery was imported from sources located outside the Palenque region. In addition, some of the non-Gloss pottery suggests that a fairly localized adaptation of Peten-based ceramic concepts may have taken place (for example, increased popularity of orange slip at the expense of red). Polychrome pottery, present for the first time, was rare. In fact, whether introduced into the Motiepa complex by trade or present as the result of indirect diffusion, all of the new, Peten-affiliated pottery had low sherd frequencies. Apart from the Late Preclassic, however, this was the time when Palenque was most strongly exposed to typically Mayan ceramic influences.

There are suggestions that during Motiepa times the principal center of Palenque may have begun to shift from the western part of the site to a new location well to the east, where the better known portions of the ruins lie. Clearly, some occupation of the eastern zone had occurred earlier, as Picota ceramics are found in mixed fill from several structures. In the eastern center, the earliest identified large-scale plaza construction dates from Motiepa, the earliest known tomb from the same period. With the probable exception of the ball court, the earliest known standing architecture is from the following Otolum complex, a temporal equivalent of Tepeu 1. At this point, Motiepa may simply be characterized as a time when effective exposure to Maya Classicism seems to have begun. This may have been on only a modest scale, as sherd frequencies suggest. On the other hand, the ceramic evidence may constitute merely the tip of the iceberg; pottery may have been accompanied by the introduction of elite-ceremonial practices of significant if undetermined proportions.

Elsewhere in the Low Sierras, Early Classic remains are spotty. The lower tomb chamber found by Blom at Yoxiha contained 11 vessels in typical Tzakol style (Blom and La Farge 1926–27:231–33), but, with the exceptions of Chinikiha and Chancala, other sites sampled in the Palenque area survey do not reflect corresponding Early Classic developments. The direct superimposition of Late Classic and Preclassic deposits is more usual.

Along the Middle Usumacinta, a population decline of major proportions may have taken place at the close of the Preclassic or Protoclassic, a reduced occupation continuing throughout much of the Early Classic. The alternative of nucleation into a smaller number of sites must also be recognized, although signs of increasing sociocultural complexity, which might be expected to accompany this process, are not apparent. The Early Classic Kaxabyuc complex of Trinidad is both poorly represented and for the most part lacking Tzakol diagnostics, but pottery of Tzakol style is not altogether unknown in the region. Orange slip, a feature having Classic affiliations, is present in the more localized pottery. Sporadic connections exist with the Picota-Motiepa tradition of Palenque. Although evidence is far from complete, Early Classic developments along this part of the Usumacinta stand in sharp contrast both to the vigorous expansion which appears to have characterized the Late Preclassic Societies and to indications of a Late Classic cultural revival.

Farther to the west, in the Chontalpa, the general absence of securely identifiable Early Classic sites is apparent from work by Berlin (1953, 1955, 1956), Sisson (1970:47), and Peniche Rivero (1973). As one turns eastward to the site of Piedras Negras, slightly outside the Northwestern Zone, the situation is dramatically different. Early Classic pottery, assignable to the Tzakol ceramic sphere, occurs abundantly in connection with large-scale ceremonial architecture. Stylistic features of temples and substructures were apparently derived from the Peten, although vaulted roofs are believed not to have been introduced until the Late Classic Period (Satterthwaite 1941). Partly because of the absence of the vault, Proskouriakoff (1950:120) has suggested that Piedras Negras may originally have formed part of a culture area "distinct from the rest of the Peten and more closely allied to southern areas of Mexico." Seen from the perspective of the Northwestern Zone, however, Piedras Negras was by this time firmly rooted in the Classic Maya tradition.

LATE CLASSIC OCCUPATION

Discussion of Late Classic developments will largely be directed to Palenque. The Otolum ceramic complex (ca. A.D. 600–700) (Rands 1974:Figs. 7, 8) corresponds to the time when Palenque emerged as a major center of Classic Maya culture. Orange-polychromes, produced at or near the site, had their greatest frequency, but clearly ceramics were not the center of cultural interest. Architectural changes took place with exceptional rapidity during the latter part of the Otolum complex. Experimentation soon led to the construction of a large number of spacious double-range galleries employing parallel vaults, a form used in both palace-type structures and temple-pyramids. Low relief sculpture, which had few known antecedents, became a prominent part of architectural design in the form of wall panels. By the end of Otolum or the beginning of the subsequent Murcielagos complex, the wall tablet was exploited as a focal point for a series of new developments—an interior vaulted sanctuary placed against the rear wall of the temple, compositional arrangements of a complex nature that were impossible to achieve within the traditional limitations of the stela cult, and the proliferation of lengthy hieroglyphic texts. It is striking that none of these evidences of high culture have been shown to be of earlier date at Palenque than Otolum and that many appear to have been essentially local developments.

Although they involve technologically sophisticated achievements, these changes may be characterized as refinements that gave new twists and directions to the Classic Maya tradition as it was incorporated in the culture of Palenque; they did not fundamentally alter the tradition. The critical question for purposes of the present volume is whether these elaborative innovations were in any way related to basic changes in the organization of society. Rephrasing the question, one might ask whether the innovative process manifested in the accelerating magnificence of the ceremonial center helped to restructure social relationships—aristocrat with commoner, adminis-trator with craftsman, Palenqueño with members of other communi-ties—so that a significantly different social order was emerging. Assuming the same population size, would the sociopolitical structur-ing have been different if the elite had been less innovative? Occupy-ing a frontier position where Classic concepts were not fully absorbed, could Palenque have maintained the support necessary to become as large as it did if it had lacked the prestige provided by skillful, creative reworking of the newly introduced Classic patterns? Such questions suggest some of the feedback components that may have promoted the success of Palenque at the beginning of the Late Classic Period.

A possible shift of the principal ceremonial precinct of Palenque from west to east, as indicated earlier, may have begun in the Early Classic Motiepa complex. Apparently the shift was not completed until well into the Otolum phase. The ceremonial complex in the west includes a small plaza, an aqueduct, a plain stela known as La Picota, and, nearby, the temple-pyramid designated the Olvidado (Blom and La Farge 1926–27:Figs. 149, 150, 157; Berlin 1942). Direct ceramic dating is unavailable for the western precinct. The presence of a standing, unsculptured stela could indicate activities which either antedated or followed Classic expressions of Maya ceremonialism. The Olvidado, dating from approximately 9.10.15.0.0, has early architectural features, such as thick walls and narrow corridors; an interior sanctuary is absent. Proportions of component parts of the vault differ from later Palenque standards. Approximately coeval with the estimated date for the introduction of the corbeled vault at Piedras Negras (W. R. Coe 1959:149–50), the Olvidado may be among the first examples of vaulted temple architecture at Palenque (Schele n.d.), although the presence of the vaulted Motiepa tomb (Temple XVIII-A Sub) may suggest otherwise. Thereafter, the erection of major pyramidal structures appears to have been concentrated in the eastern part of Palenque, although other pyramids and especially range-type structures are widespread throughout the site. The most magnificent of the double-range complexes, the Palace, is located in the eastern precinct. Apparently dating in original form from Otolum, the Palace underwent a series of elaborative changes throughout the Murcielagos Ceramic Complex (ca. A.D. 700–770; Rands 1974:Fig. 9).

Several of the great temple-pyramids of Palenque—the Conde, Inscriptions, and Cross—are ceramically dated as falling in the late facet of Otolum. Epigraphic data place other major temples, the Foliated Cross and Sun, as contemporaneous with the Cross. Hieroglyphic texts in the Inscriptions and Cross—and to a lesser degree in the other temples, except for the Conde—have been of special importance in recent attempts to reconstruct the dynastic history of Palenque (Lounsbury 1974; Mathews and Schele 1974).[5] As currently interpreted, the dynastic records of the site focus to an unusual degree on the life of "Shield-Pacal" (9.8.9.13.0–9.12.11.5.18, or A.D. 603–83) and his accession in 9.9.2.4.8 (A.D. 615). The importance given this man is indicated by the richness of his burial in the Inscriptions tomb, by his repeated portrayal in other temples at Palenque, and by the apparent desire of all later rulers to associate themselves with Pacal, as though to legitimize their reigns. Pacal's reign corresponds well with the duration of most of the Otolum ceramic complex (as given in Rands [1973a:Fig. 5]), that is, the period of Palenque's emergence as a major Classic center (see Schele n.d.). The earliest known occurrences at the site of dated sculptures, and quite possibly of major vaulted architecture, fall in his reign. It may have been under his aegis that the transfer of the major ceremonial precinct to the eastern part of the site was formalized. These findings are presented not to support a "great man" theory of historical causality but as part of the evidence relating to the surge of elite activity which I tend to interpret as marking the successful integration of newly introduced Classic features with localized, marginally Classic patterns of culture.

That Palenque had not been completely isolated from elite aspects of Classic culture is indicated by texts which apparently trace the dynastic succession back to Katun 3 of Baktun 9 (ca. A.D. 500), or perhaps even earlier. The "beginning" of the dynasty could therefore correspond to some part of the Motiepa complex, when Peten Gloss Ware was being imported to Palenque. This cannot be established on the basis of present evidence, however, and speculations linking potsherds with dynastic origins or alliances seem premature, if not idle. Questions concerning the significance of dynastic "rulers" to the Early Classic sociopolitical structure of Palenque are germane to the rise of civilization, if no less vexing to answer. I am not fully comfortable with distinctions between higher "chiefdoms" and petty "states," especially when such a classification is inferred from archaeological data. However, there may be utility in suggesting that, prior to Pacal, Palenque's social structure corresponded best to a chiefdom model but, during his reign, shifted to that of a small state. As always, it is easy to confuse symbols with social reality. It may, nevertheless, be significant that virtually all Palenque rulers prior to Pacal lack an affix compound (T74.184) apparently denoting a specific high title, whereas Pacal and his successors consistently used this title. The possibility that a chiefdomlike society existed in the Early Classic Period and was replaced by a Late Classic state, corresponds in part to the interpretation made by Sanders and Price (1968). Unlike Sanders and Price, however, I am making the suggestion only for such peripheral localities as Palenque; I am not postulating a general trend for the core area of the Maya Lowlands.

NOTES

1. The paper has benefited from extended discussions with Linda Schele, whose perspective as an art historian and epigrapher provides a useful adjunct to the more traditional anthropological studies of civilization.

2. Designations such as "Northwestern Zone," "Middle Usumacinta," and "Low Sierras" are consistent with usage in the Culbert (1973a) volume *The Classic Maya Collapse*. In that volume see especially Figs. 1 and 18 and the discussion of regional subdivisions, pages 167–70.

3. Although the term "Middle Classic" has not come into general usage and has been variously defined, it might prove useful as a period designation for Palenque. At this site, the term's significance would not be based on Teotihuacan connections, which were always feeble, but would reflect the period of tangible exposure to the Classic Maya tradition prior to spectacular developments during the reign of Pacal.

PART 3

External Areas and Influences

8

Olmec and Maya: A Study in Relationships

MICHAEL D. COE

Yale University

There is now little or no dissent from the proposition that the Olmec civilization is older than any other in Mesoamerica, including the Classic Maya. Recent excavations in both lowland and highland Mexico have proved this beyond all doubt. Now that this chronological problem has finally been solved, the task remains to discover how the Olmec pattern contributed to later developments. Of particular interest is the relationship between the Maya civilization of the lowlands and the Olmec, for it has been suggested that many of the "typical" traits of the Classic Maya were, in fact, invented many centuries before them by the Olmec (M. D. Coe 1957b).

TIME AND SPACE FACTORS

Before examining this question, I will first outline what we know of the extent of Olmec civilization in time, and its distribution in space. For many years an understanding of Olmec chronology was severely hampered by a faulty understanding of the Formative or Preclassic sequence in the Valley of Mexico, in which Olmec culture at Tlatilco was seen to appear toward the middle of the period, perhaps no earlier than 500 B.C. (Porter 1953). It is now known that Olmec and Olmec-related materials stand at the beginning of the sequence, and that the supposedly ancient El Arbolillo I phase is considerably later than once supposed (Tolstoy and Paradis 1970).

Having settled this matter, we can now see that there are really two Olmec horizons in Mesoamerica. The earliest I will call the San Lorenzo horizon, after the type site in the Coatzacoalcos drainage of southern Veracruz; it can be dated from 1200 to 900 B.C. (in radiocarbon years), and can be detected by the presence of bowls, dishes, and bottles carved with such characteristic Olmec symbols as the jaguar paw-wing motif, as well as large, hollow, baby-faced ceramic figures. At this time, the San Lorenzo site in the "heartland" reaches its height with its strange, mound-covered plateau (perhaps itself a gigantic effigy mound), and a profusion of enormous basalt sculptures, including Colossal Heads (M. D. Coe 1970). Perhaps just as large as San Lorenzo and possibly its cultural and political equal was Laguna de los Cerros. Away from the heartland, the San Lorenzo horizon can be detected at Tlatilco and Tlapacoya in the Valley of Mexico, at Las Bocas in Puebla, and in the San José phase in the Valley of Oaxaca (Flannery 1968a). Although no nonportable Olmec art belonging to the horizon can be surely identified outside the "heartland," I suspect that the polychrome paintings in the Juxtlahuaca Cave of Guerrero (Gay 1967) as well as the Pijijiapan boulder reliefs of coastal Chiapas (Navarrete 1969a) are of that period. San Lorenzo and its remarkable sculptures were destroyed about 900 B.C., but Olmec civilization continued to flourish on the Gulf Coast plain. Replacing San Lorenzo as the great Olmec center (and probably replacing Laguna de los Cerros as well) was La Venta, situated on its remote island in the swamps of western Tabasco. The site was probably the most important in Mesoamerica from 900 B.C. to about 400 B.C., when it, too, was demolished and Olmec civilization ceased to exist. It is this span of time that I will call the La Venta horizon. Gone are the large, white-slipped, baby-faced figures. The boldly carved vessels of the San Lorenzo horizon are replaced by hard, white pottery incised with the double-line break and similar abstract motifs. Jade appears for the first time, and the Olmec, particularly at La Venta and in Guerrero, prove themselves to be master carvers. The Olmec sculptors continued to produce Colossal Heads and other statuary on a gigantic scale, but relief carvings, often with highly narrative scenes, began to outnumber carvings in the round.

Spatially, Olmec civilization appears to have reached its greatest extent in the La Venta horizon, reaching up the Gulf Coast past the Bay of Alvarado, across the central Mexican plateau as far west as Guerrero, and down the Pacific Coast of Chiapas and Guatemala as far as Chalchuapa in El Salvador (Boggs 1950). It has now been established that the important trading site of Chalcatzingo in Morelos, with its spectacular narrative reliefs, belongs to the La Venta horizon and, in fact, has produced a serpentine figurine of La Venta workmanship (David C. Grove, personal communication). It is highly likely that the remarkable murals of Oxtotitlan in Guerrero were painted during the La Venta horizon (Grove 1970:32).

Imperfect though our knowledge is, there are some curious gaps in the spatial extent of the La Venta horizon. One is the Valley of Mexico, where sites of the Middle Formative such as El Arbolillo and Zacatenco seem little more than peasant villages without any of the Olmec traits that characterized the earlier Tlatilco and Tlapacoya. The other lacuna is the Maya area proper (I see no reason to include the Pacific Coast of Guatemala in this). I know of but one Olmec monument in the Maya area, the relief carving of Xoc, located in the Jatate drainage of Chiapas, on the western edge of the Maya Lowlands (Ekholm-Miller 1973). Several portable objects of Olmec manufacture, particularly of jade, have been found in the Maya country, but these do not necessarily speak of Olmec influence since they could have been carried in at a much later date; such objects, in fact, have been found in Postclassic contexts at Mayapan (Pollock et al. 1962:Fig. 25*d*) and on Cozumel (Jeremy A. Sabloff, personal communication). The one sure case of La Venta–horizon objects deposited in a contemporary context is the jade perforator in a Real-Xe cache at Seibal (Willey et al. 1968).

This means that Olmec civilization and Maya civilization show a complementary distribution in both time and space. How, then, could the Olmec have contributed to the development of Maya civilization, which does not appear until the end of the third century A.D.? No less than seven centuries separate the downfall of La Venta and the appearance of high culture in the Maya Lowlands. To answer this question, one must turn to the epi-Olmec remains of sites like Tres Zapotes, and in particular to the widespread proto-Maya civilization which has been termed "Izapan" (M. D. Coe 1965b:772–73; Quirarte 1973a and Chap. 10 below).

It is not, however, the purpose of this paper to review the evidence for direct transmission through Izapan culture. Rather, I intend to compare and contrast Olmec civilization with that of the Classic Maya to point out (1) those traits which both share and which were probably developed by the Olmec, (2) those traits which are uniquely Olmec and which failed to be adopted by the Maya, and (3) those traits which are unique to the Maya. This review may throw light on the problem of why Olmec culture failed to penetrate the Maya area, and how the Izapan civilization both passed along and filtered out important features of Olmec culture.

OLMEC-MAYA HOMOLOGIES

Perhaps the most striking of the traits which bind together the Olmec and the Maya is a sociopolitical one: an emphasis on the personality and power of individual leaders. This is in strong contrast to the impersonality of the art of Teotihuacan, Classic Central Veracruz, and Classic Monte Alban. Maya stelae and other reliefs portray the unique characteristics of definite persons, both in face and in costume; I think that most Olmec specialists are convinced that the Colossal Heads are also portraits, especially since the headgear on each is idiosyncratic. This use of headdress as individual badge must have been transmitted from the Olmec to the Maya. Furthermore, in the La Venta horizon, real persons are shown in narrative scenes, for instance on Stela 3 from La Venta, exactly as in the later Maya reliefs.

One of the principal activities of both Olmec and Classic Maya lords seems to have been warfare and the humbling of captives as shown on Olmec "altars", such as Altar 4 at La Venta, and the numerous Maya stelae showing the ruler trampling a prisoner or displaying weapons and shields. This is, of course, the main theme of the so-called Danzantes of Monte Alban, which are nothing more than portraits of slain captives, and it is surely significant that these show signs of Olmec influence.

Another activity indulged in by both the Olmec and the Maya elite was the ball game, perhaps an Olmec invention. The earliest known court for the game was discovered at San Lorenzo, in the Palangana phase which is coeval with the later occupation of La Venta. It was made of earth and clay, and was of the *"palangana"* type with enclosing ridges on all four sides. Solid clay figurines of grotesque gods attired in ball-game equipment, including the heavy belt or yoke, were numerous in the San Lorenzo phase, and elaborately garbed ball players have been found at both Tlatilco and Tlapacoya on the same time level (M. D. Coe 1965a:45, 54). In the final season at San Lorenzo, G. H. Krotser excavated, in a San Lorenzo B stratum, the remains of what appears to have been a large rubber ball; it was carbonized and in fragments, but these gave off a strong smell of burning rubber when ignited.

At one time it was thought that the Olmec religious system centered on the worship of the jaguar, but this notion is now untenable. Certainly jaguar symbolism permeates Olmec religion. But in a preliminary study which he is now revising and expanding, David Joralemon (1971) has isolated ten Olmec deities, each representing a significant cluster of symbolic motifs. Surely some, if not all, of these deities formed a pantheon which was bequeathed to the Maya and other civilizations of the Classic. His God I combines jaguar, human, crocodilian, and at times even fish features; he has eyebrows which look like stylized flames. It is his face and paw-wing which are the most frequent motifs on pottery of the San Lorenzo horizon. Without going into the details necessary to demonstrate the point, we feel that he is cognate not only with the Old Fire God/Fire Serpent complex of the later central Mexicans, but also with Itzamna of the Maya.

Another deity who surely enters into the religious systems of Classic and Postclassic Mesoamerica is God II, whose emblem is a corn plant or ear rising from the cleft at the top of the head. Surely this is the Maize God, and it is probably significant that its features appear almost exclusively incised on jade celts—an indication that for the Olmec the green celt was symbolic of an ear of corn (David Joralemon, personal communication).

Other deities shared by the Olmec and Maya are less clear. God VI is characterized by a band passing down through the eye and across the cheek, a motif distinguishing Xipe Totec, deity of springtime renewal among the central Mexicans. This god does appear among the Classic Maya, but seems to be confined to the early part of the period as the result of Teotihuacan influence; however, Xipe is present in the Maya codices as God Q. An absolutely certain identification is God VII as

Quetzalcoatl, the Feathered Serpent. However, I can find no example of this deity in any representations of the Classic Maya; those examples which have been cited by others are more likely to be a composite, ophidian creature which Thompson (1973b:61) has identified as Itzamna, supreme god of the Maya.

Certain religious paraphernalia are also shared, and suggest religious practices held in common. One of these is the pottery incense burner, usually a tall cylinder with a flat top on which the copal incense is placed, and a convex cover or lid around which the smoke swirls. The three-pronged censer is found at San Lorenzo as early as 1300 B.C., in the proto-Olmec Chicharras phase, but incense burners never attained the importance for the Olmec that they enjoyed among the Classic Maya. Monument 19 from La Venta shows a figure holding what must be an incense bag, a ritual object which appears throughout the art of Classic and Postclassic Mesoamerica.

One of the most important of all Maya rituals was ceremonial bloodletting, either by drawing a cord through a hole in the tongue or by passing a stingray spine, pointed bone, or maguey thorn through the penis. Stingray spines used in the rite have often have been found in Maya caches; in fact, so significant was this act among the Classic Maya that the perforator itself was worshipped as a god. This ritual must also have been frequently practiced among the earlier Olmec, on the evidence of the jade objects which have been called "stilettos" but which are surely penis perforators, as well as a jade effigy of a stingray spine found at La Venta in the tomb of Mound A-2. Among the Maya, the blood was spattered onto paper strips contained in a dish; the Olmec almost certainly had bark paper, but whether this was the destination of their blood is unknown. Direct evidence that the earliest identifiable Maya were using an Olmec bloodletting instrument is provided by the jade "stiletto" in the Seibal cache mentioned above.

Jade itself is a notable link between the Olmec and the Maya. There is little doubt that in the Mesoamerican mind jade was equated not only with maize but with blood; for this reason, not only the Olmec but also the Classic Maya coated jade objects with bloodred cinnabar or hematite. In the ritual bloodletting described above, jade as a precious substance quite clearly acted as the intermediary between red blood and the young, green maize whose growth it was meant to stimulate.

Among the most unusual objects that characterize Olmec civilization are mirrors. These were fashioned from iron-ore nodules which take a high polish, such as magnetite, ilmenite, and hematite, and certainly played an important role in Olmec rituals and displays of power. The most striking mirrors are concave and could have been used either as igniters or as "magic lanterns," or both. However, smaller, flat mirrors are far commoner in Olmec debris. Regardless of their ultimate function, mirrors were, on evidence from life-size statues as well as small figurines, worn around the necks of rulers, probably as a symbol of power. To my knowledge, single-piece mirrors have never been found in archaeological contexts within the Lowland Maya area. Nevertheless, several unpublished Maya pictorial vases show rulers gazing into mirrors held by subordinates; these are, to judge from their great size, probably polished obsidian. At any rate, the ritual use of the mirror seems to have been promulgated by the Olmec.

I know of two representations of Olmec personages holding what may be ceremonial bars similar to those borne by Maya rulers. The first of these is a small stone figurine of a bearded god in the American Museum of Natural History; the second is the seated ruler, apparently a woman, in Relief 1 at Chalcatzingo. There is an important difference, however, between Maya and Olmec ceremonial bars: the Maya ceremonial bars always are made up of the Bearded Dragon, sometimes with celestial markings on the body and often with the heads of other deities in the jaws, while the Olmec examples are relatively plain.

Turning to calendrics, writing, and perhaps astronomy, while it is probable that by 400 B.C. the Olmec had developed the 260-day count, the 365-day Vague Year, and thus the 52-year Calendar Round, there is no concrete evidence of this. Prior to that date, however, some features of the Maya and other writing systems had appeared. Among these is the use of bar-and-dot numbers; the large number six carved on the rocky bed of a stream at Tres Zapotes apparently belongs to the earliest known occupation of that site (Matthew W. Stirling, personal communication). Glyphic elements with definite astronomical associations in both Olmec and Maya are the U sign (Quirarte:Chapter 10 below), surely a reference to the moon; the kin sign, symbolic of the sun; Lamat, standing not only for Venus but for stars in general; and the Crossed Bands motif, apparently referring to the night sky as symbolized by the crossing of the Milky Way with the Eclyptic (Charles Smiley, personal communication).

In a paper written some years ago (M. D. Coe 1957b), I made the claim, on purely archaeological grounds, that the Olmec had invented the Maya Long Count calendar. This claim was based upon the evidence for the dating and Stirling's reading of Stela C at Tres Zapotes. While both the dating and reading have been fully confirmed subsequently, especially by Francisco Beverido's finding of the top part of the monument, it is now plain that the stela is post-Olmec. I will return to this point later. Suffice it to say that there is no secure evidence that the Olmec of either the San Lorenzo or La Venta horizons possessed the Maya calendar as we know it.

I think, however, that we may discern in Olmec art a step toward writing. This includes not only the four astral glyphs mentioned above, but also the principle of *pars pro toto* writing, in which the part stands for the whole. The hand-paw-wing motif on San Lorenzo–horizon ceramics is a good example of this: it can easily be "read" by the initiated as God I of the Olmec pantheon. The next two steps, probably taken by the epi-Olmec and Izapan scribes, would have been to use such fragmentary elements (1) as semantic indicators and (2) for their phonetic value. Once these steps were taken, the groundwork was laid for the writing system of the Classic Maya.

THE UNIQUENESS OF OLMEC CIVILIZATION

Lest I seem to be claiming that the Classic Maya were but transformed Olmec, I will stress that the Olmec civilization has characteristics which are absolutely distinctive and in some cases unique. A *cultura madre* does not produce offspring identical to the mother. One should keep in mind the immense time differential between the two civilizations: the fifteen hundred years that separate the beginnings of Olmec culture from the earliest Classic Maya are equivalent to all the time between the life of the Emperor Justinian and ourselves.

The Olmec characteristically built public monuments—at least their substructures—of earth and colored clays; the use of stone and of stucco, at least in the "heartland," was virtually unknown. These structures were laid out in a linear pattern elsewhere unknown in Mesoamerica. On the south was a large mound, with two long mounds to the north of it flanking a narrow space, perhaps a ball court; on the north was placed a smaller mound which, in La Venta at least, contained tombs. The pattern can be seen at San Lorenzo, La Venta, and Laguna de los Cerros, but Francisco Beverido has discovered through aerial reconnaissance a number of others in southern Veracruz. The orientation of some Olmec ceremonial centers is peculiar to them, also: eight degrees west of true north, an orientation which could have astronomical meaning but which also could have resulted from the use of iron-ore compasses.

I now believe that the San Lorenzo site may be a gigantic effigy mound, possibly a bird flying east; if so, it was never completed on the east side. Nevertheless, there was a definite attempt to achieve symmetry in artificial ridges and in the mounts placed on them. There is nothing like this in Maya site planning, and it allies the Olmec more closely with early cultures of the eastern United States, such as Poverty Point, Adena, and Hopewell. Gillett Griffin has also suggested to me that the entire island upon which La Venta is situated may have had artificial ridges and an outline similar to San Lorenzo's, but unfortunately that site has never been mapped as it should have been, and it may already be too late to do so.

So far, the aqueduct systems of San Lorenzo and La Venta seem unique. The one on the southwest side of San Lorenzo has been completely excavated and mapped; it seems to have been made for the purpose of carrying water from ceremonial pools to Monument 9, a duck-shaped "fountain" carved to receive the last of the U-shaped stones from which the drain was made (G. R. Krotser, personal communication). It is apparent that another system matching this is to be found in mirror image on the southeast side of the site. There is nothing quite like this in the Maya area.

Another uniquely Olmec trait is the obsession with babies, perhaps only to be matched in the Roman Catholic world with its various "Niños" or Infants—of Prague, of Atocha, and so forth. I have speculated that there is a psychological reason behind this: the affective nature of infant forms upon adults of the same species, an attested behavioral reaction among many animals (M. D. Coe 1973a:10–11). Not only does this infantile motif, usually combined with jaguar features, show up in many representations of gods, but pottery figures of nude, sexless, perhaps even pathologically Mongoloid babies were frequently fashioned; since the latter are common in household refuse at San Lorenzo (although only in graves in the Central Highlands), one might postulate a domestic function for them. What this could be is so far unfathomable.

Babies are carried by adults, however, in the Maya area—in the Bonampak murals and on the stuccoed pilasters of the Temple of the Inscriptions at Palenque. Both of these instances recall the babies on Altar 5 at La Venta. The Palenque case is perhaps indicative of the Maya, if not the Olmec function—could these little creatures suggest the notion of noble or royal descent? A careful examination of these infants at Palenque shows them to be juvenile forms of God K, surely the patron lord of the royal lineage.

I have already mentioned the concave mirrors. These were among a host of previous objects that were commonly buried as caches or offerings. While the Maya also deposited rare items under stelae and floors, and left them as offerings for the dead, nothing approaches the Olmec practice here. Hundreds of jades and literally tons of serpentine were so buried and thus taken out of circulation. The recently discovered and clandestinely excavated cache of Arroyo Pesquero, for instance, contained over twenty-five life-size jade masks and nearly a thousand jade and serpentine celts. One can only hazard the guess that the Olmec, in the face of rising jade production, and therefore of inflation, solved their problems by increasing the value of their version of money.

Lastly, apart from the narrative reliefs, which largely belong to the La Venta horizon, the Olmec sculptural art was basically three-dimensional. These people appeared on the scene around 1200 B.C. with fully developed abilities not only to carve very hard, massive rocks like basalt, but also to move them over great distances. Until the advent of the Aztec, there is nothing to equal Olmec mastery in this field. In contrast, with the exception of Tonina, Maya sculptural art is essentially flat. The same point can be made with jade carving, the Olmec working in large chunks which they fashioned into figures to be seen from all sides; the Maya, on the other hand, turned out only thin plates with reliefs on one side, or small, headlike objects.

THE UNIQUENESS OF MAYA CIVILIZATION

No one could ever mistake a Maya site for an Olmec one. There are no rooms in Olmec architecture, and whatever superstructures ever topped their pyramids must have been of pole and thatch. Because of the abundance of limestone and of lime in the Maya Lowlands, there evolved in the Peten toward the close of the Formative Period a unique style of architecture based upon the extraordinary strength of rubble-and-lime interiors. The invention of the corbel arch produced a style of architecture geared more to the production of enclosed than open space. The so-called palaces of the Maya were unknown to the Olmec.

Another feature of Maya site planning has not been found among the Olmec. These are the causeways which link outlying temples and temple complexes with the center of the site and with each other; in Yucatan, even distant ceremonial centers can be thus tied together. Whatever their function may have been, it almost certainly was ritual rather than economic.

Inside Maya centers, one does find powerful rulers like those of the Olmec, with both religious and military duties, and they are portrayed as real individuals. However, with the exception of Chalcatzingo and perhaps Stela 1 at La Venta, Olmec women never seem to play important political and social roles as women do among the Maya. I know of no other New World civilization in which females reached the degree of power that has been attested for the Maya.

Maya art is highly painterly, baroque as opposed to "classic," and almost always tells some kind of story. This is very different from the "classic" art of the San Lorenzo horizon, but very much like the Izapan style of the Late Formative from which Maya art clearly derives. Maya art relies heavily upon a kind of "whiplash" line probably derived from calligraphy, whereas the Olmec line conforms to heavier, quite logarithmic curves.

The characteristic Maya stela-altar complex is surely derived from Izapan civilization. Perhaps we should abolish the word *altar,* for I am sure that sculptures of this sort never served as such among the Maya, and Grove (1973) has proved that Olmec "altars" were really thrones. Stelae are rare in the San Lorenzo horizon, more common during the La Venta horizon, and the dominant form of sculpture in Izapan culture. They were apparently the ideal vehicle for Maya dynastic records.

Olmec pottery representations, it will be remembered, celebrate their gods. So do those of the Maya, but with an important difference: the world they show is exclusively the Underworld. I know of no civilization other than that of the Egyptians which has so concerned itself with the hereafter and the vicissitudes of the soul after death. The incredibly complex world of infernal deities seems to be unknown elsewhere in Mesoamerica, and it appears to be totally absent among the Olmec. If one explores this world, as I have in my examination of Maya pictorial ceramics (M. D. Coe 1973b), one discovers the reason for this obsession: the myth of the Hero Twins, who overcame the Underworld lords and were apotheosized as sun and moon. Surely this great myth suggested to the Maya rulers and to their subjects that they would also triumph over death, to rise again and be worshiped by members of their respective lineages and by their people.

Where did the Maya derive the traits for which they are most famous, the calendar and writing system? In the light of past and recent evidence, the crucial area and time must have been southern Veracruz, the Pacific Coast of Guatemala, and the Grijalva Depression of Chiapas from the first century before Christ to the second century after, among people who must have been the successors of the Olmec. The Long Count and the 260-day count first appear on Stela 2 at Chiapa de Corzo; in a noncalendrical text on Stela C, Tres Zapotes; and in paired glyphs in columns on Stela 1, El Baúl. Surely Maya writing, with main signs accompanied by extensive affixing, was incised on the Tuxtla Statuette, with a date corresponding to a day in the year A.D. 162. This is all post-Olmec, and it seems that we must largely exclude the Olmec from the evolution of Maya writing. Possibly the scribes of Monte Albán I had something to do with it, but the dating of the relevant monuments at that site is so dubious that they must be left out of the discussion for the present.

Maya writing and calendrics eventually became so complex that they are unique. Exclusive Maya traits include the Lunar Series (already present by 8.16.0.0.0 (A.D. 357), Distance Numbers, Period Ending Dates, Anniversaries, the 819-day Count, and Emblem Glyphs. Very early in the Classic Period the Maya were recording historical events in the fullest manner possible, and this concern with the written record eventually led to the most fully developed script in the New World. None of this can be laid at the door of the Olmec.

CONCLUSIONS

The Olmec were on the Mesoamerican scene as early as 1200 B.C. and had vanished as a cultural entity eight centuries later. During this epoch, they originated much of what we know as the typical Mesoamerican pattern of culture; these traits were diffused, by mechanisms unknown, during two horizons, the San Lorenzo and the La Venta. However, one area with few if any traces of such a diffusion is that of the Maya, both Highland and Lowland. Why, if they had reached to Guerrero and El Salvador, did the Olmec not also penetrate the Maya Lowlands? I think that the reason must be that there were few if any populations in the Maya area with which to form some sort of relationship. Present evidence, although purely negative, suggests that there were very few people in the lowlands prior to 900 or 800 B.C., perhaps because a diminished pattern of rainfall prevailed prior to that time. I have suggested that the subsequent occupants of the region might have been Maya-speaking Olmec, who could have migrated eastward from the "heartland" following the breakup of San Lorenzo civilization. The Seibal cache of Olmec jades suggests some sort of contact, but one would expect more than this: large-scale monumental sculpture throughout the Maya area. Such has not been found. The mystery remains.

Those Olmec traits that became part of the Maya pattern were transmitted by epi-Olmec and Izapan peoples who were distributed from the Gulf Coast, through Chiapas, and into the Guatemalan Highlands during the period from 400 B.C. to the third century A.D. It was in this arc, and not in the Maya Lowlands themselves, that much of Maya civilization evolved. It was these peoples who must have rejected some Olmec traits, modified others, and even moved off into new directions such as writing and calendrics. For these reasons, a concerted program aimed at sites of the Late Formative in southern Mesoamerica should be undertaken, for in that time and in those places Maya civilization took form.

9

The Mixe-Zoque as Competing
Neighbors of the Early Lowland Maya

GARETH W. LOWE

New World Archaeological Foundation,
Brigham Young University

INTRODUCTION: RIVAL SOCIAL SYSTEMS
AND ENVIRONMENTS

Compared to the usually small, culturally diversified ancient Olmec–derived communities found across the geographically disparate isthmus region of southern Mesoamerica, the Classic Maya society of the physiographically rather uniform Yucatan peninsular area is most readily distinguished by the extensive distribution of its highly developed and long-enduring artistic unity, closely stylized epigraphic inscriptions, and cut-stone architectural conventions, all characteristics of a high civilization. Rightly or wrongly, the singularly high achievements of the Maya populace in the lowland tropics are commonly attributed to social factors rather than to superior ecological potential. Regarding the intensification of growth in certain Peten Classic Maya communities, it has been postulated, for example, that nucleation was caused not by any environmental advantage but rather by the operation of belief systems and social prestige in conjunction with kin ties. (Webb 1973:388–89)

An all-important civilizing role for belief-system rituality and ranked kin ties implies a strong linkage of the supernatural with one or more dominant ancestral families:

There perhaps was a focus on some kind of ancestor cult. . . . a strong possibility exists that some of the temples found in Maya centers were dedicated . . . to ancestral deities of descent lines. (Sanders 1973: 348)

One immediately asks, To what region or peoples might Mayan ancestral beliefs be traced? Why did these eventually find greater ecological response and achieve greater cultural development in the lowland forest regions? The required appraisal of socioreligious and environmental roles in the origins of Lowland Maya civilization calls for a careful examination of the neighboring ecological regions to the west and south and their contrasting cultural attainments.

It is generally recognized that most of the Lowland Maya area was a cultural backwater for the better part of a millennium while the Ocos, Olmec, and related early western and southern cultures flowered and faded around it (Lowe 1971, 1973a; Puleston and Puleston 1971:336). The Olmec, most celebrated of the Mayan ancestors, had their domain in the greater isthmus region, an area historically and linguistically most closely aligned with the Mixe-Zoque Indians. Many, if not most, of the Lowland Maya antecedents, including their "ancestral deities of descent lines," must be traced back to this region and its older advanced culture.

The earliest and most extensive Early Preclassic culture history known within the greater isthmus area is that of southern Chiapas and southwestern Guatemala. With its large, rather dry interior valleys and its long coastal plains crossed by many rivers, southern Chiapas in particular provided a superior environment for early human occupants, including at first small groups of hunter-gatherers and then permanent village agriculturalists. To the north on the Gulf Coast, the Tabasco plain and waterways may have been equally favorable to such early occupation, but this frequently inundated region has been considerably less kind to consistent archaeological discovery. The long coastal and piedmont regions of Veracruz approximate more closely the southern

Chiapas environment (and indeed may have been even more important for the development of Early Preclassic civilization), but these regions remain less well understood and are more remote from the Classic Lowland Maya heartlands of interest here. An examination of early human occupation in the southern Chiapas and adjoining highland and isthmus regions is therefore the most feasible present avenue of comparison in our study of Maya origins models.

THE MAYAN AND MIXE-ZOQUEAN PROTOCOMMUNITY POSTULATES

One current historical-linguistic hypothesis projects an ancient Proto-Maya language or Mayan "protocommunity" in the highlands of Guatemala (McQuown 1971:69; Kaufman 1969, 1971). The present distribution of Mayan language groups is postulated by Vogt and others to be the result of a series of periodic migrations and subdivisions from this center; the beginning of this expansion is variously placed at approximately 2600 or 1800 B.C. (see summary by Vogt 1971:415–20, 431–32). The Cuchumatanes Mountains or Western Highlands of Guatemala were originally proposed as the theoretical homeland of this community (due to the concentration of a half-dozen Maya language groups there), but recent thought favors the Southeastern Highlands (Josserand 1975). According to this theory, based partly on new archaeological evidence from El Salvador (Sharer 1974), the Cuchumatanes region represents a "shatter" zone into which elements move from another core area. Regardless of which of these two ancestral Maya homeland theories is ultimately proved more correct, both postulate periodic Maya pressure against the eastern and northern frontiers of southern Chiapas, making varied inroads over time (Lee 1975).

What the original Proto-Maya expansionist model did not make very clear was which ethnic groups were being pushed around or accommodated by the Maya, assuming that the latter were not the first people to arrive in many affected regions (Vogt 1971:420). This would be a particularly sensitive problem on the borders of southern Chiapas, an area known to have been populated long before most of the postulated Maya or Proto-Maya expansion took place. It is also a problem in the western Maya margins in Tabasco and in the Yucatan

Peninsula. On the west and south, at least, the competing older populace must have been Mixe-Zoquean.

In 1964, McQuown did hypothesize that, "not before" 2600 B.C., "the Mayans . . . spoke a language whose comparatively close relatives (Totonacos and Mixeanos) were found in another part of Mesoamerica" (1971:69, translation mine). A *separation* of the Mayan and Zoquean tongues at least forty-seven centuries ago is cited elsewhere (Swadesh 1969:99–100). Glottochronology being a subjective discipline, I presume that these dates could be updated with no particular harm to historical or comparative linguistics, so that the difference between Mayan and Zoquean at 2000 or 1500 B.C. might be very small, if indeed such a distinction existed then (there is still no recognized occupation of the Lowland Maya area before or even during the Ocos horizon at about the latter date).

Kaufman's study of 1,000 cognate words in the various Mayan languages isolated a group of 11 loan words from Mixe-Zoque (more than from any other non-Mayan language). He noticed that the loan words are mainly found in Mayan languages spoken by people who are far from any Mixe-Zoque group, and who live between the Tzotzil and Jacalteco communities in central Chiapas and Guatemala. This led Kaufman to suggest that a greater extension of Mixe-Zoque occurred at an earlier time (1971:131). According to his list, the only Mixe-Zoque loan words appearing in Huastec of north central Veracruz were those for jicara, or the tree calabash (borrowed as well by the entire Mayan family), beehive (borrowed also by the Tzotzil, Tzeltal, Motocintleca, and Tojolabal of central Chiapas), and rabbit, from a Mixe dialect and borrowed by no other Mayan language (*koy* in Huastec and Mixe, *koya* in Mixe-Zoque). To this observation Kaufman appends the query (1971:134), "In the epoch of the Mixe-Zoquean invasions, which [one] separated the Huastec from the remainder of the Mayan family?"

Archaeologists and ethnologists have speculated for some time that the Zoquean linguistic group (Zoque-Mixe-Popoluca) represents a partial survival of the ancient Olmec people (see Vogt 1969:27 and partial résumé in Báez-Jorge 1973:57–63). Báez-Jorge (1973:60) draws attention to the presence of Zoquean dialects throughout the greater Olmec area, and concludes, "In any event, as Hasler (1958) has already pointed out, the archaeological Olmecs would be the Proto-Zoques, and their cultural heritage would be present not only among the Zoque-Mixe-Popolucas [of southern Veracruz] but among all groups pertaining to that trunk." The communities of the western branch of this trunk in Oaxaca, the Mixe, "form a solid block stretching east from just beyond Mitla to the trans-Tehuantepec railway" (Foster 1969:448). The Popoluca occupy the towns of Oluta, Sayula, and Texistepec near Acayucan, Veracruz. The Sierra Popoluca "live in about 25 settlements on the southern and western slopes of the 1500 m.-high extinct volcano San Martin Pajapan and to the southeast of Lake Catemaco" (Foster 1969:452).

At the conquest period the Mixe-Zoquean peoples occupied parts of western Tabasco, all of western Chiapas, part of southeastern Oaxaca, and the Pacific Coast of Chiapas into Guatemala (Foster 1969:453–54). Feldman (1973) cites curious evidence for Zoque presence at Teopisca in the central Chiapas Highlands in 1774. Foster (1969: 448) remarks that the Mixe, Zoque, and Popoluca once "almost certainly formed a solid geographical block centering on the Isthmus of Tehuantepec. . . ." According to Fernández de Miranda (1967:73), "The grouping of the Mixe, Zoque, Popolucas . . . Tapachulteca I and Aguateca II languages within the Zoquean family is recognized without discussion."

The Mixe-Zoque-Popoluca unity on the Gulf Coast appears to have been interrupted by a series of central Mexican and Maya incursions beginning in the Late Classic Period, while the Zapotecs in later times appear to have disintegrated the southern isthmus Zoquean complex (Báez-Jorge 1973:62; Foster 1969:452–56). The string of conquest-period Mixe-Zoquean towns along the Chiapas Pacific Coast no longer exists. The Indian population in that area was almost completely absorbed or decimated by the close of the eighteenth century except along the Guatemalan border (see Feldman 1973 for a summary of the confused postconquest linguistic situation).

The ancient and modern distribution of the Zoque in Chiapas is most fully discussed by Norman D. Thomas (1974).

I suggest the adoption of the model of a constant Zoquean occupation of southern (and western) Chiapas (and probably western Tabasco) from the earliest ceramic-using period, or even before, rather than the "Mixe-Zoque expansionist" model proposed by Kaufman for the Olmec (Vogt 1971:431). If we can chart some of the ebb and flow of peoples during the time of the Olmec horizons in Chiapas, it will be possible to formulate a trial "fit" of archaeological data into a

"Proto-Zoquean" community pattern of growth and decline against which, we hope, the early western Proto-Maya succession or expansion may be matched.

THE GEOGRAPHIC REGIONS OF SOUTHERN CHIAPAS

Southern Chiapas is distinguished by six major physiographic and climatic divisions (Lowe 1974). First is the narrow, rather dry Pacific coastal plain and estuary system. In the Tonala district on the northwest this region is characterized by frequent, high winds and poor, gravelly soils. In the Soconusco district on the southeast the plain is wider, with a more humid climate and fertile alluvial soils. Second is the narrow hilly piedmont section that parallels the coastal plain. This region is subject to the same orographically determined climatic regime (Lowe, Lee, and Martínez 1976) as the coastal plain; the portion in the southeastern Soconusco district is the most favored cacao-growing region of Chiapas, whereas the hill ranges on the northwest extend to the estuarine lagoons and provide little good agricultural land (but excellent defensive positions). Third is the wet Sierra Madre de Chiapas, which is lower and fairly open on the northwest and increases in height and complexity toward the volcanic peak of Tacana on the south. This entire region seems to be one of marginal potential. Fourth is the very wet tropical forest region of the Middle Grijalva River Basin at the confluence of its La Venta River major tributary, which is historically an important cacao-producing area. Fifth is the great dry interior basin or central depression of the Upper Grijalva River and its tributaries, where humid lands are restricted to the river floodplains. Sixth is the central highland valley and plateau region that crosses central Chiapas. These uplands of cool valleys and pine forests are often included with northern Chiapas, but the southeastern Comitan Valley is an important saddlelike bridge between north, south, and east (the Cuchumatanes Mountains region of Guatemala).

A system of lower wet hilly "highlands" which includes the Lacandon Forest and the Usumacinta River Zone makes up the remainder of northern Chiapas as a traditional part of the Maya Lowlands (Fig. 1.1).

The long, relatively open character of the rather low (440 to 750 meters above sea level) central depression and the long, narrow, mountain-and-sea-circumscribed nature of the Pacific coastal plain and piedmont zones crossing southern Chiapas are usually thought to have favored north-south travel through them (Navarrete 1973), with predictable diffusionary consequences (for a summary as of 1960 see Lowe and Mason 1965). The reality is that, except during periods of remarkable empire expansion, these corridors served as cultural traps. Precisely because they are narrow, they were easily blocked and divided. Particularly noteworthy is the cultural diversity, briefly described below, which characterized the opposite ends of these long, so-called natural avenues throughout most of their pre-Hispanic culture history.

MIXE-ZOQUE AREA CULTURAL HISTORY
AND MAYA RELATIONSHIPS

The Archaic Horizon Beginnings

Both the Proto-Maya and Proto-Zoque community models suppose that their eventual territories were lightly populated at the time of the recognized beginnings of pottery using and permanent village life. The all-important cultural shift to full-time sedentary villages is theorized to have begun between 2500 and 2000 B.C., but known instances in the greater Maya-Zoque area do not occur much before 1700 or 1500 B.C., before which time we have only a little information for family or community life in the Zoque area and none at all for the Maya area.

In southern Chiapas two provisionally defined preceramic hunting and gathering cultures seem to have survived into the fourth and third millennia B.C.. Within the central depression at Santa Marta Cave, the latest preceramic occupation is estimated to have ended at approximately 3500 B.C.; the overlying ceramic occupation of the Santa Marta Cotorra phase begins approximately at 1320 B.C. ± 200. This situation leads to the obvious conclusion that there must have been a "large temporal gap" in deposition at Santa Marta Cave (MacNeish and Peterson 1962:11).

In the Chantuto estuary region of the Pacific Coast of Chiapas, Voorhies (1974) has radiocarbon dated the aceramic shell mound components to between 3500 and 2000 B.C.. At one site a small Barra-phase ceramic sample (described below) was identified in the stratigraphically differentiated pottery-bearing deposit overlying the aceramic midden (Voorhies 1976).

Both of the Chiapas situations described above suggest a lack of continuity between the aceramic hunting and gathering occupations and the ceramic components of a later and presumably partly agricultural society (corn pollen was present in the Santa Marta deposit). Needless to say, a great deal more research needs to be done on the archaic horizons before conclusions can be drawn regarding the presence or absence of a transitional phase leading to the adoption of pottery and permanent village life.

The present state of research shows little or no human occupation of the Maya Lowland regions in preceramic times, but it is illogical to suppose a complete absence of humans in that large forest area before the arrival of recognizable pottery-using villagers. Nevertheless, in both the lowlands and highlands the archaic population densities must have been very light prior to and during the first ceramic horizons.

Barra, the First Ceramic Sphere

To the first carriers of ceramic vessels arriving almost four thousand years ago, the Pacific Coast littoral of Chiapas appeared much as it does now. Indeed, numerous huge preceramic shell middens scattered through some of the estuaries indicate little change from a period even several thousand years earlier. Only a series of old sandbars behind beaches very slowly moving seaward, and some sinking and filling, witness the passing of time.

Between the modern towns of Mapastepec and Huixtla numerous small rivers move swiftly down from the steep Sierra Madre slopes and quickly lose themselves in a maze of mangrove swamps and lagoons. Great swarms of migratory ducks rest here each fall and winter, and fish, molluscs, and alligators are plentiful. Moving through one of these lagoons, possibly on log or reed rafts, a small group of fishermen carrying a few clay pots came upon an island, actually a huge mound of shell, today called Tlacuachero, as big as a small city block and higher than a house.

A low place between humps on the old aceramic Tlacuachero midden provided shelter of a sort, and the small group of fisher-gatherers, perhaps a family, set up camp and possibly built a house or two. Apparently they did not stay long, for all we find are a few scattered sherds from very well-made small vessels shaped like kettle gourds or squashes, with pinched-up and grooved channels, and painted red; a small number are unpainted with only a few thin burnished lines. It is hard to understand the utility of these small, almost delicate, *tecomates* to these early island dwellers. And perhaps these people were out of place in this environment, for they appear to have soon moved away or returned to dry-land communities. The Tlacuachero midden then remained unoccupied until some fifteen hundred years later, when expanding Terminal Preclassic and Early Classic peoples found it a useful locale for renewed direct exploitation of the lagoon resources. These later occupants thoroughly mixed the lower portion of their own deep deposit of refuse with that of the much smaller first ceramic horizon (abstracted from Voorhies 1974, 1976).

Moving some thirty miles to the south through the heavy forests between the mountain foothills and the lagoons, or perhaps directly through the mangrove-lined estuarine canals behind the broad sandbars along the oceanfront, the Tlacuachero foraging group with their small clay *tecomates* would have been quite at home with their farming relatives, the Barra. The Barra culture has been identified at two inland lagoon-edge coastal plain sites near Mazatan (see Fig. 9.1). One is a presumed independent household at Altamira (Green and Lowe 1967:81–104). The other is a larger, more intensive occupation at Paso de la Amada, three miles to the north (Ceja 1974).

The Tlacuachero estuary dwellers would have found their inland Barra compatriots using a far more complex pottery inventory, with a variety of finishes and decorative techniques added to the ubiquitous small red or buff *tecomate* form; the squashlike neckless jars were complemented by various hemispherical, flat-bottomed, flaring-walled bowl, cup, and barrel forms (Lowe 1973b, 1975). The ceramic sophistication suggests that the Barra were part of a larger cultural group than that composed by our three small discovered sites, but the only other component so far certainly identified in the Zoquean or Mayan area is at Monte Alto, on the central Pacific coast of Guatemala. Elsewhere a few Barra-like grooved-red sherds are reported in the Tehuacan Valley Early Ajalpan phase (MacNeish, Peterson, and Flannery 1970:35, Fig. 26).

Complete eschewal of the early central Mexican ceramic types and forms by the Barra potters and their sharing of the early *tecomate* and

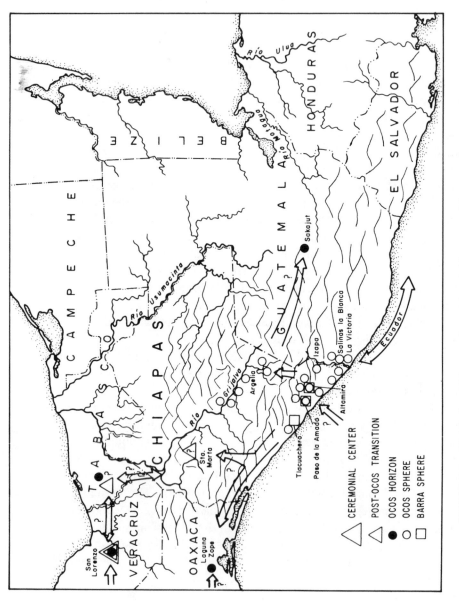

FIGURE 9.1. Distribution of known sites and probable ceremonial centers in eastern Mesoamerica, early Early Preclassic

dimpled flat-bottomed base (gourd-derived) tradition with northern South America continues to make a southern or some non-Mexican diffusion source the most logical explanation for the sudden appearance of the Barra people on the Pacific Coast of Chiapas (Lowe 1975). The possibility of long-distance diffusion affecting the greater isthmus region at about 1700 B.C. has obviously grave implications for the hypothesis of a Zoquean protocommunity developing in juxtaposition to a supposedly related but theoretically very old native Mayan protocommunity in the southeastern highlands of Guatemala and El Salvador, as discussed briefly above. Evidences of intermediate diffusion points and/or developmental stages (or proof of their absence) are, of course, needed before much more can be said intelligently about this problem.

The Precocious Ocos Horizon

The dynamism evident in the brief Barra occupations is reflected further in the almost immediate development and spread to far corners of the slightly evolved Ocos village society (see Fig. 9.1). These people, first identified by Michael Coe (1961) at La Victoria on the Guatemalan Pacific Coast near the Mexican border, have now been located on the basis of their very distinctive pottery at several other Guatemalan border sites (M. D. Coe and Flannery 1967), in the Highland Verapaz region as discussed further below, and at approximately twenty sites in southern Chiapas, including the earliest occupation at Izapa (Ekholm 1969).

A major Ocos-horizon affiliate of great importance is the Ojochi complex forming the original occupation at San Lorenzo, Veracruz, a site destined to become the outstanding Early Preclassic Olmec center some centuries later (M. D. Coe 1970). A few related sites have been tentatively identified from surface sherds in the not-far-distant Chontalpa district of central Tabasco (Sisson 1970). Isolated Ocos sherds have also been reported in the Valley of Tehuacan during the "middle" Ajalpan phase (MacNeish, Peterson, and Flannery 1970:40, 51–52, Fig. 27). One or two Ocos pottery types common at El Trapiche in central Veracruz (García Payón 1966:55–61; Ekholm 1969) suggest some unusually intense and selective interaction between this area and the Soconusco district of Chiapas involving vessels with rocker-stamped interiors. This general pattern is repeated during the Later Olmec horizon, when tripod grater bowls mysteriously become common at La Victoria, Guatemala, in a shared tradition known elsewhere only in the Huasteca of north-central Veracruz and in Ecuador. The significance of this pattern is not known.

The only good Ocos ceramic manifestations to come to light in the Valley of Oaxaca are "a few Ocos-like rocker-stamped sherds (probably from traded vessels)" thought to be from *tecomates,* and a "few sherds of polished Ocos Black" at the Tierras Largas sites (Flannery et al. 1970:96). Winter (1972:315) places these sherds and occasional "Ocos-like thickened and grooved rims" in the Late Tierras Largas phase. Significantly, there are relatively few *tecomates* and flat-based bowls in the Tierras Largas complex, and none of the typical necked water jars or hemispherical-bowl type constituting the earliest Oaxaca phase are recognized in the Ocos-horizon complexes in Chiapas (see Lowe 1971:220–22).

Kent Flannery (personal communication) thinks that an Ocos-like occupation at Laguna Zope near Juchitan, Oaxaca, investigated by Robert N. and Judith Zeitlin, represents a mixture of Ocos and Tierras Largas elements. My own impression of the earliest Laguna Zope material is that in general some of it looks like very late and provincial Ocos, which observation would seem to accord rather well with the 1350 to 1250 B.C. dates placed on Late Tierras Largas by Winter (1972:315).

The ceramic-complex proliferation at Ocos sites in Chiapas is bewildering and awesome, because most southern Mesoamerican vessel shapes are clearly anticipated at this very early date (with the exception of the missing necked water jar). In addition to form and decorative techniques already present in Barra, we now find a variety of effigy bowls, solid and hollow tripod bowl and *tecomate* supports in several shapes and sizes, vertical-walled plates, labial and medial flanges, complex silhouettes, grooved and gadrooned rims, heavy *tecomates,* and pedestal-base incense burners. Almost unique to the Pacific Coast sector are cord-impressed or shell-stamped animal effigies and both crude and finely modeled human figurines. The latter have prominent noses and mouths, narrow faces, tonsured hair, stub arms, and often exaggerated hips and thighs.

The gamut of sophisticated cord marking, textile impressions or fabric marking, and dentate and plain, often zoned, rocker stamping designs on the fine hard-fired Ocos *tecomates* can find near-parallels only in Archaic and Early Woodland and Hopewellian pottery of the United States or in Asia, according to M. D. Coe (1960; no up-to-date comparative study of the now much larger Ocos inventory from Chiapas has yet been undertaken). The great swollen and elongated tripod supports common at several Ocos sites at about 1500 B.C. (Ceja 1974) probably have no cognate forms anywhere in the New World.

The lack of Ocos contingents in either the western end of the central depression or in the western Pacific Coast plains and piedmont region is exceptional and cannot readily be explained as a result of insufficient study, since extensive surveys and excavations have been made in both areas. The somewhat Ocos-like but apparently post-Ocos "transitional" occupation of the Santa Marta Cave, as the first ceramic complex in that locale, suggests that other immediately post-Ocos and possibly Ocos deposits should appear in the western central depression. It seems quite probable that many Ocos occupations must have been very small and close to or upon alluvial lands or riverbanks which subsequently were washed away by the periodic flooding and undercutting typical of the Grijalva River and many of its tributaries. Considering the precarious and diminutive nature of the Ocos sites known on the Upper Grijalva upstream from the Angostura Canyon and along the San Miguel River tributary, in fact, there can be little doubt that erosion has taken its toll of this horizon in the principal Zoque area downstream.

The several Ocos sites identified on the uppermost Grijalva River and its tributaries are, on the other hand, in an area not known to have been occupied by the historic Zoque. The several Ocos complexes identified by Sedat and Sharer (1973) in the Highland Maya Verapaz region of Guatemala also appear to represent an enclave without present explanation. Both these regions, nevertheless, also have subsequent Early and Later Olmec–related ceramic complexes for which I suspect provisional Mixe-Zoque affiliation, so that an underlying Ocos presence is completely expectable in terms of an early Proto-Mixe-Zoque community model.

We know too little yet about the half-dozen Ocos sites on the Upper Grijalva and its tributaries to discuss community patterns in the semiarid eastern central depression of Chiapas at this time. The close similarity of content between ceramic complexes, however, leaves little doubt that they represent both fisher-gatherers and farmers moving northward and inland directly across the high Sierra Madre from sites in the coastal and piedmont regions of the Soconusco district.

Considering the preceding observations, founders of the small Ocos component reported in the Verapaz district of Guatemala noted above could easily have moved there from central Chiapas, passing through the narrow canyon and valley of the Selegua River (principal headwater of the Grijalva) eastward to the adjacent upper Negro River drainage (headwaters of the Usumacinta) and the Salama Valley. This postulate seems as probable or more so than the notion that the Ocos people had traveled southeast along the Pacific Coast and then northward across the southern and central Guatemalan Highlands without leaving any discovered evidence of their passage. Admittedly, movements could also have been in the reverse directions, if our knowledge of relative original regional occupation densities were to be modified seriously, which seems very unlikely.

An inland eastern expansion route from Chiapas for Ocos travelers would have taken them by Huehuetenango and the nearby ruin area of Chalchitan-Aguacatan (Woodbury and Trik 1953:Introduction), home of the claimed Zoquean dialect Aguateca II (Swadesh 1969:100). Further comment upon this situation is made below in the section on Early Classic affiliations, to which the reader is referred for additional evidence of the wide dispersal of Zoquean-area pottery at certain times.

With respect to beginning Early Preclassic social organization, the picture indicated is that of some true and persistent craft specialization, social stratification, and community planning. The sharply divided ceramic-form distribution pattern, coupled with community-type differences, strongly suggests widely separated social classes resulting from or related to varied subsistence activities (Lowe 1974, 1975; Ceja 1974). During the Ocos phase, vessel shapes at the small estuary-border or island sites are practically limited to well-made *tecomates* with finely polished rims, whereas a great variety of forms and finishes characterizes the coastal plain sites, as already described above. The pattern of *tecomate* dominance (up to 90 percent) at the estuary sites was rigidly maintained during the Ocos phase and even through the succeeding Olmec horizons (the Cuadros and Jocotal phases; see M. D. Coe and Flannery 1967; Pailles 1974).

One outstanding Ocos estuarine occupation (Los Álvarez) at the mouth of the Coatan River produced a mound four meters high composed only of superimposed habitation floors and hearths or ovens, with quantities of shell, a great many fine *tecomate* sherds, a very few bowl fragments, and at least one large clay human figurine (Ceja 1974). Contemporaneous with the Álvarez site and only a few miles inland, the Paso de la Amada zone includes a three-meter-high central mound surrounded by a quadrangular arrangement of very low platforms or house mounds covering several acres (Ceja 1974). This apparent evidence for very early social stratification and community planning is coupled with a suggestion of craft specialization among occupants of the different subsidiary mounds. Markedly varied obsidian-chip and clay-earspool-fragment loci frequencies and the prevalence of sophisticated pottery in a wide variety of forms combine with the community pattern to indicate the presence of ranking and of increasingly complex human interaction.

Despite the indications above that Paso de la Amada might be a small regional center, no true ceremonial center for the Ocos horizon has been recognized anywhere in Chiapas. This situation contrasts with that in Oaxaca, where for the at least partly contemporaneous Late Tierras Largas phase Flannery et al. (1970:49–51) see evidence for elite residences or temples presumably identifying ceremonial centers which date to approximately 1350 B.C.. Winter (1972:287, 293) specifies that the "Tierras Largas phase white plastered platforms possibly connected by patios" at San José Mogote and the "ten times larger" size of this site indicate that it "probably also served to some degree as a political and religious or ceremonial center." No parallel is known for the Pacific Coast of Chiapas until several centuries later, though this may be the result of inadequate excavations.

Certainly the Maya (and general Mesoamerican) penchant for plaza arrangement of large and small platforms was already evident in Chiapas during the Ocos phase. Regardless of this indication of progressive social complexity, the remarkable Ocos ceramic sophistication was to degenerate sharply in succeeding centuries; this retrogression was apparently the result of a shift in values, as an emphasis on and pride in pottery making passed to other activities when cultural norms and belief systems, perhaps, underwent a rapid evolution toward the Olmec civilization on the Gulf Coast. The post-Ocos "metropolitanization" of several centers in southern Veracruz and western Tabasco had immediate and far-reaching repercussions to the south.

The Proto-Olmec and Early Olmec Horizon Reformation

The Olmec heartland evolution or transition from the Ocos tradition (Ojochi phase at San Lorenzo) to the rather completely reformed Bajío- and Chicharras-phase "Proto-Olmec" tradition is described only by M. D. Coe (1970). On the south this reformation is usually seen as a rather abrupt change rather than as an evolution. The change is marked by the occupation of many new sites, a simplified and much more coarse ceramic inventory, and the first appearance of hollow figurines in a rather completely modified figurine complex.

The southern and eastern distribution of sites related to what I have termed here the Proto-Olmec (Bajío and Chicharras phases at San Lorenzo) and Early Olmec (San Lorenzo phases at San Lorenzo) horizons is indicated in Figure 9.2. The relative similarity of basic ceramic assemblages (rather than presence or absence of minor traits) leads me to assign sites in Chiapas and northern Central America either to closely Olmec-related spheres or to less completely related superspheres, and other sites simply to the respective time horizons.

It is to be noted that the Proto-Olmec development is poorly represented in Chiapas and undetected in northern Central America. Neither it nor the Early Olmec is clearly manifest anywhere in the Lowland Maya area except for a trace of the latter in the Lower Middle Usumacinta border region. Within Chiapas, the best Proto-Olmec transitional stages are seen, not surprisingly, at San Isidro in the Middle Grijalva Basin and upriver (beyond the Sumidero Canyon) along the lower valley of the Upper Grijalva River. The Cotorra ceramic complex, known best at Chiapa de Corzo (Pit 50 in Dixon 1959) and Santa Cruz (portions of the Burrero phase in Sanders 1961), appears to have developed rather directly out of the Proto-Olmec Chicharras complexes known at San Lorenzo and San Isidro. The Cotorra tradition was either relatively short-lived or else completely regional, inasmuch as the subsequent Early Olmec stylistic trajectory seems not to appear anywhere along the Upper Grijalva River; this in spite of its abundant presence in the western central depression and of

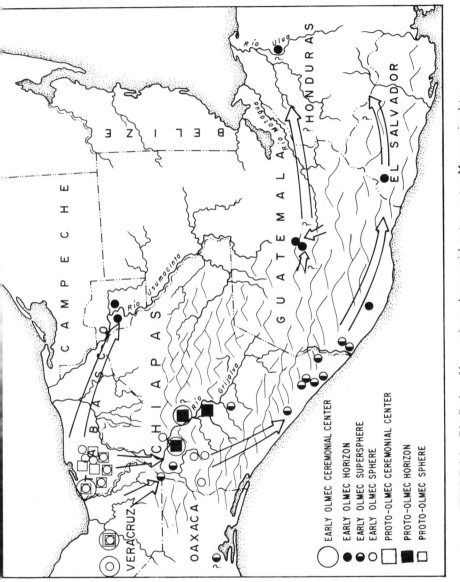

FIGURE 9.2. Distribution of known sites and ceremonial centers, eastern Mesoamerica, late Early Preclassic

EARLY OLMEC CEREMONIAL CENTER ◯

EARLY OLMEC HORIZON ●

EARLY OLMEC SUPERSPHERE ◑

EARLY OLMEC SPHERE ◯

PROTO-OLMEC CEREMONIAL CENTER ▢

PROTO-OLMEC HORIZON ■

PROTO-OLMEC SPHERE ▢

the abrupt Middle Preclassic Later Olmec stylistic resurgence all along the length of the river and its tributaries during the Dili phase, noted below.

On the Pacific Coast of Chiapas and Guatemala little evidence has been found for the obviously needed transitional stage or stages between the pre-Olmec Ocos and the much-altered Early Olmec Cuadros-phase occupations (Lowe, in Green and Lowe 1967:65; M. D. Coe and Flannery 1967:87). An even greater lack of evidence for transitional or developmental phases typifies the western end of the interior central depression, where remarkably similar Early Olmec ceramic complexes occur as the first occupations (Pac phase) at Vistahermosa (Treat 1974), Miramar, and Mirador (Agrinier 1973).

The most obvious possible explanation of the relatively numerous Early Olmec sites in southern Chiapas is that of a strong infusion of traits from the imposing Olmec centers in southern Veracruz and western Tabasco (which centers in turn may have been "fertilized" earlier by stimulation from advanced societies expanding on the north and west). With the influential San Lorenzo phase, powerful trade and other societal alliances or affiliations appear to have extended the standardized Olmec pottery complex across west central Chiapas directly to the Soconusco district of the Pacific Coast. A few related Cuadros-phase ceramic complexes appear farther south, on the Guatemala Coast and at Chalchuapa in El Salvador (Sharer 1974). Apparently Los Naranjos, Honduras, had a fair representation of this horizon style also, perhaps toward the close of its popularity (Baudez and Becquelin 1973:412, Figs. 67–77).

The preceding observations notwithstanding, the idea of an oversimplified Olmec "backwash" or expansion surging southward from the Olmec heartland (Lowe, in Green and Lowe 1967) should be treated with some caution. Increasing knowledge of the extent and complexity of the Ocos occupation across the Soconusco and elsewhere, combined with the potentialities of the huge and almost untapped "tell" at Aquiles Serdan, which has intensive occupations of both Ocos and Cuadros phases (Navarrete in preparation), makes the eventual discovery of many local survival, evolutionary, and transitional aspects of the Ocos and Cuadros cultures very probable.

Several traits shared by the Ocos and Cuadros cultures (including a continuing preference for the *tecomate* jar form and perpetuation of the fishing-gathering and farming subsistence-base diversification) may

214

indicate local evolution and cultural adaptations over time and space by the same people rather than cultural or ethnic displacement. It is true that on the Pacific Coast, at least, clay human figurine heads generally change from dominantly prognathous and narrow-faced during the Ocos phase to more orthagnathous and frequently broad-faced by full Olmec or Cuadros-Jocotal times, thus suggesting a change in racial or physical type. This possibility can better be judged after full publication of these stylistically subjective objects from both the Soconusco and San Lorenzo; it is perhaps equally probable that what is indicated is a mixed racial base and progressive modification of the most idealized physical type only.

Cultural disruption or discontinuity in Southern Chiapas in immediate post-Ocos times is indicated more definitely by the failure of recognized Early Olmec occupations to follow at the several known Ocos-horizon sites in the Upper Grijalva Valley beyond Padre Piedra. Both the ceramics and the Olmec monument at Padre Piedra on the Dorado River (Navarrete 1960:10–11, Fig. 11) are most closely related to the coastal Soconusco district across the Sierra Madre, rather than to any earlier occupation along the Grijalva River Valley.

The Pacific Coast Early Olmec–horizon sites of the Cuadros and Early Jocotal phases were linked most directly to sites rather far to the northwest along the Río de la Venta tributary of the Middle Grijalva River (Vistahermosa, Miramar-Mirador, and San Isidro), where Pac- and Cacahuano-phase ceramic-complex content similarity to the sharply stereotyped San Lorenzo pottery is very high (Agrinier 1973; Lee 1974:6–7; Lowe 1969).

There is little doubt that the sites in the western end of the central depression with nearly identical Early Olmec ceramic complexes were populated through or controlled by one or more major centers on the lower La Venta and Middle Grijalva rivers. These intermediate sites, such as San Isidro, would have governed movements either up and down the mighty but turbulent Grijalva River itself or, more probably in my opinion, over the low western mountain divide to the smaller Pedregal, Playas, or Nanchital rivers running toward the Gulf of Mexico closer to the isthmus (see Stirling 1957 and Drucker and Contreras 1953). The Nanchital River runs to below San Lorenzo on the Coatzacoalcos River within the isthmus proper, and the Pedregal and Playas run more directly to La Venta and the coastal lagoons via the Tonala River.

The very wet Middle Grijalva forest environment was both physically close to and ecologically rather similar to that of the Olmec heartland fifty or sixty miles farther north. As today on the northern slopes of Chiapas and the Tabasco plain, the cultivation of cacao may already have been important along the Middle Grijalva at this earlier time. The narrow but extremely fertile alluvial river terraces of the region (now flooded by the Mal Paso Dam) have long been an important cacao-producing territory in historic times, of exclusively Zoque affiliation and with strong archaeologic, ethnic, and economic ties to the western central depression (Lowe 1969; Lee 1974; N. Thomas 1974).

The Middle Grijalva region was highly strategic during the pre-Hispanic period of exclusively foot and river transport, since it connected the Pacific Coast and interior valleys of Chiapas with the Gulf Coast via the series of small rivers described above, which began just to the north and west of the confluence of the Grijalva and La Venta rivers. This Zoque-controlled cross-continent routing well to the east of the isthmus "neck" appears to explain the lack of obvious Olmec sites or monuments in the Pacific sector of the Isthmus of Tehuantepec. Parts of the latter region, arid, windy, and low in agricultural potential, undoubtedly were at times controlled by hostile non-Olmec (and non-Mixe-Zoquean) Zapotecan peoples before 1000 B.C.; this pattern still obtained as late as Teotihuacan times, judging from the apparent failure of that powerful society to manifest itself in the Tehuantepec region during its march to the south, elsewhere so evident.

Reviewing the pre-Olmec through Early Olmec occupational history of southern Chiapas and the northern isthmus regions, I believe the idea of a Proto-Mixe-Zoque Olmec-identified community that retained a cultural and ethnic unity through time appears acceptable. A comparison of Figure 9.1 and 9.2 shows the known geographical extent of the Ocos, Proto-Olmec, and Early Olmec ceramic horizons, between about 1500 and 1000 B.C. This distribution pattern closely resembles the historic spread of the Mixe-Zoque peoples (most of the mountainous Mixe region west of the central isthmus region remains an archaeological blank and is not considered in this discussion).

All of the Chiapas Early Preclassic site developments show a strong link to the Olmec "metropolitan capitals" at San Lorenzo, Veracruz, and La Venta, Tabasco, but none have the complexity or size of those famous centers. Chiapa de Corzo and San Isidro are postulated to have been Proto-Olmec and Early Olmec regional centers, respectively, owing to the presence of clay-floored platforms and boulder terracing, but neither site has produced stone sculpture of this date. Apparently the highly developed Gulf Coast centers commanded enough deference from a widespread populace to prevent the rise of important rival provincial centers on the south until Middle Preclassic times. The Chiapas situation may also simply reflect low population density, insufficient to spark local intensifying nucleation processes.

The small site components with stone engravings in Olmec style at Padre Piedra and Pijijiapan, assigned tentatively to Early Olmec dates (Navarrete 1974a), appear to represent shrines rather than true ceremonial centers. The stylistic faithfulness to Olmec norms (Ekholm Miller 1974) evident in these large carvings, in several smaller sculptures in the round in the Soconusco (Navarrete 1974a), and in numerous small artifacts and the Cuadros- and Pac-phase pottery strongly supports the idea of an early Mixe-Zoque Olmec community crossing western Chiapas to the southern Pacific Coast.

There is no ethnohistorical evidence for the Zoqueans in eastern Tabasco or northeastern Chiapas, but the occasional presence there of Olmec monumental carving and small artifacts (Lorenzo Ochoa: personal communication; Rands: Chap. 7 above; Ekholm-Miller 1973, 1974) and the close sharing of some ceramic types argues for at least early Middle Preclassic Mixe-Zoque occupation in the east, if the proposed Olmec Mixe-Zoque affiliation is legitimate. This original settlement of the southwestern Lowland Maya area by village dwellers would represent a normal and gradual expansion of the relatively late isthmian Olmec into all river valleys of the heavily forested and hilly Usumacinta drainage.

Beginning perhaps toward the close of the Early Olmec horizon, the eastward expansion of the isthmian Olmec appears to have achieved full force only during the "Later" and "Modified" Olmec horizons, described below. Regardless of the exact date of this development, it is obvious, I think, that it was already accompanied by firm religious beliefs and tribal alliances, including ancestral rites, all well established during the Early Preclassic Period; modifications under new ecological adaptations would occur, but no complete departure from underlying traditions. Indeed, the basic belief systems of the

Olmecs might have prevailed since archaic times and thus have been shared with any aceramic hunting-and-gathering groups native to the surrounding forest and mountain regions (see, for instance, Furst 1968; Lathrap 1972; Reichel-Dolmatoff 1975). Combinations of evolved and increasingly decadent core concepts with old conservative beliefs that had been maintained relatively unchanged on the periphery of the Olmec domains, even though brought about by socioeconomic pressures, might have resulted in feedback that created periods of religious revival and conflict. Such events may well be reflected in the archaeological record, however difficult their interpretation. We would expect many provincial Olmec manifestations to be simpler, relatively free of the complicating trade goods and intensified stylistic evolution typifying diffusion centers; they should also lack the upsetting ritual destruction and other disturbances caused by warfare and societal competition in advanced societies. This situation seems to be true of the Chiapas Early and Middle Preclassic Olmec-related areas.

The Later Olmec Horizon: Expansion and Diversification

Though little studied, an eastward expansion of the old Olmec-Zoquean populace across the base of the Yucatan Peninsula must have contributed substantially to the Preclassic Mayanization process in the lowland regions (Lowe in Green and Lowe 1967:73). As groups more and more remote from the isthmian heartland developed their own cultural and linguistic distinctions, surely they were aided toward further regional differentiation by some intermixture with peoples expanding northward from the southeastern highlands of Chiapas and northern Central America. The ethnic or linguistic affinity of most of the latter region is assumed to have been Highland Maya since very early times, but at the 1000 to 500 B.C. period with which we are here concerned the relative degree of difference between these southerners and the northern and western peoples is problematical. In the absence of other reliable guidelines, ceramic style distribution patterns should afford the best available clue to ethnic affiliations—or differences, at least.

Without adequate knowledge of the more complicated Tres Zapotes and San Lorenzo, Veracruz, and Tabascan Gulf Coast Middle Preclassic ceramic complexes, of admittedly Olmecan affinity, it is impossible to make completely reliable projections about the relative closeness of content between them and those of different adjacent regions. Published indications and firsthand observation of ceramic collections, nevertheless, lead me to the conclusion that relationships with the Los Tuxtlas and isthmian Gulf Coast regions are closer across Chiapas (and presumably Tabasco) than they are northward and westward at this time. In southern Chiapas, and somewhat less clearly elsewhere across the greater isthmus region, there is much evidence for the vigorous development of two sequent ceramic horizons, identified very generally as Later and Modified Olmec for lack of better labels (Lowe 1971). Their distribution is indicated in Figure 9.3. The "Later Olmec" designation used here is equivalent to what M. D. Coe has referred to (Chap. 8, above) as "the La Venta horizon."

The Later Olmec development and diffusion seem directly related to the beginning of Complex A construction at La Venta, Tabasco, and to what M. D. Coe (1970:28) has called an intrusive people at San Lorenzo, Veracruz, during the post–San Lorenzo–phase Nacaste phase. This group is characterized as "intrusive" because of local upsets at San Lorenzo and power shifts within the greater Central Olmec community, all of which indicates some intensified internal unevenness in that culture history (Green and Lowe 1967; M. D. Coe 1970; Lowe 1971, 1973a). The increasingly disparate directions of development are definitely but perhaps less drastically made evident in separate regions of Southern Chiapas by the appearance of the Late Jocotal–Conchas 1 and Dili ceramic spheres; the first occurs along the southern Pacific Coast and the second is found throughout the central depression. The two spheres are confused along the westernmost margins of both regions, intermingling there with strongly formalized Oaxacan Middle Formative traditions.

The Dili and Late Jocotal ceramic complexes both continue the basic pre-Olmec and Early Olmec primary dependence upon *tecomates* and flat-bottomed bowls and vases, although jars or ollas with necks usually vertical are present. There is also a persistence of Olmec-related incised and excised designs (mainly hooked and crescentic lines), but these are never very common. White-rimmed black bowls appear to continue in the Jocotal sphere but are not present in the Dili sphere, just as they were not in Cotorra. The Jocotal-related complex at the estuarine site of Pajón near Mapastepec (Pailles 1974) also lacks white-rimmed black in either its Early or Late aspects.

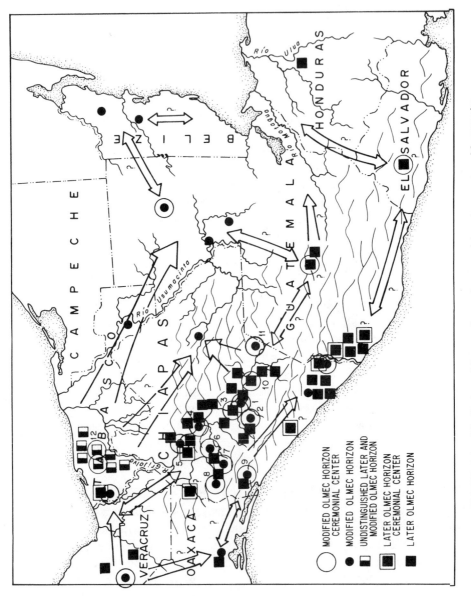

FIGURE 9.3. Distribution of known sites and ceremonial centers, eastern Mesoamerica, Middle Preclassic, with ties to Olmec centers

MODIFIED OLMEC HORIZON CEREMONIAL CENTER

MODIFIED OLMEC HORIZON

UNDISTINGUISHED LATER AND MODIFIED OLMEC HORIZON

LATER OLMEC HORIZON CEREMONIAL CENTER

LATER OLMEC HORIZON

It is of considerable interest to note that Pajón, furthermore, has little of the more complex Olmec incised design mode and lacks clay figurines (in the present sample at least), but that it does have high pyramidal platforms, and that it seems to be a community wholly dependent upon fishing and re-collection in spite of its abundant ceramics, all further indications of regional differentiation (Pailles 1976). The early Middle Formative propensity for pyramidal platform construction is noted elsewhere on the Pacific Coast, for example at Izapa in the Duende phase (Ekholm 1969), apparently at some Conchas 1 sites in Guatemala (M. D. Coe and Flannery 1967:89), and at Chalchuapa, El Salvador, during the Colos phase (Sharer 1974:169–70). The great pyramidal mound at La Venta on the Gulf Coast may in part be coeval (Lowe 1973a). Nothing similar appears in the central depression until the following horizon.

Although we lack evidence to fill out the picture, there seems nothing incongruent with the presently known Later Olmec development in the Gulf Coast centers and at Southern Chiapas and Pacific Coast Guatemalan villages (Fig. 9.3) and the perseverance of the postulated Zoquean-Olmec community. Some increasing internal diversification within the family may be reflected in the identifiable archaeological regions and subregions, however. The failure of the numerous Dili-sphere sites to produce a single identifiable ceremonial center in the well-populated Grijalva Basin is particularly puzzling; it may simply be due to a local reluctance to construct the type of large mound that would come to the archaeologist's attention, and to burial of less enduring civic-religious structures under the massive platforms common to the following horizon. Certainly it is notable that several sites having an intense Dili-phase occupation also show the bulk of their material remains gathered up in the mound fill of the ensuing Escalera-phase platforms.

Composition of the early Middle Preclassic Conchas 1 sphere within the Guatemalan segment of the Pacific Coast Soconusco district (M. D. Coe 1961) departs somewhat from the Later Olmec norms known in southern Chiapas. In general terms the ceramic form and decoration inventory, as well as the Conchas 1 figurine types, conform well to the Later Olmec standards as known at La Venta and Chiapa de Corzo (Lowe and Mason 1965; Lee 1969), but the presence of incised grater bowls suggestive of the Maya-related Veracruz Huasteca and of iridescent painting and striping suggestive of Ecuador's Chorrera phase

(M. D. Coe 1960) combine to give the Conchas sphere a significant distinction—both these traits are all but absent in Chiapas and the isthmus region. This peculiar situation on the southern and northern margins of the postulated Zoquean community provides much room for speculation and intensified investigation.

Owing to lack of familiarity with other Later Olmec–horizon pottery complexes of northern Central America, I can make no estimates regarding degree of content similarity there. It appears significant, however, as Sharer (1974:169) states, that "during the Middle Preclassic (ca. 900–500 B.C.) there is increasing evidence of Olmec cultural influence" at Chalchuapa, including specific Olmec motifs and figurines which "demonstrate apparent Olmec stylistic features."

Quite probably there was some slight movement of late Later Olmec–horizon ceramic traits into northern Yucatan and possibly the Pasión River region of the southwestern Peten. I think, however, that the bulk of the initial pottery-using population in these regions arrived somewhat later, for its ceramic complexes are well modified from the standardized Olmec norms and fit best with the following horizon.

The Modified Olmec Horizon: Nucleation and Pioneering Processes

The Modified Olmec horizon appears to reflect revolutionary times, with cultural changes that are all-important for the Lowland Maya area. These changes are seen at La Venta in the drastically modified pottery complex represented by the offerings in Complex A, Phases 3 and 4 (see chart in Lowe 1973a), and possibly in the destruction or mutilation of the Early Olmec stone monuments (this may have been done even earlier [Lowe 1973a]). In western and central Chiapas a series of formal pyramidal platform-and-plaza regional centers suddenly emerged, most of them overlying Dili-sphere occupations (Fig. 9.3). Many shallow Dili sites along the Upper Grijalva were abandoned and have no subsequent occupation, or none for another millennium. Along the southern Pacific Coast, numerous Jocotal-sphere sites were also abandoned, and others, such as Izapa, experienced a rapid expansion.

During this horizon it appears that the progressive, platform-building Gulf Coast, Middle Grijalva, and southern Pacific Coast

222

peoples dominated the related Dili sphere along the Grijalva River and its tributaries, drastically modifying the social organization and local ceramic style to conform to isthmus-wide patterns of the time. This process included the rapid building of a chain of regional, presumably administrative, centers, the first known for this area. That this activity was spearheaded from a now-modified Olmec segment in the old Gulf Coast heartland is indicated by both architectural and ceramic evidence. I am referring here to what M. D. Coe (Chap. 8, above) has called "the epi-Olmec remains of sites like Tres Zapotes."

The highly polished red-to-orange-brown ceramic ware variously defined as Cloudy Usulutan, Blotchy Resist, Polished Waxy Orange, or the Nicapa Slipped (Orange-resist) Group (at Chiapa de Corzo) is particularly abundant in the mid levels of recent deep stratigraphic trenches dug by E. G. Squier below the volcanic ash stratum at Tres Zapotes in the Los Tuxtlas region of southern Veracruz (collections in the Museum of Archaeology, Jalapa, Veracruz). This same ware is the most distinctive hallmark of the Equipac phase at San Isidro in the Middle Grijalva region (Lee 1974:9–10), and of the Escalera sphere along the Upper Grijalva River (Lowe and Mason 1965); it is also a prominent element in the Quequepac sphere of southwestern Chiapas encompassing Ocozocoautla, Mirador, Vistahermosa, and Tzutzuculi (New World Archaeological Foundation collections, Tuxtla Gutiérrez) during late Middle Preclassic times. We have recently identified a strong deposit of this ware in a coastal Soconusco village site near Altamira, and it is a prime component of the Post–Duende Escalón phase at Izapa. I think this ware is highly similar or identical to the "first appearance of Usulutan decorated pottery" during the Kal phase at Chalchuapa (Sharer and Gifford 1970:445); this is the "Puxtla Ceramic Group identified at Chalchuapa and Las Charcas Phase at Kaminaljuyu" also found at Sakajut in the Alta Verapaz (Sedat and Sharer 1972:26).

Distinctive, though highly eroded, polished-orange-ware flaring-wall and composite-silhouette bowl sherds are common at La Venta. Both they and some well-preserved refuse sherds that Rands recovered from La Trinidad on the Usumacinta River, a Middle Preclassic collection of polished brown-and-orange ware, would fit quite comfortably within the general Chiapa de Corzo Nicapa Group category (personal observation). Almost certainly some of Sisson's (1970:45) Chontalpa site collections of the Puente phase (late aspect) in Western Tabasco will also include this type and conform to the Modified Olmec horizon as herein defined.

In my opinion, the distribution pattern of the great "Cloudy-resist orange" ceramic tradition is one of the best arguments for the continuity and expansion of the Zoquean community through the Middle Preclassic Period. The apparently close relationship of this ware to some pottery in the earliest Lowland Maya ceramic complexes is a subject for important continuing research. Other widespread cultural elements of this period fortify the Chiapas Modified Olmec-Zoquean region affiliation.

Low-relief Olmec carvings, each approximately one meter square, one of a stylized serpent and the other of a werejaguar face, stood on each side of the stairway of a Modified Olmec–horizon platform at Tzutzuculi, on the outskirts of Tonala on the northwestern Pacific Coast of Chiapas (McDonald 1974a). At San Isidro in the Middle Grijalva Basin, a series of grouped, axis-aligned jade ax and pseudocelt mosaics and earplug offerings are also assignable to this horizon. Probably it is significant that none of the San Isidro celts bear incised designs. The horizon pottery is also singularly lacking in decoration other than the strikingly attractive highly polished surfaces and rare incising or grooving and occasional resist designs. Forms favored are simple small *tecomates,* open flat-bottomed bowls or plates, "cuspidors" of composite silhouette, and occasionally effigy jars in a black-and-white smudged ware. Fine paste black or white ceramic imports from the Gulf Coast are included in most of the far southern complexes.

In contrast to the almost puritan simplicity of the Escalera-ceramic-sphere content (relieved mainly by the occasional effigy vessels), the architectural composition of the accompanying Modified Olmec ceremonial centers appears to be extremely elaborate, as Figure 9.4 indicates. Even here, however, all sites of the period follow a rather closely ordered and unimaginative central layout. As demonstrated by McDonald (1974b), the several Quequepac- and Escalera-sphere sites which fortunately remain intact and uncovered by later occupations demonstrate a singular arrangement. The emphasis is upon a central axis crossing a pyramidal mound and a very long slender mound, with one or more broad flat platforms in close association. All of the numbered sites shown in Figure 9.4 have this stereotyped general layout, which McDonald (1974b) attributes to a close relationship with Group A of La Venta, Tabasco.

224

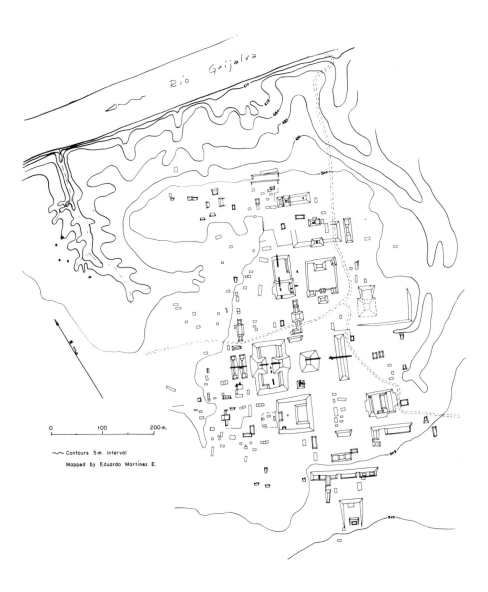

FIGURE 9.4.   Schematic topographic map of the Middle Preclassic ceremonial center of Finca
Acapulco, Upper Grijalva River, Chiapas

Finca Acapulco (Fig. 9.4; site 1 in Fig. 9.3) demonstrates the optimum formal arrangement, with the addition of a ball court. Two other Escalera-sphere sites with ball courts are Vergel and San Mateo, Sites 2 and 3 in Figure 9.3. These ball courts are the oldest so far identified in Mesoamerica (the Palangana-phase court at San Lorenzo may be nearly coeval [M. D. Coe 1970]). It is significant that these impressive sites were abandoned at the close, we think, of the Escalera phase, and it is unfortunate that all three are now covered by the waters of the huge Angostura Dam reservoir (Gussinyer 1971, 1972).

The Finca Acapulco–Vergel–San Mateo trio of regional centers is located upon high ground, with only Vergel being near any floodplain land (at the Grijalva River crossing to Chachi).

Just as in later times, the most important regional centers of the Modified Olmec horizon in southern Chiapas occupied strategic points. Each center controlled specific resources (limestone milpa lands, *nanche* forests and savannahs, gravel deposits for stone tool manufacture, and the like), critical river fords, or headwater river access routes. Sites 4, 5, 6, 7, 10, and 11 in Figure 9.3 all became major centers in later eras. It is quite probable that the Late Olmec–derived settlement pattern so visible at the abandoned zones in the semiarid central depression of Chiapas is not unique; the steady but more obscure expansion of other and perhaps related peoples into the Lowland Maya riverine and water-hole forest regions at about this same time (Lowe 1971; Puleston and Puleston 1971), as discussed above, may have had similar advanced organization in some regions. "Pioneer Maya" communities are located at right center in Figure 9.3 and are described elsewhere in this volume.

It is apparent that some of the Middle Preclassic regional centers in southern Chiapas represent unprecedented concentrations of increasingly intensive but still experimental corn farmers; in some instances such concentration must have involved expansion in new or relatively unproven agricultural lands (Lowe 1974). That all of this activity was under the direction of an established elite seems unquestionable in view of the associated formal social organization. What were the consequences of this rapid intensification? Destructive competition seems to be the answer, both between groups of men and between man and his environment. At some centers the local ecological situation seems to have become untenable after a rather short period, whereas at others a better natural and/or social environment with greater adaptation and survival possibilities facilitated perseverance and growth of the established community over many centuries. Equal or greater hardships and competition may have kept the attainment level low for many of the pioneering groups establishing themselves in the Maya Lowlands at this time (see Chap. 15, below, and the remarks on the Xe, Eb, and related cultures in other chapters).

Within the greater isthmian area it is noteworthy that both the community pattern and the ceramic-horizon content appear to conform well to the limits of the postulated Zoquean-Olmec community throughout the Middle Preclassic. We can see no clear Lowland Maya inroads back into Chiapas during this period, and little or no diffusion from the Southern Highlands either. The sophisticated regional centers are distributed across southern Chiapas right up to and beyond the Guatemala frontier both on the Pacific Coast and in the central depression; the provisional Sakajut evidence (Sharer 1974) seems to take the Modified Olmec–horizon ceramic style past the Cuchuma-tanes as far east as the Alta Verapaz, on the southern margin of the northward slopes into the Maya Lowlands. Additional studies must determine where the closest ceramic affinities really lie for these intermediate and marginal regions.

A particularly intriguing situation is that of the Las Charcas ceramic complex, which apparently develops independently in the Southern Highlands from central Guatemala southward to El Salvador. Claimed by Wetherington (1974:183) to have "only scattered representations" in the Valley of Guatemala, dating to between 800 and 500 B.C., most of the Las Charcas pottery is singularly distinct from the contem-poraneous Modified Olmec–horizon ceramics. The latter appear to have intermingled with Las Charcas at Chalchuapa, El Salvador, for example, but did not do so at any site so far known much to the west of the Valley of Guatemala and certainly at none in the central depression of Chiapas.

If Southern Chiapas during the late Middle Preclassic Period represented a strong cultural unity, resisting southern influences and contributing to or passing along a relatively uniform Olmec-derived cultural tradition, this situation was to change dramatically during the subsequent Late Preclassic Period. Widely separated northern and eastern Preclassic Maya neighbors achieved ever-greater local importance with the progress of the Late Preclassic and began increasingly to exert outward stylistic influences in apparent response to demographic pressure and perhaps to growing socioreligious forces as well.

The Late Preclassic Factions

The Late Preclassic developmental processes in southern Chiapas are of the greatest importance for comparative studies with the adjacent lowlands on the north and northeast, for it was at this time that the inhabitants of the latter area fully acquired the characteristics that establish them as Lowland Maya (W. R. Coe 1965b). It is also the time in which the southern Chiapas societies hardened their regional characteristics into a series of local cultures to be distinct from one another almost forever after.

With the agricultural conquest and control of the more humid and environmentally more uniform northeastern lowland forest regions by the Preclassic Lowland Maya, most of southern Chiapas apparently became an area of relatively inferior ecological potential; the exception was the humid Soconusco district, central locale of the Izapan civilization (M. D. Coe 1967). In the drier interior, the varied topography and vegetation patterns coupled with the exposed position and condition of the now much-denuded valley floors all seem to have contributed to an intensified regionalism as populations continued to expand during the Late Preclassic. This fracturing of the Zoquean core area apparently permitted it to compete only at a disadvantage with the Lowland Maya, who were undergoing a more continuous integrating process, to all appearances.

Figure 9.5 indicates the principal ceramic spheres in southern Chiapas during the fully developed Late Preclassic Period at approximately 100 B.C. (ignoring some transitional regional stages). These spheres, defined by the dominant local ware, also are associated with different architectural styles, which partly derive from local differences in available building materials, but also reflect the building traditions of neighboring culture areas.

Cut-stone architectural platforms show a steady process of development in the western central depression of Chiapas from about 400 or 500 B.C. (McDonald 1974a) to about A.D. 250. By A.D. 1, Chiapa de Corzo, for instance, had complex stone platforms and

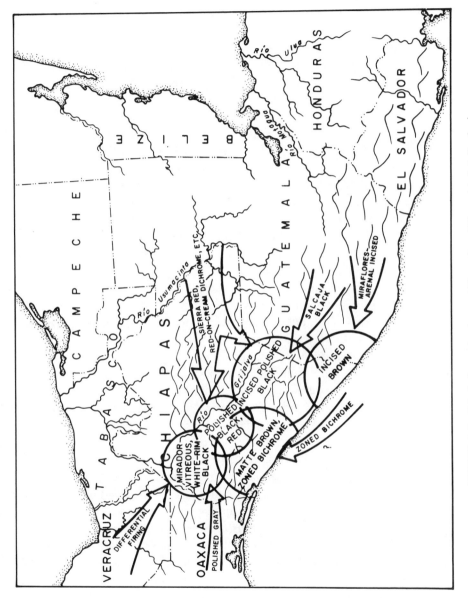

FIGURE 9.5. Principal ceramic spheres within southern Chiapas, late Late Preclassic

superstructures (Lowe and Agrinier 1960; Lowe 1962; Agrinier 1975) technologically equal (and stylistically quite similar) to the best architecture known at the time in the lowlands, and it is difficult to judge who was influencing whom. With respect to ceramics, however, a definitely elite and unmistakably Late Preclassic Lowland Maya pottery at Chiapa de Corzo and surrounding zones was coming from somewhere to the northeast. This Chicanel-horizon pottery was always an elite household- or palace-complex constituent, and a minor element rarely accepted in the abundant burial offerings of the period, but it did provide a temporary Maya gloss to the conservative Preclassic Zoque base culture. The interloping Lowland Maya ceramic types (and perhaps a new and short-lived sculptural tradition of undetermined derivation) were cut off suddenly at the close of the Guanacaste phase at Chiapa de Corzo. This event accompanied an almost exclusive elaboration of (or return to) the longstanding Zoquean societal norms emphasizing relationships to the isthmus and less so to the Southern Highlands during the Terminal Preclassic.

The Protoclassic Period all across western Chiapas saw some renewal of Lowland Maya imports in the form of Holmul I or Floral Park–like pottery, but this was amid a steadily more conservative, very non-Maya local tradition overwhelmingly favoring black smudged pottery. Significantly, the Lowland Maya imports were scarcely extended to the south and east in Chiapas during this period. The expanding Western Highland Guatemalans and the Southeastern Highland Maya, to judge from ceramics, had unprecedented influence on the eastern end of the Grijalva Trench of the central depression and on the Pacific Coast, respectively, during the Terminal Preclassic or Protoclassic periods. Neither Chiapas region ever again shared many ceramic styles with the western central depression or isthmian areas.

Unlike the stylistically integrated Late Preclassic Lowland Maya, the Zoquean population which apparently remained relatively intact in the western and coastal regions of Southern Chiapas allowed itself to become increasingly divided culturally during the Late Preclassic and Protoclassic periods, if we may judge from ceramic patterns. As indicated above, the Zoquean factionalization seems to have been brought about by their geographical exposure to expanding cultures on the north and south and to a diverse and usually inferior local environmental base. The Zoqueans of these periods failed to develop a single territory-wide great cultural tradition that we can detect, except for the western black pottery style noted above. Izapa, of course, within its moist Soconusco piedmont habitat, did create or participate in a great art and religious tradition (Quirarte:Chap. 10 below; Norman 1973), but this scarcely made itself felt in the central depression and did not survive into the Classic Period.

It is of considerable culture-historical importance that during the late Middle Preclassic and Late Preclassic apogee of Izapa, an even larger ceremonial center arose and fell on the opposite end of the Chiapas Pacific Coast, and did so without known monumental stone sculpture! Amid what we have described as the relatively poor environment of the Tonala district, the tremendous site of La Perseverancia (N. Thomas 1974: Fig. 45) became the greatest center in Chiapas for the sheer bulk and extent of its earthen mound groups. Great granite boulders face the bases of major mounds, establishing an architectural tradition extending from Tiltepec, north of Tonala, southward to Pijijiapan.

Despite its impressive statistics, and even after examination of a great riverbank cut and the excavation and analysis of a series of test pits, there is no evidence of any occupation at Perseverancia later than the Late Preclassic Period (McElrath 1973). The site participated in the conservative form modes of the Late Preclassic ceramic horizon with a lackluster brownware tradition as well as with a unique red-on-brown bichrome with incised and punctate zones that is so far well identified elsewhere only at Ocozocoautla in the central depression. Does the lack of sculpture indicate that Perseverancia was a civic center only, eschewing ritual ceremony? I doubt it, although nothing in the miserable archaeological evidence at hand sheds any light on the matter (figurines and obsidian are absent, and the site has miraculously escaped the pot-hunting which might be informative, if regrettable). There can be no doubt that Perseverancia completely controlled all movement up and down the Pacific Coast, stretching as it does from the piedmont foothills to the estuarine lagoons.

If Perseverancia was a commercial and military citadel, it had its opposite number at smaller Tiltepec, some thirty kilometers farther west (Navarrete 1959). Unlike anything at contemporaneous Perseverancia, many of the boulder platform abutments at Tiltepec were carved in what has been considered a pseudo-Olmec style, emphasizing plump human figures, some within open animal or serpent mouths, accompanied by a sort of Ahau glyph (cf. the unique example of the style from Tzutzuculi, Tonala [Navarrete 1959: Fig

8*d*]). Rude jaguar and heron figures also appear; a score of the sculptures have been removed to the museums in Tonala and Tuxtla Gutiérrez.

Not insignificantly for the postulated Mixe-Zoque community, the stone monument with the closest similarity to the Tiltepec sculpture is that reported by Stirling at San Miguel, Tabasco (1957: 225, Pl. 50). San Miguel has been described as "almost the southernmost of the sites that received a direct influence from La Venta" (Piña Chan and Navarrete 1967: 11).

The Divided Protoclassic and Early Classic Affiliations

Chinkultic, a site located in the Comitan Valley near the Montebello Lakes on the Chiapas-Guatemala border, represents an area of particular confrontation with the Northern Lowlands. Here Highland and Lowland Maya Late Preclassic, Protoclassic, and Early Classic pottery styles (Ball 1975) join with several destroyed Izapan-style sculptures to give evidence of heightened cultural interaction and strife (Agrinier 1969: 23, Figs. 26–28). Mamom- and Chicanel-horizon sherds appear at several Chiapas sites farther to the north, but there has been no program to enlighten us about the details of cultural succession in this critical area (but see Ekholm-Miller 1973; S. M. Ekholm n.d.).

In the adjacent central depression, the multipartite division indicated in Figure 9.5 for Late Preclassic times was modified drastically beginning with the Terminal Preclassic and Protoclassic periods. All of the depression area west of the Angostura Canyon and the entire Middle Grijalva region were unified in a cultural horizon characterized by black smudged pottery and platform-court room complexes often having pillared entryways. The spotty Middle Classic occupation in these regions also adapted the smudged black ware to Teotihuacan-horizon stylistic norms (Agrinier 1974, 1975).

Eastward or upriver from the Angostura Canyon, the smudged-black-ware style is absent. At Santa Rosa, the transition from Protoclassic to Early Classic has not been satisfactorily demonstrated by either Brockington (1967: 68–70) or Delgado (1965:80–81), but both show clearly the highly localized character of the site and its region during both periods, emphasizing the peculiar local efflorescence experienced during the Protoclassic. Brockington stresses the insular nature of the region, characterizing it as "provincial, in-grown, or xenophobic," and speculates that it had acquired a Highland Maya alignment following the Late Preclassic beginnings in that direction.

In relating the incised black and brown pottery of the eastern central depression most closely to the western Highland Maya, Brockington (1967:69) cites Peterson's original suggestion (1963:11) that the contemporaneous smudged and often white-rimmed black pottery of the western central depression should be related, on the other hand, to the "Mixeño (Zoque, Mixe, Popoluca linguistic subdivisions) family of languages. . . " (The smudged-ware distribution pattern conforms particularly closely to the historic lands of the Zoque tribes; see Agrinier 1974, 1975). In this regard, it is of much more than casual concern that the Early Classic tomb and burials at Zaculeu, Huehuetenango (Woodbury and Trik 1953), contained large numbers of smudged black pots with forms and incised decorations identical to those of the Early and Middle Classic periods in the Zoque area of western Chiapas (Agrinier 1974). This Zoque-area Early Classic component in Guatemala is as much an unexpected enclave in the Highland Mam Maya region as is the disputed Zoquean Aguacateca II language reported there in the early 1920s (Swadesh 1969: 100).

Within Chiapas, the eastern central depression is made to appear considerably less insular by the recent discovery that its typical incised black-brown polished-slip pottery (in several variations indicating both Terminal Preclassic or Protoclassic and Early Classic occupations) occurs abundantly together with contemporaneous Izapan coarse-incised jar types at Pacific Coast estuarine midden sites below Escuintla (Voorhies 1976). The types are not found at Izapa except very sporadically. The polished incised black type is, however, also found in some undetermined quantity in the Quetzaltenango region of western Guatemala (see Rands and Smith 1965: Fig. 13*e*). This suggests an extension of a Mayan group (for those who can accept a ceramic/linguistic equivalency) from the eastern central depression across the Sierra Madre onto the coastal plain about the beginning of our era. This might also be equivalent to, or a forerunner of, the Cabil or Chicomuceltec wedge still existing at about 1770 according to Feldman (1973:Fig. 3).

Considering the Huastec affiliations of Cabil, I am reminded of the Huasteca ceramic form (tripod grater bowls) unique to the

Guatemala Pacific Coast sector of the Soconusco (and slightly present at Izapa) during the Conchas or Middle Preclassic Period, and am caused to wonder if the Cabil-Huastec relationship does not go back to, and much beyond, the late incised-black intrusion. Regardless of this problem, the Maya wedge west of the Izapan domain is a historic fact. It left Mixe-Zoque as enclaves at Tapachula, Ayutla, and, according to Feldman (1973), possibly at Tuxtla Chico in the Izapa zone. Feldman bases this reconstruction on his study of an extinct Maa language which appears in the record in 1565 and 1735. This language appears to Feldman to be Zoquean. Navarrete (1969b) cites a Quiche surname list for Tuxtla earlier in the sixteenth century. A slightly preconquest Quiche foray from Guatemala into the Chiapas Soconusco, where Zoquean groups were conquered at Ayutla and Tapachula, is described by M. D. Coe (1961:Appendix). After the expedition the Quiche are described as returning to their homeland. It may be relevant to note also that the aforementioned Cabil wedge of the 1700s is today occupied at Tuzantan near Huixtla by the related Mam Maya (the Chicomuceltec language having been extinct for some time), the only indigenous group still extending from the Sierra Madre into the piedmont (Medina Hernández 1973).

During the Protoclassic Izapan Period, the Soconusco district witnessed one of the greatest platform-building efforts in Mesoamerica, but stone carving did not accompany this development. The increased presence of southern or local regional pottery styles at Izapa following the Late Preclassic Period (Lee 1973) suggests that this site and its hinterlands were increasingly aligned with the southern Highland Maya or other non-Zoquean northern Central American groups. The distinctive Izapan Protoclassic and Early Classic coarse-incised pottery style has not been found in the Tonala district (that is, north of Mapastepec).

We have little knowledge of the Terminal Preclassic or Protoclassic Period in the Tonala district of Chiapas unless indeed Tiltepec (Navarrete 1959) and Perseverancia entered that threshold with conservative local pottery styles little affected by the expected horizon markers, as is thought to be true of Santa Rosa in the interior; both the former sites were certainly abandoned before the Classic Period. Quite possibly the Tonala district was something of a no-man's-land for a time. Such evidence as we do have (smudged black-and-white ware at Iglesia Vieja above Tonala and offerings at San Diego near Pijijiapan) indicates that the Tonala district was fully within the western Chiapas and isthmian Mixe-Zoquean style tradition during the Protoclassic and beginning Early Classic periods (and was still Mixean during the conquest period).

By the Middle Classic Period both military and religious ceremonial functions in the Tonala district were concentrated at the hillside site of Horcones, which was rather completely dominated by Teotihuacan-style sculptural art and ceramic forms (Navarrete 1974b). Sculpture at this site, located along Cerro Bernal midway between Perseverancia and Tiltepec, included both plain stelae and altars and elaborately carved monoliths. Like Perseverancia before it, Horcones also blocked all travel along the Pacific Coast and must be considered a key defensive center.

Sculptural Evidence of Competitive Maya-Zoque Interaction

In remembered or legendary times, only the Chiapanec superwarrior group made important immigrations into southern Chiapas, apparently moving inland from the Pacific Coast through an unstable frontier region between Zoquean and Mayan speakers in the Frailesca region of the southern central Depression (Navarrete 1960). These Otomanguean intruders conquered the best river bottomlands at Chiapa de Corzo and vicinity, and enslaved Zoque groups in the vicinity for their farming, fishing, and carrying needs (Díaz del Castillo 1955:482–88).

The submission of the Zoques to the Chiapanec intruders, which apparently lasted hundreds of years, and their subsequent, apparently similar submission to the Spaniards, when compared to the fighting reception and rebellions offered by the Chiapanec and Highland Maya, may tell us something specific about the failure of a powerful local civilization to arise or endure in western Chiapas. Determining the processes leading to traditions of group submission or aggression is a hard or impossible task, but within Tabasco and Chiapas at least, I think that we are dealing with a long Zoque-Maya interaction pattern beginning back at the time of the gradual Olmec demise and the steady rise of the Preclassic and Classic Lowland Maya civilizations. This is perhaps best shown by the stone sculpture surviving across the greater isthmus area. The struggle appears to be represented most clearly in the Southern Highlands; or perhaps we should say that it is better represented—or merely preserved for the record—in the south simply because of the lesser amount of obscuring Classic overburden there. Regardless of the preservation factor, we cannot escape the fact that the earliest known monumental sculptural tradition is that of southern Veracruz and western Tabasco. Despite the precocity in the latter regions of sculpture in the round and an evolution toward relief carving there (M. D. Coe 1968) including a few early glyphs and dates, the earliest calendrical date and the only long engraved hieroglyphic texts on monuments in a Maya style appear in southern Chiapas and the Southern Highlands, respectively.

The problem of the Southern Highlands is compounded both by the Late Preclassic competition which must have existed there from the ever more sophisticated Lowland Maya groups on the north and by that which must always have been felt from the older civilized centers on the west in Chiapas and the isthmus region. The Late Preclassic Highland Maya tribes, to the degree that they were now completely non-Zoquean, probably suffered some ethnic value-system differentiation vis-à-vis the Lowland Maya groups; one might even inject a culture-shock theory related to the violent destruction of Formative Kaminaljuyu, for instance. I believe that the general rarity of carved hieroglyphs in southern Chiapas and central and southern Guatemala and El Salvador is a deliberate rejection of cultic and ethnic values foreign to the old basic, underlying Zoquean (and proto-Mayan?) character.

Despite having the earliest known dated monuments and the advanced Izapan sculptural style (summarized in Fig. 9.6), the Zoquean community was not long able to stomach or support the supreme maximization of cultic symbolism represented by Maya carved art and stylized calendrics, and they soon rejected any appearance of it almost everywhere. (A similar argument is made by Graham [1971: 264].)

The violent breaking up and burying of carved stone monuments at Chiapa de Corzo, Chinkultic, and various sites in Guatemala and El Salvador, presumably during the Late or Terminal Preclassic Period, is ample evidence of a cultic or religious overthrow (Fig. 9.6).

Of several score Preclassic monuments known at Kaminaljuyu, not one was left standing; Stela 10, with its outstanding Maya-like glyph columns, was smashed and buried beneath a Late or Terminal Preclassic floor (Miles 1965). The glyph-bearing stela at Chalchuapa and related monuments were battered and left to be "sealed" by a volcanic ash fall some time between A.D. 1 and A.D. 200 (Sharer 1974: 171–72). Does this imply that these early glyphic-monument-related stone sculpture components were everywhere destroyed deliberately when widespread seismic and volcanic activity (recall that Tres Zapotes shows volcanism more or less contemporaneous with that for the Veracruz Los Tuxtlas region) threatened, and in some cases achieved, physical destruction of the communities? Were the monuments then destroyed to appease the gods?

It is very important to note that the stone monuments at Izapa were never overthrown, or at least not broken and battered. (It is theoretically possible that they could have been overthrown and reset after the Terminal Preclassic period of volcanism.) They remain essentially intact and *in situ* to this very day (a very few were smashed and incorporated in Classic Period construction fill). I believe that the often-overlooked miracle of Izapa's monument preservation is due precisely to the fact that Izapa sculpture never adopted Maya-like hieroglyphs or the unknown regime of religious cult concepts related thereto. Izapa's sculptured themes were not exotic; they seem to have been part and parcel of the old Zoquean protocommunity value system, created by the eastern Mixe-Zoquean artisans and maintained by Mixe-Zoqueans. The Izapan descendants, however modified, remained in sufficient control of the Izapa region to maintain respect for their old monuments in spite of a series of outward cultural changes over the successive centuries to the present.

My reasoning about monument-destruction patterns as indicated by Figure 9.6 leads to two different but equally potent comparative possibilities related to the origin and development of the Lowland Maya civilization. The first possible explanation is that the hieroglyphic cult was developed in the lowlands (where chance or a policy of recarving monuments has prevented discovery of early carved examples) in general opposition to the prevailing ancestral religious practices of both the Zoquean and older Mayan communities. After its development, according to this theory, the cult was introduced to the older homeland regions on the periphery of the lowlands, where it was rejected when volcanic events indicated that the new cult was objectionable to the ancestral gods. In the lowlands, where volcanos are absent and seismic activity is minimal, the hieroglyphic cult progressed unabated. The second possible explanation is that the hieroglyphic cult was being developed by progressive or dissident

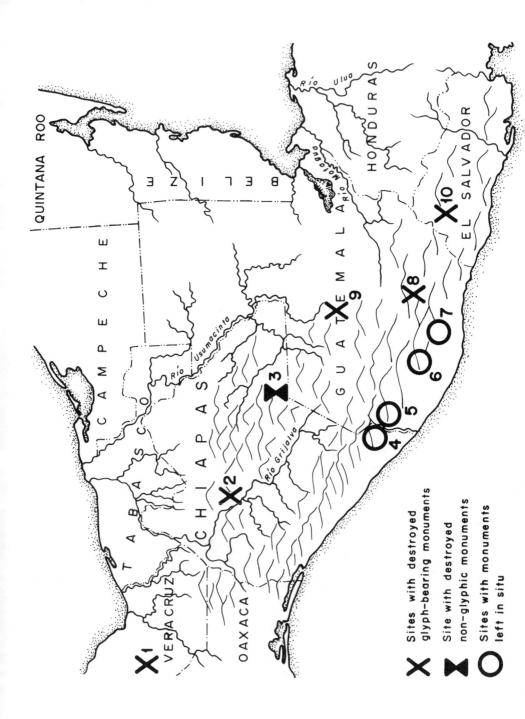

QUINTANA ROO

CAMPECHE

BELIZE

Río Ulua

HONDURAS

Río Motagua

EL SALVADOR

GUATEMALA

Río Usumacinta

Río Grijalva

TABASCO

CHIAPAS

VERACRUZ

OAXACA

X Sites with destroyed
glyph-bearing monuments

▶◀ Site with destroyed
non-glyphic monuments

◯ Sites with monuments
left in situ

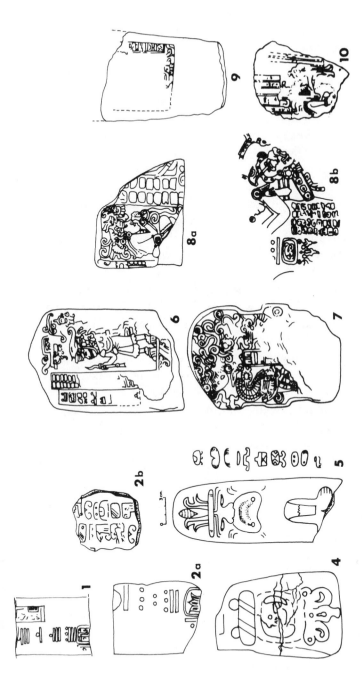

FIGURE 9.6. Distribution of Late Preclassic carved monuments and texts, eastern Mesoamerica

priestly elements among the old Zoquean and proto-Mayan populations surrounding the lowlands when volcanic events caused a reaction against it. Opponents of the cult, perhaps including the old hierarchical leaders and conservative population elements, then destroyed the objectionable monuments and conceivably forced the cult's adherents to flee to the lowland forests. There the cult protagonists took advantage of an already culturally differentiated pioneer community (lacking seismic threats) to elaborate their practice and its power-oriented societal controls toward civilization. This alternative necessitates the assumption that there were closer affinities between highland and lowland groups from early times than are indicated by available evidence. I prefer the first option.

There are other implications to my line of reasoning. Foremost is the fact that the Maya hieroglyphics were not writing in the ordinary sense. By this I mean that they do not communicate news of events, thoughts, and instructions, or record transactions, except insofar as these categories concerned a narrow range of ritual (Graham 1971:261–64). The recently acclaimed Maya practice of including bare dynastic evidence in this system seems to me to fortify, rather than weaken, the idea that Maya hieroglyphics were only cultic tools. Needless to say, the glyph system was an all-important tool, one that made concrete the Maya millennial philosophy of cosmic order, divine preordination, ancestral ritual requirements, and, no doubt, a strong concept of the ethnic superiority of the Lowland Maya elite with its fixed social classes, warfare, and slave categories (Marcus 1974). We do not see this pattern in the looser small-center Classic civilizations of Chiapas, which abstained from carved inscriptions.

DISCUSSION: ENVIRONMENTAL LIMITS VERSUS SOCIAL VALUES

Culture-Historical Problems

Arguments have been presented above to show that the known Zoquean and Mayan cultures represent two branches of an older, originating trunk society, the Isthmian Olmec, and that marked cultural differences over time have resulted from distinctive responses to varied environmental possibilities. This idea is by no means new. I have tried to show further, however, that the Barra and Ocos peoples made up a principal pre-Olmec constituency. These peoples are now known to have been well established in southern Chiapas, with much lighter densities indicated to the east, west, and north. New cultural elements from central and southern Mexico presumably were added to the Ocos base in the Los Tuxtla region of southern Veracruz, eventually resulting in the Olmec heartlands approach to civilization. Most evidence supports the idea that the heartland was of Zoquean (or, as Swadesh would say, Mixean) affiliation. (See the most recent review of the linguistic situation by Campbell [1975] and by Campbell and Kaufman [1976].)

After a long and complex internal history, summarized above, by the beginnings of the Late Preclassic Period (ca. 400 B.C.), certain groups on the eastern fringes of the Olmec heartland had established strong communities in much of the Lowland Maya area. Quite probably this pioneering was accomplished through mixing with other, possibly related, groups moving north and west out of the Southeastern Highlands in Guatemala and El Salvador, as well as with groups moving northeast out of southern and northern Chiapas. Presumably many members of these contributing groups were descendants of a postulated proto-Maya community.

Inasmuch as Zoquean and Mayan are both macro-Mayan tongues, we can leave it to linguists to debate the relative degree of Mayan-ness among the Olmec-founded communities in 1000 B.C. in eastern Tabasco and in El Salvador as far south and east as Chalchuapa, and among their respective descendants moving through or around the peninsular crescent toward each other. A critical cultural argument put forth by some archaeologists is that the southern group, so far removed from the Olmec heartland, provided a healthy and perhaps steady infusion of ceramic traits thought to be non-Olmec (that is, non-Zoquean or less Zoquean) into the Northern Lowlands; presumably some language and bloodline variations would be involved. The appearance and claimed northward spread of the late Kolos and Kal (Chalchuapa) ceramic style (including domestic ware; see Sharer and Gifford 1970) is distinguished by an emphasis upon handled and necked water jars and spouted forms, a trait constellation which contrasts sharply with the isthmian or Olmecan Early Preclassic tradition but not with sectors of the Middle Preclassic. One might even argue that the movement was the other way, that is, north to south: spouts are fairly common in the isthmian Zoquean-Olmec area by mid–Middle Preclassic times and appear within the Maya Lowlands perhaps for the first time in a possibly Dili-like portion of the Nabanche phase at Dzibilchaltun in northern Yucatan (related by Joesink-Mandeville and Meluzin [1976] and Lowe [1973a:49] to the isthmus region). Spouts also appear in the Escalera phase at Chiapa de Corzo (including one on a strap-handled whistling vessel [Lowe and Mason 1965:Figs. 10,11]), and in the apparently slightly earlier Duende phase at Izapa (Ekholm 1969: 74). Loop handles also occur on Jocotal-and Duende-phase necked jars at Izapa (Ekholm 1969:55, 70, 78, 80).

The question of mode priority and directions of movement obviously requires more careful ceramic-complex comparisons and more precise dating than has been available. Recent research, for example, shows that strap-handled ollas appear early in the north in at least one locale, the Esteros A phase (1000–550 B.C.) in "Huastec" north central Veracruz (Wilkerson 1973:39,44). Viewing the Maya linguistic affiliation of the Huasteca in historic times—and the claimed time depth of many centuries B.C. for the language group separation (Swadesh 1960; McQuown 1971:62–63)—it is apparent that any statements regarding the direction of cultural movements still remain open to question.

Southern Environmental Limitations and Geographic Liabilities

Confining the discussion for the moment to the generally assumed long Zoquean "ancestral" occupation of the western or isthmian part of Eastern Mesoamerica, how do we explain the appearance of presumably Olmec-inspired Late Preclassic Maya and Classic Maya sites across most of the northern half of Chiapas and the near absence of Classic Mayan elements in most of the southern portion? Is it just a matter of ethnic rivalry and eminent domain? A parallel question is, Why is there no great single city-state or cultural tradition dominating southern Chiapas? Why does not the naturally well-endowed large area of the central depression not have a single equivalent of Monte Alban, Teotihuacan, Tikal, Copan, or even Kaminaljuyu or Izapa? Why, viewing its very ancient population advantage, is there no equivalent or even near-equivalent in Chiapas of the Olmec San Lorenzo or La Venta ceremonial centers? Surely there was no lack of essential resources, no shortage of trade stress possibilities, no missing symbiotic opportunities, no obvious population scarcity sufficient to explain the propensity in southern Chiapas for small or medium regional centers only.

Answers to the above questions must derive from a conclusion that there *were* disadvantaging factors in the southern region's natural environment and exposed geographic position which discouraged intensifying social organization and the nucleative demands of higher civilization. It is significant that Izapa, the major early ceremonial center of the area, is located in the zone of greatest agricultural potential and on the frontier of the postulated Zoquean community. But more than a trade center or metropolis, Izapa was a religious mecca. Although it may have been primarily dependent upon the unique concentration of population in the humid lands of the Soconusco, and perhaps even specifically upon cacao production and distribution, once lzapa fell into partial abandonment during the beginning of the Early Classic Period, no other stone-carving center arose to take its place; instead myriad smaller, sculptureless centers flourished. I think that this situation was the direct result of Izapa's unessential role in the much increased coastal-route traffic between the northern and southern poles of empire which characterized the Classic and Postclassic eras in Mesoamerica; foreign control of the cacao business would have become secondary to control of the north-south trade in obsidian, whose sources and principal markets were far from the Soconusco (see arguments in other chapters of this volume). It is apparent that neither Izapa nor any other Soconusco center controlled the commerce which passed through the district after Early Classic times, however convenient it may have been as a supply depot.

Cultural instability engendered by positions upon main diffusion routes may also have held back the development of large centers and more pervasive horizon styles in the interior of Chiapas, but I think that the main limiting factor here was the environmental hazard. No matter how intensified, social controls such as those that sustained high productivity in the wet lowland forests could never maintain equal production in the great central depression of Chiapas, even on its better limestone lands, for one simple reason: the lack of a suitable moisture regime.

Annual precipitation across the central depression varies from 700 to 1,500 millimeters, most of it closely confined to the June-through-

September wet season; periodic regional drought is typical of the area (see résumé of climate by subregion in Lowe 1959:passim). The deeply imbedded rivers of southern Chiapas were never suitable for extensive irrigation at the level of technology achieved in Mesoamerica at any time, including the present. The prized river floodplain lands, often fought over, were sharply delimited and subject to frequent off-season flooding of crops; their exposed situation also made them especially vulnerable to looting.

Thus it was that the more humid Lowland Maya lands in the limestone hill country of northern Chiapas and the limestone plains of the Peten and Yucatan Peninsula operated in juxtaposition to the sharply limited production of the southern valleys with their dependence upon single-crop milpas and precarious double-cropping only on the moist strips of land along the riverbottoms or on the higher and cooler mountain slopes. With rainfall at worst (on the northern Yucatan "plains") equal to the best of the central depression, and with up to three times that much precipitation in the south (most regions showing a more constant annual distribution pattern with lower rates of insulation), the Maya Lowlands were in a distinctly superior competitive position versus southern Chiapas (except for the southeastern Soconusco district). In most northern regions, once the Lowland Maya secured adaptive maize and bean varieties, developed the social controls necessary to cope with tropical weed growth and insect problems (see Lowe 1971), and learned to make optimum use of the superior tree crops of the area (Puleston and Puleston 1971; Netting:Chap. 12 below), their power to utilize to advantage the much higher agricultural potential of their limestone rendzinic soil environment was relatively unlimited (see Ferdon 1959). In other northern regions, notably central Campeche and southern Quintana Roo, extremely prolonged dry seasons and periods of drought were also a problem, as they continue to be for the modern populace. In the low-lying Campeche region the Preclassic Maya had already resorted to extensive canal and reservoir construction in an effort to turn scarce water resources to domestic and ritual usage (at Edzna; see Matheny 1973), a practice possible in southern Chiapas only at a much smaller scale. In the droughty Quintana Roo region, extensive terracing of stony slopes, just as in Chiapas, seems never to have supported more than small centers during the Late Classic Period (Turner 1974); in both instances the rainfall regime was inadequate to restore for long the increasingly denuded lands whose forests had once supported a milpa system sufficient for a small population.

Reviewing the evidence, it appears that the citation from Webb at the beginning of this chapter must be turned around: the more intensive nucleation making possible the growth of truly large centers (and explaining the rise of the distinctive characteristics of the Maya civilization) *was* made possible by environmental advantages, which, *together with* the operation of belief systems, social prestige, and kin ties, combined to bring about the superior intellectual and community development that made possible the remarkable survival of the Maya civilization in the tropical lowlands for a thousand years. The ancestral Olmec-Zoquean peoples on their narrow coastal river levees and lateritic hills or in the dry interior valleys never had a chance in the long-run competition. Finally, constant exposure of the isthmian peoples, in their crossroads positions across communications routes, to repeated exterior interference dealt the deathblow to possibilities for steady cultural evolution. Over their long history, the southern regions are typified by change, not by constancy or the perseverance of cultural types.

Within the greater isthmian area, cultural precocity was lowest in the very dry Tehuantepec Plain and highest in the humid Gulf Coast–Los Tuxtlas hill regions on the north and in the wet Soconusco district on the south. It is perhaps not irrelevant that the surviving Mixe-Zoquean peoples are now practically restricted to the wetter slopes of the mountain regions in southern Oaxaca, southern Veracruz, and western Chiapas. The Zoques of the drier valleys and much contested humid riverbottoms of the western central depression seem to have survived one conquest after another by assuming a subservient, compliant role (Agrinier 1975). Today this same attitude is leading to their rapid assimilation into the Hispanicized mestizo culture of modern Mexico (N. Thomas 1974).

The culture-historical lessons of the isthmian area, and particularly of southern Chiapas, seem easily applied to the Lowland Maya origins problem, and bear some repetition. The factors of relative aridity or geographic marginality and of exposure to cultural change from all over Mesoamerica operated to limit nucleation in the southern regions. When reviewed in reverse perspective these same factors explain the rise of the greatest and most thoroughly Maya centers in the central Peten region. There the factors of geographic isolation and ecological advantage combined to facilitate the peculiar Maya social organization which has never been rivaled for stable control of a tropical society.

Value System Potentialities

From no other direction was the advanced social control needed for the mastery of lowland forests as likely to have come as from the isthmian area, home of the older Olmec civilization. The processes involved in this apparently fairly slow transfer and development of socioeconomic organization from the Gulf Coast floodplain eastward to the tropical forest hills and plains are subjects for separate theoretical studies (see, for instance, guidelines in Fried 1952; Ferdon 1959:18), but I think that the fact of their existence and possibilities will adequately explain the different levels of attainment or degrees of civilizational intensity achieved in the north and south in Eastern Mesoamerica.

If, for example, the ecological advantages of unusually good soil and humidity (Sanders 1973) gave Tikal its uniquely critical initial headstart at a certain point in prehistory, there were also the additional geographic advantages of central position and the freedom from the catastrophic droughts, floods, earthquakes, hurricanes, and volcanism that periodically plagued most people on its territorial margins (ironically, a series of earthquakes has just destroyed much of Chiapa de Corzo as this chapter is revised in October 1975). Once population growth began in this setting, increasing nucleation had many incentives; relative isolation and continental depth provided security against much of the unrest frequently manifest in more exposed regions. Increasingly attracted to such a stable and growing regional center would be the best technological and intellectual elements in all neighboring societies. Growing internal needs and opportunities would intensify the convergence of elite kinsmen, artisans, farmers, servants, and traders. Increased competition with rival centers would lead, quite probably, to institutionalized warfare and slave taking for prestige and economic purposes. From this point the civilizational vehicle is self-fueling; with the best ecological security available, the only danger to Tikal was foreign conquest or breakdown of the social system.

The unique Lowland Maya contribution at Tikal, and apparently at neighboring Uaxactun as well, was the application of the social organization needed to maintain growth; probably we should say the intensification of social values, for there is little suggestion of any unique social structure at Early Tikal other than scale and intensity. Whether or not this intensification featured ancestral deities, dynastic ancestors, or unusual faith in cosmic forces, there is no doubt that it did respond dynamically to challenges from demographic pressures and regional competition. The outstanding degree to which Tikal outstripped its neighbors indicates that the challenge-and-response mechanism worked very well. I am moved to remark again that Webb's comment cited at the opening of this chapter is partially in error—there was, after all, environmental advantage causing nucleation, at least at Tikal—but Webb is correct in stating that the "operation of belief systems and social prestige" kept it going (1973: 388).

If the Classic Maya people did indeed pay homage to their Olmec (and Izapan) ancestors—whose isthmian-based belief systems are everywhere present in Maya art and iconography—it was well deserved. But the real tribute must be paid to those marginal Late Middle Preclassic, Late Preclassic, and even Classic Period pioneering settlers, originally Zoquean or otherwise, who proved that adequate social organization could produce and maintain a high civilization in a habitat considered for a thousand years previously (and again subsequently) to be fit for little more than hunting and gathering.

At this point one might well ask who were the most civilized, the Classic Maya, so firmly bound to their neat stone citadels and ritual-laden lives, or their more loosely organized southern neighbors who resisted obedience to the Classic Maya cult? Modern freethinkers to the contrary, the decision must go to the Maya, if not for the elegance of their art and ritual or for their superior learning—for the southerners also had periods of literacy, technical sufficiency, and artistic sophistication—then for their sheer ability to exact so ample a livelihood for so many people for so long a time from what the world at large considers to be so hostile an environment. This is an unrivaled accomplishment.

Fully shared, deeply ingrained social values seem to have defined a different, superior, more orderly world for the early Lowland Maya, as compared to their Zoquean and other neighbors. We might view this as a distinguishable "national character," however slippery that concept may be. No doubt some conscious, visible, even tireless, effort was required to maintain this character; seemingly, commoner, priest, noble, all were willing—or required—to toe the line of custom faithfully and to work hard (the key to Maya civilization) in order to maintain their idea of what a community and religious life (was there a difference?) should be. Few today would accept such rigorously stereotyped living conditions (and apparently the ancient Zoque almost always chose not to!), but they were required in order to dominate the lowland forests for so long a period. This fact, I think, is made evident by the Maya collapse; that the Maya system could regulate the environment, overcome natural calamities, and control internal social problems is witnessed by its long survival, but it could not withstand a serious threat to the system itself from outside.

So delicately balanced were the Lowland Maya's hierarchical organization and superior self-image that they could not survive the culture shock of even partial military and/or cultural domination at the end of the Late Classic Period (see R. E. W. Adams 1973a:29–33). In the Guatemalan Peten Lowlands, where the bearers of a modified "Mexican" culture chose to intrude but did not remain long, few successors have been able to reestablish an organized way of life and none have achieved consistent return to civilization. The southern Chiapas regions, on the other hand, have fitted into a series of postclassic, colonial, and modern life styles with rather little effort (and usually little distinction). Their occupants are now once again looking northward at the lowland forests in the hope of alleviating population pressure on their own nearly exhausted lands. Without something akin to the old Maya "style" and dedicated organization, however, they will not have (and have not had) much success. The wet tropical forests still have the same superior environmental potential for agriculture, and the same liabilities. The Maya patiently learned how to play off the advantages against the liabilities, and this was a social, as well as a technological triumph. Many such living and learning processes still await modern man in the tropics.

10
Early Art Styles of Mesoamerica and Early Classic Maya Art

JACINTO QUIRARTE

The University of Texas at San Antonio

Defining the nature and structure of a style as well as its internal development is one of the art historian's tasks; establishing its links with predecessors and successors is another. The art historian performs these tasks in a number of ways. His studies of form, content, and meaning in works of art lead to definitions of style and hence enable him to classify known bodies of work. As new pieces are discovered these too are analyzed and placed within their proper stylistic context.

Art historians are further interested in establishing a temporal position for an object and in determining its historical relationship to others in the same class of objects. This makes it possible to chart the development of a style. Thus the question of dating is always important. The position of an object within a sequence will also enable the art historian to establish the duration of the style.

The development of a style within a finite duration is usually considered to include early, middle, and late manifestations. Further, the development and duration of a style can be established even if its placement in actual time is not precisely known, as Proskouriakoff demonstrated in her book *A Study of Classic Maya Sculpture* (1950). Ultimately, however, the style must be related to real time. Once the temporal position of a style is known in relation to other styles then its antecedents as well as its echoes in subsequent styles can be established.

Rather than survey all early art styles of Mesoamerica, I will concentrate on those works which have a bearing on the development of early Classic Maya art. This category includes the Izapan-style materials found in the Chiapas-Guatemala Highland and Pacific Slope sites. Mesoamericanists are generally agreed that the immediate predecessors of the Maya artists are to be found in this area. Their work, identified as Izapan in style, fits into the following chronological and developmental picture: Izapan-style artists building upon Olmec sources appear during the Late Preclassic and Protoclassic periods; they eventually influence groups to the northwest in Oaxaca and central Mexico, to the north on the Gulf Coast, and to the northeast in the Maya Lowlands. References to Izapan style configurations are found in all three areas.

For the present I will attempt to chart the ways in which the Maya artists echoed, paraphrased, and redefined solutions established by Izapan-style artists. These indicators will help us establish origins as well as trace the early development of the distinctive Maya style in the lowlands.

Three specific constituents of style in the Maya area can be identified as having developed from a variety of sources. (1) The *formal* aspects of the images—the use of line, shape, and color as well as the definition of scale, proportion, and space—can be identified as Mayan or non-Mayan or a combination of the two. (2) The *meaning* of the images is conveyed by elements, motifs, themes, and symbols. Although thematic content can remain constant within a series of successive styles without appreciable change in meaning, the manner in which it is expressed bears the unmistakeable stamp of a particular style. Since content can be altered by the form, it is this aspect of a work of art which ultimately indicates the style. (3) The *expressive* qualities of the images are conveyed by form and content and identified as Mayan or non-Mayan in origin.

The formal and expressive qualities of the works of art belonging to Izapan or Maya style will not be discussed here in great detail. Elements, motifs, and, to some extent, themes, far easier to chart at

250

this stage, will amply reflect the relationships between Mesoamerican groups during Preclassic and Early Classic periods.

ELEMENTS

Diagonal bands, crossed bands, U-shaped elements, and combinations of these appear in Olmec, Izapan, and Maya art. Although they occur in similar contexts and perhaps even in certain repetitive combinations, they do not tell us much about the creation of images by Olmec, Izapan, and Maya artists. These elements signal rather than demonstrate the attributes of human and supernatural figures. They function as signs as opposed to images which distinguish one style from another. Elements do indicate, however, that there was contact between peoples in the Gulf Coast and the Highland and Pacific Slope sites in Chiapas and Guatemala, in Oaxaca, and in the Maya Lowlands.

Among the more ubiquitous elements in Preclassic and Protoclassic monuments from the Guatemala Highland and Pacific Slope sites is a U-shaped element which appears in various contexts. References to the element are found in several early sources. It continues to be mentioned, discussed, and interpreted by Mesoamericanists. A study of the element, its settings, and possible meanings will be useful in helping us establish connections between Olmec, Izapan, and Maya groups.

Literature

In his study of Kaminaljuyu stuccoed painted vessels, Kidder (1946:223) singled out a representation of an ophidian creature which he designated Serpent X. One of the identifying features of this so-called serpent is a U-shaped element placed above the eye or within a supraorbital plate. Drucker, in his study of Olmec ceramics and art (1952:200, 204, 206), referred to an inverted U-shaped motif which suggested to him the muzzle or upper jaw outline of the "jaguar monster." T. Smith (1963:138) concurred with this interpretation. In his study of Tikal Stela 31, Barthel (1963:181–83) interpreted the U sign as "gold" and possibly the color yellow. Miles (1965:256) mentioned the incidence of a U symbol in several Izapan-style monuments. She indicated the number of times it appears in Kaminaljuyu Stelae 10 and 11 and in Chocola Stela 1. Michael Coe (1965b:759–61) also mentioned the U element found in Olmec- and Izapan-style monuments and suggested that it "may correspond to the Maya bracket element, which originally seems to have been the glyph of the moon goddess." More recently Joralemon (1971:14) has listed the U element in his dictionary of Olmec motifs and symbols as Motif 105 and designated the element as a bracket, U, or hoop.

Context, Meaning, and Function

The U element in association with crossed bands, a diagonal band, or double opposed bands appears in figurative and glyphic contexts. Its meaning is clearly linked to its association with compound creatures placed in narrative scenes and outside them as well. The compound creatures may operate as protagonists in the figurative scenes or function as borders or frames for them. Human celebrants and deity impersonators may wear the compound creature's identifying elements as pectorals or on belts and breechclouts. The same elements also appear within emblems and glyphs which may symbolize these compound creatures.

The U element as sign and symbol in conjunction with crossed bands, diagonal bands, and other elements will be discussed according to context and function in the following order:

I. Compound Creatures: Deities, Supernaturals, and Impersonators
   A. Bearded Feline Heads
   B. Mask Panels
   C. Long-Lipped Heads
   D. Winged Figures
II. Emblems, Symbols, and Glyphs
   A. Glyphs
   B. Insignia

Compound Creatures: Deities, Supernaturals, and Impersonators

The U element is most often associated with compound creatures bearing feline, serpentine, and saurian traits in Izapan and Maya art.

The compound creatures' heads have, in most cases, scroll eyes and stepped upper lips, slightly elongated; they are shown either with or without teeth. Some are predominantly feline, while others are saurian in character. In either case the U element is usually placed within the supraorbital area or within a stylized eyebrow. Related to the U shape are diagonal bands or double oblique opposed T elements, which look similar to but actually differ from the crossed bands of Olmec, Izapan, and later Maya art. The diagonal bands and oblique Ts are also related to the head or headdress.

BEARDED FELINE HEADS

The beard is prominently featured in some of the predominantly feline heads. Examples are found on Abaj Takalik Monument 1, Chiapa de Corzo bone 1, and Kaminaljuyu Stela 10 (Fig. 10.1*a, b*, and *d*). The latter two examples have U shapes within supraorbital plates. The Chiapa de Corzo head has the double oblique T shapes on the forehead and on its collar. Abaj Takalik Stela 2 has a downward-gazing human head with a beard that is barely visible within a mass of scrolls (Fig. 10.1*e*). The U element appears directly below the face at the base of a torch and within the headdress.

MASK PANELS

The same head or one related to it may be represented in the mask panels found in Olmec, Olmecoid, and Izapan monuments. The U shape occupies a central position in most of these panels.

The Oxtotitlan cave mural discussed by D. C. Grove (1970, 1973) shows a feather-winged figure seated casually on a mask panel of a compound creature bearing notched elements, crossed bands, and possibly a U element within the creature's "nose" area (Fig. 10.2*a*). Earlier examples of a similar panel are found in La Venta. However, the U shape should more properly be designated as a motif, since it forms part of a more elaborate unit which performs a pictorial as well as symbolic function. The motif frames part of the niche of Altar 5 as it does the appendages around the niche of Altar 4 (Stirling 1965:Fig. 20b).

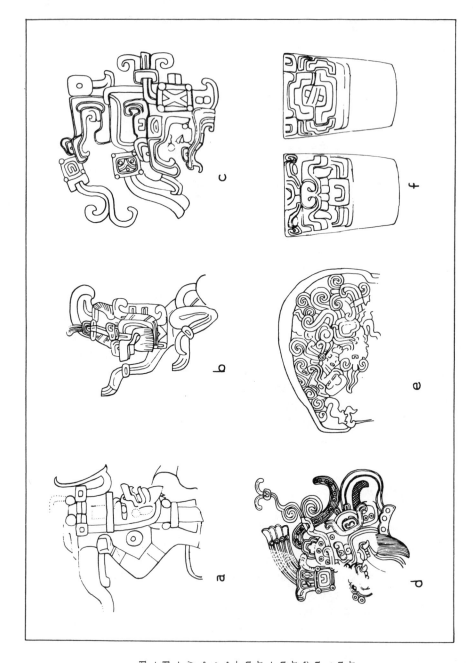

FIGURE 10.1 Bearded Jaguar figures and long-lipped head mask: deities and impersonators. *a*, Abaj Takalik, Monument 1 (formerly San Isidro Piedra Parada), after Covarrubias (1961); *b*, Chiapa de Corzo, Bone 1, after Agrinier (1960); *c*, Kaminaljuyu, Stela 11 (drawn from a photograph), after Miles (1965); *d*, Kaminaljuyu, Stela 10 (drawn from photo and rubbing), after Miles (1965) and Greene (1967); *e*, Abaj Takalik, Stela 2, after Miles (1965); *f*, Monte Alban, vessels (drawn from a photograph), after Paddock (1966).

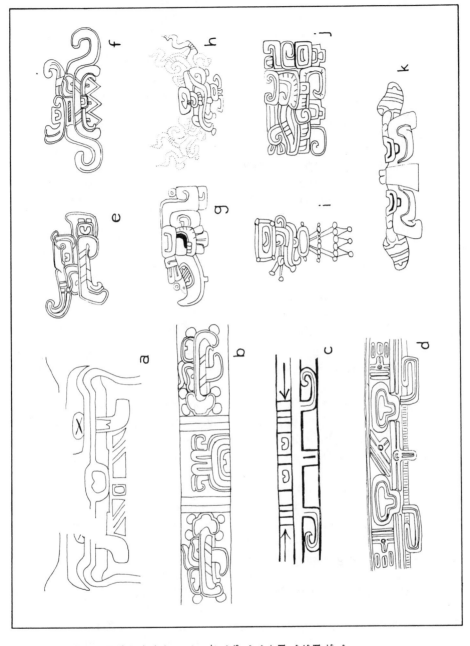

FIGURE 10.2. Top and base-line panels and long-lipped heads. *a,* Oxtotitlan, cave mural, after D. C. Grove (1970); *b,* Abaj Takalik, Stela 3, after Miles (1965); *c,* Tikal, Structure 5 D–Sub 10—first mural (drawn from a photograph from the University Museum, Philadelphia); *d,* Diker carved stone bowl, after M. D. Coe (1973a); *e,* Kaminaljuyu, Stela 11, after Miles (1965); *f,* Bilbao, Monument 42, after Parsons (1967); *g,* Kaminaljuyu, black hemispherical bowl, after Kidder (1946); *h,* Kaminaljuyu, Burial B-II stuccoed tripod lid; *i,* Kaminaljuyu, Burial A-VI stuccoed tripod; *j,* Mirador, vertical-walled bowl, after Agrinier (1970); *k,* Monte Alban, jaguar urn, after Leigh (1966)

In Izapan-style art the U element appears as an integral part of the top-line designs found on most of these monuments (Quirarte 1973a:Figs. 3, 4). It symbolizes one aspect of the compound creature used as a border for the narrative scenes. It invariably occupies the central position within the panel. By the time this tradition reached the Peten during the Protoclassic Period, the use of the U shape within the top-line border was evidently so important that it was used twice within each complete reference to this creature in the Tikal Structure 5D-Sub. 10—first mural (Fig. 10.2c).

A variation on the typical Izapan-style top-line panel is seen on the Diker carved stone bowl (Fig. 10.2d). T elements flank a diagonal with a blip on one outer edge. The latter is located in the space normally reserved for the U element.

Long-Lipped Heads

The U element is also found on long-lipped heads whose antecedents are obviously the Olmec, Olmecoid, and Izapan jaguar head with the stepped upper lip (Fig. 10.1c). Covarrubias (1961: Fig. 36) demonstrated how these developed into the later Maya Serpent X (Fig. 10.2h, i). The long upper lip is exaggerated and, as Kidder pointed out (1946:223), the long "snout" can curve downward or upward (Fig. 10.2g, j). It definitely has no beard, although, like the jaguar-head mask already described, it does appear within the terrestrial and celestial spheres (Quirarte 1973d, 1974).

The U element is prominently displayed within the supraorbital plates of the long-lipped heads used at baseline as platforms on Abaj Takalik Stela 3 and Bilbao Monument 42 (Fig. 10.2b, f). These baseline or platform heads have diagonal bands within the horizontal bar (long upper lip) which are either parallel, as in Abaj Takalik Stela 3, or opposed, as in Bilbao Monument 42. Another long-lipped head with parallel diagonal bands is attached to the front part of the belt worn by the Kaminaljuyu Stela 11 figure (Fig. 10.2e).

The U shaped element is also found on a recently discovered monument in Abaj Takalik designated as Stela 4 (Fig. 10.4e). Parsons (1972) discusses the image comprised of U shapes, double opposed Ts, bodiless heads as water suppliers, and an undulating ascending serpent-feline compound creature with a human head contained within its open jaws. Numerous U shapes placed side by side make up the underside of the serpent body.

A good example of a long-lipped head with U shape within a supraorbital plate is found on the Early Classic Maya tripod effigy bowl from El Bellote, Tabasco (Easby and Scott 1970:Fig. 26*e*).

In Monte Alban monuments the U element retains its basic position within the supraorbital area of heads which were identified as a broad-billed bird by Caso and Bernal (1952:214, Fig. 351). Leigh (1958:3, 1966:263) showed that these are two *cipactlis* shown in profile and placed back to back to form a single image in frontal view (Fig. 10.2*k*). Diagonal bands with small blips on the outer contours (T shapes) are shown on a plant form sprouting from each profile head. This is the same element seen on the forehead of the Chiapa de Corzo bone 1 bearded head and also in front of the headdress of the Kaminaljuyu Stela 10 figure (Fig. 10.1*b, d*). One of three long-lipped heads painted on a black subhemispherical bowl found in Kaminaljuyu also has the double T element on the snout and a U element in a supraorbital plate (Fig. 10.2*g*).

According to Paddock (1966:132) the U element which is usually found inscribed on the tongue of a jaguar and given the numerical value of one (or one Tiger) is commonly found joined with the representation of another glyph, which is very similar to the double oblique T element under discussion (Fig. 10.1*f*).

The Zegache vase (Paddock 1966:Fig. 21) has the double opposed Ts on the cheeks and on the eyebrows. This is identified as an effigy of the god with the mask of the broad-billed bird. The same so-called bird forms the headdress of the anthropomorphic urn found in Tomb 77 at Monte Alban (Paddock 1966:Fig. 80). This broad-billed bird is probably related to the long-lipped head from the Guatemalan Highland and Pacific Slope sites. These long-lipped heads with U shapes and diagonal bands within supraorbital plates are also found in Teotihuacan III vessels. These also have a direct relationship to Izapan-style and Classic Maya long-lipped heads (Quirarte 1973e).

The double opposed T element, like the U shape, diagonal bands, and crossed bands, was later incorporated into glyphic and emblematic contexts. All representations of the Maya rain god in the codices have a reference to this element (Glyph T 668 with Affix T 103; see Quirarte 1976).

WINGED FIGURES

The long-lipped heads associated with winged figures are to all intents and purposes identical to those used at groundline and within the narrative scene. An added feature is the crossed band element. The feather-winged figures on Izapa Stela 4 have U shapes as well as crossed bands within cartouches (Fig. 10.5a). Izapa Stela 2 and Kaminaljuyu Stela 11 figures also have the same elements in similar contexts (Fig. 10.5b, e). The crossed-bands element with an appended bifurcated tongue is worn as an earplug by the deity impersonator on Kaminaljuyu Stela 11 (Fig. 10.1c). This clearly points to a serpentine reference for the crossed bands (Quirarte 1973a).

A winged figure with crossed bands, U shapes, and other feline, ophidian, and avian features is represented on one side of a carved stone bowl (Fig. 10.6c) discussed by M. D. Coe (1973b:27). A companion figure without wings but bearing many of the traits listed above is depicted on the other side of the bowl. A variation on the top-line design is carved around the rim of the vessel.

Serpent X, also found in feather winged contexts, has prominently inscribed U shapes, crossed bands, and other elements (Fig. 10.6d). The head is found in headdresses, as part of a wing worn as a back ornament, and also under the arms (Fig. 10.6e), and is placed over an altar. The same configurations and contextual settings are borne by the later Maya Serpent Wing, Celestial Dragon, or Mythical Bird (Fig. 10.5f; Quirarte 1973c).

Emblems, Symbols, and Glyphs

The U element is found in emblematic, symbolic, and glyphic contexts during the Late Preclassic and Protoclassic periods in the Gulf Coast and Chiapas-Guatemalan Highland and Pacific Slope areas. It also appears in similar contexts during the Early Classic Period in the Oaxaca and Peten areas. The usual frame for all manifestations is a cartouche with rounded corners in which the U element is placed (see Table 10.1 and Fig. 10.3). In Izapan-style monuments as well as in those at Monte Alban, dots are placed at each corner of the cartouche (Fig. 10.3c, d, and f). This is closer to the form used in Kaminaljuyu Stela 10, where it appears in the emblem placed at forehead level of the

TABLE 10.1. U SHAPES IN GLYPHIC CONTEXTS

| Illus. This Publication | Glyphic Passage | | Object | Date | |
	Catalog (Thompson 1962)	Location	Name and Provenance	Long Count	Christian
Fig. 10.3e		A2	Stone jaguar of unknown provenance	Late Formative (Preclassic)	Ca.300 B.C.-A.D. 1
Fig. 10.3g,h, and i		2 and 4 (single column)	Jade tubular beads, Guatemala Highland and Pacific Slope area	Protoclassic, possibly Preclassic	
Fig. 10.3f			Tuxtla statuette	8.6.2.4.17	A.D. 162
Fig. 10.3j	T840		Pomona jade plug		
Fig. 10.3k	T772	A8b and A9b	Leyden plate	8.14.3.1.2	A.D. 320
Fig. 10.3l		Base panel	Stela 2, Yaxha	9.5.0.0.0±2 katuns	A.D. 534±40 (A.D. 495-573)
Fig. 10.3m	T843		Stela 31, Tikal	9.0.10.0.0 (?) or 9.3.15.17.2 (?)	A.D. 445 or A.D. 510
Fig. 10.3n	T517	E4	Stela 19, Copan	9.10.19.15.0	A.D. 651
Fig. 10.3o	67	A15	Stela D, Quirigua	9.16.15.0.0	A.D. 766

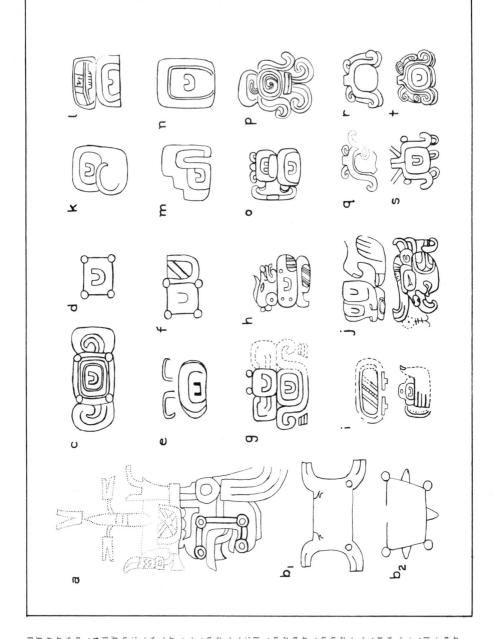

FIGURE 10.3. Glyphs and emblems. *a*, jadeite celt of unknown provenience, after Covarrubias (1961); *b*, jaguar muzzles, after Covarrubias (1946); *c*, Abaj Takalik, Stela 4, after Parsons (1972); *d*, Monte Alban, Tomb 104 slab, after Caso and Bernal (1952); *e*, stone jaguar of unknown provenience, glyph A2, after M. D. Coe (1973a); Tuxtla, statuette, glyph A5, after Pijoan and Soteras (1946); *g,h*, tubular bead, glyphs 2 and 4, after Proskouriakoff (1974); *i*, tubular bead, glyphs 1 and 2, after Proskouriakoff (1974); *j*, Pomona jade ear flare, glyph T840, after M. D. Coe (1965b); *k*, Leyden plate, glyphs A8b and A9b:T772, after Thompson (1950, 1962); *l*, Yaxha, Stela 2, base panel glyph, after Maler (1908); *m*, Tikal, Stela 31, glyph E:T843, after W. R. Coe (1962, 1967); *n*, Copan, Stela 19, glyph E4:T517, after Thompson (1950, 1962); *o*, Quirigua, Stela D, glyph A15:G7, after Thompson (1950, 1962); *p*, Diker stone bowl of unknown provenience, pectoral medallion, after M. D. Coe (1973a); *q*, Abaj Takalik, Stela 4, snout emblem, after Parsons (1972); *r*, Tikal, Stela 29, pectoral medallion, after W. R. Coe (1962, 1967); *s*, Uolantun, Stela 1, pectoral medallion, after Proskouriakoff (1950); *t*, Tikal, Stela 31, pectoral medallion, after W. R. Coe (1962, 1967)

bearded feline head (Fig. 10.1*c*). An almost identical symbol is used as the source for the upward-moving serpentine compound figure seen on Abaj Takalik Stela 4 (Figs. 10.3*c,* 10.4*e*).

The four dots of these emblems and glyphs are probably related to similar units incised on Olmecoid pieces. Covarrubias (1946:Lam. 3) shows one example of a piece with incised decoration around the mouth of a werejaguar which has four dots at the corners of a rectangular muzzle. Triangular shapes are placed midway between the dots (Fig. 10.3*b*). Covarrubias (1961:Fig. 33) shows another jaguar head in profile incised on a celt of unknown provenience which has the same bar and dot decoration around the mouth (Fig. 10.3*a*). Joralemon (1971:171) identifies this as God II or the Maize God.

The Izapan-style and Monte Alban examples are clearly related to these Olmecoid jaguar heads with bar and dot decoration around the mouth. The U element probably refers to the mouth of a predominantly feline compound creature. This would support Drucker's and Stirling's reading of the Izapa stelae's upper panels as jaguar "masks." Although the element may specifically refer to a feline, it must be borne in mind that the Olmec, Olmecoid, and Izapa mask panels refer to a compound figure with feline, saurian, and serpentine traits (Quirarte 1973a: 15–18).

GLYPHS

One of the earliest known glyphs with a U shape as a main sign is found on the Late Formative (Preclassic) stone jaguar discussed by M. Coe (1973b:25). Although its provenience is unknown, it is definitely Izapan in style (Fig. 10.3*e*).

A slightly later example of a glyph with U shape as a main sign is found on the Protoclassic Tuxtla statuette. The glyph with dots located at the corners of the cartouche (Fig. 10.3*f*) is attached to a second cartouche which has a diagonal band as a main sign. The double glyph echoes the same combination of elements found in Izapan-style monuments.

A number of examples with U shapes within glyphic contexts cannot be clearly designated as Izapan or Mayan in style. Two such examples are the jade tubular beads found in the Sacred Cenote at Chichen Itza (see Proskouriakoff 1974:82, 85, 203, 204). The beads are probably from the Guatemala Highland and Pacific Slope area and are of Protoclassic, possibly Preclassic manufacture. The two beads have a number of incised glyphs with U shapes used as main signs (Fig. 10.3g–i). The cartouches do not have the customary dots at each corner, and although the glyphs are similar to those definitely identified as Mayan, their equivalents are not found in the Thompson catalog (1962).

An Early Classic Maya example of the U shape in a glyphic context is found on the Pomona jade earplug (Fig. 10.3j). The glyph (T840) is placed directly above a compound head with a downward-curving long lip with flaring nostril. It is one of four heads placed 90° apart near the outer edge of the piece. The other three heads are clearly anthropomorphic. Each has a glyph associated with it.

Other Maya glyphs with U shapes are found on the Leyden plate, Yaxha Stela 2, Tikal Stela 31, Copan Stela 19, and Quirigua Stela D (Fig. 10.3k–o). Thompson (1962:119) does not interpret these glyphs except to say that the Copan example (T517) "is an infix of some early glyph" (Fig. 10.3n).

In Monte Alban the U shape within a cartouche with dots at each corner functions more as a sign or symbol than a glyph, for it usually stands alone. The U element is used on the sealing stone of Monte Alban Tomb 4 and painted over a niche on the north wall of the tomb (Fig. 10.3d). Caso and Bernal (1952:Fig. 117a, b) identified the serpentine head placed directly above the sign in both instances as *dios del moño en el tocado*. According to Caso (1938:77) the same sign is painted on the ceiling of Tomb 7. Here the symbolic references are obviously to the interior of the earth. This is in keeping with the use of the same element to frame the niche on La Venta Altar 4.

Another Monte Alban example of the U element with dots at the corners of the cartouche is used as the place glyph on Stela 2 (Paddock 1966:Fig. 143). A profile figure wearing the skin, head, and claws of a jaguar stands on the ("mountain") glyph. His hands are bound behind his back.

INSIGNIA

Deities, supernaturals, and impersonators of these beings wear scrolls, U shapes, diagonals, double opposed Ts, and crossed bands as identifying features. These insignia may be identical to those forms found in glyphic passages. Only the contexts differ. Thus, the U shape within a cartouche with dots at each corner is worn on parts of the body on belts and headdresses. The seated figure on Kaminaljuyu Altar 1 wears such insignia at belt level. It is placed on the nose of a long-lipped head worn in the headdress of Kaminaljuyu Stela 11 figure (Fig. 10.1c). Other examples are shown on the supraorbital plates of some of the Kaminaljuyu Tripod heads found in Tomb A-VI (Fig. 10.2i).

The U element is also worn on breechclouts and pectorals. It appears upside down in the breechclout of the Leyden plate figure (M. Coe 1967: Fig. 16). A pectoral with prominently incised U element is worn by the figures on Uolantun Stela 1 and Tikal Stela 31 (Fig. 10.3s, t). Tikal Stela 29 figure wears an identical pectoral but without the U element (Fig. 10.3r). The identical format for this unit is perched and becomes part of the snout of the serpentine-saurian creature's head shown on Abaj Takalik Stela 4 (Figs. 10.3q, 10.4e).

A similar configuration for a pectoral with scroll infix is worn by the winged figure seen on the Diker stone bowl (Figs. 10.3p, 10.6c).

Other examples of U shapes not discussed above are found in figurative contexts on a number of objects: a Holmul black lacquer bowl with effigy cover (Merwin and Vaillant 1932:Pl. 21); a seated jade figure with incised U elements within cartouches above the eyes found in Uaxactun (Kelemen 1946:Pl. 242c); a Tikal cylindrical tripod vessel (W. R. Coe 1965a:36) depicting warriors and temples of Teotihuacan. The U element is inscribed on the sides of the temple platform within tablets flanking the stairway. The temple has the typical Teotihuacan talus-tablet arrangement.

Summary

The earliest examples of U elements, diagonal bands, and crossed bands are found in Olmec and Olmecoid sculptures and paintings. The same elements appear in later Izapan sculptures in association with similar compound creatures which are placed in unique thematic and formal structures.

The interchangeability of parts, whether elements, signs, or motifs, in Izapan-style art is amply shown in the depiction of the compound creatures bearing saurian, serpentine, and feline traits. Sometimes the compound figure's "head" is used to frame the narrative scene. The use of top-line and base-line designs in these stelae demonstrates the Izapan artist's propensity to abstract the compound creature's qualities by signaling its presence by a number of elements in specific arrangements. The U element in these contexts signals the feline traits of the compound creature used as frame as well as participant in the narrative scenes of Izapan-style monuments and portable pieces. Diagonal bands refer to the crocodilian traits in some cases and to an iguana in others (Izapa Stela 2). Crossed bands clearly point to the serpentine traits of the compound figure.

The U element within cartouches was apparently formulated and fully developed by Izapan artists. It passed from the Guatemala Highland and the Pacific Slope sites to the Maya Lowlands. Its appearance in Monte Alban during the same period demonstrates contacts between the Chiapas-Guatemala Highland and Pacific Slope sites and Oaxaca.

THEMES IN IZAPAN-STYLE ART AND CLASSIC MAYA ART

Clusters of elements can also be used to identify compound figures in early Mesoamerican art. Joralemon (1971) has made efforts to identify deities in Olmec art along with his compilation of elements and motifs. Elements combined with physiological characteristics of compound figures have formed the basis for these identifications. Their structures and contextual settings have been studied in efforts to understand them better. No such effort has been made with regard to Izapan-style art.

Elements as well as motifs, such as the numerous compound figures found in Izapan-style art, can be used to establish convergent solutions as well as connections between Olmecs, Izapans, and Mayans. A thorough study of these figures in Izapan-style art within their respective contextual settings will help us identify the thematic structures in these works. If and when specific compound figures can be identified as well as the range of activities in which they operate then such relationships can be determined. Knowing who or what a figure represents and what its function in a specific context may be, as well as its configuration, will help us determine whether similar concerns are manifest in the art of successor cultures. All previous efforts to disentangle the images in terms of elements and motifs were and continue to be necessary. This is the initial step which should lead to identification, analyses, and definitions of themes. Part of this process involves identifying who the actors are, what they do, what happens to them, and what they may represent.

Themes in Izapan-style art appear to comprise deities, deity impersonators, other celebrants, worshipers, and just plain observers. The bulk of the images contain representations of deities and supernaturals as well as their impersonators. The numerous worshipers found in Izapan-style art will be mentioned only in passing, for they appear to be a distinctly Izapan-style characteristic and do not appear in later Maya art.

Deities and supernatural beings appear in at least three contexts in Izapan-style art: (1) as object toward which an action by a god impersonator is aimed, as in a mythic combat; (2) as a presence in a power- or protection-conferring image, to be observed, impersonated, and/or worshiped in ritual and ceremony; and (3) as personification of earth and sky and as a source for water. Deity impersonators constitute a fourth category for thematic contexts. (See Table 10.2.)

Deities and Supernatural Beings as Object: Mythic Combat

One of the few scenes in which a deity or supernatural being is involved as the object of a specific action, in some cases violent, is one which can be described as a mythic combat. I have discussed this elsewhere as a confrontation scene between compound or polymorphic creatures and a two-headed serpent (Quirarte 1973a:23–24). More specifically, a god impersonator bearing feline-saurian serpentine attributes and wearing stiff wings is shown holding a two-headed serpent with upraised arms on Kaminaljuyu Stela 19 (Fig. 10.4*a*). The same god impersonator is shown on Kaminaljuyu Stela 4 holding the serpent's "tail" head—a scroll-eyed head—which has been severed (Quirarte 1973b:Lam. 12). A similar event may be depicted on Izapa Stela 3 (Fig. 10.4*b*). A god impersonator with more pronounced serpentine attributes stands over a large serpent whose "tail" head has been severed and is shown on the left side of the narrative scene.

The winged feline figure, perhaps now depicted as a deity, is seen

TABLE 10.2. MOTIFS AND THEMES IN IZAPAN AND MAYA ART

Motifs and Themes	Middle Preclassic	Late Preclassic	Early Protoclassic	Late Protoclassic	Early Classic	Late Classic
DEITIES AND SUPERNATURALS						
(1) As Object: Mythic Combat						
Two-Headed Serpents	I St. 3* Kam St. 4	Kam St. 19	I St. 50			
(2) As Presence: Symbol of Power/Protection						
Two-Headed Serpents (Maya Serpent Bar)			?	⟵ AT St. 4 ——→ ? EB St. 1 Hauber St.	Leyden plate	
Feather-Winged Figures (Mythical Bird)		I St. 4 Kam St. 11 I Altar 20	I St. 2, 25 and 60	Diker bowl	Tikal low gourd bowl; Kam vases	Pal. TC and TFC panels
Bodiless Heads			I St. 7 AT St. 1		Tikal St. 29, 4, and 31	
(3) As Personification: Earth, Sky, and Water						
Two-Headed Serpents as Earth and Sky	I St. 6 and 11		I St. 2, 5, 12, and 7			Pal. TC panel
Bodiless Heads as Water Suppliers	I St. 1 and 23		AT St. 4 ——→ ?			
	? ⟵ I St. 22 and 67 ——→					
DEITY IMPERSONATORS						
Feather- and Stiff-Winged Figures	Kam St. 4	I St. 9, 4 Kam St. 19 and 11			Kam vases	Tikal Bu. 196 vase

*The following abbreviations are used:

AT	Abaj Takalik	Bu	Burial
EB	El Baúl	St	Stela
I	Izapa	Kam	Kaminaljuyu
Pal	Palenque	Ox	Oxtotitlan
		TC	Temple of the Cross
		TFC	Temple of the Foliated Cross

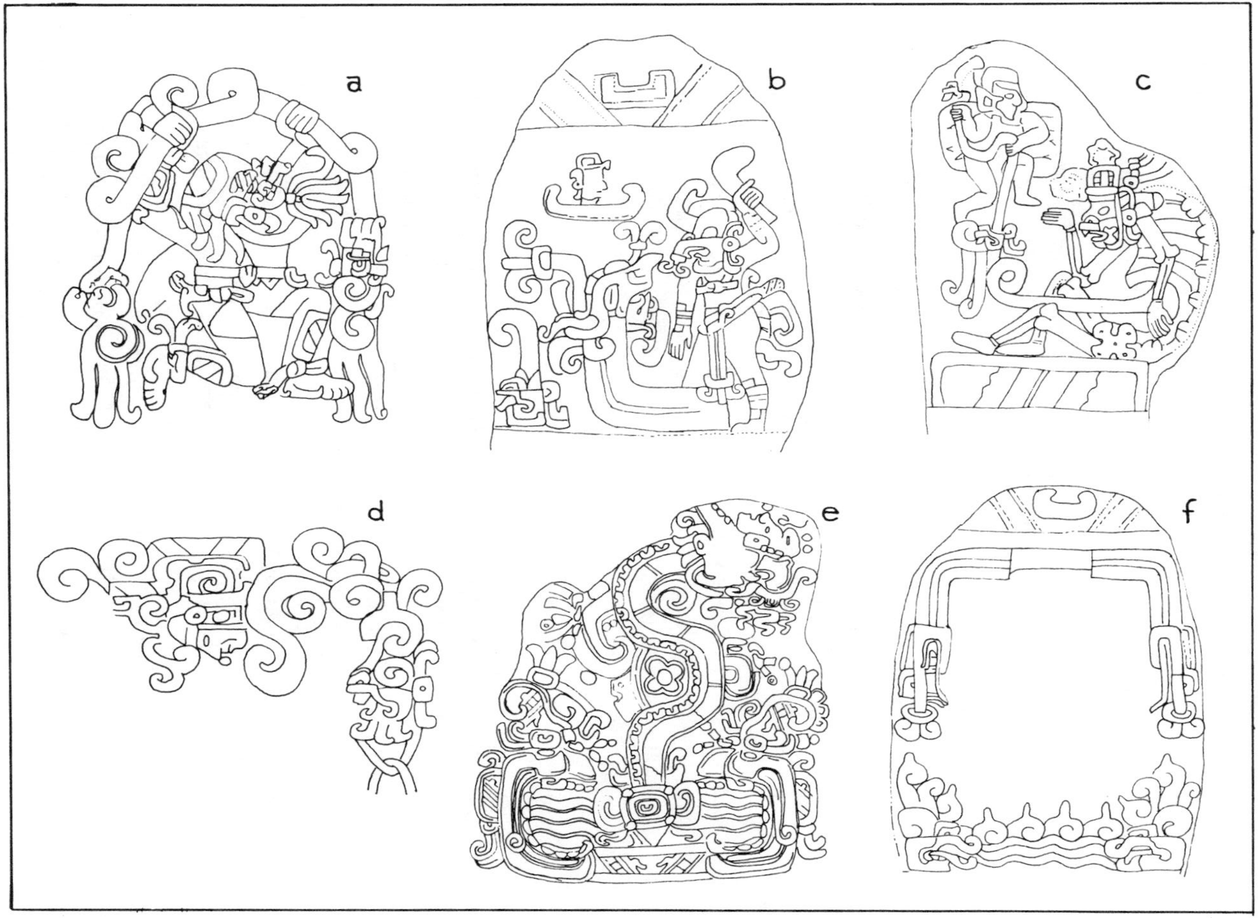

FIGURE 10.4 Double-headed compound figures in "mythic combat" scenes: serpents and scroll-eyed heads. *a*, Kaminaljuyu, Stela 19, after Proskouriakoff (1968); *b*, Izapa, Stela 3, after Norman (1973); *c*, Izapa, Stela 50, after Norman (1973); *d*, El Baul, Stela 1 (drawn from a photograph), after Parsons (1967); *e*, Abaj Takalik, Stela 4, after Parsons (1972); *f*, Izapa, Stela 23, after Norman (1973)

on Izapa Stela 50 vigorously pulling a serpent which also functions as the umbilical cord of a large skeletal god of death (Fig. 10.4*c*).

Although similar compound creatures bearing feline and skeletal attributes are found in later Maya art, they do not appear in this type of scene.

Deities and Supernatural Beings as Presence: Scenes of Power and Protection

Two-headed serpents and other supernatural beings appear as symbols of power and protection. Other deities appearing in similar contexts are feather-winged figures shown descending, hovering, or recumbent on the ground. Sometime they merely gaze down upon the narrative scene from the uppermost portions of the stela.

TWO-HEADED SERPENTINE FIGURES

The two-headed serpent appears to have moved from its position as object in the mythic-combat context to an emblematic role as a symbol of power under whose protection the human figure shown directly below moves and acts as a deity impersonator, ruler, or priest. The clearest example of this is the late Protoclassic Stela 1 at El Baúl. A two-headed serpent is shown on this stela attached to the human figure's back; the serpent extends upward to contain a downward-gazing human head within its bracket inscribed with double opposed diagonal bands (Fig. 10.4*d*). There is no question that the same double-headed serpent is represented here.

A similar theme is represented on the miniature Hauber stela (Easby and Scott 1970:Fig. 169). The articulation of forms and the definition of the constituent parts establishes this stela as an interim piece between Izapan-style art and early Classic Maya art. The motifs and their definition are very close to similar configurations found in the Early Classic Tikal Stelae 28, 1, and 2. The primary difference is in the definition of space around the figures in the respective pieces. The actual space around the Hauber figure is closer to Izapan than to Maya practices.

The downward-gazing head of the Hauber stela is contained within the open jaws of a serpent head with U element inscribed on its snout. The body of the serpent extends downward, is held by the masked figure, and continues in parallel fashion down to the lower side of the narrative frame where the small "tail" head can be seen.

Until recently there was no image dating from the Preclassic or Early Protoclassic periods that would correspond to the Late Protoclassic and Early Classic images of human heads contained within the jaws of double headed serpents. Lee Parsons (1972) discusses the representation of a related theme depicted on Abaj Takalik Stela 4 (Fig. 10.4e). Although there are no human participants in this scene that would qualify it for discussion under this heading, the representation of such a compound creature demonstrates enough parallels in form, function, and possible meaning to warrant inclusion here.

An upward-facing human head is shown within the open jaws of a large ascending serpent which emerges from a body of water shown at the bottom of the stela (Parsons 1972:Figs. 1, 2). The serpent does not have a "tail" head. However, a closer reading of the images indicates that these heads were not always presented in figurative terms. Often a sign was sufficient to indicate the head or "tail" of this compound figure. An example is the use of double opposed diagonal bands in El Baúl Stela 1 to symbolize the serpentine-saurian head of the compound creature (Fig. 10.4d). The "tail" head of this double-headed serpent demonstrates feline and serpentine traits. It is identical to the bodiless scroll-eyed heads shown as water suppliers on Izapa Stelae 1 and 23 (Fig. 10.4f). The heads in the latter are actually the "tail" heads of the double-headed celestial serpent shown directly below the top-line register (Quirarte 1974:131). The same breakdown of parts and presentation may be intended in Abaj Takalik Stela 4. The U shape refers specifically to the feline. Its inclusion here may signal the presence of the "tail" head.

FEATHER-WINGED FIGURES

The descending feather-winged gods with prominently inscribed crossed bands and U-shaped elements on Izapa Stelae 4 and 2 have no equivalents in later Maya art (Fig. 10.5a, b). This is also true of their positions as hovering on Izapa Altar 3 and recumbent on the ground on Izapa Stela 60 (Fig. 10.5d). There may be a parallel between the same

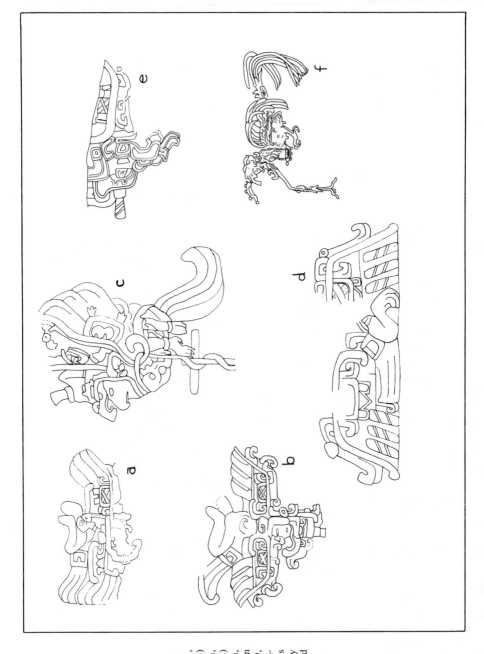

FIGURE 10.5. Feather-winged deities. *a*, Izapa, Stela 4, after Stirling (1943) and Norman (1973); *b*, Izapa, Stela 2, after Stirling (1943) and Norman (1973); *c*, Izapa, Stela 25, after Norman (1973); *d*, Izapa, Stela 60, after Norman (1973); *e*, Kaminaljuyu, Stela 11, after Miles (1965); *f*, Palenque, sanctuary tablet, Temple of the Foliated Cross, after Blom (1950)

deity shown perched on a stylized tree staff on Izapa Stela 25 (Fig. 10.5*c*) and the mythological bird shown perched on the stylized maize plants represented on the sanctuary tablets of the Palenque Temples of the Cross and Foliated Cross (Fig. 10.5*f*; Quirarte 1974:132–33).

Other related winged deities are shown gazing downward on Kaminaljuyu Stela 11 (Fig. 10.5*e*). A downward-gazing head evidenced by surviving earplug is seen on Izapa Stela 7 (Norman 1973:Pl. 14).

WORSHIP

The feather-winged god is worshiped by human figures with outstretched arms on Izapa Stela 2 and by a lone seated figure on Izapa Altar 20 (Norman 1973:Pl. 59).

Deities and Supernatural Beings as Personifications of Earth, Sky, and Water

Representations of earth and sky in Izapan-style art are extremely varied in contrast to later representations of the same creatures in Maya art. The earth monster can be the major protagonist, as on Izapa Stelae 11 and 6, or he may simply form the stage for activities represented within the narrative panels as a baseline (Izapa Stelae 7, 60, and 4) or as a frame (Izapa Stelae 12 and 5).

On Izapa Stelae 11 and 6 a fat crocodilian-saurian creature with tail and serpent bodies and heads acts as a receiver or supporter of protagonists placed directly above them within the narrative frame.

Stela 11 shows a frontal representation of a squatting crocodilian-saurian-serpentine compound creature (Norman, 1973:Pl. 22). In contrast to the predominantly feline cast of most Olmec and Olmecoid heads to which it is related, the Izapan figure has a crocodilian-type head. Another unique feature is the serpent bodies with heads extending to the sides and up to the level of the creature's head.

The serpent bodies with identical heads are probably attached to the tail of the fat crocodilian-saurian creature whose body is parallel to the picture plane. This is clearly seen on Stela 6, which shows a profile view of the same fat creature. The feline-serpent head with bifurcated tongue is seen on the lower part of the creature's back. The artist has brought the tail of the compound creature around and placed it on either side of the frontal figure. It was essential that the tail be duplicated for purposes of clarity. Since the articulation of forms followed strict frontal and profile views of objects and figures, the artist was unable to show the front and back views of the creature simultaneously. An angular view of the creature would have made it possible to do this.

On Izapa Stela 7, although represented as a full-bodied serpent, the earth creature is relegated to the baseline (Norman 1973:Pl. 14). On the left the head is physically connected to the downward-peering celestial serpent.

A segment of the terrestrial body is represented on Izapa Stelae 12 and 5 as a flat panel with serpent bodies extending up to the top-line design to form a frame for the narrative scene (Norman 1973:Pls. 24 and 10).

The earth creature has foliage or a tree growing from its tail or head on Izapa Stelae 25 and 2, as on Izapa Stelae 5 and 12. On Izapa Stelae 50 and 4 the reference to the earth creature is completely abstracted.

Two-headed serpents also personify the sky and are so represented within the upper portions of the stela as on Izapa Stela 23. The sky serpents extend downward, while the "tail" heads are shown at ground level as water suppliers (Fig. 10.4f).

The "tail" heads of the double-headed serpents discussed above are shown detached and facing each other at ground level on Izapa Stelae 1, 22, and 23 and on Abaj Takalik Stela 4 (Fig. 10.4e).

Finally, on Stela 3 an earthbound sky figure appears to control the earth serpent whose tail sits on the left of the stela (Fig. 10.4b).

The use of compound creatures to personify earth and sky is continued in Early Classic Maya art. The Maya artist retained these creatures but placed them within peripheral positions in relation to the narrative scenes. The Maya artist further standardized and subjected the compound figures to an abstraction process so that the serpent bodies if not the "heads" were eventually depicted as a series of signs and glyphs. This is particularly true of Late Classic Maya art at Palenque (Quirarte 1974).

Early Classic examples of terrestrial and celestial figures echo Izapan sources. A two-headed compound creature constitutes the platform on which a human figure stands on Tikal Stela 1 (W. R. Coe

1965a:32). The head on the right is a long-lipped head with fleshless mandible and the Tikal emblem glyph as a headdress. A glyphlike unit without a main sign occupies the position of the other "head." It is not known what was represented at baseline since only the upper half of Tikal Stela 29 is presently available (Shook 1960:32).

Tikal Stela 28 demonstrates the Maya practice of depicting a prisoner used as a platform on which the main figure stands. The captive or victim, tied at the wrists, is lying face down with the head and arms extending beyond the main figure's feet and upward on the side of the narrative scene. The overlapped legs on the other side complete the symmetrical arrangement. The figure incised on the Leyden plate has an identically positioned figure at his feet (M. D. Coe 1966:Fig. 16). He does not actually stand on this victim but it is clear that such a position was intended. Tied victims are found in other Tikal monuments. Although no such scene exists in Izapan-style art, victims are depicted in Izapa. The best example of this is the decapitation scene represented on Izapa Stela 21.

The Leyden plate, like the Diker carved stone bowl, stands as an interim piece between Protoclassic and Early Classic thematic and formal programs. Its Maya-style traits are as follows: (1) the pose of the figure, (2) its standing position on a victim one-third its size, and (3) a double-headed serpentine compound creature with small figures emerging from the open jaws of each head (ceremonial bar) cradled in its arms. The articulation as well as the individual elements and motifs are close to Izapan sources. The breechclout, comprising crossed bands, inverted U element, and stylized bifurcated tongue, clearly echoes Izapan representations of this unit. The long-lipped head with flared nostril, scroll eye, nose plugs, and a scroll emanating from the corner of the mouth, behind the tripartite inner fillet, is close to Izapan representations. The head appears upside down as the uppermost unit in the multitiered anklet on the figure's left leg and above the unit with double crossed bands directly behind the figure's earplug. It forms part of the headdress, which is primarily comprised of a feline head with serpentine references. A U element appears within the supraorbital plate of the uppermost head of the headdress.

The heads emerging from the open jaws of the double-headed serpentine creature held by the figure demonstrate features also seen in Izapan examples. The bearded head on the left is a feline serpentine head with the Y-shaped element inscribed in the headdress.

This appears repeatedly in Izapan style examples (Kaminaljuyu Stelae 10 and 11, and Izapa Stela 25).

Feather-Winged Deity Impersonators

One of the most persistent themes cutting across all representations in Olmec, Izapan, and Mayan art is the feather-winged deity impersonator. A clear parallel exists between the cave painting of a winged figure discussed by D. C. Grove (1970:8–11, 1973:132–33) and the one shown on Izapa Stela 4. The identifying features of the Izapan figure are the feather wings, the prominently inscribed crossed bands, the feline-saurian headdress mask, and diagonal bands on the breechclout. A similar combination of elements and attributes is found on the Late Protoclassic Diker carved bowl (Fig. 10.6c) discussed by Michael Coe (1973).

The Diker carved stone bowl is a key object, for it portrays a figure whose antecedents are found in the monuments mentioned above. It points to other Early Classic representations such as the seated and dancing winged figures represented on Kaminaljuyu polychromes (Fig. 10.6d) discussed by Kidder (1946:222–23; Figs. 205f, 227, 207e) and in turn is echoed by later Maya artists as demonstrated in a Classic Polychrome found in Tikal Burial 196 (Fig. 10.6e) reported by William Coe (1967:52–53).

Specifically, the parallels to Izapan-style antecedents are shown on the Diker carved stone bowl (Fig. 10.6c). The top-line register, although differing in details, is nonetheless related to similar representations in Izapan-style monuments (Fig. 10.2d). The feather-winged god impersonator shown on one side clearly demonstrates its relationship with the feather-winged figures mentioned above. The configuration of the long-lipped head with feathers attached under the arms points the way to the representation of the serpent wings found in later Maya art.

The Diker carved stone bowl winged figure has the characteristic long-lipped head just under each feather-winged arm. The head has some of the traits listed by Proskouriakoff (1950:46) for the Maya serpent. These also correspond to a trait breakdown for Izapan-style long-lipped heads (Quirarte 1973e: 15) and Kidder's Serpent X. The identical serpent segment is contained within the inner side of the

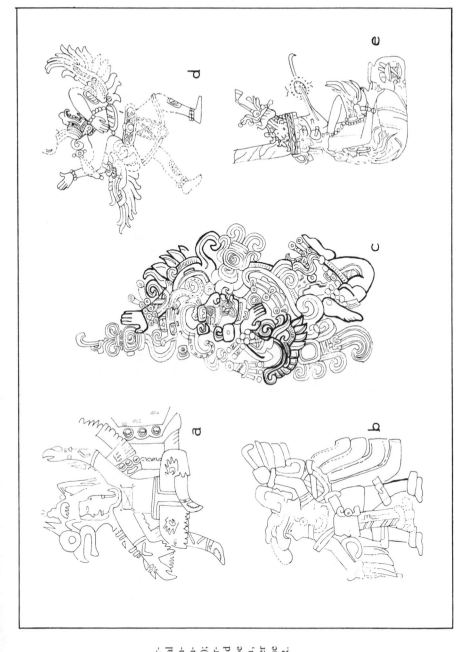

FIGURE 10.6 Feather-winged figures and mythical birds: deities and impersonators. *a*, Oxtotitlan cave mural, after D. C. Grove (1970); *b*, Izapa, Stela 4, after Norman (1973); *c*, Diker carved stone bowl, after M. D. Coe (1973a); *d*, Kaminaljuyu, stuccoed vessel, after Kidder (1946); *e*, Tikal, Polychrome vase, Burial 196, after W. R. Coe (1967)

wing(s) of all Classic Maya representations of the Serpent-Wing, Celestial Dragon, or Mythical Bird.

The Diker winged figure wears thigh cartouches and feline-serpentine buccal attachment with inscribed diagonal bands, bracelets with inscribed crossed bands, U shape within the supraorbital plate, and a feather wing in lieu of the eye. A scroll infix is contained within elaborate cartouches with pendant scrolls at uppermost headdress level and directly in front of the head (Fig. 10.3*p*). The same scroll infix is contained within the bracket with double opposed diagonal bands couching the downward-gazing head on El Baúl Stela 1 (Fig. 10.4*d*). The scroll infix also appears attached to the front of the headdress of each feline-serpentine head depicted on the Becan cylindrical tripod (Ball 1974b:4–5).

It is evident that the same deity and deity impersonators are depicted on Izapan and Maya examples. Variants on the seated figures represented on the Becan vessel are shown as dancing winged figures on a Kaminaljuyu vessel discussed by Kidder (1946:227; see Fig. 10.6*d* this volume). The stuccoed surface was in fragments, but enough remained to make a reconstruction of the scene possible. Unfortunately, only two of the masked heads were found in a complete state. One is a death mask while the other is a long-lipped head with feline, saurian, and serpentine traits. The latter is also shown on the inner side of the feathered wings. The head has a supraorbital plate in the shape of a U. Crossed bands within cartouches are worn by all figures on the belt and breech clout. Diagonal bands within cartouches are worn on the legs and attached to a beaded necklace. There is no question that this is the same figure represented on the Diker carved stone bowl, which in turn is related to the winged figures painted in the Oxtotitlan cave murals and on Izapa Stela 4.

Possibly related are the figures wearing stiff wings on Izapa Stela 9 and Kaminaljuyu Stela 11. The latter definitely shows all of the same traits—the long-lipped heads worn as a headdress, as a mask, and at belt level with the U shape, diagonals, and crossed bands included.

Twin Scroll-Eyed and Cross-Eyed Heads

The feather-winged figure and its companion depicted on the Diker stone bowl have additional references to the two-headed compound creatures discussed above. Thus this theme is further linked to earlier Olmecoid and Izapan as well as later Maya pieces.

Specifically, the bodiless heads, attached to the lowermost portions of the figures represented on the Diker bowl, demonstrate two distinct sets of traits. A predominantly feline head with nose plugs is located below the flexed legs of the winged figure on one side, while a predominantly saurian compound head is seen on the other (Fig. 10.7d_1, d_2). The latter is in the same position and is associated with a figure assuming a pose identical to that of the winged figure but demonstrating slightly different attributes. This figure wears no mask and no feather wings. The bodiless head near his foot has a U shape within cartouches on the top and on the rear of the head as well as within its open jaws. The most significant feature is the placement of the stylized iris of the eye which makes the head appear cross-eyed (Fig. 10.7d_2). In contrast the head on the other side of the vessel attached to the winged creature has a "normal" eye; its most distinguishing feature is a hooked element on its forehead (Fig. 10.7d_1). At least two Izapan-style heads have the hooked element in the same position: Izapa Stelae 69 and 3. (Fig. 10.7a, b). The first is probably a winged figure; the second is an earthbound anthropomorphic figure with feline-serpent snout.

One other feature of the cross-eyed head associated with the wingless figure on the Diker stone bowl is a gently sloping element attached to the forehead. This element is featured on another "earthbound" long-lipped head shown on Abaj Takalik Stela 3 (Figs. 10.2b, 10.7c). All of the elements seen on the saurian side of the ledger are associated with this head. Among them are the double contoured diagonal band and the U shape within the supraorbital plate.

Efforts to find clear-cut antecedents for the Diker bowl heads are difficult because the differentiation between heads is not as clearly defined in the Izapan-style examples. Antecedents for them can nonetheless be traced by studying the compound creature's heads and their location to determine whether these occupy the "head" or "tail" positions.

A predominantly feline head with serpentine references appears as a "tail" head on Kaminaljuyu Stela 19 and El Baúl Stela 1 (Fig. 10.4a, d). When these heads are placed in a baseline context and function as water suppliers, they are bodiless and shown in duplicate fashion. Examples of this are seen on Izapa Stelae 1 and 23 and Abaj Takalik Stela 4 (Fig. 10.4e, f). In the case of Izapa Stela 23, the two-headed

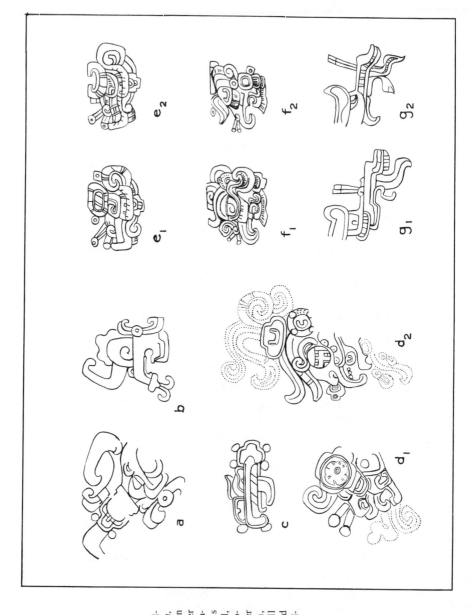

FIGURE 10.7 Twin scroll-eyed and cross-eyed heads. *a*, Izapa, Stela 69, after Norman (1973); *b*, Izapa, Stela 3, after Norman (1973); *c*, Abaj Takalik, Stela 3, after Miles (1965); *d*, Diker stone bowl, after M. D. Coe (1973a); Teotihuacan, tripod vessel, after Quirarte (1973c); *f*, Becan, tripod vessel, after Ball (1974b); *g*, Holmul, painted vase, after Merwin and Vaillant (1932).

compound creature is presented in quadruplicate fashion; that is, each head is presented twice. On Izapa Stela 1 and Abaj Takalik Stela 4, only the "tail" head is duplicated as on Izapa Stela 23.

Thus, regardless of how the two-headed creature is multiplied, its basic components are the heads which represent two distinct sets of traits: a saurian-serpentine head on one side, usually the "head," and the feline-serpentine head as the "tail." As will be seen below, similar heads bearing the scroll-eyed and cross-eyed traits as well as the "hook" and "cowlick" on the forehead appear in Classic Maya images.

Examples of Protoclassic and Early Classic heads bearing the distinct sets of traits discussed above appear in contexts which differ from those established by Izapan-style artists. The heads are no longer merely attached to a serpentine body or presented as bodiless heads within baseline panels. The heads are either (1) attached to anthropomorphic figures with body markings and other insignia which indicate that a deity or supernatural is depicted; or (2) presented as bodiless heads with no other indication of meaning or function, such as that already indicated for the Izapan-style scroll-eyed heads seen at baseline. The bodiless heads may appear on opposite sides of a vessel or on the obverse and reverse sides of a stela.

Heads associated with anthropomorphic figures are seen on the walls of a Becan cylindrical tripod vessel discussed by Ball (1974b:2–9). The heads are attached to almost identical seated figures represented on the extreme left of two large horizontal panels carved on opposite sides of the vessel (Fig. 10.7*f*). Over half of each panel is taken up by an upward-gazing feline-serpentine head with U-shaped elements forming part of the headdress. The seated figures probably emerge from the open mouths of these compound heads. A plantlike element grows from the uppermost cartouche containing the U element placed on the headdress of these heads. A long-lipped head with scroll eye and a supraorbital plate in the shape of a U is located on the right side of the headdress; directly in front of it is a glyph with a scroll infix along with part of a long-lipped head with flared nostril and nose plugs.

The heads of the Becan seated figures clearly represent the two distinct sets of traits discussed above. The figure on the left has a scroll eye while the one on the right is cross-eyed (Fig. 10.7f_1, f_2). This is in keeping with the list of traits found on the corresponding heads of the Diker carved stone bowl (Fig. 10.7d_1, d_2). A similar profile and sloping forehead "cowlick," as well as the prominently inscribed U shape, are present on the cross-eyed head. The scroll-eyed head on the other side has a hooked element instead of the cowlick.

The same two supernatural beings appear together as bodiless heads on a number of vessels found in Teotihuacan by Sigvald Linne (1934:Figs. 28, 29) in the early 1930s. These vessels have long been accepted by specialists as examples of typical Teotihuacan III pottery. I have shown elsewhere (Quirarte 1973e) that these are alien to Teotihuacan in style; in fact their possible origins may be found in the Chiapas-Guatemala Highland area (Fig. 10.7e).

The long-lipped head with scroll eye and a diagonal band placed within the supraorbital plate is seen on one side of the Xolalpan vessel, while the U shape as supraorbital plate is placed above the cross-eyed long-lipped head shown on the other side of the vessel.

This combination of traits associated with twin heads is retained in a number of Late Classic Maya images. One example will be sufficient to demonstrate this traditional arrangement. The lowermost long-lipped heads forming part of the triple-tiered back attachments worn by human celebrants represented on opposite sides of a Holmul painted vase have the traits discussed above. One head is scroll-eyed; the other is cross-eyed (Fig. 10.7g).

Summary

There is no evidence of a theme in which a compound serpent is the object of a "mythic combat" in Early Classic Maya art.

The Izapan-style double compound serpent is retained in power-conferring themes in Early Classic Maya stelae (Tikal Stelae 29, 28, 1, 2, and 31) as a ceremonial bar or equivalent object held by deity impersonators, priests, or rulers. The downward-gazing head (Tikal Stelae 29, 4, and 31) links these thematic arrangements to Izapan sources (Kaminaljuyu Stela 11).

Specifically, as in Izapan-style art, the double-headed compound creatures are presented in duplicate and quadruplicate fashion in Maya art (Izapa Stelae 1 and 23). The identical heads constituting the ceremonial bars probably correspond to one of the double-headed compound creature's heads presented in duplicate fashion. It is only in the unique articulation of the Maya manikin scepter and the heads and half figures emerging from the open jaws of the double-headed serpents that the distinct dual traits of the Izapan style double-headed compound creatures are presented.

The personification of earth and sky with compound creatures bearing feline, saurian, and serpentine traits in Izapan-style art is retained by the Maya and other Mesoamerican groups. A terrestrial dragon head, as seen on Izapa Stela 2, becomes a standard arrangement for most "presence" or power and protection scenes in Classic Maya art.

The clearest indicator of Izapan and Maya relationships is demonstrated by the feather-winged deity impersonators depicted on the Oxtotitlan mural, Izapa Stela 4, Diker carved stone bowl, Kaminaljuyu Burial B-II cylindrical tripod, and Tikal Burial 196 cylindrical polychrome vessel.

Finally, the Early Classic twin heads bearing distinct identifying features such as the "normal" and cross-eyed look are related to similar articulations in Izapan-style art and possibly earlier Olmecoid art.

Conclusions

Mythic events dominate the thematic content of Izapan-style art. Deities, supernatural beings, and their human impersonators and worshipers are the primary motifs constituting the themes of this art.

The Izapan-style artists rely alternately on figuration and abstraction in the creation of images. Both approaches can be used simultaneously within the same image. Figurative solutions can range from a stylized representation of a compound creature, such as the hovering winged figure of Izapa Stela 25, to realistic portrayals of animals, such as the crocodile with foliage growing from its tail on the same stela. Abstraction is best exemplified by the use of elements to present similar—and, in some cases, the same—compound creatures above and below the narrative scenes in most Izapa stelae.

The arrangement of figures within primarily vertical formats in Izapan-style art follows a similar unpredictable alternation between symmetry and asymmetry. While some themes may be presented in bilateral fashion, most are presented asymmetrically. Small (human) and large (deities and supernatural) figures do not balance each other out in established patterns. What is seen on one side is not necessarily echoed on the other. Each theme appears to dictate the manner of its presentation, with motifs moving freely between terrestrial and celestial bands into and out of the narrative scenes. There is no clear-cut distinction between narrative scenes and their borders. While some of the compound creatures may frame the scenes, they do not necessarily perform a secondary function either visually or thematically (See Quirarte 1974).

Although Izapan-style images appear overly complicated at first glance, the fact is that the repertoire of elements, motifs, and themes is not that extensive. Neither is their presentation. The curvilinear aspects of Izapan-style art, the most immediately apparent characteristics, give this art that "busy" look. Yet the artist(s) took great care to define figures and objects as precisely as possible according to established pictorial conventions. The contours of all elements and motifs define their shape as well as their volume. Inner fillets are rarely used to enhance the surface of the relief sculptures. Most early pieces are read primarily as a series of positive and negative spaces. The area around and behind each object is given sufficient importance to ensure that the figures—that is, all positive areas—do not become the central issue in these images. The negative areas do not ever become simply the background. There is always tension between the two so that one does not dominate the other.

In Maya art the difference between figurative and abstract approaches, positive and negative areas, symmetrical and asymmetrical arrangements, borders and narrative scenes are all subdued and under control.

The arrangement and placement of figures as well as their poses and postures are simple, predictable, and straightforward. With few exceptions almost all Maya images are symmetrically arranged.

Lateral displacement of images and texts (glyphs) is extremely sophisticated. Subtleties between positive and negative areas are one of the distinguishing achievements of Maya art. The positive areas are defined in such a way that the negative areas, literally the background, enhance their presentation. The relief surface is usually defined with equal distinction. Figures and objects are freely elaborated in terms of contours, double contours, and inner fillets. The surface is further altered by a vast array of cuts, from fine incised lines to others of varying width and depth which demonstrate a fine calligraphic quality.

There is rarely any visual confusion between images, glyphic texts, and narrative borders. Each is accorded its place. Narrative scenes, extrapictorial glyphic passages, and borders are accorded their respective functions. Everything is ordered in this fashion.

Finally, the Maya artist does not have to contend with all of the constantly opposing tendencies and tensions presented by elements, motifs, and themes, as in Izapan-style art. All aspects of the image-making process are firmly under control.

PART 4

Processes and Models

11

Environmental Heterogeneity and the Evolution of Lowland Maya Civilization

WILLIAM T. SANDERS

The Pennsylvania State University

This chapter attempts to offer a body of environmental data to support Webster's competition model (Chap. 13, below) for the evolution of Maya civilization. Basically, the argument is that population growth produced a shortage of agricultural land, leading to intra and inter-societal competition. This, in turn, produced inequities in the control of the most critical commodity in the Maya economy, agricultural land, which in turn led to ranking and ultimately to stratification.

Among the problems encountered in previous attempts to use this model were a number of misconceptions about the Lowland Maya environment. The area is huge, and to the casual observer it seems relatively homogeneous. Until recently we believed that Maya settlement was relatively light, uniform, and based on a very extensive system of land use. The absence of evidence of large-area political integration of the Aztec type and our misinterpretation of the subject matter of Maya art, furthermore, led us to believe that militarism was lacking in Maya culture. Recent evidence shows, however, that population was not in fact evenly distributed: some areas were very densely settled. We have also recently learned that the subject matter of the art is essentially secular. It involves a complex web of political alliances and intrigue, and much of it does, in fact, relate to warfare.

I will attempt to justify Webster's model by focusing on the heterogeneity of the area. This heterogeneity is not really comparable to that found in Highland Mesoamerica, but it was sufficient to have conditioned the pattern of Maya settlement recovered by archaeological research.

Although environmental heterogeneity could be demonstrated in a number of ways—by examining rainfall, coastal versus inland conditions, topography, or surface drainage, for example—I will focus here on variability in soil characteristics. This approach is justified by the fact that soil quality seems to be the major problem in adaptation of agriculturalists to the humid tropics. Unfortunately, we do not have regional soil surveys for the Maya Lowlands outside of the Southern Zone on a scale useful for the present analysis. As a primary source of data I will draw on a publication by Simmons, Tarano, and Pinto called *Clasificación de reconocimiento de los suelos de la República de Guatemala,* published in 1959 by the Guatemala Ministry of Public Education and circulated by the Ministry of Agriculture, Instituto Agro-Pecuaria. I am aware of the large scale of the study and probable inaccuracies in local detail, but such problems are inevitable in any regional survey of this type.

Simmons, Tarano, and Pinto present a succinct summary of the soil situation in the Peten which translates as follows:

An analysis of the data shows that 354,394 hectares (9.76 percent of the total) of the Peten consists of savannah soils. These are very acid, highly leached, and not recommended for cultivation or grazing without special techniques. Of this extent 73,144 hectares (2.01 percent) are characterized by good drainage and structure and 281,250 (7.75 percent) by poor drainage, including large swampy areas.

Some 3,216,348 hectares, or 89.84 percent of the area, are covered by a dense forest that would make it relatively expensive to prepare the land for agriculture. The greater amount of these soils have a moderate fertility level, but of them 1,178,257 hectares, or 32.5 percent, have poor or deficient drainage, many of which would need, besides the effort of deforestation, special works to correct the noted defects before being cultivated. About

397,385 hectares, or 10.98 percent, are deep soils with good drainage and occupied by great forests, among which there is fine quality lumber, which to a certain degree constitutes an obstacle in the preparation of the land for cultivation. About half the area, or about 1,640,706 hectares, or 46.36 percent, is represented by shallow soils with good drainage and characterized by rockiness or steep slopes, making them impractical for mechanized agriculture. They could, however, be utilized under primitive and rudimentary methods, but this would provoke a rapidly accelerating process of erosion.

Examining the soil picture more closely, the authors define 26 types based on the nature of the parent material, drainage, depths, texture, fertility, and topographic setting. These are grouped into two major categories: savannah (I) and forest (II) soils. The first is then divided into Ia (deep, well drained), Ib (deep, poorly drained), and Ic (shallow, poorly drained). The forest soils are divided into four major subgroups: IIa (deep, well drained), IIb (shallow, well drained), IIc (deep, poorly drained), and IId (shallow, with some drainage impediment). Figure 11.1 shows these distributions in the area.

The group I soils are all soils characterized by very low fertility, savannah vegetation, and generally poor drainage. There is no evidence that they were ever utilized by the Classic Maya.

Subgroup IIa includes three specific soil types: quinil, sebol, and sotz. They occur primarily in the south and west of the Peten on slopes of less than ten degrees. They make up 11 percent of the area. All three have friable surface soils and hence could be intensively cultivated using hand tools. All are characterized as moderately fertile, and both sotz and quinil soils are stated to have a tendency to become sticky when wet.

Subgroup IIb includes a high percentage of the soils of the Peten and is of special interest since the Classic Maya occupation tends to be closely associated with it. The subgroup includes seven types: cuxu, chacalte, guapaca, ixbobo, jolja, sacluc, and yaxha. They are concentrated in the south central and northeastern portions of the area. Two of them (guapaca and ixbobo) are rated as having a moderate fertility level (3 percent of the total area of the Peten) and the rest are rated as high. Another major difference within the group is that the cuxu, chacalte, guapaca, and ixbobo types all occur on unusually steep slopes (often exceeding 50 degrees) and hence are subject to par-

289

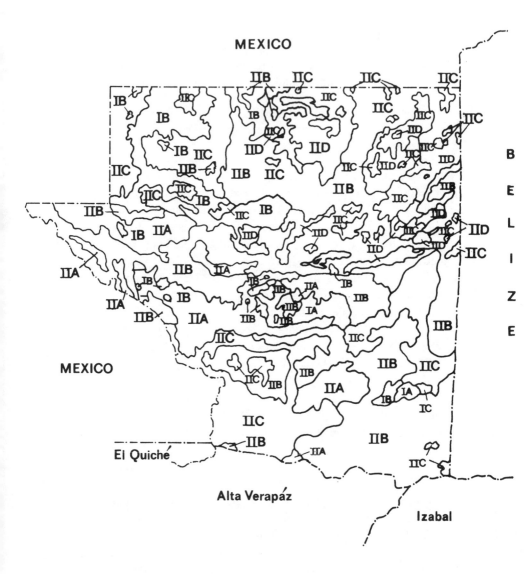

FIGURE 11.1.   Map of Peten showing soil group locations (after Simmons, Tarano, and Pinto 1959: Fig. 76)

ticularly severe erosion compared to the subgroup as a whole. This problem also occurs over an unspecified area occupied by yaxha soils. A further complicating factor is that the jolja soil type is characterized by low friability; thus only the sacluc and some yaxha soils are ideal for primitive intensive agriculture.

The IIc subgroup comprises several major types—chapayal, chucup, mopan, petexbatun, sarstun, usumacinta, and yoloch—and makes up 24 percent of the surface of the Peten. All but the mopan, petexbatun, and usumacinta have heavy plastic surface soils that would be difficult to cultivate intensively with hand tools. In terms of natural fertility the yoloch type is rated as low, mopan and usumacinta as high, and the balance as moderate. This group is distributed throughout the Peten.

Finally, subgroup IId includes two types, macanche and uaxactun, and makes up 8 percent of the area, primarily in the northeastern portions. Their high natural fertility and moderate friability would seem to make these soils excellent for both extensive and intensive cultivation with primitive tools. They also have the advantage of lower susceptibility to erosion than the IIb group. The authors, unfortunately, do not provide us with an estimate of what percentage of the area occupied by these soils presents serious drainage problems.

I have summarized the major characteristics of the 26 soil types in terms of their value for cultivation in Table 11.1. These soil statistics suggest a number of leads in understanding the evolution of Classic Maya civilization, in terms of the overall process, of the kind of civilization that evolved, and of the specific spatial distribution within the region.

The model presented here, essentially a direct application of Ester Boserup's agricultural evolution model (1965), postulates the initial phase of colonization as one of a rapid expansion of swidden farmers with a crop complex based on maize. The Peten offers an ideal setting for this type of cultivation with an unusually high percentage of the land (for tropical soils) rated as highly productive under forest or bush fallowing. All of the IIa, b, and d soils would be so classified; in other words, all the well-drained forest soils. These soils occupy 65 percent of the region. Of course, microtopographic variability would reduce this figure somewhat—a fact not taken into account in the percentage calculations of zonal soil distributions—possibly to as low as 40 percent. Nevertheless, a 40 percent cultivability ratio is extraordinarily high. A bush or forest fallowing system would permit a density of

TABLE 11.1.   SOIL CHARACTERISTICS OF THE PETEN MAYA LOWLANDS

Soil Types	Fertility	Friability	Erodability	% of Area
I. Savannah Soils				9.76
Deep, well drained				2.03
Chachaclun	Low	Moderately friable	Low	1.76
Poptun	Low	Moderately friable clay loam	Low	.27
Deep, poorly drained				7.66
Bolon	Moderate	Plastic clay	Very low	2.13
Exkixil	Low	Moderately friable silty clay	Low	.23
Machaquila	Low	Moderately friable clay	Low	.28
Saipuy	Very low	Plastic clay	Very low	5.02
Shallow, poorly drained				.09
Sachachin	Low	Friable clay	High	.09
II. Forest Soils				89.84
Deep, well drained				10.98
Quinil	Moderate	Moderately friable clay	Low	7.41
Sebol	Moderate	Friable clay loam	Low	.05
Sotz	Moderate	Friable clay	Low	3.52
Shallow, well drained				45.36
Cuxu	High	Plastic clay	Very high	8.49
Chacalte	High	Friable clay	Very high	9.77
Guapaca	Moderate	Friable clay	Very high	.44
Ixbobo	Moderate	Moderately friable clay	Very high	2.45
Jolja	High	Plastic clay	Moderate	5.33
Sacluc	High	Moderately friable clay	High	3.31
Yaxha	High	Moderately friable clay	Very high to high	15.57
Deep, poorly drained				24.11
Chapayal	Moderate	Plastic	Low	3.67
Chucup	Moderate	Plastic	Low	7.33
Mopan	High	Moderately plastic clay	Very low	2.82
Petexbatun	Moderate	Friable sandy loam	Very low	.59
Sarstun	Moderate	Plastic clay	Low	2.81
Usumacinta	High	Moderately friable clay	Very low	.55
Yoloch	Low	Plastic clay	Very Low	6.34
Shallow, deficient drainage				8.39
Macanche	High	Moderately friable clay	Very low	5.11
Uaxactun	High	Moderately friable clay	Low	3.28

40–50 persons per square kilometer of cultivable land, or an overall population of 560,000–700,000 (yielding an overall density for the area of 16–20 per sq km). Assuming an essentially swidden system for most of the Mesoamerican Lowlands through most of the pre-Hispanic sequence, this datum provides us with an understanding of the unusually highly developed civilization in the Peten.

The soil distribution also offers an explanation for the great apparent variability in the distribution and concentration of Classic Maya centers and, inferentially, Classic Maya population. The soil map does not capture all pertinent factors, so we have summarized and further refined it in the form of a diagram of agricultural productivity (see Fig. 11.2). Our procedure was to divide the area into a grid, each grid covering 300 square kilometers. The diagram includes the depths of Isabal and a portion of Alta Verapaz as well as the Peten. To simplify the diagram and to bring into greater relief the variability, any grid in which over 50 percent of the soil fell into one of the major subgroups was shown as though all of the unit was so classified. We also split IIb into two subgroups, one with soils very highly susceptible to erosion, the other highly susceptible.

The diagram dramatically illustrates the relationship between soils in the area and Classic Maya settlement, and clearly demonstrates the' unusual potential of the northeastern Peten—the area where we have the largest concentration of Classic Maya centers. The diagram also suggests that the maximum growth of population and its specific distribution in Late Classic times was in fact related to a process of agricultural intensification.

If we exclude all soils characterized by high plasticity, moderate or lower fertility ratings, or very high susceptibility to erosion and poor drainage, leaving those soils most adaptable to intensification with primitive tools, then the following picture emerges:

group I	no soils		
group IIa	no soils		
group IIb	Sacluc	3.31%	
	Yaxha	15.57%	(but some have very high erodability)
group IId	Macanche	5.11%	some areas of
	Uaxactun	3.28%	impeded drainage
		27.27%	

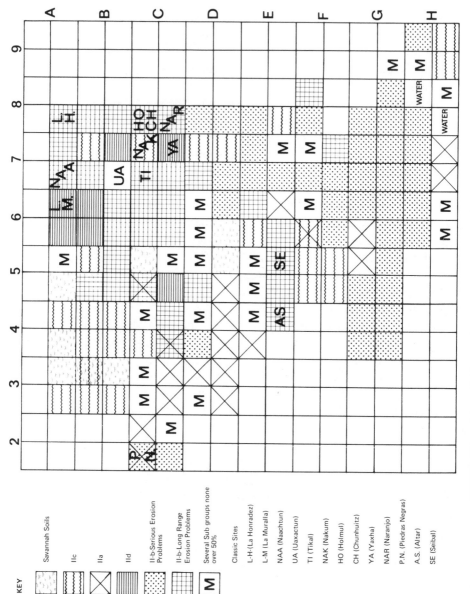

FIGURE 11.2. Schematic diagram showing correlation of soils in the Peten with major Maya
sites

KEY

Savannah Soils

IIc

IIa

IId

II-b-Serious Erosion Problems

II-b-Long Range Erosion Problems

Several Sub groups none over 50%

M Classic Sites

L-H-(La Honradez)

L-M (La Muralla)

NAA (Naachtun)

UA (Uaxactun)

TI (Tikal)

NAK (Nakum)

HO (Holmul)

CH (Chunhuitz)

YA (Yaxha)

NAR (Naranjo)

P.N. (Piedras Negras)

A.S. (Altar)

SE (Seibal)

What the data suggest is that no more than 20 percent of the land surface of the Peten is easily adapted to primitive intensive agriculture. Virtually all of the soils of this category are limited to the northeastern Peten with a much smaller comparable area along the Middle Pasión. The northeastern Peten, from the soil data alone, emerges as a kind of nuclear area. In an area measuring 6,000 square kilometers the following major sites occur: La Muralla, Naachtun, La Honradez, Uaxactun, Tikal, Nakum, Yaxha, Naranjo, Holmul, and Chanhuitz. The noted four soil types of groups IIb and IId occupy 75.2 percent of this area, whereas they occupy only 27.27 percent of the Peten as a whole.

If we reduce the figure of 75 percent to perhaps as low as 50 percent, to exclude areas of very high susceptibility to erosion or impeded drainage, and assume an overall density of 200 per sq km (see Sanders 1973) then the area could have supported a population of 600,000 at the peak of the Classic Period.

The capacity of the much smaller Middle Pasión area (1,800 sq km) calculates as follows:

	Middle Pasión Core	
group I soils		30 sq km
group IIa		300 sq km
group IIb	optimal conditions	915 sq km
group IId	severe erosion problems	555 sq km
		1,800 sq km

Not only is this core considerably smaller in overall size, but also only 50 percent falls into the optimal soil category. If we assume a comparable reduction of quality land due to erosion and impeded drainage, then the 600 sq km of optimal agricultural land under intensive cultivation would support 120,000 people, or one-fourth that of the Peten core.

The overall soil data, then, point to the unusually high potential of the Southern Maya Lowlands for swidden farming and their highly variable potential for intensive agriculture. These two factors, I believe, relate to the specific patterning of Maya growth. The data seem easily adaptable to Webster's competition model in the evolution of Maya civilization. The emergence of some level of political centralization and ranking—in other words, the basic sociological process we call civilization—could have occurred in Late Preclassic or

Protoclassic times as the product of population pressure over swidden land. In much of the Maya Lowland region, during most of the succeeding Classic Period, the agricultural system may have proved inadequate either because it did not evolve further or because attempts to intensify agriculture may have produced a rather rapid deterioration of the soil resource.

The actual population of the area necessary to produce social competition would not even have to reach our estimated carrying capacity of 500,000–700,000. Evidence from a number of studies suggests that carrying capacity as low as 30–40 percent may engender severe conflicts over land. I leave it to my colleagues to judge, on the basis of the admittedly spotty data, whether a demographic setting of this nature characterized the Maya Lowlands at the end of the Formative Period. The dramatic cultural explosion in Late Classic times in a few key areas, I am now convinced, is related to unusually high population levels made possible by intensification of land use. This level of land use, furthermore, must have operated as a major stimulus toward further centralization of the political system and increasing social stratification. In the long run, as I argued in a previous paper (1973), this process failed, and Lowland Maya civilization went through a final phase of collapse.

An additional question raised in Webster's chapter and at least implicit in a number of papers on Maya political organization is not only why major centers developed where they did, but also why or whether larger political units than, say, the local state centers, or such centers as Tikal or Uaxactun, occurred during the Classic Period. There is, of course, convincing evidence of widespread ideological contact between Maya centers and military alliance networks, and the enormous size of several Maya centers versus nearby smaller ones (say Tikal compared to Uaxactun) suggests some type of supralocal organization. My impression, however, is that the dominance of particular Maya centers over others was rather ephemeral, and that such dominance was constantly shifting. A quick glance at the Basin of Mexico in Classic times is perhaps useful at this point. The Basin is roughly the size of our northeastern Peten core. During the Classic Period the area witnessed the rise of Teotihuacan, a city whose peak population was perhaps 125,000—four times the size of Tikal. The most important comparison, however, does not lie in this direction but in the difference in size between Teotihuacan and the next largest community in the Basin. The data indicate that the city was ten times as large as the next largest community. In contrast, although we do not have population studies, a comparison of the size of public buildings at other centers in the northeastern Peten indicates that such centers as Naranjo, Nakum, Yaxha, and Naachtun were not much smaller than Tikal—certainly no less than half its size. The situation in the Basin was not exceptional during the Classic Period. Throughout the history of the area there were recurrent cases of political centralization of a comparable nature. The population of Tenochtitlan, for example, was at least five times, possibly ten times that of Texcoco, the next largest center, and Tula's population was at least five, possibly ten times the size of the largest other Mazapan site.

These differences probably relate to the much greater disparity in internal population distribution and agricultural productivity within the two areas. In the Maya case the productivity within the key areas—and these were relatively large and continuous—was relatively uniform, hence inhibiting stable political centralization above the small-state level, which in turn would inhibit the achievement of political dominance by one of the Peten centers over more lightly settled peripheral areas. In fact, if our calculation of Maya Lowland carrying capacity is reasonable, the demographic advantage of core areas over peripheries in the Maya Lowland is not comparable to that of, say, hydraulic cultivation over rainfall cultivation in central Mexico.

12

Maya Subsistence: Mythologies, Analogies, Possibilities

ROBERT McC. NETTING
University of Arizona

It is interesting to speculate on whether the anthropological investigator may take on in the course of time some of the characteristics of his subjects, whether a kind of sympathetic resemblance grows from the absorption of a student in a particular society or region. If this is indeed the case, we might expect Mayanists to form a brilliant if somewhat parochial elite among archaeologists, concerned with what seem to be cultural irregularities and the development of a civilization which appears anomalous rather than typical. No native plants or animals invite comparisons with other cradles of domestication, no rich alluvial plains suggest the growth of hydraulic politics, no current inhabitants of the lowlands provide a clear living link to the glories of the past. Rather we are confronted with a people whose greatest mystery is their abrupt departure from the stage of world history, a collapse often seen as reflecting something inherently fragile or fundamentally unworkable in the structure of Maya society.

Though an intellectual attraction to the exception is perhaps understandable among Maya scholars, it may have fostered a certain unwillingness to prove any more general rule from the apparently unique factors of their case. The question of life support in the tropics, more specifically of rain-forest agriculture, has been particularly intractable. Reading directly from present-day preferences and practices in the Peten, Mayanists agreed that shifting cultivation of maize was basic to Maya subsistence at all periods. Though the first reports and experiments showed that this technique was highly productive and afforded its devotees plenty of leisure time for temple building and stargazing, there remained a nagging doubt. Would the frequent fallowing necessitated by soil exhaustion and rapid weed growth allow maintenance of a population sufficiently dense and stable to support an elaborate religious system, monumental architecture, craft specialists, and literati? Either the jungle had to be a more beneficent environment than any temperate-zone farmer suspected or the feckless Maya had slashed-and-burned themselves to a spectacular dead end in a classic example of ecological overkill. In recent years, this pervasive myth of the milpa has come under increasingly vigorous attack from archaeologists convinced that man does not necessarily live by tortillas alone and that those multitudes of house mounds in the sprawling sustaining areas of Maya suburbia were fairly continuously inhabited by a goodly number of warm bodies.[1]

Perhaps the time is ripe to suggest some alternative and less familiar models of intensive tropical agriculture depending neither on wet rice (which the Maya did not have) nor on complex irrigation systems (which they did not need). I have in mind a system of infield-outfield cultivation with permanent kitchen gardens producing root and tree crops in a pattern of dispersed settlement. Such an adaptation is found among indigenous Ibo populations of eastern Nigeria where the natural environment, crops, settlement layout, and perhaps community integration exhibit possible parallels to those of the ancient Maya. In order to show that similar processes were at work, I must resort to the suspect and much-maligned use of ethnographic analogy. I take heart from the fact that even archaeologists in good standing have sought comparisons as far away as Cambodia (M. D. Coe 1957a), and that as a garden-variety ethnographer who has never set foot in Mesoamerica, nothing more substantive could be expected from me.[2] I make no claims to illuminate authoritatively the darkness at the heart of tropical ecosystems but rather offer some might-have-been alternatives to the just-so stories of the Maya milpa.

NATURAL ENVIRONMENT

A comparison of the Lowland Maya area, by which I mean the Yucatan Peninsula of Mexico, Belize, and the Peten of Guatemala, with the homeland of the Ibo-speaking peoples east of the Niger River in southern Nigeria is not beyond the stretch of geographical imagination. Table 12.1, showing gross features of precipitation, temperatures, soils, flora, and general climatic zones, indicates a number of similarities. Variations within each region from higher rainfall and more dense tropical forest in the south to a drier, savannahlike environment in the north are roughly parallel. Pronounced differences—like the Ibo replacement of much lowland forest by palm bush and, farther north, by derived savannah—may represent the effects of present population pressure in contrast to the situation in the Peten, whose high forest today shows the marks of human intervention mainly in the prevalence of economically useful wild species (Lundell 1938:38). A major distinction between the two areas is in soil composition, with the Yucatan rendzinas and terra rosas derived from a limestone base (Ferdon 1959; Stevens 1964) while the red earths of Iboland have weathered from sedimentary sandstones. Both favor quick seepage except in alluvial areas, but the calcimorphic soils may retain their fertility longer than the quickly impoverished African counterpart. Very much the same types of crops are suited to both regions and a certain amount of fruitful exchange has taken place between them, suggesting at the very least that we are comparing not apples and oranges but something more akin, perhaps, to two varieties of tropical citrus.

THE IBO

Agricultural Intensification

Superficially, food production among the contemporary Lowland Maya bears very little resemblance to that among the Ibo. The conventional picture of Maya agriculture is of temporary cultivation of maize with perhaps some beans, squash, and chile. Observations of rapidly declining yields and the testimony of the farmers themselves reinforce the impression that "the only kind of farming possi-

TABLE 12.1 ENVIRONMENTAL COMPARISONS BETWEEN THE MAYA LOWLANDS AND THE IBO REGION OF NIGERIA

	Maya Lowlands		Ibo Region	
Annual Rainfall (in millimeters)	1. Peten, band across base of Yucatan Peninsula. Tikal and Belize on 2,000 mm line. Usumacinta drains center of area.	2,000–3,000	1. Southern section (heavy showers leading to erosion)	1,800–2,000
			2. Northern section	1,000–1,800
	2. Most of Yucatan	1,000–2,000		
	Quintana Roo	1,200–1,500		
	Campeche	900–1,700		
	3. Northwest Yucatan	500–1,000		
	Progreso	470		
	Mérida	913		
Temperatures (Centigrade)	Variability: 10–40° Monthly mean: 25–26° with variation from 22.7–28.5° Never below 18° limit of tropical lowlands		Monthly mean: highest 35°, lowest 26°	
Soils	1. Hydromorphic glei soils from Tabasco across Peten. Intermittent waterlogging. High organic content where drainage restricted. 2. Calcimorphic rendzina developed from limestone base. Central and east Yucatan, much of Peten. 3. Terra rosa laterized in wet-dry season climate, high calcium content. Northwest Yucatan from south of Campeche to northeast tip of peninsula.		Derived from sedimentary rocks, red earths, or acid sand; poor in mineral nutrients; coarse texture favors quick seepage, rapid leaching. Above Udi escarpment derived from soft red sandstone, easily worked but impoverished, fertile when cleared but rapidly depleted by cropping.	

Flora	1. High lowland forest (150 ft) with some deciduous trees. Real rain forest in only a few places. Forest shows human interference: middle story of Brosimun, Achras, Talisia; understory of palms, avocado, mamey, copal. 2. Interspersed savannahs with coarse grass, stunted trees in Peten, southern Campeche.	1. Lowland tropical forest (120 ft) with three strata, rain forest along streams, replaced by palm bush. 2. Derived savannah with relict forest north of 2,030 mm isohyet; villages form forested islands in poor upland grasslands.

Climatic Zones	1. Afẃ—Tropical rainforest: at least 60 mm rain per month. Brackets Usumacinta, widens to include coast of Honduras.
	2. Amẃ—Tropical monsoon: short dry period in winter, at least 1 month less than 60 mm
	   Chetumal 3 months 30 mm or less
	   Cozumel 3 months 57 mm or less
	3. Aw—Tropical wet and dry, November-May dry season. Desiccation of grass, seasonal leaf fall. Lowland Veracruz, northwestern Yucatan.
	   Campeche 7 months
	   Merida 6 months
		1. Amẃ—Tropical monsoon (Guinean): 2,000–2,600 mm rainfall, less than 3 months dry season (Orlu, Owerri, Abak)
		2. Aw—Tropical wet and dry (sub-Guinean): 1,400–2,000 mm rainfall, 3-to-5-month dry season (November-March) with less than 60 mm. Summer rainfall twin peak; precipitation is temporally and spatially irregular.

	Sources: Vivo Escoto 1949, 1964; Stevens 1964.	Sources: Buchanan and Pugh 1955; Morgan 1959; A. T. Grove 1951.

ble . . . in the Maya lowlands is . . . a shifting, slash-and-burn system under which the forest is permitted to regenerate at intervals" (M. D. Coe 1967:25). Usually a plot is cultivated for two years followed by four to seven years of fallow in the Peten or fifteen to twenty years in Yucatan. With the research into shifting cultivation that has gone on in Southeast Asia (Freeman 1955; Conklin 1954; Geertz 1963; Spencer 1966) and South America (Carneiro 1961; Harris 1972a) in recent years, there can be no doubt that such a system is not only viable but perhaps also maximally efficient under tropical conditions. It is equally clear that shifting cultivation has a real limit defined by the ratio of population to available land. When this balance is exceeded, integral and self-perpetuating subsistence is threatened and the signs of erosion, replacement of forest by less productive grasslands, and human malnutrition become rapidly evident. Among the possible social responses to such a situation of deteriorating man-land relationships is the option of achieving a more stable and dependable food supply by maintaining smaller plots of land per capita in continuous production through the application of increased amounts of labor and new technology—in short, by means of agricultural intensification. Such a course requires perhaps less initiative than a mass migration and less courage than an immediate attack on one's slightly less hungry neighbors. Nevertheless it is a practical and undramatic alternative which seems to have occurred with amazing frequency to peoples whose population, for whatever reason, had gotten out of equilibrium with their means of production (Boserup 1965).

Though we have been reliably informed on a number of occasions (see Meggers 1954) that such a possibility is not available to those locked into the tropical regime of high temperatures, leaching rainfall, lateritic soils, and competing jungle growth, it is plain that intensification can take place even under a humid southern exposure. The Ibo experience indicates that a change from tropical swidden cultivation to fixed-plot horticulture is neither contradictory nor abrupt—comes the revolution and no one need be aware it is happening. Basic principles are not altered. As the fallow cycle shortens, the cultivator continues to rely on "mixed plant assemblages of trees, shrubs, climbers, herbs, and root crops which take over spatial and functional roles similar to those fulfilled by wild species of equivalent life forms in the natural forest ecosystem" (Harris 1972b).

The southern root economy characterizing most of the forest zones of West Africa relies on the bush fallowing of yams and manioc, with maize, rice, and beans as subsidiary crops. Clearing and burning is followed at the first rains in March by the planting of yams and corn, plus pumpkins, melons, and calabashes. After the first corn harvest in June, beans, manioc, okra, and cocoyams are planted. Yams are dug in September or October, and the second harvest of maize takes place from October to November. The farmer may return for one or two years to gather later-maturing cocoyams and manioc. The preferred fallow period allowing adequate restoration of fertility is eight to fifteen years (Buchanan and Pugh 1955:105). Where this must be reduced due to land scarcity, a rudimentary sedentary cultivation is gradually introduced, based on rotation of crops, more careful selection of seeds, and sequential planting. In a sample rotation from Nnewi in Onitsha Province (Table 12.2), legumes such as beans and pigeon peas are consciously used as soil builders, and wild crotolaria is used at the end of a cropping cycle as a ground cover to bind the soil and protect it from climatic elements (Floyd 1969). When woody plants no longer regenerate spontaneously, the shrubs *Acioa barteri* and *Macrolobium macrophyllum* may be planted to help restore fertility during the fallow period (A. T. Grove 1951; Morgan 1959). A succession of crops not only shelters the land and extends the harvest but also guarantees that at least one crop will succeed under varying weather conditions (Morgan 1955). The close correlation of declining field size and shorter fallows with increased population density is

TABLE 12.2.   CROP ROTATION AT NNEWI, NIGERIA

First Year	Second Year	Third Year
Yams	Maize or cocoyams	Late manioc
Beans	Beans	Pigeon peas or cucurbits
Vegetables	Vegetables	Crotolaria fallow
	Early manioc	

Source: Floyd 1969:179.

TABLE 12.3.   IBO POPULATION DENSITY AND AGRICULTURE, NIGERIA

Area	Population Density	Length of Fallow (years)	Average Holding (acres)
Aba	over 1,000	3	3
Nvosi	436	5	4
Ndoki	148	7	10 or more

Source: Morgan 1955.

apparent in Table 12.3. It is also noteworthy that the more crowded Ibo areas feature four or five crops of major importance (yam, manioc, cocoyam, maize, pigeon pea), while their neighbors with more abundant land rely on two or three crops or even an imperfect monoculture (Floyd 1969:187). Though the most desirable food crop remains the yam, its production is declining in favor of manioc. Because manioc does not require rich soil, it gives higher yields under conditions of shortened fallow. It also takes less time than the yam to grow, can be harvested when no other fresh food is available, and may be processed into a flour called *gari* which is easily stored and transported (Morgan 1955).

Along with more continuous use of outer farmlands, intensive use has altered the composition of remaining wild vegetation. High forest has been practically eliminated from much of southern Iboland, being replaced by dense stands of self-seeded oil palms. This tree grows best in moist yet well-drained soils and can flourish on sands of relatively low nutrient status. In the Ibo uplands, though water soaks away rapidly, the soil remains moist at depths of five feet or so even in the dry season. This factor accounts in part for the success of tree crops (A. T. Grove 1951). The palm provides a vitamin-rich edible oil from both the fleshy outer layer of the fruit and the kernel. Its sap, slightly fermented as palm wine, is an important part of the daily diet. Leaf ribs are used in building, leaves in thatching, and fibre in rope (Buchanan and Pugh 1955:132). Because palm oil is sold on the international market, the tree is a mainstay of the Ibo cash as well as domestic economy. By protecting young trees while eliminating competing vegetation, tapping the trees, and regularly collecting their fruit, the Ibo have intensified gathering activities along with the more explicitly agricultural activities. Organic materials are also transferred from the forest to farmlands by leaf mulching, a labor-intensive activity involving spreading litter from the forest floor on fields. This also cuts down the loss of soil water evaporation (Floyd 1969:180). The same effect can be achieved by dry mulching, tilling the surface of the soil at intervals during the dry season.

Though manuring and composting practices are being extended to the outer farmlands, they are most highly developed on small plots immediately adjoining the residential compounds. Undoubtedly certain vegetables and condiments along with fruit trees have always been cultivated near dwellings or in small patches within compound walls.

Land scarcity and diminishing yields from outer farmlands have led to the raising of basic starchy foodstuffs such as yams and cocoyams by methods of permanent horticulture on the compound plots. Kitchen gardening of this type is found in virtually all Ibo rural villages today, and it has been extended into outer farmlands on the peripheries of settlements in areas of highest population density from Onitsha to Uyo (Fig. 12.1) and on the Udi Plateau (Floyd 1969:181). In the village of Oko on the Awka escarpment, an average family of five may be supported by about 2 acres of compound farm with an additional half acre of swidden cultivated after four to six years under grass fallow (A. T. Grove 1951). Kitchen gardens may also be scattered in small plots of 0.1 or 0.2 acre each.

> The impression gained is one of a multi-tiered system of farming with several levels of crops being maintained on the same few square yards of soil: an ingenious technique of mixed and sequential cropping. Lowly groundcreeping plants such as the cucurbits are shaded by the foliage of root crops, which in turn are found growing within the shade of the smaller "economic" trees such as the banana, plantain, orange, mango, breadfruit, native pear, cashew, castor bean and kola; the ubiquitious oil palms grow taller varying in height from some thirty to sixty feet, and only eclipsed by scattered specimens of forest giants from the original rainforest, especially cottonwood trees. In sum, as many as a dozen food-yielding, beneficial plants may be struggling for survival and fruition in hard proximity. (Floyd 1969:181)

Far from being a primitive and inefficient alternative to modern specialized agriculture and monoculture, mixed cropping may be highly beneficial under tropical conditions. The variety of vegetation provides better maintenance of soil fertility, requires fewer chemical fertilizers and pesticides, is less subject to invasions by pests and diseases, and prevents the decline of nutritive value in cereal grains and vegetables (Igbozurike 1971).

Richer kitchen garden soils maintained by the composting of household waste and ashes, dead leaves, stalks, and vegetable peelings, plus the dung of goats and chickens, allow the growing of demanding crops such as tobacco, sugarcane, bananas, various vegetable and leaf plants, peppers, pineapple, and papaya. Night soil is systematically collected in areas of severe land shortage such as Ezza in Abakaliki (Wallace 1941). With a higher organic content, the

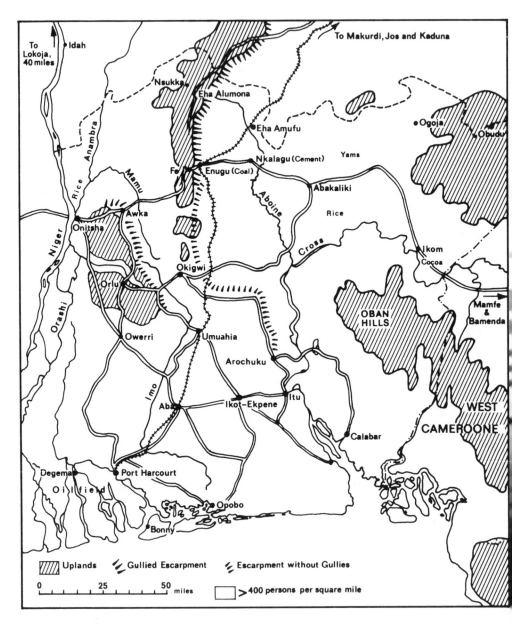

FIGURE 12.1.   Map of Eastern Nigeria

garden soils retain moisture for a longer period, receive extra water from roofs and courtyard runoff, and are protected from the direct action of sun and rain by shade trees (Morgan 1969a). The earth may be ridged with compost buried in the furrows of the previous season and depressions between the ridges retaining rain water. Further seed and top dressings of organic matter are made at planting time (Floyd 1969:182). On hilly tracts, terraces with dry stone retaining walls are constructed (Floyd 1965).

A multiple land-use system combining permanent kitchen gardens with more distant shifting cultivation provides not only nutritional variety and insurance against crop failure but also a more efficient distribution of labor. The garden needs little dry-season labor but considerable weeding during the rains (4–10 man-days per acre) as well as manuring (10 man-days per acre for digging, carrying, and spreading three tons of compost) (Morgan 1969a). Fine-comb cultivation techniques are more elaborate, more careful, and more time-consuming than those required for shifting cultivation. Residence in the immediate vicinity of the plot allows selective harvesting of produce and fruit, protection from pests, and prevention of theft. Travel time to and from the field is reduced to a minimum. Horticultural tasks can be readily performed by women and children, thus enlarging the available work force. For the more distant bush fallows, the maximum labor demand is in the dry season for clearing and burning. Tillage techniques are cruder than in the gardens, and less weeding is done. Crops grown by shifting methods need to be fairly tolerant of weed infestation and have some resistance to pests and plant diseases. It is probable that total labor input increases with agricultural intensity, and that some effort previously absorbed by gathering and hunting is redirected into farming as accessible forest areas shrink.

I am not contending here that Ibo agriculture is either an ancient and stable pattern of subsistence or that it is an optimal adaptation to a tropical environment. The southward movement of Ibo-speaking populations into a heavily forested zone may well have become important only from the seventeenth century onward (Morgan 1959). American domesticates such as maize, manioc, peanuts, sweet potatoes, tobacco, and various citrus fruits were probably introduced by the Portuguese through Benin in the sixteenth century. Steel machetes traded in from Europe made possible easier and more rapid forest clearance, though drier northern woodlands could be opened effectively by ringing and later burning the trees. Palm oil became important commercially only after the decline of the European slave trade in the nineteenth century. The point to be made is not the antiquity of intensive agriculture among the Ibo but the very rapidity of its development and elaboration under conditions of land scarcity and growth in population density. Crop diversification and rotation, use of soil-building plants during fallow periods, composting, ridging, kitchen gardening, and higher, more continuous applications of labor all contributed to this intensification. It is clear, however, that in many areas high forest was eliminated, savannah grasslands spread, and soil deterioration was marked. Removal of timber from certain watersheds hastened some spectacular examples of gully erosion (A. T. Grove 1967). Where rural population densities surpass 1,000 per square mile, even the most intensive local agriculture cannot support the entire population, and imports of foodstuffs (chiefly fish and beef) must be paid for with proceeds from trading and migratory wage work (Udo 1964). Where kitchen gardening is dominant, as many as 60 to 70 percent of adult males may be absent at any one time. Agricultural intensification appears, then, as a possible and practical means of coping with land scarcity in the tropics, though not as a final or sufficient solution to all problems of ecosystem imbalance.

Settlement Pattern and Land Tenure

If intensity of land use indeed varies directly with population pressure, we might expect such social factors as residence location and rights to the means of production to show correlated changes. A relatively pure system of shifting cultivation in the presence of abundant virgin or fully regenerated forest with population densities of 25 to 30 per square mile could be carried on from a hamlet whose location changed occasionally for purposes of convenience. As land became less easily available and bush fallowing took on a more regular sequence, the nucleated village on a permanent site offered certain advantages. From this central point, the lands encircling the village were relatively equidistant, and a plan of farming each sector of the land in turn while protecting the fallowed fields from incursion could be administered. The maintenance of paths radiating from the village and initial clearing operations could be cooperatively organized. A larger nucleated settlement could better defend its territory, and before the end of the slave trade and tribal wars, compounds were often built within a ring of thick forest or earthworks (Udo 1965). A village core with dependent hamlet clusters might number 1,000 to 5,000 inhabitants and occupy up to 15 square miles (Floyd 1969:56). Allotments of usufruct rights in village or clan lands could be made annually in accord with the needs of each household. A network of parent and daughter colony villages of this type spread through the Ibo uplands where light, well-drained soils were easier to clear, better adapted to root crops, and more suitable for oil palms. Communication was maintained by footpaths along elevated watershed ridges, avoiding the seasonal swamps and dense underbrush of low-lying areas (Floyd 1969:48). The major locational problem may have been the distance to dependable water supplies during the dry season, when surface water disappeared into the porous soil.

Continued population growth without the possibility of migration encouraged the increased reliance on kitchen gardening and at the same time led to the disintegration of nucleated settlements. "It is reasonable . . . to suggest that under conditions requiring more intensive use of land, a dispersed settlement pattern brings population into closer contact with the land than does a pattern of settlement nucleation" (Prothero 1972). Morgan (1955) has estimated that a rotation requiring three acres under cultivation for a family of 7 with a minimal three-year fallow period could support some 373 individuals per square mile of farmed land. When a critical density of 382 to 490 is reached, shifting cultivation is no longer adequate and various measures of intensification must be introduced. Under such circumstances, compounds become dispersed, each household being located in the midst of its own kitchen garden-orchard. Dispersed settlement—as opposed to nucleated villages, street villages, and compact hamlets—shows a strong correlation with Ibo areas having populations in excess of 400 per square mile; where densities reach 1,000, the dispersed compounds are practically continuous (Figs. 12.2, 12.3). On the uplands between Awka, Enugu, and Nsukka, "towns" each containing between 10,000 and 60,000 people in dispersed compounds have appeared (Morgan 1965). As compounds fill up a village territory, farmlands formerly under shifting cultivation are put under permanent cultivation as compound gardens. Open farmlands and forest may practically disappear from an area in less than thirty years (Figs. 12.4, 12.5). Evidently convenience to

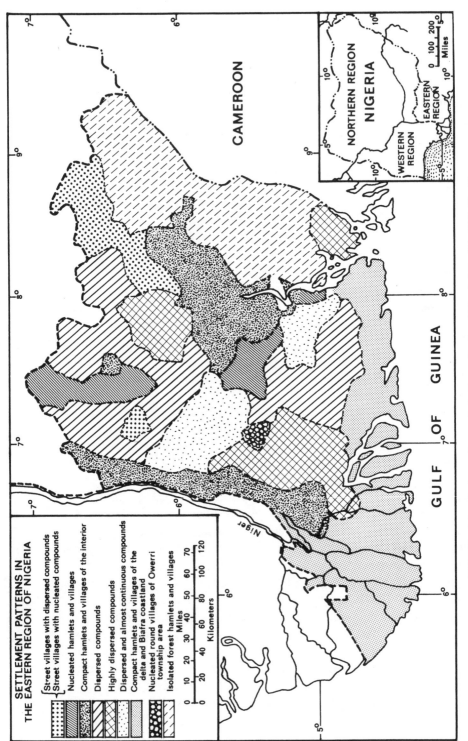

FIGURE 12.2. Settlement Patterns in the Eastern Region of Nigeria (after Udo 1965: Fig. 1)

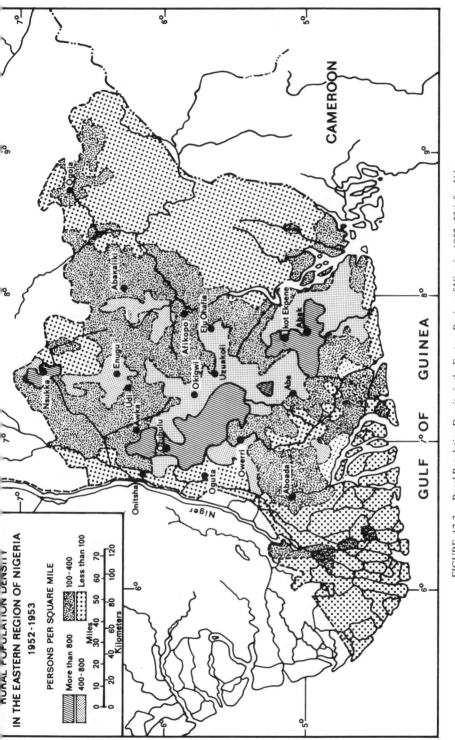

FIGURE 12.3.   Rural Population Density in the Eastern Region of Nigeria, 1952–53 (after Udo 1965: Fig. 2)

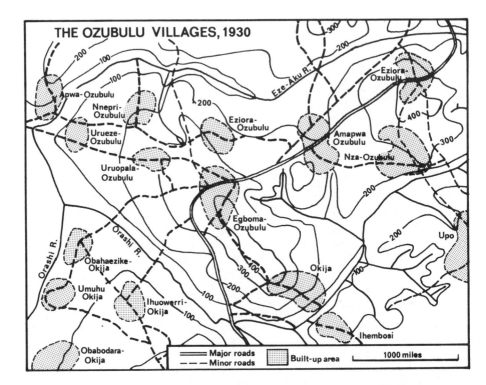

FIGURE 12.4. The Ozubulu Villages, Eastern Nigeria, 1930 (after Udo 1965: Fig. 6)

agricultural land rather than the location of water determined compound siting. Some households lived as far as eight miles from permanent water sources, and clay-lined catch pits at the compound were usually unfit for drinking purposes (Morgan 1955).

When communal lands could no longer be allotted by the elders in adequate amounts to all households, demands for individual tenure appeared. Private or *okpulu* land, usually that occupied by the compound and its associated gardens, has always been regarded by the Ibo as belonging to an individual or family by title comparable to freehold, except that it could not be alienated (Morgan 1955). The conversion of community land to residential and kitchen garden use brought about the dominance of individual ownership without radically changing cultural rules or the traditional association between land use and land tenure. Only with personally owned land could a man find

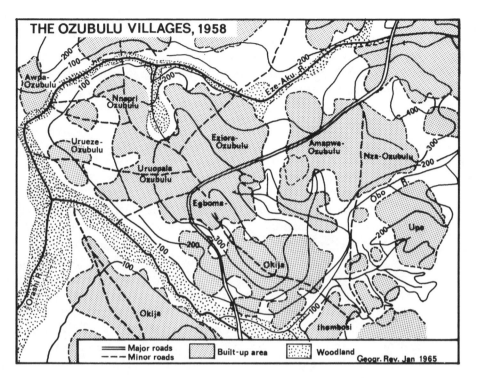

FIGURE 12.5.   The Ozubulu Villages, Eastern Nigeria, 1958 (after Udo 1965: Fig. 7)

security, and arrangements for pledging, renting, and selling property
rapidly appeared (Chubb 1961; Jones 1949). As increasing demand for
farmland led to disputes, heirs enforced their claims by building on a
plot (Udo 1965) and planting the economic trees or permanent
vegetable beds indicating continuity of possession (Morgan 1969a).
Lineage members may also have dispersed to the borders of their
territory to defend it better from incursions of competing kin groups.
Fragmentation of communal lands and the advantages of residence on
or near the garden have also contributed to the breaking down of large
extended family households in detached houses (Udo 1965; Netting
1969). With individual tenure and nuclear family households replacing
communal village landholdings and the cooperative extended family
compound, it is obvious that economic differences should become
pronounced and that wide variations in access to productive resources

315

should ensue. Along with the tendency to individual tenure under conditions of crowding, one observer has noted the appearance of more permanent rectilinear plot shapes in what may be the minimum useful size (Morgan 1955). Fields reached by regularly spaced parallel paths have narrow frontages of about nine yards, approaching a standard of one-fifth of an acre, useful in measurement, inheritance division, exchange, and sale.

Commerce and Politico-Religious Integration

The obverse of agricultural intensification is what might be called economic extensification. The same pressures threatening local subsistence self-sufficiency also increase the selective advantage of craft specialization and exchange networks. A denser population concentration of farmers needs supplementary foods, fibers, cutting and digging implements, and processing materials for milling, cooking, and so forth which cannot be easily supplied from accessible forests, streams, or quarries. Imported luxury goods for social display and ritual purposes may also be in greater and steadier demand. In upland areas where chronic food shortages exist despite the emphasis on labor-intensive horticulture, the Ibo have long been involved in textile weaving, palm-produce processing, blacksmithing, and other specialties. For the salt, yams, and smoked fish of the Niger riverine region, they traded iron tools, cotton fabric, palm oil, livestock, and, formerly, slaves (Henderson 1972:36). From the seventeenth century on, lowland Ibo shipped camwood and slaves downriver in exchange for European copper bracelets and manufactured goods and also transmitted ivory and potash north to the Benue confluence. The great entrepot in this trade was Onitsha, situated above the Niger floodwaters and providing direct access to the densely settled uplands. Onitsha, almost alone among Ibo centers, qualifies as a city with a state organization focused on a sacred kingship.

The number and size of domestic markets in the uplands reflects the dependence of these villages on foodstuffs from the lowlands (A. T. Grove 1951). Most villages have markets once every four to eight days and are attended by as many as 4,000 people from a radius of ten miles. Villages may develop reputations for particular crafts, as in the case of blacksmithing for Awka, or Inyi pottery, which is traded over distances of about thirty miles. It is also from congested districts of continuous gardens that migration is most apparent. Men go to plant yams in the lowlands (Udo 1964) or become laborers, petty traders, or clerks in modern towns. Education is most popular in areas where farming opportunities are limited. Such observations, supported by comparative material from peasant China, Russia, and England (Netting 1974), suggest that craft specialization and expanded trade are less the result of rural affluence and leisure than of an agricultural squeeze in which the production of inadequate land resources must be supplemented with part-time occupations of other sorts. Though trade may eventually bring wealth, it seems to be in the first instance a final resort of the poor farmer whose preference for the security and independence of self-sufficient agriculture remains clear. The relative convenience and lightness of most tasks connected with kitchen gardening and arboriculture also means that the continuous presence of mature males is not required.

Though Ibo political organization has conventionally been treated as small-scale and fragmented, with authority exercised by a variety of clan councils, village heads, and title societies, it is now becoming apparent that more exclusive structures of common ritual and symbolic hegemony did exist. The origin myth of the Nri king narrates his coming from the north, his initial growing of yam and cocoyam from the heads of his sacrificed son and daughter, and his production of a sacred medicine rendering yams edible (Henderson 1972:60). He and his siblings founded a chain of communities in what is now the most densely populated part of the Ibo uplands east of Onitsha. They collected an annual tribute in return for the use of their yam medicine. The descendants of the Nri king traditionally established the annual ritual calendar of these communities as well as the schedule of weekly markets. Men of the royal village who had achieved the ritual purification represented by the *ozo* title were free to travel in safety through Ibo country, carrying their sacred staffs and the medicines that enabled them to cleanse other communities of social abominations. They could confer *ozo* titles on others and dispense the sacred yam medicine. "This symbolic charter and the rights formulated by it defined a dependence among these Ibo groups upon Nri for their subsistence, law, and attainment of prestige" (Henderson 1972:61). It is not asserted that the Nri king exercised direct political control over the largely autonomous local groupings of Ibo, but rather that he embodied shared religious ideas and used ritual means to promote communications, settle disputes, and legitimize the power of village leaders. That this role carried with it superior prestige and considerable wealth can be seen in the richness and artistry of grave goods in the royal burial at Agu-uku (Shaw 1970).

A more recent but still functionally similar pattern of politico-religious integration can be seen in the network of Aro Chuku colonies whose resident agents guided Ibo suppliants to the shrine of a powerful oracle (Ottenberg 1958). I have suggested elsewhere (Netting 1972) that conflicts arising from heightened competition for agricultural land could be mitigated or resolved by such supernaturally sanctioned adjudication, and that magically protected trade routes and merchants could greatly increase commercial activity in the absence of a strong, centralized government. The establishment of spiritual supremacy demonstrated in fundamental agricultural ritual, the scheduling of public occasions, the administration and protection of trade, and the mediation of serious disputes may have been a frequent precursor of more formal and authoritative institutions of statehood. When the problems faced by a group arise from the internal dynamics of their ecosystem rather than from an external military threat, there may be an advantage to voluntaristic, religiously sanctioned organization of the Ibo type as opposed to the direct imposition of coercive or exploitative mechanisms.

THE MAYA

Reconstructing Maya Agriculture

The purpose of the lengthy excursion into the farming and society of the West African Ibo was to provide a single detailed model indicating the possibility of agricultural intensification in the humid tropics and the evolutionary association of this process with population increase, growth in occupational specialization and trade, and new types of politico-religious integration. I submit that there may be functional similarities between the Ibo and the Preclassic Maya, though close resemblances in form and in the details of the two systems are not to be expected. A look at some of the evidence on Lowland Maya agriculture, along with the inferences we may make from other

Mesoamerican ethnographic cases, should show whether or not we have our parallels straight.

The most solid proof of intensive agricultural techniques among the Maya is the remains of drained or ridged fields along the Candelaria and Usumacinta rivers (Puleston and Puleston 1971; Siemens and Puleston 1972). Similar ridged fields along the Hondo River are tentatively assigned to the periods of late Preclassic through Classic (Hammond 1976:11). Though drainage techniques are less dramatic than the irrigation and chinampas seen in other parts of aboriginal America, their presence probably indicates a population exceeding the carrying capacity of more easily cultivated land (Denevan 1970). Obviously considerable amounts of labor were expended in constructing ridges 25 to 30 meters long, 5 meters wide, and 1 meter high. This suggests permanent or repeated use and at least a partial dependence on techniques other than those of the shifting milpa. While land itself may not have been limited, the rich alluvial bottomlands handy to sources of aquatic animal protein, neither waterlogged nor seasonally dried out, and reachable by boat were clearly in scarce supply. The annual process of cleaning out the ditches, though laborious, would have both ensured drainage and fertilized the ridge tops with muck, thereby allowing production without periodic fallowing. It is possible that fruit trees and long-maturing root crops like manioc could occupy the ridge tops while water-loving xanthosoma and a catch crop of maize could grow in the channel during the dry season. If a riverine or littoral environment offers the best possibilities for hunter-gatherers who are incipient cultivators in the tropics, as Carl Sauer (1958) suggested, the river routes into the Yucatan Peninsula may have been the scene of early demographic pressures and agricultural experimentation.

Drainage techniques in low-lying *bajos* and savannah depressions were supplemented by extensive terracing in eastern Guatemala, Belize (Wilken 1971), and the Rio Bec uplands. "Tens of thousands of relic terraces crisscross the hillsides of southern Campeche and Quintana Roo, encompassing an area exceeding 10,000 square kilometers" (Turner 1974). The system of rock embankments collecting the eroding soil of sloping fields plus elevated walkways controlling runoff and allowing easy movement during the long wet season is inconsistent with any notion of long-fallow agriculture. The gradual emergence of such intensive techniques is credited by Turner to enlarging populations during the Late Classic Period. No single method of food production is claimed here (Wilken 1971), and indeed the key to effective permanent agriculture is its employment of a range of techniques specifically adapted to local differences of terrain, moisture, and soil. Changes in the physical environment through time or because of the demands placed on it by the human population should also be sensitively registered by the subsistence system.

Another sort of intensification is that promoted by exceptionally fertile areas, often either volcanic or alluvial, where rainfall is sufficient to grow two or three crops a year. "High-performance milpa" is familiar in the Guatemalan Highlands (Wilken 1971). Double cropping of maize with a short fallow cycle is possible in the pioneer area north and south of Poptun reported on by Culbert, Magers, and Spencer (1974). If shifting techniques alone could produce sustained yields, an area such as this might be, at least temporarily, a kind of agricultural Eden. However, the rapid growth of population which seems always to accompany such frontier conditions would almost inevitably lead to a shrinking per capita land base and efforts to raise or at least artificially maintain high production. Emigrants from a favored region might also be motivated to duplicate such cultivation where deficiencies of soil or climate made this difficult.

The Ibo model suggests to me that a locally adjusted mix of (1) milpa with multiple cropping where possible, (2) drained fields in alluvial or swampy areas, (3) terraces on slopes, and (4) fixed-plot kitchen garden-orchards may have formed the base for Maya subsistence at densities reaching 300 to 500 per square mile.[3] The relative importance of maize, roots, vegetables, tree crops, and wild forest produce would vary according to the local environment and the pressure of population, but intensification could proceed rapidly and effectively without the need for a radically altered technology, new crops, or outside domination.

Looking High and Low for Maya Crops: Fruits and Roots

The first successful challenges to the prevailing dogma of the mandatory Maya milpa were mounted by Bennet Bronson (1966) and Dennis Puleston (1968), emphasizing respectively the potential importance of root and tree crops. Focusing on the sweet potato, the yam bean or jicama, manioc, and xanthosoma or yautia, Bronson argues that these plants had a long history of cultivation in the lowlands, that they produce a great many more calories per unit area than does grain, that they are less demanding of soil fertility or labor than maize, and that they are more drought resistant.[4] The diversity of sweet potato, yam bean, and xanthosoma types suggests that the Maya area may have been the center of botanical variation, and the ritual role of the sweet potato bespeaks its ancient economic importance.

At the risk of going round and round in an unprovable Kulturkreis debate, it might also be noted that several students have postulated an ancient lowland agriculture based on manioc and other vegetatively reproducing plants (O. F. Cook 1935; Kidder 1940; Sauer and Armillas cited in Kelly and Palerm 1952). Many of the root crops occur naturally in marginal transition zones or ecotones such as that between uplands and lowlands, at forest-edge habitats where tree cover gives way to more open country, or where woodland abuts on swamp, river, or coast (Harris 1972a). The biological productivity of such contact zones tends to be high, and they provide good opportunities for foragers to combine the gathering of wild plants with hunting and fishing. To the extent that Maya actually occupied areas with a monsoon or tropical wet-and-dry climate, they would find an optimum root-growing environment. "Tropical root crops, with their underground organs specialized for starch storage, are adapted to survive dry seasons and to grow quickly once the rains return. It may be assumed that their wild ancestors were native to areas of pronounced dry season and that man's earliest selection of shallower-rooting forms with larger tubers, corms, or rhizomes took place in such areas rather than in humid tropical forests" (Harris 1972b). A widespread South and Mesoamerican "noncenter" for such domestication has been proposed (Harlan 1971). The later partial displacement of root crops by seeded plants such as cereals is familiar from Southeast Asia and Africa as well as Mesoamerica (Harris 1972a). A "predilection for propagation through planting rather than seeding" has been remarked among the Totonac, carrying over into their ready adoption of sugarcane and banana, which accord well with the native pattern (Kelly and Palerm 1952:148).

The available root crops of Mesoamerica also fit neatly into a variety of microenvironments present in the lowland area. For clarity's sake, I have listed the names of Mesoamerican root crops in four languages in Table 12.4.

TABLE 12.4   ROOT CROP NAMES

English	Spanish	Maya	Latin
Yautia	Malanga	Cucutmacal	*Xanthosoma* spp.
Manioc	Yuca	Tsin	*Manihot esculenta*
Sweet potato	Camote	Iz	*Ipomoea batatas*
Jicama	Jícama	Chicam	*Pachyrhizus erosus*

Manioc thrives from sea level to 3,500 feet in the tropics and can produce from 4 to 12 tons per acre (Oyenuga 1959). Xanthosoma, on the other hand, does best under conditions of a long wet season with rich alluvial soils. It requires a high water table and is often planted under the shade of orchard trees in Ibo kitchen gardens. Yields of 4,000 to 8,000 pounds per acre have been recorded in Nigeria (Oyenuga 1959:173). It was raised in quantity along stream banks in Yucatan and Veracruz, and the Spaniards, who regarded it only as emergency rations, noted that the Indians seemed very fond of it (McBryde 1947:140). The sun-loving sweet potato flourishes in well-drained soil, but earth too rich in organic materials will exaggerate its production of vines and leaves. The central Peten has been characterized as generally poor for root crops, especially manioc, because of its inadequately drained, shallow soils, which naturally support only savannah grassland (Cowgill 1971). Similar edaphic conditions are no bar to the production of tubers in West Africa, and the typical mounding techniques may actually raise the roots above impermeable soil layers. Salvaging heavy clay soils from waterlogging due to a four-to-five-month inundation and fitting them for the growing of root crops may be the purpose of the ridges and raised fields previously described (Turner 1974).

In terms of their nutritional values, root crops may have been somewhat unjustly maligned. The comparison of digestible crude protein as percentage of dry matter presented in Table 12.5 shows xanthosoma as having about 60 percent as much protein as maize.[5] Xanthosoma is also a fair source of oils and fats, while 4 to 7 percent of the starch in sweet potatoes occurs as sugar. Sweet potatoes contain many essential amino acids and are rich in carotene, which is a good source of vitamin A (Oyenuga 1959:27–29). Perhaps more striking is the protein content of xanthosoma leaves (14.23 percent) and sweet

TABLE 12.5.   PERCENTAGES OF PROTEIN IN FIVE ROOT CROPS

	Protein (% of dry matter)	
Root Crop	Oyenuga*	FAO†
Manioc root (peeled)	1.37	1.6
Xanthosoma corm (peeled)	5.04	2.2
Sweet potato (peeled)	4.76	1.3
Maize	7.82	9.5
Lima bean	22.30	19.7

*Oyenuga 1959:15
†FAO 1970

potato leaves (9.61 percent), both of which may be cooked as palatable spinachlike greens. Manioc leaves are similarly nutritious and tasty (B. Bronson, personal communication). Certain vegetable products are highly nutritious as well. The squash seed (pepita guesa; in Maya Top'sikil) used by the Maya in many of their dishes has been analyzed as having 36.90 percent protein (J. M. Andrews, personal communication). The collection of further nutritional information on food plants and simulation of various possible mixes of root crops, vegetables, maize, and fruits should provide better evidence of Maya dietary balance (Olga Puleston, personal communication). Preparation of roots for eating is also easy. Jicama, a white turniplike root, is consumed raw, and the more frequently grown sweet variety of manioc is boiled or cooked as a sweet with sugar or honey. Starch balls of manioc prepared in the Guatemalan Lowlands are taken in large sackloads to highland markets (McBryde 1947:139). Wild varieties of manioc, sweet potatoes, and jicama are known to contemporary Yucatec Maya (J. M. Andrews, personal communication). Manioc, used in the Peten for starch, a drink, and baby food, can be sun-dried and stored for months (Reina 1967). Olga Puleston has recently recorded 43 species of edible plants growing in the kitchen gardens of Dolores and another 40 species occurring as weeds or transplanted from the jungle into milpas (O. Puleston, personal communication). That root crops as an old, widespread, productive, nutritious, and easily grown food should have been ignored by the Maya strains the limits of probability.

That a variety of economic trees figured in both the milpa and possible kitchen garden regime of the more densely settled Maya communities seems to me equally beyond dispute. In addition to the fruit, fiber, nuts, and sap which it produces, a permanent orchard could provide partial shade and conserve moisture in the ground below, fertilize the soil with its leaf mold, and draw nourishment from lower and otherwise untapped ground levels. Trees pass easily from wild to domestic and back again in Mesoamerica. The native fruit trees of Guatemala are usually a fortuitous growth, but a seed may be planted or a seedling taken by an Indian closer to his house (McBryde 1947:147). The Tajin Totonac casually plant fruit trees in the house clearing where birds are less likely to attack the fruit and the trees can be better protected from the ravages of the arriera ant (Kelly and Palerm 1952:141). That the original forest vegetation of the middle parts of Yucatan has been altered and to some extent replaced by trees dispersed with the help of man is a thought-provoking assertion (Lundell 1938; Wagner 1964:232). The direct statistical association of *Brosimum* (the ramon or breadnut) with house mounds in Tikal provides one fascinating confirmation of this process (Puleston 1968).

Economically important fruit is provided by the following native trees:

Avocado *(Persea americana)*
Guava *(Psidium guajava)*
Anona *(Annona reticulata)*
Matasano *(Casimiroa edulis)*
Zapota mamey
 (Calocarpum mammosum)
Papaya *(Carica papaya)*
Sapodilla *(Achras sapota)*
Injerto *(Lucoma multiflora)*

Jocote *(Spondias mombin)*
Cacao *(Theobrama cacao)*
Caimito or star apple
 (Chrysophyllum caimito)
Nance *(Byrsonima crassifolia)*
Cashew *(Anacardium occidentale)*
Jurgay *(Talisia olivaeformis)*
Jobo *(Spondias purpurea)*

Some provide several products such as the beverage and soap made from mamey seeds (McBryde 1947:147) and the edible shoots and buds in addition to fruit of the jocote. Imported trees have been so significantly integrated into this complex that bananas, plantains, and mangos are the principal means of subsistence for the Chorti after their maize stores have been exhausted (Wisdom 1940:63). Citrus has also been introduced; although I do not know whether its requirements resemble those of the native trees, it is interesting that Peten soils as mapped by the Food and Agriculture Association–Fomento y Desarrollo del Peten are on the whole much more suited to citrus than to milpa. Fruit trees such as avocados or chirimoyas are specialties of particular Tarascan Lowland towns, and it is suggested that they entered into prehistoric trade to the Sierra, being consumed especially at religious festivals (West 1948:46). The Chorti also have square, fenced orchards, often irrigated from springs (Wisdom 1940:58).

Perhaps neglected in discussions of Mesoamerican arboriculture have been the palms, which form a substantial part of the Peten forest understory (Wagner 1964:231). The valuable Ibo palm bush may have a counterpart in the Western Hemisphere. The cohune palm *(Orbignya cohune)* provides leaves for roofing, fire fans, rain capes, and brooms, as well as an edible palm cabbage. The flesh of its fruit is eaten, and the seed kernel yields an oil used by Indians in British Honduras for lighting and cooking. The woody trunk is strong enough for construction purposes (McBryde 1947:145). The closely related corozo palm (*Scheelea* spp.) yields good kernel oil (Bomhard 1945:77). The coyol palm *(Acrocomia mexicana),* whose name—along with those of the sweet potato, manioc, corn, yellow squash, chile, avocado, and cacao—appears in all the major branches of the Maya linguistic stock (Bronson 1966), has a sap which makes a fermented palm wine. The consumption of this drink was apparently a pre-Columbian practice (McBryde 1947:145). If Mesoamerican palm wine were comparable to the West African variety, one liter might contain 3 mg of iron, 2 g of protein, 5 g of alcohol, and a fair amount of thiamine, riboflavin, and nicotinic acid (Oyenuga 1967:85). The royal or pacaya palm has edible shoots commonly baked or boiled during the dry season. These palms are frequently transplanted by the Chorti to their orchards (Wisdom 1940:64). The Maya may also have sought out and protected the incense bearing *Protium copal* and *Bursera simaruba* as well as harvesting the timber of the tropical cedar *(Cedrela mexicana)* and mahogany *(Swietenia macrophylla)* (Wagner 1964).

That tree cropping could become a specialized, intensive, and commercially significant activity is demonstrated by the familiar role of cacao. Because it requires rich soil and abundant rainfall, it will not grow everywhere, but wild trees are found in areas in the Peten as well as in parts of Veracruz and coastal Honduras. The Central American type has probably been subject to human selection for 3,000 years or more, but it remains extraordinarily delicate, requiring constant care to protect it from wind and cold, shade it from the sun, drain it and cut weeds in the wet season, and irrigate it during a long dry period (MacLeod 1973:68, 72). Where production for the market was observed along the Pacific Coast plain in historic times, cacao was constantly replanted after blights and parasite infestations, had to be started from seed in special beds, and yielded nothing for the first five years. The production of the beans, valued both as the source of a stimulating (and nutritious?) drink and as a form of standard currency, depended on intensive techniques, skilled labor, and investment, leading in some areas to a monocrop, mercantile economy (McBryde 1947:33). Maya who both produced and consumed cacao as well as celebrating it in their origin myths (Quiche and Cakchiquel) were presumably competent arboriculturalists. Cacao is known to have been an important crop in the Chetumal area of Yucatan, in Caribbean coastal regions of Guatemala, and on the northern coast of Honduras (Millon 1955). There was considerable commerce in cacao along the Dulce River and the tributaries of the Motagua River in the vicinity of Quirigua and Copan, and Millon (1955) also mentions extensive waterborne trade, with Chontal Maya of Tabasco and Honduras exchanging cacao for salt, cloth, honey, and slaves of central and northern Yucatan. Hammond makes the intriguing suggestion that cacao, with its need for moisture, would be an obvious orchard crop on the ridged fields along the swampy margins of the Hondo Valley in Belize. This commercial crop—combined with fish trapped in the channels between fields; root crops, maize, and vegetables from milpas on the limestone ridge; and breadnut from orchards around the settlements—would have provided an efficient and diversified economy (Hammond 1974a:186–87).

Fixed-Plot Horticulture

There are a number of reasons for minimizing the infield or kitchen garden-orchard as a possible source of Maya subsistence. The premium accorded to cereal cultivation by both indigenes and Spanish conquerors, the storage potential and portability of maize as a trade good, and the supposed insignificance of vegetables and fruits produced largely by women and consumed domestically all contribute to this impression. The major factor is, however, that contemporary Lowland Maya provide almost no examples of this adaptation, probably because, as Culbert, Magers, and Spencer (1974) point out, the underpopulated Southern Lowlands still contain almost unlimited areas of virgin rain forest and there are no demographic reasons for the adoption of labor-intensive systems of agriculture. Where subsistence from the milpa alone is inadequate, chicle gathering and wage labor provide more attractive options because they produce cash rather than food (Reina 1967). Lundell (1938), however, specifically mentions as Maya dooryard vegetables squash, pumpkins, chayote (whose fruits, tender shoots, flowers, and tuberous roots are all edible), chaza *(Jatropha aconitifolia),* and palmera or izote *(Yucca elephantipes).* Where dooryard gardens do exist in neighboring regions, they have the sort of multitiered, highly diversified composition that we would expect to find in the tropics. In addition to many of the roots and trees already mentioned, the Totonac plant kidney and lima beans, squash, pumpkins, arrowroot, chile, tobacco, cotton, four condiments, and six medicinal plants as well as gathering small tomatoes and chile which grow as volunteers in the maize fields (Kelly and Palerm 1952). Tarascan house-lot gardens, cultivated by women using wooden digging sticks and metal hoes, contain maize for roasting, sweet local beans, chayote, tomato, chiles, European cabbage, medicinal plants such as tobacco, datura, euphorbia, and castor beans, as well as flowers (West 1948:45). Small Chorti vegetable gardens include sweet potatoes, Irish potatoes, six varieties of chile, manioc, cherry tomatoes, and mustard greens, either separately or together. Condiments and tobacco are planted in large pots or wooden vessels above ground (Wisdom 1940:54–57). In Highland Guatemala, milpa may be almost continuous with contour furrows, fertilizing with leaf litter and manure, mounding, and complex maize-bean rotations. Perennial güisquilea or vegetable pear vines provide fruit, edible greens, and roots. Along Lake Atitlan, a bed of manioc 15 meters square was bordered by 7 orange trees, 5 limes, 12 jocotes, and 6 mangos, as well as matasanos, injertos, and bananas (McBryde 1947:26).

Perhaps the best described example of garden-orchards comes from Nicoya, a peninsula on the Pacific side of Costa Rica with a wet-dry climate having annual precipitation of over 1,750 mm but less than 20 mm in January, February and March (Wagner 1958). In villages near the southwestern coast where the natural vegetation is a dense, three-layer forest, small gardens are tended by women, especially widows and spinsters. From a small space near the house, drought-resistant crops, trees, and a variety of seasonal crops can "provide for a family fairly well throughout the year" (Wagner

1958:215). Five levels of plants flourish together: large fruit trees; lower fruit trees like anona and cashew; small trees such as plantains and bananas; herbaceous and bush plants, especially root crops; and twining plants like yams and procumbent cucurbits. Xanthosoma and yams grow in the shade, and sweet potatoes compete so successfully with weeds that they can produce in incompletely cleared fields. The largest part of the fresh vegetable food is furnished by cucurbitaceae such as ayote *(Cucurbita moschata)*, pipian, cohombra *(Sicania odorifera)*, and chayote *(Sechium edule)*. Five types of palms and eleven other native tree crops are named, with maranon (cashew), jicaro, and cacao dominant in settlements. Diagrams (Fig. 12.6) of individual gardens show the frequency and relative importance of the various plants as well as their spacing on the ground.

SOCIAL CORRELATES OF INTENSIVE AGRICULTURE

Sedentary communities with dense populations permanently exploiting scarce resources by intensive techniques show certain regular differences in social organization from sparsely settled swiddeners. The smaller the plot of land, the more likely it is that labor will be provided by an individual or a small group such as a nuclear family. The statistical dominance of the nuclear family among Kofyar homestead farmers and the change to extended families when new land allowed large-scale shifting cultivation has been explained in this manner (Netting 1965). Work groups usually include sons and brothers only on contemporary Maya milpas of more than five acres (Reina 1967). Continuous tending of a variety of kitchen-garden and tree crops calls for the steady application of effort by small residential units. If Maya horticulture indeed followed such a pattern, house mounds might frequently support only a single married couple, with their adult offspring moving to vacant garden-orchards when they established new households. Though unilineal descent groups may be maintained under such circumstances, they cease to be coresident and no longer hold and reallocate land as a corporate group. Residential dispersion and the declining power of the lineage characterize the Ibo case outlined above (pp. 314–15). A quantitative comparison of several Maya communities in Highland Chiapas shows a very similar correlation between descent group attenuation and land scarcity.

> Family organization into units deeply extended in the male line, reflected in local residential clustering or otherwise, and interpersonal attitudes of authority, respect, control, and obedience between patrilocally related kinsmen are confined to communities with substantial farm land, while the two communities almost devoid of patrilineal emphasis have almost no land at all. This leads to the hypothesis that in the Maya culture area, patrilineal emphasis in social organization is strong where land is highly valued as a resource and available in amounts great enough so that it can serve as a mechanism, through inheritance, for binding together the affairs of a man and his heirs. (Collier 1975:76)

While ancient Maya household composition and kin-group structure must remain matters of speculation, there is at least reason to question the postulated predominance of extended families and strong descent groups (Sanders 1973; Eaton 1976). This does not negate the presence of a marked lineage ideology, great genealogical depth, and emphasis on favorable alliances with other kin groups among wealthy, highly ranked, or royal families. Indeed a stratified population may glorify descent at the top while undermining its importance as a major social principle among the poorer farmers and craftsmen who make up the bulk of the society.

When numbers of people dwell in close proximity to each other over time and when there is necessarily some competition for resources in short supply, rights to these means of production become more rigidly defined and individualized. The fixed location of trees plus the dependability and nutritional value of their production spanning a number of years encourages the development of private ownership concepts. Though modern *milperos* in the Peten reject individual tenure of milpa because of the demands of shifting cultivation, the fruit trees they plant can be claimed as private property (Reina 1967). Ethnohistoric sources document similar practices, with Maya sons inheriting from their fathers improvements to the land consisting of houses and trees (Millon 1955). The establishment and tending of orchards could also create valuable property for succeeding generations and further economic differentiation within the population. Restricted access to house plots and the marketable tree crops of their surrounding groves may well have been associated with domestic authority and a modicum of social stratification among the Maya.

329

FIGURE 12.6. The widow's garden, Costa Rica (after Wagner 1958)

KEY TO GARDEN PLANS

Achiote (Bixa)

Ahuacate (Persea)

Algodón (Gossypium)

Anono (Annona)

Arroz (Oryza)

Ayote (Cucurbita)

Banano & Plátano (Musa)

Cabuya (Furcraea)

Cacao (Theobroma)

Café (Coffea)

Caña (Saccharum)

Cardón (Pedilanthus)

Chile (Capsicum)

Cohombro (Sicania)

Coyol (Acrocomia)

Daguillo (Yucca)

Frijol (Phaseolus)

Gandul (Cajanus)

Guácimo (Guazuma)

Guayabo (Psidium)

Higüerilla (Ricinus)

Jenjibre (Zingiber)

Jícaro (Crescentia)

Jocote (Spondias)

Madero negro (Gliricidium)

Maís (Zea)

Maís pujagua (Zea)

Marañón (Anacardium)

Nancite (Byrsonima)

Naranjo, etc. (Citrus)

Níspero (Achras)

Ñame (Dioscorea)

Ñampí (Colocasia)

Ñanjú (Hibiscus)

Palma de Coco (Cocos)

Palma real (¿Scheelea?)

Papaturro (Coccoloba)

Papaya (Carica)

Paste (Luffa)

Pina (Ananas)

Piñuela (Bromelia)

Quelite (Jatropha)

Sacuanjoche (Plumeria)

Seso vegetal (Blighia)

Sontol (Andropogon)

Tiquisque (Xanthosoma)

Tomate (Lycopersicon)

Yuca (Manihot)

Zapote (Calocarpum)

Zapotillo (¿Calocarpum?)

Ornamental bushes

Ornamental & medicinal herbs

Wire

Other symbols represent non-cultivated species.

ALTERNATIVES AND IMPLICATIONS

A voyage into prehistoric Maya agriculture by way of Eastern Nigeria is a little like sailing the Kon Tiki to Yucatan. Showing that it could have been done does not prove that it was. The entire excursion has been motivated by the manifest difficulties of accounting for the seemingly stable and secure subsistence of dense populations over at least six hundred years in a tropical environment. Total reliance on long-fallow, milpa cultivation appears unlikely. It neglects both the evidence of intensification by drained-field agriculture in alluvial areas and presumed changes in natural forest vegetation indicated by the presence today of economically useful frees in formerly settled areas. It discounts the flexibility of infield-outfield cultivation in adapting to land scarcity resulting from population pressure by shortening fallows, decreasing farm size, and increasing labor input. By restricting intensification to examples of irrigation or the introduction of plow farming, students of Mesoamerican agriculture have not noted the advantages of diversified and stratified crop complexes including root and tree produce maintained in permanent associations by rotation, fertilization, protection, and other horticultural techniques. A set of complementary cultigens were available to the Maya, could have provided substantial and dependable nutrition, and are grown contemporaneously with traditional technology by ethnographically attested Indian societies in more crowded corners of the Mesoamerican Lowlands. Moreover, the pattern of continuous dispersed residences in the sustaining areas of Maya religious centers is precisely what one would expect if fixed plot kitchen garden-orchards were being effectively exploited to provide a significant part of domestic subsistence. That a rapid growth in numbers, correlated with intensifying local agriculture and regional economic exchange, demanded the equally impressive development of sociopolitical integration is attested by the Maya remains, monuments less to enigmatic civilizational achievements than to the mundane processes of culture change and reasonable florescence in the tropics.

NOTES

1. Recent reviews of this controversy, documenting sources of the milpa *idée fixe* and the gradual accumulation of contrary evidence, are contained in Bronson (1966),

Sanders (1973), Turner (1974), and Culbert, Magers, and Spencer (1974). Experienced earlier observers suggested that the ancient Maya may well have had more intensive techniques and linked the ubiquitous contemporary milpa to the abundance of land (Ricketson and Ricketson 1937:12; Lundell 1933:77, cited in Wilken 1971).

2. For graciously attempting to remedy some of the more glaring gaps in my knowledge of the Mesoamerican environment and its botanic inventory I would like to thank Bennet Bronson, Dennis and Olga Puleston, and Tony Andrews. Help in tracking down the names and uses of native palm varieties was provided by Ed Ferdon, Ellen Basso, and Fran Stier. Comments and suggestions on earlier drafts of this manuscript by seminar participants Pat Culbert, Bill Sanders, and Joe Ball were particularly useful.

3. Estimates of population density supportable by swidden cultivation include 100–200 per square mile near Lake Peten, and 73–220 for the Rio Bec (Turner 1974). Whereas these figures represent a maximum carrying capacity, most guesses at average Maya density have fallen between 10 and 76 persons (S. F. Cook 1972). Intensive agriculture might well have maintained between 600 and 700 per square mile (Sanders 1973; Turner 1974), and housemound counts for urbanlike centers reach densities of perhaps 1,800 per square mile (Haviland 1972).

4. Jicama should perhaps be considered as a snack food rather than a possible staple (B. Bronson, personal communication).

5. The figures cited for Nigerian crops (Oyenuga 1959:15) give higher protein values for root crops and somewhat lower values for maize than those contained in the FAO compilation. Granting the fact that samples are small and that protein content may vary with soil and other growing conditions, it is perhaps premature to make any definitive statements on the nutritional value of Mesoamerican tubers.

13
Warfare and the Evolution of Maya Civilization

DAVID L. WEBSTER

The Pennsylvania State University

Analyses of the origins and development of Lowland Maya civilization have usually focused on (1) the potential of the environment to support a complex society (Dumond 1961; Meggers 1954); (2) patterns of colonization and initial settlement (Puleston and Puleston 1971); (3) evidence for the emergence of various institutions, such as social stratification, which are symptomatic of complex cultural development (Haviland 1967; Rathje 1970); or (4) the dynamic processes of developing Maya society (Rathje 1971). The following discussion takes the fourth approach. Specifically, I wish to investigate the role that warfare may have played in the evolution of Maya civilization.

The notion that conflict is a crucial process in the development of complex societies, particularly in the emergence of social stratification, is a venerable one in the sociological and anthropological literature. It has been espoused recently by Service (1962), Carneiro (1970), and Fried (1961, 1967) in connection with the development of the state. A survey of the recent literature reveals that conflict is regarded as an important mechanism in the generation of "pristine" states, including Highland Mexico (R. M. Adams 1966; Sanders and Price 1968), Mesopotamia (R. M. Adams 1966, 1972) China (Chang

1968), and Peru (Carneiro 1970). Current theories on the processes of state formation involve complex feedback relationships between demographic factors, concentration of wealth and authority, subsistence strategies, and conflict (Flannery 1972a). The following discussion emphasizes conflict as one of a set of such interacting variables, not as any sort of prime mover.

A traditional and continuing debate in Maya archaeology has centered on the question of whether or not the Lowland Maya ever achieved the level of the state. For the purposes of this chapter this question is in a sense irrelevant, since few archaeologists would disagree that the processes of state formation were under way—even if Maya society had not developed to a fully urbanized stage—by the time of the collapse of the core area in the ninth and tenth centuries A.D. A second basic assumption of this paper is that processes of cultural evolution in the Maya Lowlands were largely indigenous, and consequently that the Maya should be considered a "pristine" civilization. This is not to deny that the Maya Lowlands were involved in a large Mesoamerican interaction sphere, and that wide-ranging contacts, especially with Highland Mexico and the Gulf Coast, might have affected the pace of development. I contend, rather, that the basic processes of cultural evolution were generated by internal factors, and can fruitfully be investigated in this perspective.

Warfare and militarism must be seen in the context of very dynamic culture change. These processes have been vehicles for upward social mobility and the emergence of status differentiation in many societies. Warfare mushrooms in importance after the formation of state-type institutions (Padden 1967). But while the most spectacular aspects of militarism may appear after the state has been established, we cannot underestimate the role of warfare in the formative process itself.

Until quite recently it would have been possible to point to the Lowland Maya as an exception to the general idea that conflict has played an important role in the emergence of most, or all, "pristine" civilizations. Traditional reconstructions of the Lowland Maya developmental sequence emphasized its peaceful, "theocratic" qualities (for example, Thompson 1954). Ethnohistoric data from the Postclassic Lowlands abundantly document endemic warfare and political factionalism, but these examples of conflict have usually been explained away as deviations from Classic norms under the influence of "militarists" from elsewhere in Mexico.

This picture has changed considerably in recent years. Evidence of foreign intrusions with militaristic overtones at the end of the Classic Period has been found at several sites, notably in the Usumacinta-Pasión drainage (R. E. W. Adams 1971; Willey and Smith 1963, 1967). Accumulating artistic data, such as the Bonampak murals and numerous carved monuments from Tikal, Calakmul, Yaxchilan, and other sites, suggest that warfare was a conspicuous aspect of political structuring during much of the Late Classic. Proskouriakoff's inscriptional studies at Piedras Negras and Yaxchilan seem to indicate that local dynasts were consolidating their positions through warfare during the eighth century A.D. (1961, 1963–64). The discovery of large-scale earthworks at Tikal, the largest Maya center, suggests intercommunity conflict of a more lethal nature than mere raiding for slaves or sacrificial victims (D. Puleston and Callender 1967), and there is a distinct possibility that these earthworks were constructed during the Early Classic (D. Puleston, personal communication). Even in the face of all this evidence scholars have only grudgingly pushed back into the Classic Period patterns which are still seen as essentially Postclassic. Thompson, for example, states that there was a period of "unrest throughout the last century and a half of the Classic Period" (1971:215).

My own work at the fortified site of Becan, in southern Campeche, Mexico, suggests that the inception of large-scale conflict was much earlier. At Becan massive defensive earthworks were constructed at the very beginning of the Classic Period (ca. 250–450 A.D.), clearly indicating that periods of "unrest" were much earlier than previously thought (Webster 1972, 1974). It seems to me that we must now seriously consider whether warfare might not have been an important process in the evolution of Maya society from its very beginnings, and not merely a symptom of its dissolution in the latter part of the Late Classic.

DEMOGRAPHIC TRENDS AND CONFLICT IN MAYA CULTURAL EVOLUTION

A major factor in the dynamic cultural systems of developing societies is population growth, in terms of absolute size, distribution, and density. Unless checked by natural or cultural factors, population growth may cause disequilibrium, thus necessitating adaptive readjustments. Competition or conflict may be viewed both as symptoms of stress and as adaptive responses that may lead to higher levels of organization.

A basic assumption of recent demographic studies is that human populations, like many animal ones, possess the reproductive capability to overpopulate rapidly. Despite this capability, population density seems to be maintained well below carrying capacity in many situations (Binford 1968; Lee and DeVore 1968). Among the equilibrium-maintaining mechanisms that inhibit human population growth are such internal, culturally mediated practices as child spacing, abortion, and infanticide, all of which are subject to conscious control. A few words should be devoted at this point to the notoriously slippery concept of *carrying capacity*. The concept in its most simplistic form refers to the maximum amount of food available to a population, but may also include many other constraining factors, such as water or climatic variables. Attempts to determine the carrying capacity of any particular environment are enormously complicated, not only because of difficulties of observation and measurement, but also because of the potentially variable behavior of many organisms. On the human level, the problem of defining carrying capacity is complicated by the dynamic quality of cultural adaptation—that is, cultural readjustments, in terms of new technology, new forms of social organization, or new subsistence patterns, may quickly redefine carrying capacity. Nevertheless, rough estimates of carrying capacity may be produced, assuming a given set of extractive practices, and to a certain extent this is easier to do with agricultural than with hunting and gathering economies. It seems undeniable that humans *perceive* limitations on basic productive resources; whether these perceptions are accurate or not is beside the point. Boserup (1965) has argued that perception of limitations, however accurate or inaccurate, is precisely what spurs many kinds of cultural readjustments, particularly agricultural intensification, and this assumption is followed in the discussion below.

Although the Maya Lowlands seem to have had agricultural populations much earlier than previously expected (see Rice 1976 for a review of the evidence), we can perceive major increments of population only after ca. 1000 B.C.. The origins of these early agricultural colonists are obscure, but Puleston and Puleston (1971) argue, I think persuasively, that routes of migration followed river systems from the west or northwest (Usumacinta-Pasión drainage) and the east (Belize system), with the former routes being most important. Both of these routes funneled migrant groups into what was later to become the "core" area of Maya civilization, the Tikal-Yaxha lake region of the northeastern Peten, an area which exhibits high demographic potential and precocious cultural development. Regardless of the routes of migration, the fact remains that the lowlands were an open niche being filled up by frontier populations of agriculturalists. Under these conditions we may assume that the internal mechanisms which operate to stabilize population growth were relaxed, since equilibrium could effectively be maintained by continual fissioning, a contention adequately borne out even by our very fragmentary knowledge of population growth and spread for the region as a whole.

A question crucial to any understanding of developmental aspects of Maya society is the extent to which various kinds of stresses may have been generated in the Preclassic Period (before ca. 250 A.D.), particularly stresses relating to population densities and agricultural systems. Any attempt to demonstrate that competition may be generated by real or perceived limitations on basic resources (particularly land) requires an overall estimate of the carrying capacity of the Preclassic subsistence system. Here we run into two basic problems. First, we do not have sufficient archaeological information to define the details of Preclassic agricultural patterns, and are forced to fall back on reasonable analogies based on studies of ethnohistoric or modern subsistence activities in the Maya area. Second, and this problem seriously affects the first, our knowledge of modern subsistence activities is confused, both by the many different observations made by many different scholars and by the variability inherent in Maya agriculture itself.

A detailed model of Preclassic cultural energetics is beyond the scope of this paper. In the following discussion I will attempt, rather, to define the Preclassic carrying capacity of the Lowland Maya region as a whole, to define rates of population increase in order-of-magnitude terms, and to assess their implications for stress and competitive behavior. An assumption is made that Preclassic peoples practiced some pattern or patterns of swidden agriculture with maize as the staple crop. The possibility of more intensive forms of agriculture is acknowledged, and there is evidence for them, but none can be shown to have been operative until well into Classic times.

Generations of anthropologists have been plagued by the question of the capacity of the modern Maya swidden system to support human populations. Steggerda (1941) used data from his experimental milpas in northern Yucatan to calculate modern population densities of 15–20 persons per square kilometer, but this figure is based upon production of considerable surpluses for market exchange and domestic animals, and hence upon large amounts of land in cultivation per producer (average of four hectares). If these surpluses were invested in added support of the local population, densities approximately four times as great could be maintained per hectare of good agricultural land.

If we assume that the Preclassic Maya practiced swidden agriculture, and that maize was the subsistence crop, contributing about 75 percent of the caloric intake as it does for the modern Yucatec Maya, what kinds of overall population densities could be maintained? In extrapolating present agricultural practices back into the Preclassic several adjustments must be made. First, the use of stone rather than metal tools would necessitate about 4.4 times as much labor in one of the most crucial agricultural operations—clearing of land (Townsend 1969). Using metal tools, the modern Maya farmer manages to clear fields which average about 4 hectares in area (Steggerda 1941; Vogeler n.d.). The use of stone tools would, at first glance, seem to reduce this effective total to 1 hectare or less, but there are two other crucial variables. If the Preclassic farmer had been willing to put in more *labor* than his modern counterpart, and if there was no scheduling problem in terms of *time*, more than 1 hectare could have been put into cultivation by a single producer, and this increased expenditure would probably have been necessary to support a household. That more than 1 hectare could be cultivated using only stone tools seems to be suggested by Steggerda's reference (1941:111) to the Xiu family papers for the mid seventeenth century. According to the Xiu account a single dependent producer was *expected* to clear and plant 60 mecates, or about 2.4 hectares. At that time stone tools were probably still in general use in Yucatan, as they were in the Valley of Mexico (W. T. Sanders, personal communication). The implication is that neither time nor labor limitations precluded cultivation on this scale, but given an extractive colonial economy, 2.4 hectares is probably about maximum.

Using a bush-fallowing system, modern farmers clear land at an average rate of about 3 mecates per day (Steggerda 1941:126, Vogeler n.d.), so 20 days would be needed to clear 2.4 hectares. Corrected for stone tools, the figure would be about 88 days, raising the total time involved in agricultural pursuits to around 250 days as opposed to the 200 days invested by the modern Yucatec farmer. My impression is that this amount of time is about the maximum which could be devoted to agriculture, especially since clearing of land is often squeezed into the end of the growing season when other agricultural tasks are light.

Sanders (1973) has suggested that stone technology would have made bush-fallow systems (with a 1:3 ratio of cultivated land to fallow) more attractive than forest-fallow systems (1:6), even though there is some decrease in returns. This preference seems to be reflected in Cowgill's (1961) work near Tikal, where frontier populations still have available forest but prefer a cyclical pattern utilizing old swidden plots to a linear, forest-fallow pattern. If this pattern was widespread in Preclassic times a single holding would require about 10 hectares if 2.4 hectares were in cultivation annually. Thus a square kilometer of high-quality agricultural land would contain 24 hectares under cultivation at any given time.

We must now face two related questions: did the Preclassic producer find it *necessary* to plant as much as 2.4 hectares, thus maximizing his labor output, and if so, what population densities are implied? Again following Sanders (1973) about 800 kilograms of maize are currently produced per hectare. Allowing a one-third decrease in yield because of the more primitive varieties of maize being used in the Preclassic, this figure is adjusted down to 528 kg, and consequently a 2.4-hectare milpa would give a total yield of 1,267 kg. This amount of maize would be quite sufficient to support a single household of 5.5 persons, the figure used by Steggerda in evaluating his Yucatecan data. If, as seems likely, Preclassic households were somewhat smaller, cultivated fields of 1.5–2 hectares would have been sufficient, with corresponding decrease in labor expenditure.

Because of the high labor input per area of cultivated land, Preclassic farmers could produce only very small surpluses, but population densities would accordingly be somewhat higher than modern ones. Moreover, with no effective taxation, trade, tribute, or domestic animals, whatever surpluses were produced could be used to support more people rather than leaving the local population as they do today and as they probably did in Classic times. The fact that potential surpluses were available, even on a small scale, has important implications for subsequent sociopolitical evolution.

Let us assume on the basis of the above discussion that (1) approximately .5 hectare was necessary for the support of each individual in the Preclassic household and that this amount (ca. 1.5–2.5 ha) could have been handled by a single household cultivator; (2) that bush fallow (3:1) systems were preferred; and (3) that 40 percent of the total Lowland Maya area (100,000 sq km) was high-quality agricultural land. Total carrying capacity may be calculated by plugging these estimates into Carneiro's (1961) formula for slash-and-burn carrying capacity, which is based upon four variables: T, total cultivable land available; A, amount of land which must be cultivated annually to support each individual; Y, length of time each field is cropped before it is put to fallow; and R, the number of fallow years. The formula is

$$\text{Total population (carrying capacity)} = \frac{\frac{T}{R+Y} \times Y}{A}.$$

Assuming a bush fallow system, total carrying capacity would be 1,250,000 people. A forest fallow system, alternatively, would only support 714,300 people. If, as seems likely, the Preclassic system was characterized by bush fallow systems on productive soils and forest fallow systems on more marginal ones, the actual carrying capacity should be somewhat greater than that calculated for bush fallow systems alone. I would suggest an order-of-magnitude figure in the neighborhood of 1,500,000 people. The crucial question now becomes how quickly populations might have built up to this level, and how early stresses relating to land shortages and competition may have occurred.

In a recent paper Hassan (1973) has evaluated the mechanisms of population growth during the Neolithic. His basic conclusions are (1) that the only effective means of internal population control is to eliminate a large proportion of children at or before birth; and (2) that average annual increases for Neolithic populations as a whole were on the order of .1 percent per year, but under some conditions could be as high as 1.77–2.65 percent, thus comparing favorably with "explosive" rates of growth in many parts of the world today.

Although we have little information on prehistoric Maya demographic trends, there seems to be an undeniable upward trend throughout the Preclassic, as reflected in Willey's Belize Valley study (Willey et al. 1965; see Sanders 1972:123 for a summary graph). Indirect but more striking evidence for rapid overall increases is the enormous geographical spread and internal homogeneity of the Chicanel ceramic sphere (Willey, Culbert, and Adams 1967). The inevitable conclusion is that during the first two millennia of agricultural colonization of the lowlands, the Maya, far from stabilizing their populations, were expanding at a rapid rate—in other words, internal mechanisms of control were relaxed in a frontier environment where fissioning could effectively provide for local equilibrium.

If we accept a fairly modest annual rate of population increase of .7 percent (well below Hassan's maximum figures), total population would double in about 100 years. The implications of this rate of growth are startling. Given a small population of 1,000 people in 1500 B.C., the entire lowlands would have filled to carrying capacity in about 900 years, or by 500 B.C., even if there were no increments of population from elsewhere.

I will be the first to admit that I am in a sense playing with figures in proposing the above levels of population and rates of increase, but the exercise is by no means a futile one on that account. Many of the calculations are *minimal* ones; the population explosion of the lowlands and consequent conflict may have occurred even faster than suggested for several reasons: (1) the estimate of 40 percent high quality land may be too high for the lowlands as a whole; (2) there may have been greater initial selectivity of productive land than we realize; (3) factors other than agricultural subsistence potential may have restricted the desirability of some portions of the landscape (in the Maya Lowlands, for example, water sources may have been critical, especially in the drier north); or (4) population stress may have been *perceived* (however accurately) at levels far below actual carrying capacity (Binford 1968).

My conclusion is that while population pressure and concomitant stresses producing adaptive conflict patterns must have appeared *at least* as early as 500 B.C., there is a strong possibility that they were actually present long before that date. Thus we may postulate a long period of adaptive competition among Preclassic Maya populations on a relatively egalitarian level, similar to that documented for many ethnographically known slash-and-burn cultivators. By about 400 B.C. identifiable centers with permanent civic architecture begin to appear, indicating the presence of new organizational forms consistent with the development of small-scale ranked societies. Warfare, in other words, may have been partially responsible for the evolution of the earliest chiefdoms in the Maya Lowlands as well as the more complex organizational forms discussed more fully below.

COLONIZATION, POPULATION, AND CONFLICT

The processes of agricultural colonization and population growth in the Maya Lowlands were complicated by a number of factors. First, the region is not so environmentally homogeneous as many have thought. Very significant differences exist between the lush, well-watered tropical forests and comparatively deep soils of the Peten and the more xerophytic vegetation and thinner soils of Yucatan. Some areas are well provided with surface water in the form of swamps, or *bajos,* while in other areas subsurface drainage is more pronounced. River systems rising in the highlands to the south traverse the southeastern and southwestern sections of the Maya Lowlands, but over most of the Yucatan Peninsula there are few permanent streams of any size.

On a more local level there are often striking differences in topography, soil type, slope, drainage, and susceptibility to erosion. Simmons, Tarano, and Pinto (1959) have identified 26 varieties of soils in the Peten, with significant differences in fertility and problems of cultivation—such as poor drainage, grass cover, thick texture, erodibility—for farmers using stone or wooden tools.

A surprisingly high proportion of the soils of the Tikal-Yaxha region are of high fertility, which is one reason why this area seems to have had a demographic advantage throughout Maya prehistory (see Sanders 1973:335–40 and Chap. 13 above for a summary of the work of Simmons, Tarano, and Pinto). Agronomic studies of other parts of the lowlands would probably show similar local variations. The point is that early colonists would have been presented with a series of microenvironments of markedly different capacity in terms of swidden agriculture.

Routes of migration would also have affected the initial patterning of populations in a number of ways. If many of the earliest colonists worked their way upriver from the lowlands of Tabasco to the west, we might expect an early preference for riverine environments, possibly reflected in the pre-Mamom ceramics at sites such as Altar de Sacrificios (R. E. W. Adams 1971). Moreover, colonists following these river systems would naturally have been funneled into zones of high fertility in what was later to become the core area of Maya civilization. Although we do not possess sufficient information from archaeological or ecological studies to specify the initial patterns of colonization, it is clear that the lowlands cannot have filled up randomly. Land was cultivated in discontinuous pockets, reflecting the preferences of the cultivators themselves and the varying capacities of local environments to support populations. Centers of population were also discontinuous in terms of size, density, and rates of increase, and any conflict model must take this into account.

Given the potential for perceived or real limitations on basic resources, especially land, by 500 B.C. or shortly thereafter, a number of possible solutions were available:

1. acceptance of declining standards of living;
2. internal limits on population growth, that is, elimination of children at or before birth;
3. emigration of excess population; or
4. expansion of local subsistence resources.

As Dumond (1972:288) notes, the decision to make one or another of these choices involves three considerations: "the satisfaction of material wants, the satisfaction of affective relationships (including purely symbolic ones, as with gods), and the expenditure of least effort." The first choice, except in very short-range terms, is not really a choice at all. According to our limited information on population trends, the Maya seem to have been unwilling or effectively unable to make the second choice, control of local populations using internal mechanisms. Here we are probably running up against "affective" considerations, to a certain extent: since population controls had not been present or necessary in Maya society for at least a millennium, they could only be initiated at considerable social cost in terms of the traditional value systems.

The third choice, emigration, had always been open to the Maya, and is reflected in the enormous spatial spread and internal homogeneity of the Chicanel ceramic sphere, which embraced most of the Maya Lowlands and was present even in areas which were later to fall outside the lowland culture area, such as Chiapas. The rate of expansion and the extent of late Preclassic populations over an area of at least 100,000 square miles is all the more remarkable considering that travel by water, so important in other areas of extensive agriculture, such as the Amazon Basin, was highly restricted. Much of this early expansion had, moreover, been achieved only at social and ecological expense; areas which were probably marginal in terms of carrying capacity and attractiveness, given the traditional swidden system, were rapidly filled up. Thus by about 500–300 B.C. emigration may no longer have been a viable choice, especially in the core areas where populations had established themselves early and increased at a rapid rate and where social circumscription (in Carneiro's sense) was therefore most strongly felt.

At this point expansion of local resources, the fourth choice, would have been the only course open to many groups. In terms of the traditional subsistence system, this could only be accomplished by acquiring more land (note that in this sense expansion of resources and emigration are not separate choices). Increased population density meant more mouths to feed and more available labor for subsistence activities, but without the acquisition of new land more labor was useless in providing for increased production. (The Maya could, it is true, have turned to more intensive systems of cultivation, such as grass fallowing, raised fields in fertile *bajo* areas, or terracing, and these were probably used under conditions of extreme population pressure in the Late Classic; but these systems would have involved significant increases in labor expenditure.) I feel that at this point continued expansion was still a viable choice in some areas, but such expansion now involved conflict, as it could be undertaken only at the expense of other social groups.

Sanders's assertion that bush-fallow systems were more economical than forest fallow in terms of available technology carries a number of implications about demographic patterns and conflict. First, cyclical swidden systems, as opposed to linear ones, would have slowed the centrifugal tendencies of fissioning and created a certain stability in local populations. Yet the marginal frontiers continually absorbed excess elements of the populations whose only immediate choice was linear forest fallow. Since not all regions were equally productive, we must envision a disjunctive distribution of short-cycle systems with locally high population densities surrounded by marginal, low-density zones. The implications for subsequent political development are obvious.

Bush-fallow systems in themselves may offer pretexts for conflict, quite apart from population pressure. Vayda, in his studies of New Zealand populations (1961), has shown that second growth is often so preferred by cultivators using stone tools that it becomes a valuable capital resource itself—something worth fighting over even when expanses of virgin forest are still available.

Abstract discussions of adaptive solutions often imply that we are dealing with only one population and one suitable choice. In a developing cultural system such as that of the Maya, we are confronted with a much more complex situation. Numerous local groups were experiencing stress, and a variety of adaptive choices was open to each group at different times and under different conditions. Consequently we must conceive of constraints on adaptive choices not only in terms of internal or natural variables, but also in terms of the choices made by other groups. One group, for example, may indeed have chosen to place internal limits on population growth, but if another chose instead to expropriate land through conflict, the first group would be at an obvious competitive disadvantage. In other words, choice is conditioned by information from the larger system of interacting populations. If, consequently, aggressive expansion were undertaken by only a few groups, probably those in the core areas with greatest population densities and suffering most from social circumscription, other groups would be forced to make choices which would increase their own competitiveness. Selection of militant expansion in heavily populated zones (perhaps concurrently with other solutions, such as certain kinds of intensification), with its resultant feedback into social organization, helps to explain the precocious development of some areas such as the northeastern Peten.

It must be emphasized that in the context of the larger Maya system aggressive expansion to acquire land was not in itself a viable long-term solution, since it provided neither for an increase in overall productivity nor for a decrease in overall population. Rather it was a short-term, local solution growing out of local perceptions of the problems of land shortage. The real adaptive significance of the choice is seen in increased sociopolitical integration, which in turn offered or

347

enforced other solutions, such as lowered standards of living or agricultural intensification. In fact, the juxtaposition of aggressively expanding populations with tighter political organization probably resulted, by late Preclassic or Protoclassic times, in concentrations of populations with unpopulated or underpopulated zones between them. In other words, as a result of demographic and political reorganization, in part related to conflict, land was actually *removed* from cultivation even as land shortages increased.

Warfare as an adaptive choice is seen as self-reinforcing: successfully expanding groups are likely to continue this competitive behavior, with concomitant organizational changes, and groups which are competitively disadvantaged are either decimated, subordinated, or forced to make appropriate defensive and organizational adjustments of their own. What kept the Maya situation from stabilizing at a level of fairly constant though inconclusive petty struggles were the rapid, though disjunctive, rates of population growth and the variable demographic potential of the lowlands as a whole, which gave some regions a decided edge in military capability and developmental precocity.

SOCIOPOLITICAL EFFECTS OF WARFARE

Explanations of Lowland Maya cultural evolution have long been unable to identify obvious adaptive functions for an emergent elite organization. Many "managerial" functions that appear to be fundamental to the growth of pristine states elsewhere seem inappropriate to the lowland situation. Strong authority structures, for example, were apparently not needed to initiate and control extensive hydraulic systems or to effect regional exchanges of basic commodities, as they were in Highland Mexico. Rathje (1971) has maintained that the florescence of Maya centers and the high-status personnel associated with them grew out of long-distance trade in certain "necessary" commodities (such as salt, igneous rock, and obsidian). Like many other archaeologists, I remain unconvinced that these commodities were necessities in any absolute sense, and consequently that their acquisition provided a stimulus for hierarchical development. Rathje's ideas do have considerable merit, but in my opinion long-distance bulk trade such as he envisions was a comparatively late development and was an *acquired* function of already-existing high-status groups, rather than a factor in their initial appearance.

I suggest that by the time we see the first hints of hierarchical sociopolitical organization and the emergence of centers (at ca. 400 B.C.), indigenous processes of population growth, colonization, and land use such as outlined above had produced sufficient stresses in Maya society so that hierarchical organization and increasing political centralization had great adaptive value. Organization for the initiation, conduct, and resolution of warfare provides one "managerial" role for high-status Maya groups or individuals, and may be seen as one adaptive process (among others) related to basic ecological stresses.

After about 400 B.C. ranking becomes a conspicuous sociopolitical feature of the core area of the lowlands. Highly ranked individuals or groups served the following functions:

1. they provided focal points of group identification and cohesion;
2. they played an important role in adjudicating internal disputes (over land, women, and so forth) which would have provoked constant fissioning in small communities;
3. they facilitated the redistribution of basic commodities through ceremonial feasts or other exchanges, thus evening out shortages resulting from inequities in quality or quantity of land distribution or production (such inequities were no doubt responsible in large part for the ascendancy of particular kinship units in the first place); and
4. they provided the organization for successful offensive-defensive military operations and for the maintenance of political relations with similarly constituted, adjacent groups.

The most crucial problem from the point of view of this paper is the relationship between warfare and hierarchical status differentiation. My own assumption is that conflict stimulates organization as an adaptive response; an organized group is a more competitive group, and the pressures to organize for warfare may have evolutionary potential at many political levels. Here I would take issue with Fried (1967), who, though recognizing the prevalence of warfare on many levels of sociopolitical integration, would restrict its evolutionary significance to the process of state formation.

Success in war has been a vehicle for upward social mobility in many societies. Even on the egalitarian level, headmen may acquire considerable personal prestige in relation to their skills as war leaders, as among the Yanomamö (Chagnon 1967). Nor is prestige their only reward. Aggressive headmen may have privileged access to women, more offspring, and hence more extensive and valuable interpersonal relationships than the average man, thus reinforcing their positions. On more complex levels the potential exists for the translation of situational leadership in times of war into permanent statuses or roles with even greater political and economic, as well as military, prerogatives (see, for example, R. M. Adams's [1966] discussion of the metamorphosis of the role of *lugal,* or war leader, into that of secular king in Sumerian society). Military offices or roles may, in other words, be springboards to the differential accumulation of personal wealth in terms of land or booty, which can in turn be reinvested in client-patron relationships which further increase political and economic influence. The formula is superficially a simple one: an individual's success in military leadership makes him a valuable resource, to be rewarded with prestige and economic favors. Eventually the support of military leaders, and their families and retainers, may be underwritten by the group as a whole and distinct social gulfs may appear, eventually be be institutionalized as social stratification.

In reality, of course, the process is not so straightforward. Obviously the evolutionary potential of war leadership in an egalitarian society which does not generate surpluses (as most hunter-gatherer societies do not) is very limited. An effective agricultural economy in which surpluses are produced (or can be stimulated) is a necessary precondition. Moreover, I would agree with Fried's (1967) contention that the primary evolutionary significance of warfare lies in its ability to institutionalize preexisting principles of ranking or economic stratification, which are, in turn, related to ecological problems in the first place. I would disagree, on this basis, with Carneiro's assertion that warfare can be identified as *the* mechanism of pristine state formation (1970:734).

It seems highly likely to me that by the time warfare had become an attractive adaptive "choice" in the Maya Lowlands there were already present a number of conditions which could quickly have been intensified or modified by chronic warfare and its organizational concomitants. As we have seen, stresses relating to population pressure were being felt by ca. 500 B.C., but Maya farmers could still produce small-scale surpluses. There was at least incipiently developed ranking, with semisacrosanct groups directing redistribution, exercising judicial and ritual authority, and establishing advantageous prestige relationships. It also seems quite probable that by this time there was some degree of differential access to land, if not in terms of quantity, at least in terms of quality of landholdings.

The crucial question from the evolutionary point of view is how incipient *economic* stratification can emerge from or be reinforced by preexisting traditions of sacred leadership or situational military leadership. Under conditions of land shortages, increasingly restrictive notions about land tenure may be expected to emerge. At the same time, aggressive expansion may allow the incorporation of new land and perhaps new population elements, but the problem of what to do with these new acquisitions immediately arises. Here the opportunity for differential access to these resources presents itself. Successful military leaders (or more particularly their kin groups) may acquire more or better lands than others, especially if these leaders already possess other sanctions giving them slightly advantageous status. Such acquisitions seem especially likely if the traditional role of a high-status individual is to gain prestige largely by giving away goods, thus creating dependents and obligations. For such individuals there will be a strong tendency to attempt to maintain control over a disproportionately large amount of the newly acquired resources, or at least to enlarge their prestige relationships by judicious redistribution of them.

If newly acquired resources are not sufficient to even out shortcomings effectively, then pressure will continue, and those who are economically still somewhat disadvantaged (now perhaps including members of conquered groups) must continue to seek out favors from important or highly ranked individuals or groups at precisely the same time that those individuals or groups are acquiring effective control of more resources which can be manipulated for their own ends. Thus the ideal situation for emerging economic stratification would *not* be the one in which expansion through warfare is so successful that it opens up *vast* new areas by eliminating competing populations, but rather one in which small amounts of land are gradually accumulated and the groups formerly occupying them subordinated. Such a situation would produce attendant problems and opportunities for differential redistribution and extension of client-patron relationships. I suggest that this was the dominant pattern in the Maya Lowlands, as well as being an evolutionary process common to many emerging states (Webster 1975).

Again I emphasize that military leadership is only one of a series of important adaptive functions which gravitated to, and eventually defined, emergent high-status segments of Maya society during the Late Preclassic and Early Classic. Netting has argued that under conditions of population growth and resource limitation the structural weaknesses of a society based on localized, highly autonomous units must be overcome, and that "to integrate a number of such units or to allow an existing unit to expand without fission, ways must be found to keep the peace while enlarging personal contacts beyond the range of kin group and locality" (1972:233). In his view (illustrated by a number of examples drawn from African ethnology) incipient political leadership based upon sacred or symbolic prerogatives is one effective way of overcoming these structural weaknesses.

> The overwhelming need is not to expand existing political mechanisms (they are in certain respects radically inelastic) but literally to transcend them. The new grouping must be united not by kinship or territory alone, but by belief, by the infinite extensibility of common symbols, shared cosmology, and the overarching unity of fears and hopes made visible in ritual. A leader who can mobilize these sentiments, who can lend concrete form to an amorphous moral community, is thereby freed from complete identification with his village or section or age group or lineage. (1972:233)

Presumably the germ of such a development is found in the "Big Man" role common to a number of egalitarian societies (Sahlins 1963). Netting's ideas are obviously compatible with the "theocratic" flavor of early Maya society, but the use of the word *theocratic* should not overshadow the very real ecological advantages of sacred leadership in promoting effective redistribution, adjudicating conflicts over basic resources, and maintaining wider political and economic relationships, including those based upon conflict.

We know very little about the development of status differentiation among the Maya, but its undoubted direction was toward increasingly well-defined differentiation which seems to have culminated in social stratification *at least* by Late Classic times (Rathje 1970). Haviland's nutritional studies of Maya burials, though unfortunately based on an inadequate sample, suggest differential access to basic foodstuffs and marked status (class?) differentiation by the Early Classic (1967). At precocious centers such as Tikal, elaborate burial practices push status differences back into the Preclassic (Culbert 1974:15–19). All this evidence suggests that centralization of political decision making occurred quite early, especially in high-density areas. Assuming that status differentiation reflects increasingly effective and adaptive organization, I suggest that it also, in part, reflects adaptive sociopolitical restructuring related to problems of burgeoning populations, limitations on land, and conflict resolution.

A number of authorities have postulated relatively decentralized institutions of political and religious control for the early Maya, such as the *cargo* system advocated by Vogt (1963), for which Rathje (1970) has produced evidence in the form of burial distribution and content. If these institutions existed in the lowlands, and they may have, they would seem to me to have been ephemeral under the conditions of stress, including competition, found in Preclassic society. They would not have provided stable enough or predictable enough leadership. If they existed, their importance probably lay in the ease with which they could be short-circuited, or could themselves provide the preconditions for status differentiation which could quickly have become more rigid as the necessity for effective leadership grew more pressing. Subsequently they may have been incorporated as subunits in societies with effective social stratification, since they allowed at least limited participation in (and satisfaction with) the overarching political and religious institutions and thus served valuable functions of integration. At the same time concentration of wealth, an increasing monopoly of elite groups, was discouraged among the sustaining cultivators.

Conflict, even on a fairly small and disorganized scale, presents distinct problems for swidden agriculturalists. One of the frequent adaptive responses to the stresses of warfare in many societies is population nucleation (R. M. Adams 1972), a solution which was not really viable on a landscape most effectively exploited by small, scattered populations residing in hamlets or farmsteads. An effective compromise is the development or intensification of a number of organizational features. One such compromise might be the strengthening of interaction on the local level without drastic changes in settlement patterns—that is, the elaboration of mutually supportive relationships, whether in terms of offensive-defensive operations or redistribution of food to those driven from their homes or deprived of their crops. Such interaction may be envisioned on the basis of bonds of kinship or less personal political alliances, as among the Yanomamö (Chagnon 1967). As noted previously, the Maya were in a sense preadapted to the crystallization of relatively well-defined local groups, given concentrated areas of high productivity and population and the centripetal tendencies of bush-fallowing systems.

Among the consequences of intensified local bonds might be increased definition of "territory," greater endogamy to solidify supportive kin relationships, and perhaps even production of culturally defined local shortages, stimulating small-scale craft specialization and complex forms of redistribution, again found among the Yanomamö. It is under such conditions that the first recognizable centers may have appeared in the Maya Lowlands after about 500 B.C.

Archaeologists have always been hard pressed to explain the functions of Maya centers. The traditional label attached to them has been "ceremonial" centers, and indeed there is no doubt that centers performed ritual functions and were foci of ritual interaction. But why should the Maya need ceremonial centers when other folk agriculturalists have done perfectly well without them? And why do they appear relatively late in the Preclassic, and then only in a few areas?

I suggest that we use a new label, *organizational centers*—a term sufficiently vague to allow speculation about a variety of possible adaptive functions. Ceremonialism is thus seen as a *symptom* of organization, not as an end in itself. In light of the above discussion organizational centers may be regarded as another compromise response to population stress and conflict in lieu of nucleation, and several primary functions may be postulated:

1. On the symbolic level the center helps to define the local community through common awareness of and participation in *ritual activity*. The development of such focal points of ceremonialism, particularly associated with ancestor worship (traditionally strong among the Maya) has been singled out by Flannery (1972b) as a mechanism of territorial definition.

2. *Economic redistribution* would be another possible function. We previously suggested that conflict itself would necessitate some redistribution of basic commodities, if some members of the community were driven from their lands or deprived of their crops or

354

stored surpluses. Redistribution of artificially created "scarce" resources has also been alluded to. Given land shortages and unequal distribution of some kinds of land, along with early impulses toward intensification, basic foodstuffs might also have been redistributed under conditions of seasonal or occasional shortages. For example, dry-season crops grown in moist, fertile *bajos* might be redistributed annually, or under conditions of drought. Alternatively, in wet years or seasons, *bajo* cultivation might be impossible due to excessive moisture, necessitating redistribution of crops grown on better-drained slopes.

3. Perhaps the most important functions of the centers would involve group decision making, that is, *political or administrative functions*. On the local level these would include decisions concerning distribution of resources, organization of ritual, and most important from the point of view of this paper, problems in boundary maintenance or expansion under conditions of conflict—in other words, coordination of conflict.

The establishment of centers, then, is probably symptomatic of a series of organizational adjustments. Among other things, even the earliest centers had military functions, and individuals or groups residing in them provided necessary leadership as warfare became chronic.

The position of war leader has a respectable antiquity in Maya society. *Nacoms* were important under the fragmented political conditions of the Postclassic Period (Tozzer 1941). The careers of Bird Jaguar and his ilk in the Late Classic at centers such as Yaxchilan (Proskouriakoff 1961, 1963–64) have decided military overtones. Artistic representations of bound or downtrodden enemies or armed warriors at Tikal, Calakmul, Bonampak, and other sites push this pattern back into the Classic. Given the potential for conflict under conditions of ecological stress, I suggest that military functions were not late acquisitions of the Maya elite, but rather helped to generate this class in the first place. By Late Classic times we may have fully developed military aristocracies, though perhaps not as complex as those of Central Mexico.

In terms of developing stratification linked to conflict, the concepts of "self-serving" and "system-serving" should be introduced here, following Flannery (1972a). War leaders, adaptive (system-serving) in terms of the local cultural system when they first appeared, may quickly have become maladaptive (self-serving) in that system as their status was institutionalized. If, as has been maintained, the emergence of centralized authority, due at least in part to the need to organize for military purposes, was originally adaptive, it also triggered changes in the system—changes which may have intensified stresses rather than lowering them. As competition became more pronounced the positions of successful war leaders were strengthened, their component in the population increased, and they attracted or subordinated new populations from which unusually high surpluses could be extracted. They acquired more "essential" functions (and here Rathje's [1971] ideas about long-distance trade are probably most useful) and were able to initiate changes in other institutions which had previously been impossible, such as agricultural intensification in the forms of terracing or raised-field systems. Warfare itself may have been manipulated by perceptive leaders who saw their own fortunes linked to military success, and such conflict would ultimately have become self-serving and destructive of the wider system.

Many of the "adaptive" choices made in this tremendously dynamic political milieu were, in fact, maladaptive in the long run. Intensification of agriculture may not only have produced environmental destruction and diminishing yields in terms of labor input, but also have encouraged population growth to provide additional labor even as productivity declined and the demands of nonproducers increased. These new stresses, however, are more properly seen in the context of the collapse of Maya civilization (Culbert 1973a).

PATTERNS OF WARFARE AND MAYA CULTURE HISTORY

By late Preclassic times, if the preceding estimates of population growth and carrying capacity are reasonably accurate, conflict and related adaptive organizational responses were producing numerous local centers. This process, by no means uniform, was greatly accelerated in areas of high population density and social circumscription. It was in these areas, at first through internal conflict and later through extension of conflict to surrounding, marginal, low-density regions, that status differentiation related to warfare was most marked.

At the present time, to my knowledge, we have no direct knowledge of patterns of Preclassic warfare, with a possible exception. Baudez and Becquelin (1973) have tentatively identified defensive earthworks at the site of Los Naranjos in northern Honduras, and on the basis of ceramic affiliations suggest that they were originally constructed some time between 800 and 400 B.C. If correct, this identification of extensive fortifications in a Preclassic (Olmec-related?) context near the southern limit of Mesoamerica bolsters my contention that competition came surprisingly early to the Maya Lowlands. Unfortunately for the archaeologist interested in warfare as a mechanism of cultural evolution, intergroup conflict is often difficult or impossible to infer from prehistoric remains (see Webster 1972:13–17 for a more complete discussion of this problem). One generalization can be made: *negative* evidence is meaningless, since many forms of primitive warfare lack specialized weaponry, military architecture, or other obvious and preservable paraphernalia. I recently asked Napoleon Chagnon what clear evidence there would be for Yanomamö warfare on the basis of their material culture and settlement pattern alone. His answer: "None."

Given the probable small sizes of local political units, rather inefficient authority structures, and logistical problems, the basic pattern of conflict was probably the raid, although there may occasionally have been larger, more formalized or ritualized contests such as those of the Dugum Dani and other New Guinea peoples (Heider 1970). Note, in this connection, that Maya warfare, when admitted to have occurred at all, is traditionally thought to have emphasized small-scale raiding, primarily for the capture of slaves or sacrificial victims (thus reflecting Postclassic patterns). An implication of this traditional point of view is that because of its small scale, conflict in Maya society was of little significance. Few archaeologists have pointed out that although the *scale* of conflict may be small in terms of duration, numbers of combatants, or casualties, its political and demographic consequences may be very significant indeed (Larson 1972; Webster 1972).

Raiding on a more or less constant basis serves to delineate local groups (thus reinforcing we-they distinctions fundamental to organized intergroup conflict) and also functions to maintain boundaries and to space population. Chagnon has argued that where there is sufficient vacant land, tendencies toward fissioning in small communities may produce chronic warfare in the form of raiding (1967). Indeed, the very possibility of flight or migration may make a belligerent stance an effective adaptive choice. Chronic warfare also adds a supracommunity dimension to Yanomamö politics, in that intercommunity alliances (albeit shifting ones) are apparently necessary for the survival of most communities. Such a situation of chronic raiding could have existed in the Maya Lowlands at ca. 500 B.C., setting the stage for intense conflict over land. It may, in other words, have been a preparation for the formation of non-kinship-based alliances and the appearance of regional centers as integrative mechanisms. It should be emphasized that centers and the high-status personnel residing in them probably functioned to resolve conflict as well as to organize for it. In many areas where primitive warfare has been observed ethnographically (for example, New Guinea) elaborate feasts and conciliatory rituals are necessary to *terminate* hostilities formally as well as to cement military alliances between politically autonomous groups. Production of "surpluses" would seem essential for this process to operate.

It should be noted in passing that the processes of population movement which were responsible for the initial occupation of the lowlands may have involved small-scale conflict in very early times. If large increments of tropical agriculturalists moved in from the Tabasco-Veracruz coastal zone, as seems likely, after 1000 B.C., these movements may have been related to population growth under conditions of complex sociopolitical development in the Olmec "heartland," assuming, as many have, that the Olmec were Maya speakers. If the breakup of Olmec society is related to fissioning of communities into more marginal zones to the east, rapid deculturation would be expected and seems to be reflected in the archaeological data. But relic organizational features of Olmec society may have been retained, and these may have included rather well-developed authority structures. Prestige ranking of lineages can apparently endure even where deculturation in a sociopolitical sense occurs (as among the Maori), and such ranking can be the germ of new forms of organization.

As land shortages became strongly felt after 500 B.C., raiding became more significant in its scope, incidence, and consequences. Warfare was still quite limited in scale, however, for the reasons noted above. Another limiting factor, one common to many preindustrial societies, was the highly seasonal nature of the agricultural cycle.

Significant numbers of combatants could be mustered only during slack seasons, such as the end of the rainy season, when crops were ripening. This limitation affected the Postclassic Maya (Roys 1943) and was in large measure responsible for the failure of the great Maya rebellions of the mid nineteenth century (Reed 1964). The very fragility of the agricultural cycle, however, could have made the raid an effective political and military weapon. Even small-scale raiding could disrupt such necessary tasks as clearing, planting, or harvesting and could destroy maturing crops or stored surpluses. Raiding could have been, in a sense, a kind of bullying tactic in which groups with demographic superiority would have had a decided edge in the long run. Such large groups could have fielded more raiders more often and, on the other hand, would also have had a *defensive* advantage in their home territory. What I am suggesting is that constant attrition of marginal populations, even if casualties were few, would have had serious demographic consequences, forcing some groups to flee or subordinate themselves.

Under conditions of widespread and chronic raiding, many emerging centers were probably fortified with ditches and/or timber palisades, as were some of the Postclassic towns seen by Cortés on his march to Honduras. Such defenses would have been quite effective, given the logistical problems of Maya warfare and the numerical advantage usually held by defenders. Here again the raid would be the most effective form of offensive action. With direct assaults or sieges either too costly or impossible, the only effective way to eliminate competing centers rapidly would have been quick, unexpected penetration of enemy defenses, with consequent dispersal or destruction of those residing at the center.

If warfare in the form of raiding was a common element in Preclassic Maya society, certain organizational responses would have been very adaptive. For example, any local group which could support even a small number of quasi-professional warriors would possess both an offensive and a defensive advantage, since the limitations of time and labor would not affect them. It seems very likely that this is one function that accrued to high-status lineages residing in organizational centers, since their support would already have been partly underwritten by their redistributive functions. The emergence of such warrior groups would not only be adaptive in terms of external rivalries, but might also establish a special interest group with loyalties apart from the network of wider kin relationships—the beginnings of centralized control of physical force.

After 400 B.C. organizational centers were fairly numerous and some, such as Tikal, grew to impressive proportions. Status differentiation, probably on the basis of highly developed ranking, becomes conspicuous in the archaeological record (see Culbert 1974 for a summary of the Tikal data). By Terminal Preclassic times (ca. A.D. 150–250) regional centers are numerous and well established. Highly ranked kin groups, probably already enjoying advantageous control over basic resources, in part through successful military expansion, no doubt eagerly sought to monopolize religious functions to consolidate their gains further, lacking as they did a firm monopoly of physical force. Thus the strong "theocratic" quality of early Maya society was functionally related both to the necessity of maintaining effective organizational centers for dispersed populations in a highly competitive ecological situation and to the emergence of an eventually self-serving elite class. If this suggestion is correct, the traditional assumption that "theocratic" societies are peaceful is highly suspect (Webster in press).

There is some evidence that by Late Preclassic times warfare had become very significant in its scope and effects. As a result of my 1970 fieldwork I dated the massive defensive system at Becan, in southern Campeche, Mexico, to the initial stages of the Early Classic (250–450 B.C.). I noted, however, the distinct possibility that initial construction of the earthworks may have occurred in the Late Preclassic (Webster 1974:127). Joe Ball, ceramist of the Becan project, feels on the basis of close scrutiny of an enlarged ceramic sample from excavations subsequent to my own that this possibility is very likely correct; he would place initial construction at about A.D. 100 (personal communication), and I concur in this chronological realignment. The Rio Bec region near Becan is extremely productive in terms of swidden agriculture, and our preliminary work suggests a very dense Late Preclassic population. Prior to the Late Preclassic the area seems to have been vacant. Here again is evidence for rapid population growth and movement, related, significantly enough, to large-scale warfare. Another indication of increased political definition of territory, a process intimately related to warfare, is the gradual disintegration of the formerly highly homogeneous Chicanel ceramic sphere.

The period most crucial to an understanding of Maya cultural evolution is the Early Classic (ca. A.D. 250–600). Not only does status differentiation become increasingly marked at this time, but new stresses in the form of foreign influences appear, probably from El Salvador (Willey, Culbert, and Adams 1967; Sharer and Gifford 1970). Disjunctive changes in the ceramic sequences at a number of sites such as Altar de Sacrificios and Barton Ramie suggest not only that new population elements appeared, but that in some places these new elements were dominant after fusion with local populations, perhaps indicating well-developed class distinctions (Willey, Culbert, and Adams 1967; R. E. W. Adams 1971:155–56). Perhaps we may see in these influences some anticipation of the military adventuring which later becomes such a conspicuous feature of Mesoamerican society. Significantly enough, larger centers such as Uaxactun and Tikal show no disruption of local sequences, which probably reflects their already strong organizational structures and military capability.

A further foreign influence may also have contributed to stress and conflict between centers at this time. Contacts with the burgeoning highland state of Teotihuacan may be earlier than previously thought. Pendergast (1971) has found evidence of some sort of Teotihuacan presence at Altun Ha, in British Honduras, sometime during the second century A.D. Such early exploratory probings of the lowlands by highland groups probably represent attempts to establish initial commercial relationships, and one might expect contacts at a number of centers as they felt out the political and demographic situation. Eventually, as might be expected, Tikal became a focal point of influence during the fifth century, since it was strategically situated to dominate trade from the west and south and had the most impressive political structure and certainly the demographic base to maximize commercial exchanges.

It seems very likely that the establishment of Teotihuacan commercial influence at Tikal further stimulated the development of that center in a number of ways. It provided the emerging local elites with exotic status symbols and strengthened their managerial functions insofar as they effectively manipulated a lucrative foreign trade and allowed some of its products to trickle down to all levels of society.

This new commercial dimension, of course, caused additional stresses in the already competitive political environment of the lowlands. Tikal, and possibly other favored centers, had to take steps to gain firm control of trade routes and were able to engage in a sort of economic imperialism with regard to other, more peripheral centers, which possessed their own high-status leaders hungry for prestige objects and fearful of the rising power of the northeastern Peten. It is not surprising that new evidence for the increased importance of warfare appears during the Early Classic. At Tikal itself, Stela 31 pictures a dominant Maya lord flanked by warriors armed in a fashion more typical of the highlands, raising the possibility that foreign mercenaries may have been used in lowland conflicts. Impressive earthworks, which seem to be hinterland defenses, delimit the Tikal sustaining area (D. Puleston and Callender 1967). Although they are not securely dated, Puleston (personal communication) believes they could be of Early Classic origin.

At Becan the impressive defensive system was certainly functioning during the Early Classic (if not earlier, as previously noted). There appears to have been a rather drastic population dislocation during much of this period; very little habitation refuse has been found outside the ditch and ramparts.

There is presently, in my opinion, no evidence to suggest the sort of direct Teotihuacan military intervention in the lowlands that may have occurred at Kaminaljuyu. No doubt this was in part due to the already vigorous indigenous political systems and to locally heavy populations; in fact, Tikal's population may have reached its maximum during the Early Classic. That the Teotihuacan presence exacerbated lowland political tensions, however, seems very likely. The economic dimension has already been mentioned. It is also possible that new political and military ideas were introduced into the lowlands, but this should not be understood in the same sense as other claims that "militarism" was a highland introduction. Conflict was already an important factor in Maya society and probably had been for hundreds of years. Significantly enough, the earliest evidence for large-scale warfare in all of Mesoamerica is found in the Maya Lowlands (the Becan fortifications) and *not* in the presumably more "militaristic" highlands.

I have elsewhere (Webster 1972:289–94) outlined the probable relationships between the Becan defensive system and the Peten Maya sphere of influence to the south. Briefly, there are three major possibilities: (1) that the defensive system at Becan was built to protect a peripheral Maya center (or alliance of centers) against expansive

Peten Maya political influence; (2) that the center was fortified as an outpost of Peten Maya influences; and (3) that the construction of the defensive system had nothing to do with expansive influences from the Tikal region under Teotihuacan influences.

Although which of these explanations is correct cannot be determined on the basis of the present evidence, the acceptance of *any* of them indicates quite clearly that the lowlands had an impressive tradition of indigenous warfare, and that by A.D. 300–500 conflict was being conducted on a large scale.

Before the rapid spread of "Classic" traits after ca. A.D. 550 there may have been a rather marked regional disjunction in sociopolitical development between the more mature, precocious centers of the northeastern Peten and those farther north in Yucatan, where "non-Classic" chiefdoms were appearing. Joesink-Mandeville (1972) suggests that the southern, Classic manifestation was the product of Cholan speakers, the north being densely populated by Yucatec Maya. While contacts were certainly well established between these two gross regions, there may have been zones of tension along a political and linguistic frontier somewhere in southern Campeche, including the Rio Bec area where the fortified center of Becan is located.

By Late Classic times (after ca. A.D. 600) evidence for warfare becomes reasonably abundant in the archaeological record, and I will not review it here. At this point I would like to make what I feel is a very important distinction between *warfare* and *militarism,* two terms which we unfortunately tend to use interchangeably. A definition of warfare itself is beyond the scope of this paper; rather I would like to offer a definition of militarism as a special form of warfare. Militarism is the effective institutionalization of warfare and its accoutrements in the social organization, ideology, and symbolism of complex societies (states). Its particular characteristics, when contrasted with simpler forms of warfare, are the following:

1. Its aims are territorial aggrandizement or the acquisition of other capital resources, such as trade routes, resource areas, or even people.
2. Decision making on the initiation of conflict, organization, and strategy is in the hands of relatively few high-status individuals and is exercised as part of a conscious political policy. Positions of leadership in actual military operations are also highly restricted.

3. There are distinct economic gains in addition to prestige, and access to the rewards of successful conflict is weighted heavily toward the decision makers.

4. Participation in conflict for most combatants is not a matter of free choice, but is enforced by sanctions more effective than public opinion. The warrier, in short, becomes the soldier.

5. Effective political consolidation of new territory and populations is possible.

6. Groups of semiprofessional warriors appear, and while this role and the rewards that go with it are often monopolized by privileged classes, there may be opportunities for limited upward mobility through warfare (see, for example, the Aztec *techutli*).

7. Specialized weaponry, military architecture, and organizational systems appear, the scale of warfare is increased, and combat becomes more lethal.

Many of these characteristics may be present in more primitive forms of warfare, but when taken together they constitute true militarism, a "new and intensified form of warfare that came about as a new aspect of governance" (Service 1967:169).

It is on the level of militarism that warfare is very likely to become "self-serving," both as an institution in itself and for those who control it. I suggest that, throughout the Late Classic, militarism, as defined above, was a constant element in Lowland Maya culture, in its self-serving capacity responsible in part for generating the stresses which ultimately produced the sudden decline of Classic Maya civilization.

As a "Big Tradition" solidified, relations on the elite level between various Maya centers became strongly developed. Elite interconnections, on the one hand, by cementing relationships between centers, served to avoid conflict or facilitate its resolution and the formation of new political alliances. On the other hand, actual kin relationships and recognition of mutual interest in maintaining the hierarchical status quo need not be seen as inhibiting conflict. Ethnohistoric accounts indicate that during the initial period of Aztec expansion in the Central Highlands common understandings between the elite from overtly antagonistic political units were fairly common (Durán 1964:192–94). Militarism, at least at some of the larger centers, probably also served important functions in the maintenance of internal social cohesion. Elite classes in Late Classic times were faced with the problem of *controlling* their own dispersed populations, a reversal of the Preclassic situation in which *protection* of a local population was the overriding concern. Insofar as the local elite groups effectively monopolized the use of armed force it could be used as a pragmatic sanction of their by now rather oppressive domination. On the other hand, the small surpluses which could be generated by the Maya farmer at the base of the social pyramid meant that only a comparatively small number of nonproducers could have been supported. This would have severely limited the usefulness of military threat in maintaining the hierarchical system. A related factor is the lack of any real technological differential in military capability on various social levels. In the Old World such a differential existed in Bronze Age societies, where elite groups effectively monopolized metal weapons and armor, chariots, horses, and so forth, but it was obviously absent in the Maya Lowlands, and indeed in Mesoamerica as a whole. Naked force, then, was not very effective in maintaining the sociopolitical status quo. This is one reason why kin ties and religious sanctions were so necessary in Maya society, and why it retained, even in its mature stage, a strong theocratic flavor.

Internal social cohesion may have been reinforced, however, by the artificial stimulation of external conflict or tension between centers or alliances of centers, an Orwellian idea that is probably not restricted to industrial states. Chronic conditions of warfare and tension produced and manipulated by the Maya elite would have strengthened the managerial role of that elite; here again relations on the elite level *between* competing centers may still have been maintained. Such manipulation of conflict for essentially "self-serving" ends seems to have characterized at least the earlier phases of Aztec expansion. Durán, noting the secret connivances of various supposedly antagonistic rulers in the Central Highlands, writes that "the reason for all of this secrecy was that they did not wish the common people—soldiers and captains—to suspect that kings and rulers made alliances, came to agreements and formed friendships at the cost of the life of the common man, and the shedding of his blood" (1964:193–94).

A conspicuous feature of the political structuring of the Late Classic Maya is the apparent lack of widespread political unification, except where old, established centers grew up in close proximity but experienced different rates of growth and possessed different capacity in terms of absolute size of supporting populations (Tikal, for example, probably maintained some sort of dominant relationship with Uaxactun from the Early Classic on). Although this may seem paradoxical in light of my contention that militarism was chronic in Late Classic Maya society (assuming that militarism is an important mechanism in hammering out large-scale political structures), a number of explanations can be advanced.

1. Given the low resource diversity of the lowland environment, there was comparatively little incentive to establish widespread political hegemony and, more important, no marked tendency for widely separated areas to hang together as units of economic interdependence even if such hegemony was momentarily established.

2. Regions of high productivity and high density, and their concomitant impressive political developments, were unevenly distributed, which reduced the feasibility of overarching political structures.

3. The Maya elite class itself was never very numerous, given the small per capita surpluses generated by the peasant producer, and the sanctions supporting it were comparatively fragile. Thus a great deal of energy was necessarily expended to ensure local ascendancy and control local supporting populations; by the time militarism is most marked, these problems of local control were also most severe.

4. The populations that actually sustained even the largest autonomous Maya political units were never very large (in comparison, for example, with highland states)—say on the order of 40,000–60,000 people. Maya hierarchical organization was geared to societies of this magnitude, and incorporation of further large increments of population, especially at considerable distances, proved unworkable.

I am not denying that supracenter political unification did occasionally occur (as in the Usumacinta drainage) or that taxation or tribute was imposed by one center on another. But such unification was on a very small scale and appears to have been quite unstable, for the reasons suggested above.

A factor contributing to the internal fragility of Maya polities throughout the Classic Period was the traditional, strong emphasis on kin linkages and lineage ranking as basic frameworks for authority structures. Even if sufficient social gulfs had appeared by Late Classic times so that we might speak, however tentatively, of social classes, Maya politics was probably often characterized by the instability more common to high-level chiefdoms—that is, by the competition for power among various elite lineages within a single polity. Such competition, perhaps involving actual conflict, may have occurred in large centers and would have been even more pronounced if a *number* of centers, each with its own potentially independent ruler, formed a temporary political unity. Such a fluid and competitive internal political environment made expansion highly risky, and even where successful expansion occurred, effective political consolidation of multicentered states was impossible on a long-term basis.

While the Maya elite undoubtedly manipulated Late Classic Maya militarism for self-serving ends, some aspects of the ecological imperative for conflict were still operating. Long-distance trade was well developed and involved not only the movement of such products as salt, cacao, and igneous rocks within the lowlands themselves but also in areas outside the Maya region, especially Tabasco and Honduras. Resource zones of raw materials and the routes over which they traveled were sources of potential conflict.

By Late Classic times, too, in some areas various forms of intensified agriculture must have become increasingly important, or even necessary, to feed the burgeoning populations in high-density zones such as the northeastern Peten. These new techniques probably included *bajo* cultivation on a large scale, terracing, grass fallowing, and dependence upon valuable orchard crops. Such intensification may have stimulated conflict in a number of ways. First, portions of the landscape which had formerly been either unpopulated or only marginally populated were occupied and, in fact, redefined as valuable basic resources. Examples might be the extensive *bajos* around major sites, and extensive grasslands such as found south of the lake region in the northeastern Peten. Many of these new resource zones were on the peripheries of major centers and may indeed have constituted political buffer zones. Their colonization and effective exploitation might consequently have presented problems in terms of intracenter political relationships, and conflict may very well have been generated over their possession. Another factor related to certain forms of intensification is that of capital improvement. Effective exploitation of some microenvironments obviously required substantial investments of labor. An example is the large system of canals and drainage ditches to the south of Edzna, which seems to have been designed to drain a swampy area for agricultural purposes. Such improvements produced extremely valuable capital resources. It is not unreasonable to suppose that capital improvements of this sort stimulated conflict, since in many cases the "social cost" of acquiring them through conquest would have been less than the initial investment of labor required to produce them.

A factor indirectly related to agricultural intensification is that of environmental degradation. If some heavily exploited zones of the lowlands were experiencing environmental destruction through certain kinds of intensification, such as reduction of the fallowing cycle, as some authorities have maintained (see Sanders 1973), serious dislocations of populations may have occurred, resulting in the florescence of some centers at the expense of older, well-established ones (did Yaxha, for example, grow at the expense of Tikal?). This process would have caused rapid shifts in demographic potential and concomitant political structuring, as well as problems of internal population control, and the already intensely competitive atmosphere of Lowland Maya political alignments would have been further heightened.

Conflict and warfare, then, expressed especially in the form of militarism, can be seen as a major factor in the buildup of stresses in the Late Classic which ultimately led to the collapse of Maya hierarchical society in the "core" area in the eighth and ninth centuries A.D. Late Classic militarism was, however, the logical outcome of stresses that had been present in Maya society from its inception.

SUMMARY

In order to summarize the foregoing discussion of evolutionary processes related to warfare, I have constructed three models of the dynamic Maya cultural system, representing three different states of the system along its developmental continuum (Figs. 12.1–12.3). These models are oversimplifications to a very high degree, emphasizing those features of the system which are most closely related to warfare and sociopolitical evolution.

State 1, before ca. 400 B.C.

During the initial period of agricultural colonization and population growth, fissioning effectively corrected temporary imbalances between population concentration and productive resources. The system (or series of similar systems) was consequently in a state of unstable equilibrium, since an increase in social circumscription (and corresponding decrease in ability of groups to fission into vacant land), eventually produced by population growth and fissioning itself, produced readjustments in the system. Warfare, if it occurred at all, had little evolutionary potential at this stage.

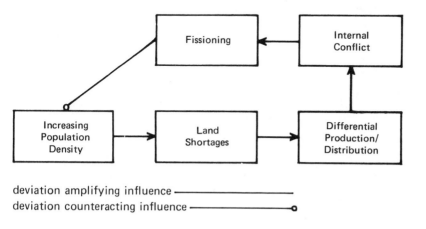

deviation amplifying influence ———————————
deviation counteracting influence ———————o

FIGURE 13.1. Maya system before ca. 400 B.C.

State 2, ca. 100 B.C.

From the point of view of the evolutionary potential of warfare this is the most crucial state. When fissioning into vacant land ceased to be possible, differential access to land and differential production simultaneously created economic stresses in the system (internal conflict) *and* incipient economic stratification. Internal conflict necessitated the appearance of various managerial roles (especially redistribution and adjudication), and personnel to fill managerial roles were recruited from those groups with advantageous access to basic resources in the first place. Such personnel formed the nuclei of high-ranking, sacrosanct lineages. Aggressive expansion (or, alternatively, successful defense of the local population) was one

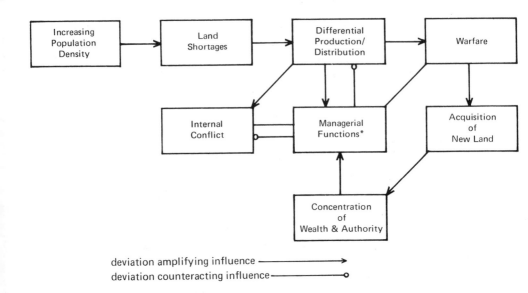

FIGURE 13.2.   Maya system at ca. 100 B.C.

---

*"Managerial Functions" refers to the related processes of sacred leadership, redistribution, suppression of internal conflict (adjudication), and maintenance of external political relationships (including organization for and resolutions of warfare).

solution for land shortages, and leadership in warfare became an important managerial function. Successful expansion incorporated new land (though probably in small amounts). This new land was, in effect, a basic resource which was "external" to the traditional system (no local lineages or individuals had claim to it) and so could be advantageously manipulated by the highly ranked managerial groups, in terms of differential access to it and/or politically judicious redistribution of it. Through this process the already present incipient economic stratification was heightened, and leveling mechanisms which might have corrected this process of concentration of wealth were unable to do so because of the highly adaptive functions of the managerial groups in a politically competitive environment. The necessity of maintaining an aggressive stance made local population increases still adaptive, and subordinated populations increased local densities as well. Subordinated populations were also, in a sense, "external" to the system (they had no kin ties to managerial groups and

370

could be depressed economically) and contributed to hierarchical development. State 2 was extremely unstable and dynamic.

State 3, ca. 750 A.D.

At some point the developing system became involuted, in the sense that aggressive incorporation of new land was no longer feasible for environmental or political reasons. Intensification of agriculture was one answer to this problem, and resulted in valuable capital resource production. Intensive agriculture contributed to further increases in population density to provide labor. Intensification created new problems of labor organization and redistribution, reinforcing the managerial roles of the high-ranking groups still further, and facilitated additional concentrations of wealth and authority, now in the form of taxation or tribute. The rich were getting richer.

Warfare assumed militaristic proportions and was still system-serving in that it protected local capital resources and occasionally allowed expropriation of such resources from neighboring political units. Its self-serving aspects became important, however, in suppressing internal conflict (i.e., in maintaining the socioeconomic status quo), as well as in defending the hierarchical polity from external encroachment. Effective concentration of wealth and authority stimulated trade in common and especially in luxury commodities, again reinforcing the managerial statuses through new redistributive functions and display of status symbols. The direction of the system was toward well-developed social stratification, and emergent elite groups fostered further militarism, perceiving it as an essential process in their own rise to and maintenance of power. This Late Classic involuted system was extremely unstable, and endured for several hundred years at the most.

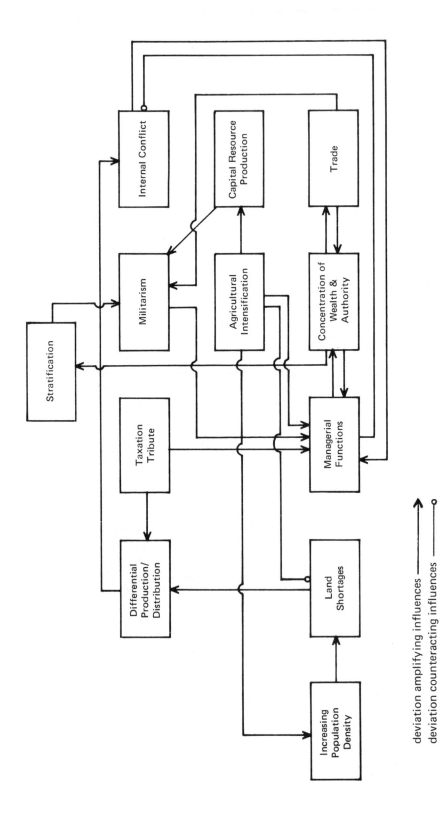

deviation amplifying influences ————————►
deviation counteracting influences ————————o

FIGURE 13.3.   Maya system at ca. A.D. 750

14
The Tikal Connection

WILLIAM L. RATHJE
University of Arizona

Currently in archaeology one idealized method for studying complex civilizations is a multidimensional systems approach, in which various interrelated general processes (see Flannery 1968b, 1972a) and specific factors (population growth, warfare, agricultural and other subsistence strategies, trade, and others) are analyzed to evaluate the ways in which their synergism affected specific cultural developments. Few archaeologists find fault with the methods or goals of this research strategy.

A simple ordering of priorities, however, suggests some value to a much more limited approach to the study of Maya cultural development. This chapter briefly explains my use of this limited approach and attempts to relate it to an ultimate goal, a total systems reconstruction of the specifics of Maya history (see Rathje 1975 for a more general systems model of Maya development).

Any systems analysis requires more than simply a "consideration" of a number of interacting factors. The specific interaction among factors must be identified and quantified in detail. Given general systems processes, specific local factors must be weighted in terms of their effect on each other in order to generate the actual parameters

373

of a culture's development and failure. The specific weighting of any single factor is a difficult undertaking. At the present time, very few variables have been analyzed to a degree where they can be interrelated in a quantified model.

Population growth is a good example. Due to the work of Boserup (1965) and others, population growth has been clearly identified as an important variable in the increase of cultural complexity. However, the parameters on rates of population growth are unclear. For the Maya, there are few detailed models which discuss in a concrete manner how agricultural productivity, warfare, disease, social organizations, or trade patterns promote or constrain births and deaths. Many models, in fact, simply take population growth of an unknown magnitude as a given.

It is important to study population growth and other variables carefully. The relationships among population growth, warfare, and agricultural productivity described in this volume are critical to developing a productive model of Maya cultural development. Several models have been proposed, however, that are somewhat incompatible with the actual archaeological data.

Many models suggest that population growth and resulting stresses on resources led to the introduction of both agricultural intensification techniques and competitive warfare as significant components in early Maya subsistence systems. The complex organizations that would have been needed to implement such activities are proposed to have led to the archaeological manifestations of Maya civilization, including temples, palaces, elaborate burials and caches, and stelae. Many of these archaeological remains first appeared in a cohesive large-scale format in the central Maya area, a zone identified by Sanders (Chap. 11, above) as containing especially fertile soils and hence the potential for high agricultural productivity. Therefore models which explain the rise of Maya civilization as a product of population growth and the resulting resource stresses require hard evidence both of rapid population increase and of competition over resources in this central Maya region, relative to other parts of the Maya Lowlands, during the Preclassic.

The problem is that Preclassic Tikal (Culbert, Chap. 2 above) seems to have had a lower population (both in absolute numbers and relative to Late Classic levels) and a slower rate of growth than other scholars have found at sites outside the Central Zone where the evidences of

Maya civilization are earlier, but smaller and less sophisticated. It therefore remains to be demonstrated that population pressure in one principal area of Maya cultural development had reached a level by Early Classic times that led to drastic forms of economic intensification, either major changes in basic subsistence techniques or competition in the form of warfare. Obviously, more detailed quantitative data are needed to evaluate archaeological evidences of differential population growth and their relation to intensification activities.

Another problem area for population and warfare models is Early Classic population levels. In Belize, population continues Preclassic rates of increase into the Early Classic. In the Usumacinta-Pasión drainage, population seems to have been dramatically reduced. Within the central area, in contrast, population climbed significantly in spite of the possibility of migration to the seemingly sparsely populated Southeastern Lowlands. The population pressure and warfare models do not make the reasons for this variability clear, especially in the central Maya area.

A further example of the difficulty of using only these variables is provided by the Chicanel horizon. Most models which emphasize competition for resources see this period as a time of intensive, even conquest-oriented, warfare, preparatory to the spread of a unified Maya cult during the following Early Classic Period. Certainly warfare might be expected to produce a marked regionalism in pottery styles. Instead, the Chicanel horizon is a time of homogeneity in the production of pottery from northern Yucatan to the edge of the Guatemalan Highlands (see Ball, Chap. 5 above). Few models have been proposed to reconcile this apparent contradiction between heavy warfare over resources and widespread homogeneity in pottery production techniques and results.

These points are not raised to depreciate the significant effects of population growth, warfare, or differential agricultural productivity on the development of Maya culture. However, they do lead to one conclusion—that individual factors must be much better defined and understood before complex systems models can be developed which interrelate these variables.

As a result, I have chosen to concentrate on defining as fully as possible the effect of household-level economics (specifically, the need to obtain nonlocal basic resources) on aspects of Maya cultural development (cf. Rathje 1971, 1972, 1973). The goal is to combine these data with information on other factors to construct a systems model of the specifics of Maya cultural development. I will not reiterate here the Maya trade models that have been reported in detail elsewhere. Instead I will simply provide an outline of trade constructs which can be used in conjunction with population and warfare models to soften some of the abovementioned inconsistencies between archaeological data and these models.

The study of the development of Maya culture must use a dynamic model that incorporates growth and change. One way to view a system's growth dynamically is from an economic perspective. In a review-article, Keeble (1967) observed that economists have begun to devise spatial models of economic development in reaction to static equilibrium models which assumed that regional variations in economic development would tend to equalize through time. The constructs he outlined are essentially variations of only one general growth model which involves three basic processes: cumulative causation, backwash, and spread.

The hypothesis of *cumulative causation* states that once growth begins it sets in motion a series of feedback loops. These result in accelerated development of economies which require a minimum demand in order to operate, but which produce effects that stimulate further growth once the economies have crossed critical thresholds. Once these thresholds are crossed, often by a number of separate organizations experiencing economic development as a result of cumulative feedback interactions, a growth center is established.

The second concept, *backwash,* holds that the growth center will attract labor, capital, and commodities from surrounding areas. Backwash is directly related to cumulative causation, which suggests that large organizations will become successful in attracting resources, both human and material.

The third concept is *spread*. This process counteracts backwash, because it holds that the growth center will also stimulate demand in surrounding areas (for agricultural products, minerals, and manufactured goods). If the demand becomes strong enough to overcome backwash, a new center of growth will be established. The spread concept subsumes the proposition that less successful centers will continually attempt to adopt or outperform their competition's methods to challenge more successful centers.

376

Successful competitors do not stand idly by; often, for two important reasons, they directly stimulate the growth of their less successful competition. The first reason is based on the proposition that when two systems interact, the closer their levels of organization, the more efficient their interaction becomes in exchanging materials and information (cf. Service 1955). Thus successful growth centers often try to minimize the size and complexity of their own organizations by supporting the development of organizations elsewhere which can serve their needs in areas that are logistically hard to support. The second reason that growth centers stimulate their potential competitors is related to the first. Since many growth-center exports may be manufactured status goods or specialty items, growth centers expand the markets for their own products by supporting outside development. This process of supporting the development of outside organizations may backfire if those organizations cross thresholds which turn them into competitive growth centers. The postwar relations between the United States and Japan are a good example of this process. During Japan's early postwar development, it was a major U.S. market, but as the Japanese economy developed, it succeeded in turning the tables in many product areas.

The history of the development and disintegration of the British Empire and its colonial holdings is a familiar case of the dynamic interaction among cumulative causation, backwash, and spread.

This economic model also has a demographic implication. Because of competition and because of threshold effects related to commodity production and demand, rapidly expanding populations can be used profitably in systems undergoing economic growth through trade. The development of models of the nature of growth opportunities will provide a framework for an economic and population model of ancient Lowland Maya cultural systems.

Warfare and agricultural intensification are not the only responses to population pressure on resource availability. A major opportunity for economic growth is provided by trade (see Renfrew 1969; Webb 1973). From an economic perspective, it is assumed that, beyond a certain threshold, procuring high-turnover resources provides a return substantial enough to support complex resource-production and exchange organizations (Vance 1971). This market does not directly "create" exchange organizations; trade models of this kind simply point to one direction in which complex management organizations could profitably expand. The potential for rapid expansion of procurement and exchange functions affects the tempo of growth processes, and this brings us to the specifics of Maya development. The growth potential of Maya trade can be derived from a previous economic construct, the core–buffer zone model (Rathje 1971, 1972, 1973).

The core–buffer zone concept, an essentially mercantile perspective, has its weaknesses, but it has one important advantage over other trade constructs applied to the Maya. It cannot be the basis of an equilibrium model; it must be incorporated into a disequilibrium model based on competition between groups with differential geographical access to desired resources.

The model proposes a large and profitable market for several high-turnover, or "basic," resources (salt, obsidian for cutting tools, hard stone for metates) involved in the efficiency of household-level subsistence. Since the resources in question must be imported from the fringes of the Maya Lowlands or beyond and must be distributed over a wide area, the effects of competition for these resources will be regional in scope rather than confined to individual centers. Differential access to these resources, due to geographic and ecological variety, can be used to divide the Maya Lowlands into large regions. A Central Lowland core area is farther removed from basic resources than a peripheral buffer zone. From the perspective of large organizations involved in long-distance trade, the competition for resources can be seen to affect regional growth, both in economic development and in population size.

With this background, Maya specifics can be added to Keeble's general economic-growth model of cumulative causation, backwash, and spread.

1. *Cumulative causation*. The model begins as a system crosses a developmental threshold and steps up its rate of growth due to cumulative causation. In the Maya Lowlands the core area seems to have crossed this threshold earlier than many peripheral regions, for several reasons. Differential soil fertility has been suggested as one (Sanders, Chap. 11 above). Trade patterns are another. Together they could mean a growing population resulting in a growing demand for basic high-turnover resources. Although the market for basic resources is not seen as requiring complex exchange organizations, it can be seen as providing an opportunity for the development of such organizations and for the advantageous utilization of growing populations. It follows

that once there were enough people so that a demand threshold was crossed which made basic resource procurement profitable for a large organization, core centers grew rapidly to expand long-distance trade made difficult by geographic and other disadvantages and by buffer-zone competition. The core—the area with a sizable market potential and the greatest need for efficient large-scale basic resource procurement organizations—was among the first to develop the material symbols of large-scale organizations in the Preclassic.

This reasoning does not affect buffer-zone areas like Belize. Such regions were obviously developing not because of a local lack of resources but because of the local availability of resources (Hammond suggests cacao) in demand by other groups. Thus, for different reasons, both the core and the Belize buffer zone were becoming more complex during the Preclassic. A perspective emphasizing the importance of trade and interaction among lowland groups during early stages of Maya cultural development also explains why the Late Preclassic Chicanel horizon was a time of homogeneity in Lowland Maya pottery.

2. *Backwash*. More specifics can now be added to this model around the process of backwash—the pulling of resources and people from the buffer zone to supply and staff rapidly expanding core production and distribution organizations.

Perhaps the most significant early trade contact in Belize was the influx of Q-Complex or Floral Park ceramics from Salvador, the first polychrome pottery in the Maya area. These wares and their occurrence in burials were significant because they opened a new type of resource demand at ceremonial, and perhaps even at household, levels—a demand for manufactured exotic cult items.

A second important outside contact just before the Early Classic Period was with Teotihuacan. Altun Ha data indicate an early interest in Belize on the part of Teotihuacan (Pendergast 1971). As stated elsewhere (Rathje 1973), Teotihuacan trade organizations must have opened a large-scale-demand market for lowland products. Teotihuacan's market organization, extending several hundred kilometers from its home base in central Mexico, would obviously have wanted to minimize its efforts in collecting and exchanging goods. It would have wanted ideally to make contact with a well-developed trade organization which could minimize Teotihuacan's need to expand its operations further.

At this point the contrast between the lowland core and the buffer zone was relevant to Teotihuacan. At the end of the Preclassic, a long-distance exchange organization was developing in the core. Tikal, and probably similar core sites, were ideal areas for Teotihuacan contact. All that remained was for *Tikal* (which here, in italics, will stand for all other similar core sites) to find a mechanism to buy into resource areas in other parts of the lowlands. The necessary opening was provided by the demand for exotics started by the Q or Floral Park complex of exotic ceramics. With their differentiated internal organization, Peten sites like Tikal were able to produce what I will call a Barbie-Doll cult complex based on their own local cult items (it is perhaps significant that sites like Tikal seem not to have bought the Q-Complex themselves). When consumers purchase a Barbie Doll, they do not buy one doll. They buy into a whole system of optional but related sets of clothes and furniture for Barbie, friends and relatives for her, and clothes and furniture for Barbie's friends and relatives. In other words, *Tikal* was able to produce a whole range of interrelated cult items—pottery and other portable cult paraphernalia, an exotic writing system, stelae-cache dedication systems, and various types of ceremonial structures. The purchase of one must often have required the purchase and simultaneous use of many others. The popularity and spread of this cult (cf. Rathje 1971, 1972) gave *Tikal* a handle on many other resource areas and perhaps the balance of payments necessary to collect lowland products for Teotihuacan trade. From this perspective it is not surprising that after the beginning of the Early Classic and the spread of the core cult, almost all material evidences of Teotihuacan contact are restricted to the core area.

It is important to note again that warfare and agricultural intensification are not the only responses to population-resource stress. Increases in specialization and trade are equally useful. Thus it is not strange that an area with a background in organization for local and regional collection, manufacture, and exchange should attempt to enter into a potentially lucrative trade situation.

Warfare, however, was certainly one component of the expansion of *Tikal* market organizations into other resource areas in the lowlands (see Webster, Chap. 13 above). For example, Becan was fortified during the Terminal Preclassic (Webster, personal communication), just before the core Barbie-Doll complex began to spread into other areas. During the Early Classic Becan did not buy into the core system, and its material inventories included green obsidian, probably from Teotihuacan. But that situation changed. Webster (personal communication) has evidence that Becan was threatened and perhaps even attacked during Sabucan times. Also, during the same period, Becan was "Petenized"—the *Tikal* complex was introduced en masse as the manufacture of local cult items was largely discontinued.

During the expansion of the *Tikal* cult in the Early Classic, Belize, an important resource producer, continued to expand in population. The central core area, the middleman trading the Barbie-Doll complex into Belize for control of collection-redistribution activities, expanded at an amazing rate evidenced by large building projects, a fantastic array of trade commodities, and rich caches and burials. Population changes in other areas can be partially attributed to the backwash factor and the potential of a rapidly expanding large-scale trade organization to stimulate and soak up population increases. The "depopulation" of the Usumacinta-Pasión drainage in the Early Classic may be one example of the effect of this process.

3. *Spread*. Once core systems were well established, new growth centers spread into the buffer zone, the area between core systems and basic resource sources. The major spread, however, occurred in the Late Classic after the *Tikal*-Teotihuacan connection had broken (Willey 1974). The rapidity and scale of the Late Classic development of centers like Palenque, Piedras Negras, Yaxchilan, and Copan exemplify the tremendous potential of spread and of competitive success provided by the ecological and geographic advantages of the buffer zone.

Owing to the nature of exponential growth patterns and the specifics of the rapid development of Maya civilization, the possibility of overshoot related to outrunning resources is implicit in the model. The specifics for this possibility are outlined in more detail elsewhere (Willey and Shimkin 1973; Rathje 1973).

There are weaknesses in this specific Maya growth model. Most seriously, there are possible objections to various assumptions made by core–buffer zone trade concepts about the use, source, and procurement difficulty of basic resources. However, this speculative model provides one starting point for more detailed analyses to explore the amount of cultural change that can be related to trade and exchange

15

The Rise of Maya Civilization: A Summary View

GORDON R. WILLEY

Harvard University

T his chapter is intended as a summary and, to a degree, a synthesis of the exposition, argument, and discussion that have been presented in the foregoing chapters and that were developed in the course of the seminar proceedings.[1] Its organization follows that of the book and falls into the same three essential parts, covering (1) the basic archaeological data from the Maya Lowlands; (2) the external influences that are presumed to have impinged on Lowland Maya cultural developments; and (3) the cultural processes involved and the models that have been designed to explicate them.

As will be evident to the reader, there is a descending scale of agreement among the seminar participants as we progress in this organization. For the most part, there is a concordance on the archaeological data bases although even here divergences in interpretation may set in at primary or low levels of inference. Beyond this, disagreement arises as we attempt to understand the nature of external influences that bore upon Maya cultural growth and upon cultural process in this growth. I have indicated some of this disagreement, but, in the interests of summarization and brevity, admit to not having done full justice to it all. Thus, whatever I have done, my summary is biased, although I have tried to keep my biases to a minimum and can only urge the reader to return to the individual chapters to appraise various lines of argument.

As what I have to say here is obviously based on the preceding papers, I shall not cite these papers specifically in all instances; however, where speculation and theoretical opinion come to the fore, I will refer to specific names. Additional backup literature will not be referred to, as a rule, since it is cited in the other papers, but I will provide references for those few occasions which were not so covered.

THE LOWLAND MAYA DATA BASES

The basic data, especially as presented in the chapters by Culbert, Hammond, Adams, Ball, Willey, and Rands, pertain to the Mesoamerican cultural subarea known as the Maya Lowlands. This territory, of southern Mexico and portions of Central America, is well defined in many source books, and it has been very specifically plotted and subdivided into regions or zones in an earlier work by Culbert (1973a:Fig. 1).[2] As each of the above authors has provided a regional or zonal presentation, I shall not recapitulate here in that fashion, but instead will summarize by horizons or time periods. These periods correspond to those of Mayan (and Mesoamerican) archaeological chronology. The reader's attention is called to J. W. Ball's chronological chart (Fig. 1.3), with its zonal columns, major period divisions, and B.C.–A.D. dates. This chart is an important adjunct to the study of this summary or to the reading of any of the chapters in this volume.

The Early Preclassic Period (2000–1000 B.C.)

There is, as yet, no clearly defined cultural horizon for the Maya Lowlands prior to or during the Early Preclassic Period. Scattered possible preceramic finds have been reported, but these "assemblages," if they can be dignified by that name, are neither well defined nor dated. Hammond has referred to a radiocarbon date on a maize pollen core from Lake Yaxha, in the Peten, which is given as 2000 B.C.; but we need to know more about the cultural context of this date—as well as to have others of a comparable chronological range—before we can arrive at any well-grounded conclusions. Besides this, there are hints that pottery-making peoples may have been present along the western and eastern margins of the Maya Lowlands a little before 1000 B.C. The earliest Chontalpa-region pottery, on the western side of the Maya Lowlands proper, dates to the Early Preclassic Period (Molina and Palacios phases—see Fig. 1.3); from Cuello, in northern Belize, Hammond reports an early radiocarbon pottery date of 1020 B.C. This last, of course, is a single date, and it is close to the Early Preclassic–Middle Preclassic dividing line. The fact that pottery-making and farming peoples were well established in the Early Preclassic Period in other southern Mesoamerican subareas, at no great distance from the Maya Lowlands, does make it strange that these lowlands were not also so occupied at the same time; but such are the facts to date.

The Middle Preclassic Period (1000–300 B.C.)

The earliest firm and reasonably abundant evidence for Maya Lowland occupation comes from the Pasión Valley region or zone of the southern Peten Department of Guatemala. This is the Xe pottery complex of the sites of Altar de Sacrificios and Seibal. Xe pottery occurs as unslipped or monochrome wares, occasionally incised and punctated, and featuring flaring-sided, flanged-rim plates and *tecomate* jars. It is similar to Early Middle Preclassic pottery of the Gulf Coast Chontalpa country, which, in turn, derives from the tradition of Chontalpa Early Preclassic pottery to which we have just referred (see Fig. 1.3). The wider relationships of this ceramic tradition are with other early southern Mesoamerican pottery groups of the Chiapas Pacific Coast and to Gulf Coast pre-Olmec and Olmec levels. The Middle Preclassic Chontalpa pottery (the Puente and Franco phases) may have provided the source for the Xe pottery of the Maya Lowlands, via early settlers from the Gulf Coast–Usumacinta country. The Chihuaan phase of the Trinidad locality may be a link in such a line of relationships which lead on up the Usumacinta River to the Pasión drainage. Hammond argues for such a Xe entry, suggesting that these earliest immigrants into the Maya Lowlands were following out and exploiting a landscape that would offer aquatic riverine as well as terrestrial resources. Subsequently, in the course of Middle Preclassic cultural change, they, or their descendants, were forced into less desirable nonriverine, as well as other riverine, site locations. An alternative source for Xe ceramics, and for a first peopling of the Maya Lowlands, is out of the highlands to the south, in Salvador or Guatemala. Xe-like pottery is reported from the Guatemalan sites of El Portón and Sakajut. I have tended to prefer this as the starting point for the Xe immigrants, although the majority of the seminar participants argued for a Gulf Coastal source. The relative datings, which would be crucial to the resolution of such a question, are still too uncertain for a final decision, at least to my way of thinking. One difficulty in all of this is that we are dealing with an interrelated southern Mesoamerican ceramic evolution, one that has earlier manifestations in the Early Preclassic potteries of the Chiapas Pacific Coast (Barra, Ocos), as well as on the Gulf Coast (Ojochi, Bajío, and Molina), so that there is a strong possibility that descendant complexes may have been carried into the Peten from either direction.

Pottery definitely identified to the Xe ceramic sphere has not yet been reported elsewhere in the Maya Lowlands. Culbert describes the Eb complex, the earliest at Tikal and a possible contemporary of Xe, as being distinct from Xe although showing some resemblances to it. The same could be said for the early facet of the Jenney Creek complex of the Belize Valley. Hammond's Cuello pottery, which he dates to his pre-Mamom-horizon Swasey complex, is also described in preliminary comments (postconference commentary from Hammond) as being distinct from Xe. In reviewing the situation as a whole, the seminar group tentatively agreed that, while a Gulf Coastal or northwestern source seemed the most likely, it remained a distinct possibility that the earliest ceramics of the Maya Lowlands may have had diverse origins—as did the people who brought these ceramics with them.

Xe and Eb sites are small and few. They are, in effect, small refuse areas and house locations found beneath later cultural deposits at Altar, Seibal, and Tikal. The inferences drawn from this are that the first Peten settlers were few in number and widely scattered. It is highly probable that these people were farmers. They built perishable houses either on the ground level or on very low artificial platforms. No clearly identifiable public architecture was found at any of the sites, although it is just possible that an inner mound platform (within a much larger and later structure) at Tikal does date from late Eb. However, owing to the very limited excavation exposure (a tunnel), and the possibility of earlier sherds being included in later fill materials, the Eb-phase identification remains uncertain. The settlement and architectural implications for Xe and Eb are, thus, those of peoples living in simple, egalitarian societies. At the same time, we should not forget that Xe and Eb peoples must have been aware of more complex societies in the contemporary communities of the Gulf Coast Lowlands or Chiapas. Here, the village-cum-ceremonial-center settlement system and at least the beginnings of nonegalitarian social orders were in existence in the Middle Preclassic Period and had been even earlier. That there were contacts with the outside as early as Xe-Eb times is attested by the fact that obsidian was traded into the Maya Lowlands on this horizon.

By about 700–600 B.C., Xe ceramics began to be replaced by those of the Mamom pottery sphere. Mamom appears to have developed out of Xe, and it persisted throughout the latter part of the Middle Preclassic Period. In the Central Zone and the Pasión Zone, as well as elsewhere, Mamom pottery marks a trend toward greater uniformity and standardization in manufacture. Ball, however, viewing the situation from Yucatan, is inclined to reject this "uniformity" as superficial, and stresses, instead, regional differences. From his descriptions, these differences do, indeed, set the north apart from the south at this time. He relates this regionalism to segmentary tribal settlement of the Maya Lowlands as the descendants of the original Xe riverine communities spread away from the river locations into the internal hinterland and filled up the Maya Lowlands. While I am in agreement with Ball's concepts of fission and spread of tribal societies, I do think that there is a discernible overall trend from ceramic heterogeneity to homogeneity in the three to four hundred years of the Mamom horizon. That there should be such a trend is not surprising. As populations increased and the country became filled, communication between communities must also have increased.

Mamom-sphere pottery has little that suggests sumptuary wares for burial or trade. This is in keeping with the profile for other archaeological remains of the sphere. The sites themselves, while more numerous than those of the Xe horizon, are still small village areas.

Public architecture is lacking or rare and of modest size. At Altar de Sacrificios there is an artificial platform, four meters high, that dates from late Mamom (San Felix), and this is in a modest cere-monial-center-type setting of a plaza arrangement with other, smaller mounds. At Nohoch Ek, in west central Belize, there is a small Mamom-horizon platform with cut-stone masonry and lime-stucco plastering, constructional traits that continue and flourish with the Maya (Coe and Coe 1956). In northern Yucatan the Nabanche phase at Dzibilchaltun has some platform structures that also look like corporate labor constructions. Elsewhere, however, even this small-scale elite architecture is lacking. This applies to such Mamom-sphere phases as the Escoba at Seibal, Tzec at Tikal, Mamom proper at Uaxactun, Jenney Creek in the Belize Valley, López Mamom in northern Belize, Acachen in the Rio Bec, and the pre-Picota and Xet phases in the Northwestern Zone.

The Late Preclassic Period (300–50 B.C.)

The chronological definition which Ball (see Fig. 1.3) has given to this period is a compromise and reconciliation of a number of regional sequence columns. The authors of the several data-base papers offered slightly varying dates, and this was complicated by the fact that some, but not all, operated with the concept of a Protoclassic Period. Ball has included such a period on his chart (50 B.C.–A.D. 250), and it is a useful device in our tracing out the events leading up to the Maya Classic Period; however, some authors in their descriptions of local phases often melded Late Preclassic and Protoclassic together. Here I shall be at pains to try to make a distinction, and we shall take up the Late Preclassic first.

Chicanel and Chicanel-like ceramics are the diagnostic of the Late Preclassic in the Maya Lowlands. Chicanel very clearly develops from the Mamom sphere. For the most part, the pottery complexes of the Chicanel sphere are highly standardized. The ware has a characteristic "waxy" surface, usually in red, black, or cream monochromes. There are also bichrome wares, and these tend to be more common in the later facets. To generalize further about the Chicanel-linked cul-tures, this was a time of marked population increases. Sites become more numerous, are individually larger, and the first major ceremonial-center architecture appears. Specific architectural features herald later Classic Period developments. There is a trade now in luxury items, such as marine shells and stingray spines from the coast and jade imported from the highlands. Differentiations in grave goods signal status differences. The implications of all this are those of a society, or series of related societies, expanding and developing a nonegalitarian sociopolitical structure.

At the same time there are notable regional differences to these generalizations. Indeed, these were some of the most important findings to emerge from the seminar, bringing together as it did regional specialists from all parts of the Maya Lowlands. Among these differences were the pace and timing of population expansion, ceremonial center construction, and indications of elite-commoner dichotomies. At Tikal, in the Central Zone, it is the early part of the Late Preclassic Period, the Chuen phase, that sees the big population upswing. This was accompanied by public architectural construction, including such anticipations of later Classic Period features as apron molding on pyramid-platforms and corbeled-vaulted tombs. Such tombs were presumably the burial places of members of an emerging elite class and were accompanied with such things as jades and stingray spines. In contrast, the latter part of the Late Preclassic Period, the Cauac phase, was a time of either population stabilization or, perhaps, decline. This Tikal diachronic configuration of the Late Preclassic differs from that of the Pasión Zone as seen in the stratigraphic record at Altar de Sacrificios, where there are indications that ceremonial elaboration, and probably population as well, built up through the Late Preclassic, climaxing at its very end. In Belize, also, in the northern Corozal–Orange Walk sector, the Cocos Chicanel phase, which shows a fourfold increase in site-unit occupation over earlier Mamom-sphere times, seems to show a more or less steady growth, or at least there is no noticeable decline in the latter part of the period. In the Northwestern Zone we know that Chicanel pottery is associated with the first sizable mound structures of the region, in the vicinity of Palenque, in the Chacibcan phase of Trinidad, and in the Pinzon complex nearer the coast; however, there is still too little information to say anything about the timing of developments within the Late Preclassic Period.

The Northern Plains Zone has a Late Preclassic developmental profile more like that of Tikal or, perhaps, even more pronounced. The

Komchen phase, which Ball dates at 250–100 B.C., was a cultural peak, with large populations and architectural constructions of great size. The ceramics of Komchen, while showing some relationships to Chicanel, differ from those of the south. In the succeeding Xculul phase, which Ball dates at 100 B.C.–A.D. 250 and thereby carries over into the Protoclassic Period, there are indications of population decrease and a cessation of public building. It should be noted, however, that this developmental pattern derives from the great site of Dzibilchaltun. Elsewhere in the north, at Soblonke and Yaxuna, for example, the Xculul drop-off is not apparent.

In the Rio Bec Zone, in the south central part of the Yucatan Peninsula, there is still another developmental story. While the Pakluum phase of the Chicanel sphere registers a population increase over earlier times at its inception, there is no major architectural development at all in the 300–50 B.C. period. This all comes later (50 B.C.–A.D. 250), in the Protoclassic Period.

This regional irregularity in Late Preclassic Period developmental profiles is most interesting and certainly not yet well understood. Tikal peaked in the first half of the period. One wonders if this was true of all of the northeast Peten region, or Central Zone. Dzibilchaltun, in northern Yucatan, did the same. Were the causes similar? In this connection, it is worth noting that the two phenomena do not seem to have been closely related historically. Dzibilchaltun was, in its Komchen phase, the most divergent of any of the early Late Preclassic ceramic complexes, with its Chicanel-sphere status most dubious. At Tikal the Cauac phase of the later part of the Late Preclassic was at best a time of stabilization of population. At Dzibilchaltun the contemporaneous Xculul phase was definitely one of population drop-off and cultural decline. At the same time, this was not the case in other sites in the Northern Plains Zone. This latter finding is both interesting and disturbing. Must our attempts at generalization and our search for developmental regularities be further complicated by site-to-site as well as region-to-region variability? In the Pasión Valley the Late Preclassic has been adjudged to be a time of mounting population growth and constructional buildup, with the climax at the end. The same seems to hold for the Rio Bec Zone, as this is measured at Becan, although the pace is slower, and the climax, at least for ceremonial architecture, is delayed until the succeeding Protoclassic Period. The best we can come up with out of all this is that while the

390

Late Preclassic Period was the time of the first rise toward population density and the kind of settlement organization and public construction one associates with civilization, this must be viewed in broadest chronological perspective. When we construct a finer-grained spatial-temporal framework in which to examine events, we are confronted with variation. This variation is almost sure to have been important in the course of civilizational growth in the Maya Lowlands.

The Protoclassic Period (50 B.C.–A.D. 250)

In Maya archaeology there has been some conceptual confusion about the "Protoclassic." It has three aspects or meanings. A Protoclassic Period of time has generally been defined as the early centuries A.D. This is the chronological definition on Ball's chart—50 B.C.–A.D. 250. Obviously, all Maya Lowland regional cultural continua passed through such a period. A second meaning of the Protoclassic pertains to cultural content. This content refers mainly to ceramics, to vessel-form features such as mammiform tetrapodal supports and to surface decorative techniques in the Usulutan-resist manner or to positive painted imitations of this. There are also a distinctive orange monochrome ware and red-and-black-on-orange polychromes (e.g., Ixcanrio) which presage the Early Classic Maya polychromes. One of the better known ceramic complexes of this kind is the Floral Park of the Belize Valley. Holmul I and the Salinas phase at Altar de Sacrificios also fit here. It is generally thought that these pottery traits were introduced into the Maya Lowlands from the Salvadoran-Guatemalan Highlands. A third Protoclassic meaning is a little harder to define, but it has, essentially, a cultural-stage connotation. It refers to the terminal climax of the Late Preclassic Period and to the transition from that period into the Maya Early Classic. This is expressed in architectural forms, as well as in ceramic decoration, and in tomb paraphernalia and other indications of the rise of an elite class. As we review the several lowland zones, let us keep these three definitions or meanings in mind.

At Tikal the Floral Park kind of ceramic complex is present during the late Cauac and Cimi phases, which date to the 50 B.C.–A.D. 250 time bracket; however, this kind of pottery does not appear in sufficient volume for Culbert to postulate a site-unit intrusion of people bearing such a complex. Nor was there any population growth or major increase in architectural activity at Tikal during this period. Still, some of the Protoclassic "stage" developments do make an appearance in such things as tomb and temple wall paintings of the Cimi phase. These depict individuals in the high-status dress and paraphernalia, similar to those of the succeeding Classic Period, and in some of these paintings there are definite clues to Izapan stylistic influence. Uaxactun, the other major Central Zone politico-religious center for which we have detailed information, has much less Floral Park or Holmul I–type pottery than Tikal; but the stucco-ornamented E-VII-sub temple at that site undoubtedly dates to the Protoclassic Period, and its sculptures are another indication of the Protoclassic "stage" transition into the Classic.

Along the Peten-Belize border, as at Holmul, and in both the Belize Valley and the Corozal–Orange Walk district to the north, the Floral Park ceramic complex is present at several sites. In the Belize Valley this was a time of population increase in the house clusters of Barton Ramie. To the north, in the Corozal–Orange Walk sector, Hammond reports the presence of the Freshwater Floral Park–phase ceramics at several sites, including the important center of Nohmul, where they are associated with major architecture. In his opinion, a center such as Nohmul was in process of becoming an important governmental locus at this time for the direction of agricultural production and the control of trade for the region. Here it is of interest to note that agricultural intensification, as indicated by the ridged fields of the Río Hondo locality, dates as early as this. Hammond makes the point that not all sites in northern Belize show the Floral Park ceramic complex. While its absence might possibly mark a hiatus between Late Preclassic and Early Classic in their occupation, he feels that this is unlikely—and so do I. Apparently here, as to the west at Tikal and Uaxactun, the time period designated as the Protoclassic (50 B.C.–A.D. 250) was not everywhere characterized by Floral Park–complex pottery. In Hammond's opinion the cacao production of the Belize Zone was an important trigger in the processes leading to the rise to civilization, not only in northern Belize, but, indirectly, for the rest of the Lowland Maya.

The other place where the specialized Floral Park–like ceramic content of the Protoclassic Period is found is in the Pasión Valley, at Altar de Sacrificios. The ceramic relationship may express a connection out of original highland prototypes rather than a direct one across the southern Peten. While no case can be made out for a population increase, Salinas was a phase of architectural activity which set the local scene for the Classic; but, while this was going on at Altar de Sacrificios, Seibal, some distance upstream to the east, was undergoing a definite population decline and cessation of building activities in the late facet of the Cantutse phase.

In the Northwestern Zone, Rands says, Protoclassic pottery (presumably that of Floral Park–Salinas styles) is rare but present. This does not, of course, necessarily indicate any population or cultural decline along the Usumacinta at this time. The Northwestern Zone sites, like those of the Central Zone, may simply have been too remote from, or in some other way out of the orbit of, Floral Park–Salinas ceramic styles.

In the Rio Bec, the later Pakluum-phase facets mark a cultural peak, both in the ceremonial-center constructions at Becan and in the peopling of the surrounding countryside. Becan at this time consisted of a ceremonial center of plazas, platforms, and pyramids covering some forty acres. This was surrounded by a moat and wall of obviously defensive purpose—the earliest defense work, at least of great size, in the Maya Lowlands. Thus, in the sense of a developmental climax, the Protoclassic is well represented in the Rio Bec Zone. At the same time, as both Adams and Ball stress, the Protoclassic Floral Park–like pottery is not found.

For the Northern Plains we have already recounted what happened at Dzibilchaltun during the Xculul phase, which subsumes the Protoclassic Period. It was a time of population and constructional decline at that great site—trends which are in no way consistent with the Protoclassic buildup in the south. This decline, however, is modified somewhat by the apparent continued heavy activity at other Northern Plains sites during the same period. In ceramics the north did not participate in the Floral Park or any closely related sphere.

The overall Protoclassic Period picture for the Maya Lowlands, as I see it, then goes something like this. In the south, particularly in the Peten, the Protoclassic phases come at the end of a Late Preclassic era of populational growth and cultural buildup. In this growth and buildup Tikal and the Central Zone had taken an early lead and then slacked off somewhat; along the Pasión these upward trends seem to have continued more or less steadily up to the Protoclassic. The Protoclassic was a time of stabilization and crystallization, with the latter term applying to the fact that certain cultural forms take on a definite "Classic" appearance at that time. Along the far eastern edge of the Peten and in western Belize the Protoclassic cultures were given a new and somewhat different "flavor" by the appearance of exotic ceramic traits, generally thought to be of Salvadoran or Guatemalan Highland origin, and referred to, collectively, in the Lowlands as the "Floral Park complex." The Belize Protoclassic cultures enjoyed a florescence at this time, and it is possible that they served to transmit new ideas of various kinds, along with new ceramic elements, into the Central Zone of the Peten, where Maya Classic culture was to make its first appearance a century or two later. Floral Park–like ceramics are also seen in the Protoclassic along the far western edge of the Peten at Altar de Sacrificios. In the Rio Bec Zone the Protoclassic Period was a time of cultural climax, both demographically and architecturally; however, there is no sign of the Floral Park ceramic complex in this zone. In the Northern Plains the data indicate a populational and cultural buildup beginning early in the Late Preclassic. At Dzibilchaltun this buildup is terminated in the Protoclassic, which is a period of decline for that site; elsewhere, however, there is the strong possibility that such a buildup was maintained. This zone is without Floral Park ceramics.

The Early Classic Period (A.D. 250–600)

The formal definition of the inception of the Early Classic Period is the appearance of Initial Series–dated monuments in the Central Zone, especially at Tikal and Uaxactun, in the half-century between A.D. 250 and A.D. 300. These monuments may be said to have put the seal of official and authoritarian recognition on the social and political hierarchies that had been developing during the Late Preclassic and Protoclassic, especially in the three centuries of the latter period. While concerned with astronomical events to a degree, their hieroglyphic texts and Long Count calendric dates were the validations of a ruling aristocracy. In the Central Zone the Tzakol ceramic sphere replaced the Chicanel sphere. Culbert notes that many of the new ceramic traits had been present before, in the Protoclassic Period at Tikal, but that now these formerly minor traits assume a position of numerical dominance. Many other new Tzakol features would appear to have been introduced via Floral Park influences, and there are also Teotihuacan ceramic features as early as Early Manik (the beginning of the Tikal Early Classic). But Culbert sees this Tikal Early Classic development as a local synthesis and rejects the hypothesis of a new population influx of the site-unit intrusion type. The Early Classic brings demographic changes at Tikal. Early Manik gives little evidence of population growth over the antecedent Cimi phase, but by Middle Manik times Culbert postulates a doubling of former population. Architectural construction enjoys a boom, but actual ceremonial center layout and architectural features continue in the plans and modes that had been laid down as early as the Late Preclassic.

The Central Zone "stela cult" of Initial Series dedicatory monuments had spread to Altar de Sacrificios on the lower Pasión by A.D. 450, as had Tzakol pottery, including the polychrome vessels (of Floral Park ancestry) and the tripod jars (of Teotihuacan inspiration). The Early Classic was not a time of population growth at Altar de Sacrificios, but, judging from the hieroglyphic monuments, the site continued as an important center. During this time, Seibal, the other major Pasión Valley center, located upstream from Altar, was virtually abandoned.

The Early Classic and the Nuevo Tzakol ceramic sphere are well represented in Belize. While the stela cult does not seem to have spread this far to the east, at least on this time level, the ceramic ties binding the Central and Belize zones are strong.

In the Northwestern Zone, Rands describes the Picota complex as being essentially unlike the Tzakol, although contemporaneous with it. No Picota-phase architecture has yet been identified at Palenque, although refuse and fill sherds suggest that ceremonial construction probably began this early somewhere in the site locality. In the succeeding Motiepa phase (the latter part of the Early Classic Period) there was an introduction of the Peten Gloss wares of the Tzakol sphere, plus some polychrome pottery. These new traits, however, are modified and integrated into local patterns and styles. There is large-scale construction identified with Motiepa. Elsewhere in the Northwestern Zone, as along the Middle Usumacinta, the Early Classic seems to have been a time of population decline. Rands considers the possibility that this might be a nucleation of population into fewer but larger sites, but he is inclined to reject this hypothesis for lack of indication of sociopolitical complexity in the sites that are occupied.

Again, however, regional or even subregional differences must be commented upon. Northward, on the Gulf Coast, the Early Classic is better represented; and southward, in the upper Usumacinta Zone, the site of Piedras Negras was an important Early Classic center. The stela cult is represented by Early Classic Piedras Negras monuments, and the pottery there belongs to the Tzakol sphere. In all of this, Piedras Negras, as well as Yaxchilan, farther upstream, are much more closely allied to Altar de Sacrificios than they are to the Northwestern Zone sites.

In the early part of the Early Classic Period in the Rio Bec Zone the population expansion and architectural florescence that had characterized the preceding Protoclassic Period came to a stop. At some point in the A.D. 250–450 period, known as the Chacsik phase, the inhabitants of Becan appear to have been, in effect, besieged in their fortified city. There is no evidence of the stela cult, hieroglyphics, or other distinctive Peten Central Zone traits. Later, in the Sabucan phase (A.D. 450–600), the political situation may have changed. There is evidence to indicate that the great defensive moat at Becan was no longer maintained as it had been formerly. This may have been related to more peaceful conditions, although Webster (postconference commentary) cautions that this neglect may reflect only higher priority labor use elsewhere, and continued reliance on a fortification which even in a somewhat shoddy condition remained perfectly defensible.

In the Northern Plains Zone, Dzibilchaltun, which had declined notably in the preceding Xculul phase, was abandoned in the earlier part of the Early Classic (A.D. 250–450); however, we know that other northern sites, such as Yaxuna and Acanceh, were active at this time, so events were not uniform for the entire zone. Nevertheless, looking at all of the north, including the Puuc, Chenes, Rio Bec, and Northern Plains zones, Ball makes the generalization that the early Early Classic saw a reduction in the number of ceremonial centers and in individual size of sites. A little later (A.D. 450–600), Dzibilchaltun was reoccupied during the Piim phase, and, in general, the late Early Classic saw something of a revival in the north. Throughout, the cultural changes are those noted for the Rio Bec Sabucan phase. Southern, or Peten, influences appear in ceramics and occasional stelae and hieroglyphic inscriptions.

The Classic Hiatus Phenomenon
(A.D. 534–593)

The Classic hiatus in stela dedication lasted from shortly after 9.5.0.0.0 (A.D. 534) until 9.8.0.0.0 (A.D. 593). This is the end of the Early Classic Period following Ball's chronological chart (Fig. 1.3); however, the short hiatus interval might be said to form the dividing line between Early and Late Classic. In the data chapters I was the only one to direct much attention to the hiatus. It is a phenomenon of the Southern Lowlands, especially the Central, Pasión, (upper) Usumacinta, and Southeastern zones. From Piedras Negras, in the west, to Copan, in the east, there is a marked drop-off in stela carving and dedication for an interval of about sixty years; there is evidence to indicate that ceremonial construction also slackened during this time. Elsewhere, however, the hiatus either is not clearly registered in the archaeological record or fails to exist. It is not noticeable in the Palenque sequence, where the late Early Classic Motiepa phase seems to have been a time of growth and construction. Nor is it present in any clearly defined way in the north. In fact, in some northern sequences the sixth century A.D. is, relatively, a time of cultural vigor, as in the Sabucan and Piim phases. Without attempting to offer explanations or processual statements at this point in the summary, but merely trying to set down the basic data, it appears that the Classic Hiatus is a southern phenomenon and, especially, a Peten phenomenon.

The Late Classic Period
(A.D. 600–900)

This period takes us essentially beyond the story of the rise of Maya civilization, but its configurations are of some interest. Throughout the Maya Lowlands it was a time of demographic growth and cultural elaboration. For most regions this Late Classic peaking, in contrast to developments that had gone before, was most impressive. In fact only in the Central Zone, at Tikal and perhaps Uaxactun, and probably in the Belize Zone do Early Classic achievement and growth even come close to rivaling those of the Late Classic. The Late Classic was the time of the Tepeu ceramic sphere,[3] and the centuries of growth and climax were the Tepeu 1 and 2 subphases of that sphere (ca. A.D. 600–800). In general, ceremonial centers multiplied in numbers and were individually enlarged architecturally. Outlying house-mound occupations, insofar as we have archaeological information on this, increased in number in almost all parts of the lowlands. In the south this was the era of the stela cult in full glory, with sculptural portraits of rulers and hieroglyphic texts recording the deeds and pedigrees of royal personages. In the south and especially the north the Late Classic saw the largest and most impressive architecture. Palenque, Piedras Negras, and Yaxchilan in the west, Copan in the east, and the Rio Bec, Chenes, Puuc, and Northern Plains centers of the north grew in size to rival Tikal.

In the latter third of the Late Classic Period, the time of the Tepeu 3 subphase (ca. A.D. 800–900), a decline set in that led to the desertion, or near desertion, of the southern cities by the end of the ninth century. This "Maya collapse" has been discussed and documented at length in an earlier seminar presentation (Culbert 1973a). In the north this decline seems to have been somewhat later. Here it occurred somewhat earlier in the southern zones, such as the Rio Bec and Chenes, later in the Puuc and Northern Plains. In the latter regions substantial ceremonial construction lasted until A.D. 1000, or into the Early Postclassic Period. After that portions of the north fell under Toltec dominance for a time (Chichen Itza) and then continued in a Mexican-Maya cultural tradition (Mayapan, Tulum).

EXTERNAL INFLUENCES ON LOWLAND MAYA CULTURAL GROWTH

In the foregoing section we have referred, by way of descriptive identification, to the presences of what are unmistakable external cultural influences in the Maya Lowlands and in the Maya Lowland cultural continuum. Except for the evidences of the earliest cultural remains, and the question of the "first peopling" of the lowlands, we have offered no discussion of these influences. In this section of the summary I will bring together what I consider to be the salient points of the seminar's opinions about these matters. The principal sources and source areas for the foreign influences that impinged upon the Lowland Maya are: (1) the Olmec Gulf Coast (treated primarily by Coe, but also by Lowe and Quirarte); (2) southern Chiapas (treated primarily by Lowe, but also by Quirarte and Coe); (3) the Guatemala-Salvador Highlands (referred to by Lowe and others); and (4) central Mexico (referred to by most of the seminar members). While it would be possible to take up the questions of external influences under each of these headings, a better integrated and interactive picture of events through time can be obtained by organizing our discussion period by period, in the same manner that the basic *in situ* lowland data were presented.

Southern Mesoamerica in the Early Preclassic Period (2000–1000 B.C.)

Some background on the Early Preclassic Period in southern Mesoamerica is a prerequisite to our understanding of the influences that created Maya Lowland culture. The earliest known ceramic complex of southern Mesoamerica is the Barra of the southern Chiapas coastal region, dating to 1600 B.C. (see Fig. 1.3) or even earlier. It and the immediately later Ocos-phase pottery of the same region represent an early pottery tradition that may have spread from southern Chiapas, across the Isthmus of Tehuantepec, and into the Gulf Coastal Olmec country of southern Veracruz-Tabasco. The Gulf Coastal Ojochi, Bajío, and Chicharras phases are developments out of this tradition, as are the later San Lorenzo A and B phases of "classic" Olmec and the Cuadros phase of southern Chiapas. Lowe regards this ceramic tradition as the creation of peoples of Zoquean (Mixe-Zoque-Popoluca) speech. Zoquean, along with Mayan, belongs to the more inclusive Macro-Mayan language group. This cultural-linguistic linkage is a speculation, but a speculation based upon the geographical position of Zoquean-speaking peoples in the historic period, especially with reference to the position of the Maya; upon archaeological continuities; and upon the probabilities that tribes speaking these Zoquean languages were the old residents of this territory, antedating such nations as the Chiapanec and Nahuas. Others of us in the seminar, including myself, have suggested that the Early Preclassic Olmec were Mayan-speaking. This is, of course, a possibility, although I admit to being impressed by Lowe's line of argument. It should also be kept in mind that Zoquean and Proto-Mayan may have been much more closely related in the 1600–1000 B.C. period than were Maya, Zoque, Mixe, and Popoluca in historic times.[4]

Other southern Mesoamerican ceramic complexes that may relate to this Barra-Ocos-Ojochi (possibly Zoquean) tradition include the Molina of the Chontalpa country (to which we have already referred in discussing Maya Lowland origins), the Pre-Chiuaan of the Trinidad locality, the Cotorra of the Grijalva Trench (Chiapa de Corzo), and the Tok of Salvador. All of these complexes are thought to be Early Preclassic in date. It is also possible that the Salama Valley complexes of the northern Guatemala Highlands which have been described briefly by Sedat and Sharer (1972), and to which Lowe refers in his chapter, date this early; however, some seminar members expressed doubt on this point. Pottery-making villagers do not appear to have been this early in the central Guatemalan Highlands, nor is there a matching occupation in the Maya Lowlands (excepting the Chontalpa and Trinidad finds as essentially marginal to those lowlands).

The general culture status of all of these Early Preclassic peoples of southern Mesoamerica is not fully known; however, there are indications that some of them already had hierarchically ordered, nonegalitarian societies. This certainly was true of the Olmec-region peoples during the San Lorenzo phases, with their large earth constructions and monumental stone art, and, in Coe's opinion, it was probably also true of the earlier Chicharras and Bajío phases. In southern Chiapas earth mounds are associated with the Ocos phase, although Lowe can identify no definite ceremonial centers.

The Middle Preclassic Period (1000–300 B.C.)

It is to these surrounding regions, which were participating in an early southern Mesoamerican pottery tradition and which were, at least in some places, the settings for centrally controlled, hierarchical societies, that we must look for the first settlers to the Maya Lowlands. As has already been stated, the Xe and Eb complexes of the Peten appear to have been derived from this same early southern Mesoamerican pottery tradition. Xe-Eb pottery is, of course, of Middle Preclassic date, rather than Early Preclassic, and its closest resemblances are to the contemporaneous Middle Preclassic phases of the surrounding extralowland territories—to Duende, Conchas 1, and

Dili, of Chiapas; to Nacaste of the Olmec region; to Puente in the Chontalpa; and to Colos of Salvador. Based on pottery criteria, it was the unanimous opinion of the seminar that the Xe-Eb pottery-making immigrants first entered the Maya Lowlands at the very beginning of the Middle Preclassic Period.

Lowe suggests that these earliest settlers were groups who were marginal to or disaffected from the somewhat more prosperous and advanced societies to the west and south. Indeed, he argues, they were "commoners," and "desperate commoners," who were moving out into hitherto unexplored lands, motivated essentially by hunger resulting from increased population pressure in the "old lands." As we have seen, the Xe and Eb communities were small and their cultural repertory modest. There are no public structures, no sumptuary goods. The social profile is an egalitarian one. Yet if Lowe is correct, and I am inclined to think that he is, these Peten "pioneers" were aware of more complex social structures than their own. Archaeological evidences of extra-Lowland contacts bear this out. Furthermore, these commoner settlers aspired to greater things; and, following Lowe's thesis, these aspirations fired an ethnic rivalry between the emigrants and their more established relatives that led to the rise of a separate Maya Lowlander religious and political identity in the succeeding Late Preclassic Period.

Exactly who were these first settlers of the lowlands, and where did they come from? Lowe concurs with his colleagues that Olmec ceramic traits (Nacaste phase) were carried into northern Yucatan from the Gulf Coast at this time and that the Usumacinta, Pasión, and Peten may also have been peopled from this direction at the beginning of the Middle Preclassic. However, with reference to this last point, he expresses a preference for another migration down from the Salvadoran-Guatemalan Highlands. These migrations, in his opinion, mark a split between Zoquean- and Mayan-speaking populations; seen in this light, the highland-to-lowland route was the most likely one for Mayan groups to have taken.

The Late Preclassic and Protoclassic Periods
(300 B.C.–A.D. 250)

Both Coe and Quirarte make convincing cases for Olmec iconographic elements and themes in the later art of the Classic Maya.

401

One of the problems of southern Mesoamerican archaeology is just how this transfer took place. As Coe points out, there seems to have been little direct contact between Olmec and Maya. For one thing, this could not have been possible on a Classic Period level. By that time the ancient Olmec were long gone. The first Olmec horizon, so designated by Coe, was between 1200 and 900 B.C., the period of the San Lorenzo A and B phases. As far as we can tell, this was prior to the first settling of the Maya Lowlands. The second horizon, from 900 to 400 B.C., is pretty much the period known as the Middle Preclassic. La Venta was the dominant Olmec center during this time. It was during this time that the Maya Lowlands were settled, at least in part by peoples who were marginal Olmecs or related to the Olmecs; however, virtually nothing of Olmec art or symbolism seems to have been carried by these Middle Preclassic settlers. The jade bloodletter that Coe mentions, which was found in a Xe cache at Seibal, is one of the few truly Olmec ritual items found in a Maya Lowland Preclassic context. It is, of course, possible that Olmec religious and ritual concepts were a part of the ideological heritage of the first Maya Lowland settlers, even though they brought or made little attendant material paraphernalia to accompany this mental culture. Lowe suggests this possibility with his hypothesis that early concepts involving the jaguar were carried into the Maya Lowlands from Olmec country at this time. Later, these jaguar concepts were replaced by others in the Olmec–southern Chiapas Zoquean territory but were retained by the Lowland Maya as unifying cultural symbols in their ethnic confrontations with the Zoqueans. By this time the period is that of the Late Preclassic, and the Maya Lowlanders had adopted or evolved (both, probably) an elite class system and were constructing major ceremonial centers. By this time, also, Maya Lowland Late Preclassic cultures were in contact with the Izapan culture of southern Chiapas and its related manifestations in the Guatemalan Highlands at Kaminaljuyu. This Izapan culture was an important and demonstrable link between Olmec and Lowland Maya.

Both Coe and Quirarte stress the Izapan linkage between Olmec and Maya, and there can be little doubt but that contacts between Pacific Chiapas and the Guatemalan Highlands, on the one side, and the Maya Lowlands, on the other, were vital in introducing a certain ideological content and form to Classic Maya civilization. This could have taken place even though the bearers of Izapan culture were Zoqueans and the

Late Preclassic Lowlanders were Mayans. Modes of religious and political organization can transcend ethnic rivalries, as can the iconographic elements and motifs that may be used to express them. Indeed, these rivalries may even promote borrowing, although, as Lowe argues, the patterns and emphases may be different. In the Izapa–Lowland Maya contacts it is also highly probable that Kaminaljuyu, in the Guatemalan Highlands, was a vital node in the transmittal of ideas. The odds are that Late Preclassic Kaminaljuyu was Mayan rather than Zoquean, and it is significant that an Izapan-style monument at that site (Stela 10) also bears hieroglyphs very similar to those of the slightly later Classic Lowland Maya stelae. Coe has listed iconographic elements and themes shared by Olmec and Maya; and many of these, as Quirarte indicates, such as the U-shaped moon symbol, the composite creatures of saurian, serpentine, and feline forms, and the feather-winged deity impersonators, are also present in Izapa art. In Coe's opinion the Olmec had a "proto-writing" and also some elements of Mesoamerican calendrics. Long Count dating and hieroglyphic systems probably developed in Izapan and related Late Preclassic cultures on the western and southern borders of the Maya Lowlands. In these inventions the role of Oaxaca and the Zapotecs is not to be discounted, although the geography of the situation would suggest the Izapan and epi-Olmec cultures of the Gulf Coast played a more direct role in the influencing of the Maya.

As we have seen in the basic lowland data papers, Maya iconographic and architectural elements that are the obvious immediate antecedents to those of the Classic begin to appear in the Late Preclassic ceremonial centers and come into better definition in the Protoclassic. It cannot be denied that the synthesis of these takes place in the lowlands and is peculiarly Maya, just as it cannot be denied that there has been borrowing and influencing from the Late Preclassic and Protoclassic Period cultures lying outside the Maya Lowlands. This Late Preclassic–Protoclassic influence can be definitely identified, in many instances, as we have already noted, as Izapan in style; quite possibly it passed to the lowlands via Kaminaljuyu. It is also probable, following Lowe's hypothesis, that earlier the Olmec-Maya Middle Preclassic established certain ideological bonds that made for a more ready acceptance of the Late Preclassic Izapan-Olmecoid traits in the Maya Lowlands.

Two other currents of influence affected the course of Maya

Lowland development in the Protoclassic. One of these is best registered in ceramic traits—Usulutan wares, imitation positive-painted Usulutan, polychromes, and specialized vessel forms such as the mammiform tetrapodal bowl and the Z-angle bowl—in brief, what is sometimes called "Protoclassic Period pottery" or, now, the Floral Park complex. In the regional data papers we have noted particularly heavy occurrences of these traits in Belize and along the Belize-Peten frontier, on the eastern side of the Maya Lowlands; they occur, also, at Altar de Sacrificios, on the western or southwestern edge of the Lowlands, Their source almost certainly is highland, in Guatemala or Salvador. Usulutan ware, one of the Floral Park– complex traits, dates back to the Kal complex in Salvador; this dating is Middle Preclassic, or substantially earlier than its appearances in the Maya Lowlands. In the Altar de Sacrificios sequence the Floral Park influences make a first and somewhat minor appearance in the Late Preclassic Period but become pronounced in the Protoclassic. Does the appearance of these new ceramic traits in Belize, on the eastern edge of the Peten, and at Altar de Sacrificios signal an invasion or partial population replacement? It is a question that has vexed Maya archaeologists for some time and that, as the papers in this volume indicate, is still with us. That the Floral Park pottery, of Salvadoran-Guatemalan Highland inspiration, should occur on the very threshold of the changes that usher in the Classic Period suggests the invasion hypothesis—the arrival of groups with an elite social class organization who subjugated the simpler resident Lowland Maya and, in effect, "lifted" them up to the status of civilization. This is a possibility, but I am inclined to doubt it. Many important sites and regions show little of the Floral Park complex. Tikal and the Central Zone are prime examples. Here we can trace a very steady buildup in cultural elaboration from the Late Preclassic, through the Protoclassic, and into the Early Classic Period with little or no tangible sign of the Floral Park complex. Of course, it could be argued that only certain rather marginal sites were directly affected by the "invaders" and that these marginal establishments, along the Belize-Peten border or at Altar de Sacrificios, in turn influenced more centrally located sites and regions. It is possible that physical anthropological research on skeletal series may some day be able to help us resolve this "invasion or diffusion" question. As yet, however, such research has not been done. Appraising the evidence that is available at present, I am inclined to see the Floral Park ceramic complex as an indication of extraterritorial trade and contact, processes that were increasing as Lowland Maya culture grew more centralized politically and more differentiated socially. In saying this, however, I should call the reader's attention to Ball's statement that he thinks a Protoclassic Period invasion of a new population group into northern Yucatan is a distinct possibility, so that the question, important as it may be for an understanding of the rise and growth of Lowland Maya civilization, must remain an open one for the time being.

The second current of influence referred to derives from Central Mexico, in particular from Teotihuacan. I use the term "current of influence" because, again, as with the Floral Park–complex case, the processes of this influence are not clearly understood; however, for Teotihuacan I believe that direct contacts, brought by emissaries from that Mexican Highland metropolis to the Maya Lowlands, are highly probable. As Teotihuacan influence upon the Lowland Maya was heaviest in the Early Classic Period, I will refer to these probable processes of contact below. For the Protoclassic Period we know there were some contacts, direct or indirect, between Teotihuacan and the Lowland Maya. A cache of specialized obsidian artifacts from Altun Ha, in Belize, can be cited as hard evidence. Just how important these early Teotihuacan contacts may have been in transforming Lowland Maya Protoclassic culture to the Classic stage is more difficult to determine.

The Early Classic Period (A.D. 250–600)

As indicated, Teotihuacan continued to exert a major influence upon the Maya Lowlands in the Early Classic Period. It is highly likely that this influence was in some way mediated by or involved with the great site of Kaminaljuyu in the central Guatemalan Highlands. Sanders describes two sequent "waves" of Teotihuacan influence at Kaminaljuyu. The first left its imprint in architecture, and Sanders is inclined to relate this to the presence and power of important Teotihuacan nobles or emissaries at Kaminaljuyu. The second wave is documented in ceramics and manufactures and, perhaps, represents the descendants of the Teotihuacan visitors in a more settled or acculturated situation in the Highland Maya cultural context. It is possible that these two waves are also registered in the Tikal record. Some of the earliest Teotihuacan influences there are seen in stela inscriptions and portraiture, dating to the late eighth and early ninth baktun, or very early in the Early Classic Period. These Teotihuacan evidences might very well pertain to the arrival, presence, and intermarriage of Mexican Highland aristocrats. Subsequently, in the range of A.D. 400–550, Teotihuacan influence is fairly common in ceramics. It is this later kind of influence that is found in most other Maya Lowland sites and regions, so that the strongest Teotihuacan ceramic impress in the Tzakol sphere pertains to Tzakol subphase 2 and the early part of 3.

The question referred to in our discussion of the Protoclassic Period—to what degree is Maya Lowland civilization indebted to Teotihuacan for its origins and growth?—is also important for the Early Classic. Was Teotihuacan influence or tutelage, in either the Protoclassic or Early Classic periods, responsible for the centralization of Lowland Maya polity? Again, this is a question that must be left open. While it is true that the strongest "wave" of Teotihuacan influence, insofar as this can be measured in the archaeological record, is in the A.D. 400–550 time band, there are stelae and other indications of a Teotihuacan presence a century or two earlier—early enough to have been significant in the crystallization of Classic Maya culture. After A.D. 540–50, the beginning of the hiatus, Teotihuacan influence disappeared from the Maya Lowlands. Did a break with Teotihuacan precipitate the hiatus or semicollapse, as I have suggested in my chapter? Or did Teotihuacan influence stop because of a locally generated crisis within the Maya Lowlands? Once more we are puzzled by, and seek information about, the Teotihuacan–Lowland Maya relationship.

The Late Classic Period (A.D. 600–900)

During most of the Late Classic Period no single external area influenced the Maya Lowlands more than any other. To some extent the lowlands may be said to have flourished in "splendid isolation" for two hundred years. This does not mean that there were no contacts or exchanges with other Mesoamerican subareas. In both raw materials and manufactures there was a vigorous commerce with the Guatemalan

Highlands, and there must also have been contacts with and knowledge of Oaxaca, Gulf Coast, and central Mexico. The results of some of these contacts are seen in the Late Classic art of the Maya, particularly along the western edge of the Maya Lowlands and spreading into the Yucatan Peninsula (Proskouriakoff 1951; Sabloff and Willey 1967). Alien, or at least non–Classic Maya, elements appear integrated into Classic iconography. Anything like an invasion seems an unlikely explanation; perhaps we are seeing a reflection of the assimilation of some foreign elite persons into the local Maya aristocracies.

In the last century of the Late Classic, along with the decline of Classic civilization in the Southern Lowlands, there are various clues to foreign presences in some sites. Fine Paste pottery wares, made in Tabasco or the Gulf Coast Lowlands, are a part of the Tepeu 3 (A.D. 800–900) pottery complexes along the Usumacinta and in the Peten. A new figurine style, associated with the Fine Paste wares, depicts a non–Classic Maya individual. At Seibal, on the Pasión River, stela portraits of the ninth century are those of nontypical Maya personages. J. E. S. Thompson (1970) has suggested the Chontal, or Putun, Maya, from the Gulf Coastal region, as being responsible for these alien introductions into the heart of the Maya Lowlands, and most Mayanists agree, at least in general, although some prefer variant interpretations (see R. E. W. Adams 1973b; Sabloff 1973). This Terminal Late Classic impingement on the Southern Maya Lowlands is the theme of the previous seminar on the Maya (Culbert 1973a), and several of the papers issuing from that conference evaluate the degree to which this late external influence was responsible for the fall of Classic Maya civilization. As an epilogue to the story, the central Mexican Toltec invaded northern Yucatan a century or so later, at about A.D. 1000 , and this invasion had a profound effect on Maya civilization in the Northern Lowlands.

PROCESSES AND MODELS

The chapters by Sanders, Netting, Webster, and Rathje are all concerned primarily with processes of culture growth and change, and these processes and the formulation or selection of models to explicate and systemically relate them will provide the core of the discussions that follow in this section of the summary; however, as is evident from a reading of the papers in this volume, all seminar participants were involved with processual interpretations, and I will try to integrate their views in my comments.

I have arranged these comments under five headings: (1) ecology-subsistence-demography; (2) warfare; (3) trade; (4) ideology; and (5) what I have called the "overarching model," or my attempt to interrelate opinion and interpretations into a unified synthesis. Such a breakdown is designed for clarity and emphasis in presentation and, as the several authors have made clear, does not indicate a faith in monocausal explanations on the part of any of my colleagues. On the contrary, all authors have been at some pains to place their particular models and the processes which these subsume into broader contexts of systemic interaction.

Ecology-Subsistence-Demography

Sanders sees the natural environmental heterogeneity of the Maya Lowlands as the underlying reason why Maya civilization developed as it did. This lowland heterogeneity is by no means as marked as that of some other Mesoamerican subareas, such as the central Mexican Highlands; nevertheless, it is a condition, too often overlooked, that had an important effect in social and cultural growth. Man's ecological adaptation to the regional diversity of the Maya Lowland natural environment related directly to subsistence and demographic systems and patterns; and this systemic complex of ecology-subsistence-demography, in turn, provided a matrix for the growth of Maya civilization that was, in many of its features, restrictive and determinative. Sanders's evaluation of environmental heterogeneity is based on soil analysis. While he admits that this is not a total environmental evaluation, he feels that it is, within the Lowland Maya setting, the crucial factor in appraising agricultural adaptation. The soil analyses classify soils by types and subtypes and rate these on a fertility scale, especially with reference to the swidden farming of maize. These various soil types are plotted on a map of the Peten, following the research of Simmons, Tarano, and Pinto. Unfortunately, comparable data were not available for other portions of the Maya Lowlands.[5] With the data at hand, however, Sanders notes an exceptionally good soil fertility rating for the northeast Peten, or the Central Zone of the Maya Lowlands—the region in which Tikal, Uaxactun, and a large number of other major Maya ceremonial centers are located and in which Classic Maya civilization first emerged. The total acreage of highly favorable soils for this zone exceeds that of any other Peten zone.

According to the Sanders model, which is an adaptation of the Boserup model, this natural environmental advantage of the Central Zone made possible a population buildup which, in turn, resulted in a shortage of agricultural land, which led to competition, and thus to inequities in control of the land, and so on to social ranking and ultimately stratification. Such a sequence also transpired elsewhere in the Maya Lowlands, but it occurred earliest, or got off to an earlier start, in the Central Zone. A review of the archaeological evidence, at least in the Southern Lowlands, supports this contention. Of course, it is a circumstance that was known a priori, and Sanders's hypothesis and model are attempts to explain it. The one other lowland region where there was a contemporaneous developmental precocity (as measured by population concentration and architecture) is the Northern Plains of Yucatan. Here, however, the developmental upcurve seems to have been broken prior to full Classic-type achievements. In the Central Zone, the Tikal data show a continuity, although there is, perhaps, a slackening or lag in population growth in the latter part of the Late Preclassic and Protoclassic periods. At the same time there was, however, a Late Preclassic and Protoclassic development of what is interpreted as centralization and ranking which led into the Early Classic.

Culbert was the only contributor to challenge Sanders's basic environmental appraisal. He did this by citing the high fertility potential of the Southeastern Zone (the location of Copan, Quirigua) which, he states, did not have a well-developed Late Preclassic occupation. The nature of Southeastern Zone soils are not specified, and, as I have said, this portion of the Maya Lowlands was not included in Sanders's soil map. My own opinion of the fertility of the zone, based on a brief survey of the Copan Valley, would correspond to Culbert's; however, we need more information on the Preclassic there, for its developmental status might be somewhat better than Culbert's rating. Nevertheless, Classic Maya civilization does not appear to have been established in the Southeastern Zone until one or two hundred years later than it was at Tikal and Uaxactun, so Culbert has a point. Why didn't the apparently favorable soil conditions make the Southeastern Zone the "cradle of Maya civilization"? We cannot give a certain answer to this question, but I suggest that it has something to do with geographical marginality, quite possibly related to ethnic differences. The Southeastern Zone is on the edge of the Maya Lowlands, and it may not have been a part of the territory settled by the Middle Preclassic pioneers who moved into these lowlands from the Gulf Coast, the Guatemalan Highlands, or both. It is possible that it was not occupied in Early Preclassic times; and in Middle Preclassic times its population may not have been Maya, but related, instead, to the peoples of the Ulua Valley to the east. This Ulua Valley, incidentally, is prime agricultural land, yet it was never the scene of civilizational attainments of Maya Classic status. At best, in the Late Classic, it displayed a marginal and reduced variant of Maya Classic culture. Following out this line of argument, I think it probable that factors of centrality and marginality within the Maya Lowland sphere may have to be taken into account in explaining the beginnings of the Maya florescence. Another geographical factor might have been locational advantages with reference to sources of outside stimuli. Perhaps the Central Zone was, in some way, more strategically placed to assimilate trade and other contacts from Chiapas and the Guatemalan Highlands than was the Southeastern Zone.[6]

On balance, I think the Sanders environmental heterogeneity model has much to recommend it. Significantly, it is essentially consistent with the models and hypotheses advanced by Netting, Webster, Adams, and Ball; and it is not inconsistent with those interpretations which accord diffusion and ideological influences a role in Classic Maya growth.

Netting's model is a historically documented ethnographic one. He describes the ecological, settlement, and general cultural adjustment of the Ibo tribe of Nigeria. Living in a tropical forest environment somewhat similar to the Maya Lowlands, the Ibo practiced a system of "infield-outfield" cultivation. Household garden plots were maintained for some crops; others were grown more extensively, at some distance from dwellings and villages, in a swidden-fallow pattern. A variety of crops were cultivated, including roots, cereals, and trees. Netting suggests convincingly that a change toward increasing sociocultural complexity can be equated with and causally related to the growth of Ibo populations and their density. Did the Lowland Maya follow a similar ecological system, and is the model for a change toward such cultivation intensification applicable? Netting reviews the arguments that have been made for Maya crop diversification, including root crops and orchards. He also notes the evidence that has been coming in recently for techniques of intensification, especially the ridged fields in certain Maya Lowland regions. He concludes that reliance solely on long-fallow milpa cultivation of maize seems most unlikely. He observes that the Maya settlement pattern of ceremonial or politico-religious centers and of continuous dispersed residences is similar to that of the Ibo and that the spacing of households is consistent with infield or kitchen-plot agriculture.

Netting's model has the great value of offering a life situation for comparative analogy with the Lowland Maya. We see an ecological adaptation together with its settlement and sociopolitical systems, and we understand something of their integration. All of this has particular bearing on Maya Classic Period developments, especially changes between Early and Late Classic. As an adjunct to his Rio Bec regional data paper, Adams offers a model of Maya development. As a part of this diachronic model, he sees a first "florescence," as a climax to population growth, in the Late Preclassic–Protoclassic–Early Classic. A second florescence follows in the Late Classic with, again, population increase and attendant competition and sociopolitical development. This second florescence was made possible by agricultural intensification techniques and crop diversification of the kind Netting is talking about. A related overview model has also been devised by Peter Harrison (1975). Harrison did not participate in the seminar nor contribute his paper to it directly; however, his formulation, which has grown out of field research in southern Quintana Roo, just east of the main Rio Bec sites, is germane to this consideration of Lowland Maya food production and population. Harrison emphasizes "crises" rather than "florescences." It is his opinion that food production remained ahead of population growth from Preclassic times up until A.D. 500, or almost through the Early Classic Period. At that point the Maya began to suffer from food shortages, and this first crisis corresponds, more or less, to the sixth-century stela dedication hiatus. Soon after, though, the situation was improved through agricultural intensification; evidence for this intensification includes not only the ridged fields of the Rio Bec country but the grid patterns in the *bajos* of southern Quintana Roo, which total over 10,000 square kilometers in extent. This *bajo* cultivation is, in effect, a chinampa-type system, similar to that used in the lakes of central Mexico, and its productivity can be very great. It supports Netting's projection of the African Ibo model onto the Maya with even greater force. Harrison's second crisis is the Maya "great collapse" of the ninth century, a crisis again precipitated by population outrunning food production.

I note one omission in both the Adams and Harrison models. This is the indication, in some of the archaeological records at least, that there was an earlier crisis than the one at the end of the Early Classic Period. I have suggested in my Pasión-region data paper that population density began to present serious problems as early as the Late Preclassic, and that the competition arising from this pressure led to serious settlement rearrangements and new political patterns. In keeping with the larger curves of the Adams and Harrison models, the new political institutions of centralization and wider spheres of governance and, perhaps, food-production regulation then allowed for continued growth through most of the Early Classic. Adams, in discussing competition and warfare, alludes to this development, and I think that Ball's Northern Plains Zone data could also be accommodated to this general interpretation. The Protoclassic "decline" in the far north is what I have in mind here; and the somewhat delayed Early Classic revitalization in that region may have been abetted by the spread of southern political patterns in that direction.

The Adams and Harrison models do not explain everything about Classic Maya growth (and decline)—and here I should pause to note that neither author claims that they do and that Adams, quite pointedly, discusses many other factors in his developmental model—but they nevertheless establish for us, along with the contributions of Sanders and Netting, some basic ecological-subsistence-demographic guidelines and restraints and suggest some causal relationships among these systems. By way of caution, Netting has added (in post-conference commentary): "Intensification [of agriculture] is not an alternative to conflict over resources or to trade—rather I tend to see all three as adaptive responses to the conditions of changing man-land ratios following the pioneering occupation of a new area." And this cautionary comment is a fitting prelude to our next model.

Warfare

All of the abovementioned authors have alluded to warfare and competition in their models, but Webster focuses his attention on this institution. He disclaims it as a prime mover in civilizational growth, and, if I understand him correctly, he means by this that it is secondary to the subsistence-demographic complex. It is an "option," given certain demographic conditions. But, given the "circumscribed" nature of the Maya Lowlands, to use Carneiro's term and concept, it seems a very likely option. The archaeological evidence seems to indicate that it was an option often chosen.

Using computations derived from productive capacities of Maya Lowland land areas under long-fallow maize cultivation, plus available archaeological settlement information, Webster concludes that by the Late Preclassic Period there would have been land shortages and no room for further geographical expansion into unfilled territories. New agricultural techniques would have been one possible response to this difficulty, but apparently they were not the solution turned to at this time. Instead, there was expansion at the expense of other populations. The earliest expansion radiated out of the Central Zone (at least in the south; the Northern Plains may have been another zone of early aggressive expansion), where population pressures were greatest. Such expansion was achieved by warfare, and this development fed back into the sociopolitical organization to begin the formation of incipient states. This feedback effect worked both for the original aggressors and for those who set up defenses against them. As Webster points out, warfare was not a viable, long-term solution to the problems of food production and overpopulation, but there was a long-term adaptive significance in the rise of sociopolitical complexity. Among some of the more immediate results were, ironically, the depopulation of territories between aggressively expanding and competing political units. Such depopulation would have taken some land out of cultivation, and this process may be reflected in the Protoclassic Period "stabilization" or "decline" that has been noted for some regions. Another result was that the Maya Lowlands did not become "Amazonianized"—that is, they did not end up in a patchwork of more or less equally strong, endlessly competing polities. Some regions had the decided edge. This, I think, was true of the Central Zone and of

Tikal, in the Early Classic Period. Later, in the Late Classic, the region was more "Balkanized," splitting into a series of powerful ceremonial centers with some forty to sixty thousand adherents.

Webster examines the functions of a ceremonial-center elite. He prefers the term "organizational center," rightly arguing that this broader designation more appropriately refers to the broad range of militaristic, governmental, managerial, and ritual activities that must have gone on in these places. He sees the role of the warrior as highly important among those managerial roles acquired by Maya elites, being especially essential in the processes by which a ranked society was transformed into a primitive state. By Late Classic times, warfare had become the firmly established institution of militarism. High-ranked individuals were the focal points for tribal or "national" identification, and their contacts were widened and their prestige increased by their sacred or symbolic identifications with deities. They and their immediate kinsmen were in charge of goods redistribution and trade, adjudicated disputes, and served in other managerial ways. The managerial tasks would include duties related to construction and maintenance of agricultural intensification projects, such as the ridged fields or the *bajo* grids. Webster's discussion of an organizational center, its personnel, and their functions recalls Netting's analysis of Ibo society.

In this brief summary I have not mentioned the archaeological evidences of warfare. I would agree with Webster, however, that "negative evidence is meaningless," especially in the Maya Lowland situation. There are, nevertheless, evidences, both direct and indirect. Scenes of violence, particularly with reference to the humiliation of captives, are common in Maya art, both in sculpture and painting. These, of course, are largely confined to the Late Classic Period. For the Protoclassic, the period at which Webster postulates the first serious warfare, there is the walled organizational center of Becan in the Rio Bec region. There is also a defensework on the outskirts of Tikal, apparently delimiting its immediate sustaining area, that is believed to be of Early Classic date. The more indirect evidence has been mentioned, including changes in territorial settlement-pattern organization. For these, other causes are possible, but the reader is referred back to Webster's detailed arguments, which I find persuasive.

Trade

Rathje's model emphasizes long-distance trade as a vital process in Lowland Maya culture growth. He makes no monocausal claims, however, observing that trade is one factor among many, and his model incorporates population growth, food resources, and competition among groups. Indeed, the postulates underlying Rathje's model are much the same as those of the other models. Briefly, in the competition for desirable resources, whether they be arable lands or trade items, larger and more complexly structured social units enjoy an advantage over smaller, less internally segregated units. In the ensuing competition more successful units may incorporate less successful ones, and this incorporation is a process that enlarges the success potential of the successful. While there are limits of growth in both size and internal structuring, the limiting conditions that operate in this regard are more relevant to the fall of a civilization than to its rise.

With regard to the Lowland Maya, Rathje argues, as did other seminar members, that the Central Zone, or the "core area," was the first to cross the developmental threshold to complex society. It did so at the beginning of the Late Preclassic Period. The core area, with its large population, provided the earliest great market potential for large-scale resource procurement, and this procurement system, which was, in effect, long-distance trade, had an important feedback into the sociopolitical development of the core area. Thus, while Rathje does not insist that trade was the prime or only essential mover in the processes of civilization, he sees it, since it involves both exchange and goods production, as an important option—just as warfare is an option—once societies have reached a certain size and density of population. More specifically, if core area development precedes "buffer zone" development—as it appears to do in the Early Classic Period—then organized trade was a very significant process in Maya culture growth, especially in the Late Classic.

Two obvious and very important trade contacts for the Lowland Maya were those of the Salvadoran-Guatemalan Highland Floral Park system and of the Teotihuacan system. The Central Zone "core area," as represented by Tikal and Uaxactun, appears to have been on the outer periphery of Floral Park contacts; but Rathje believes, and I think he is correct, that the Floral Park system had created a market demand in the populous Central Zone for craft items and esoteric knowledge. Shortly after this, Tikal seems to have established itself as the major lowland center for the Teotihuacan, or Teotihuacan-Kaminaljuyu, trading system, a system that was to have a far wider influence on the Maya Lowlands than that of Floral Park. But both of these trading relationships were undoubtedly significant in the growth of Lowland Maya civilization.

Ideology

No one offered a formal model to explicate the role of ideology in the growth of Maya civilization, but it is difficult to look at the monuments and remains of this civilization without believing that this role must have been an important one. As we examine the record for evidences of population growth, subsistence resources, warfare, and trade, there is a tendency to relegate ideology to an epiphenomenal position, to reject it as a significant causal force or a "prime mover," but, leaving aside for the moment the question of initial or prime cause, there are indications that idea systems played an important part throughout the course of Maya development. Lowe touches on this subject on Early-to-Middle Preclassic Period levels with his concept of ethnic rivalry and ethnic identification. We have seen that the early Peten "peasants" were in contact with more complex societies that had developed religious iconographies. Beginning with the Late Preclassic an externally influenced but locally reformulated Maya Lowland iconography appears, and this, along with a "literature" in hieroglyphics and a highly involved and evolved calendrical system, flowered during the Classic Periods. This total ideology, rich in symbolism and ritual, must have been crucial in maintaining the entire Maya cultural system as it was directed from its ceremonial or organizational centers. It was also instrumental in bringing the system to decline and termination. All of the contributors to this volume have offered some suggestions as to how this could have come about. Netting, with his Ibo model, has provided comparative insights from the use of ideology, ritual, and symbol by an African elite. He has also reinforced his original remarks with an additional statement (postconference commentary): "Though warfare was probably a significant factor in the growth of Maya civilization, the response of channeling work effort and restraining conflict through the manipulation of sacred symbols and religiously sanctioned social hierarchies still seems to me *the particularly creative strand in this society*. Ideology, rather than being an epiphenomenon, would certainly play the central role in such peaceful management of conflict. The question of the degree to which voluntaristic mechanisms such as the acceptance of ritual hegemony and the peaceful facilitation of inter and intraregional trade were more important than military coercion is still unclear" (italics added).

A major difficulty in all of this is that we do not know—and probably will never know—the nature of the ideas involved. To be sure, ideas, rituals, and symbols were used to validate the position of a ruler, to propagate his image, or to win allegiance to his cause, but we do not know just how they accomplished these functions or in what way some ideas were more efficacious, more successfully adaptive, than others. To go back to Lowe's example, one wonders what was the nature of "jaguarism" as opposed to the cult of the "wind god"? The symbols in themselves tell us little. Undoubtedly they stand for some idea that was, for a time, transcendent, compelling. Are the differences here sheer happenstance? While the symbols may have been, I do not think that the ideas behind them were historical accidents. Rather, they must represent significant differences in world views, ideas that had adaptive value. If we knew what these ideas were, we could, perhaps, see how they interrelated with other systems, how they exerted feedback influences, negatively or positively, on the whole cultural system of the ancient Maya.

Considering this difficulty, is it worthwhile even to attempt to struggle with this dimension of civilization, given the archaeological methods and means available for the study of the Maya past? Should we not, instead, simply assume that ideological content is a constant, that it is not very important, and that we should turn our efforts to the more tangible systems that we can cope with more readily? Some archaeologists appear to think so; I do not. I realize, however, that it is incumbent upon me, and upon those who think similarly, to demonstrate how ideology may be "reconstructed" from the archaeological record. So far, it is fair to say, we have not done so.

The Overarching Model

Lest anyone be misled by this somewhat arrogant subhead, let me hasten to say that I make no attempt to replace, supplant, or transcend the models we have been summarizing and discussing. By "overarching" I mean, instead, a sort of canopy that will cover the models and processes which all of us in the seminar have put forward. It is an attempt, too, to arrive at some sort of consensus, although, as I said at the outset of this summary, I cannot hope to be unbiased in the way I have reviewed and tried to synthesize opinion.

Our model for the rise of Maya civilization is defined much as we defined the model for the collapse of that civilization. "A precise statement of the characteristics and dynamics of a system," the model here proposed is a "qualitative and general one which will be compatible with the known facts and which will suggest leads for more complicated models and, particularly, for models which will be ultimately quantified" (Willey and Shimkin 1973:489). It is viewed as a systemically related set of hypotheses and a research design as much as it is an explanation. Diachronically and developmentally, the model for the rise of Maya civilization precedes and overlaps with that described for the collapse. Again, in briefest form, and in general terms, our model postulates population growth in a previously unoccupied area as the preparatory base for the advance to the civilizational threshold. This threshold was attained through the development of an elite culture by means of intergroup competition and rivalry. The success of the system was stimulated by extraareal cultural contacts through trade and other mechanisms, and this success produced further growth of population and competition between groups. Beyond this point, as we have described in our model for the collapse, internal stresses and external pressures resulted in an increasing rigidity in the system, leading to system failure and collapse. The model as devised here owes much to the form and organization of other model presentations in this volume, especially to the one offered by Rathje.

The model can be broken down by period as follows:

1. At the beginning of the Middle Preclassic Period (ca. 1000 B.C.) populations from the Mexican Gulf Coastal Lowlands, from the Guatemalan-Salvadoran Highlands, or from both of these Mesoamerican subareas entered the Maya Lowlands. This was

418

the first occupation of the territory by a farming people, and it seems quite probable that such peoples had been marginal to more advanced cultures. The immigrants were of Zoquean or Mayan speech or of both. During the Middle Preclassic Period (1000–300 B.C.) these peoples increased in total numbers. Groups multiplied by fissioning. Communities, however, remained small and, probably, essentially autonomous. Trade and perhaps other contacts were maintained with parent populations outside the Maya Lowlands; social and political organization, however, was simple. Culture was generally similar throughout, although regional differences are evident in such things as ceramic manufactures.

2. In the Late Preclassic Period (300–50 B.C.) population continued to increase, although population growth rates exhibit some region-to-region differences. The Central Zone of the northeastern Peten reached a Preclassic population peak early in the Late Preclassic Period, as did the Northern Plains Zone of Yucatan. Elsewhere, however, increase continued through the Late Preclassic and, in places, even into the Protoclassic Period. These differentials in population growth rates are attributed primarily to differing environmental potentials for long-term-fallow swidden cultivation of maize. Population pressures led to competition and warfare for agricultural lands. Such intergroup and interregional competition promoted political organization and centralization and the rise of an elite leadership. The sociopolitical focal points were ceremonial or organizational centers. While such centers may have been present in earlier times it was not until the Late Preclassic Period, with its demographic and competitive pressures, that they became marked by a permanent public architecture. It was also during this period that emergent Maya Lowland civilization was assimilating ideologies from more advanced cultures such as the Izapan. The symbolic value of these centers as the seats of elite leadership was commemorated in monumental art. The functions of the centers, and of the resident elite, included military leadership, political governance, economic management, the organization of trade, the direction of craft goods manufactories, and the maintenance and propagation of religious and intellectual authority.

3. In many Maya Lowland regions the Protoclassic Period (50 B.C.–A.D. 250) was a time of crisis and political reorganization. Some regions and centers achieved dominance over others. Many former Late Preclassic centers were abandoned as a result of the intensification of competition and increasing incorporation of weaker polities into stronger ones. New ideas and ideologies (and, perhaps, peoples) were introduced into the Maya Lowlands from the outside. The maintenance of foreign trade relations became very important and also highly competitive. Architecture, art, and burials in the ceremonial centers all indicate the further consolidation of an elite-class leadership and a prevalent elite ideology.

4. The Early Classic (A.D. 250–600) saw the crystallization of Maya Lowland civilization in the Central Zone of the northeastern Peten. Architectural, ceramic, sculptural, and other arts flowered. Hieroglyphic inscriptions pertaining to calendrical and, probably, dynastic matters made their appearance. During this period the stela cult spread from the Central Zone to other parts of the Maya Lowlands. Tikal appears as the largest and probably the most important of the ceremonial centers of the south. Its ideological ascendancy was achieved early and long maintained. The prestige of Tikal was undoubtedly enhanced by its relationships with Teotihuacan and Kaminaljuyu, which involved trade in both utility and luxury goods, dynastic ties, and religious and ideological bonds. It is possible that there was a centralized state, ruled from Tikal, which dominated the Southern Lowlands at this time; certainly the Early Classic Period was an era of stability following one of flux and change.

5. In the last half of the sixth century A.D. the era of Early Classic stability was disrupted. This is the time of the stela hiatus, and the archaeological evidence suggests a breakdown of centralized authority. The most probable causes for this are new increases in population, which placed a strain on Lowland Maya agricultural productivity; the difficulties inherent in sustaining a large-scale political state directed from Tikal and the Central Zone; and, possibly, a cessation of trading and other contacts with the Teotihuacan system. It is, however, possible that the cessation of Teotihuacan contacts came about from the local lowland breakdown rather than the reverse.

6. A new stability was established during the first two centuries (A.D. 600–800) of the Late Classic Period. Stela dedication was resumed; architecture and the arts enjoyed new vigor; old ceremonial centers were revived; new ones sprang up. While Tikal and the other cities of the Central Zone flourished, they were rivaled in size and magnificence by the great centers of the Usumacinta in the west, by Copan in the east, and by Rio Bec, Chenes, and other northern sites. The impression is one of several competing regional polities sharing common cultural bonds but with no single center or region achieving political dominance for any length of time. Increased agricultural production through intensification techniques (ridged fields, *bajo* cultivation, terracing) and greater crop diversification (garden-plot cultivation, root crops, arboriculture) relieved population pressures for a time, making possible this Late Classic flores-cence. Warfare continued, however, and became institutional-ized into militarism.

7. In the last century of the Late Classic Period (A.D. 800–900) a cultural decline set in throughout the south and, to a degree, in the Rio Bec region. It is believed that this was brought about by the population pressures that had been mounting during the two previous prosperous centuries, by food shortages, and by sharpened militaristic competition between regional centers. This was further exacerbated by external pressures in the west from the Mexicanized Putun Maya. There were probably shifts of southern populations northward in this century, and the far northern regions of the Puuc and Northern Plains flourished somewhat later, until A.D. 1000, the date of the Mexican Toltec entry into the Northern Lowlands.

This model, as cast here, is obviously a very "historical" one. With this historicity stripped away, it places demographic pressure—in its systemic complex with ecology and subsistence productivity—in the position of prime mover or prime cause of the rise of Lowland Maya civilization. This is satisfactory up to a point. Numbers of people and their physical well-being are basic to the maintenance of any society, particularly a large and complex one. But these are self-evident truths—essentially biological conditions. Without these forces and factors, to be sure, nothing would have happened. And yet the forms that they assumed are not, to my mind, really comprehensible from so

421

distant, so superhuman a perspective. Beyond population pressure, a drive for survival through competition represents a second level of causality. Complex social, political, and economic organizations are adaptive mechanisms for survival, but they take many forms. It is at this point that ideas and ideologies enter the picture. When we begin to consider these, and to attempt to achieve understanding on a more human scale, we come to "historical explanation"—something that is decried by some as no explanation at all. Maybe so, but in the study of human events I cannot rid myself of the feeling that this is where the real interest lies.

NOTES

1. This summary was prepared in the months following the seminar conference. It was then circulated to all of the other participants during the summer of 1975. Most of them replied with some comments and suggestions for revisions. I have incorporated many of these into a revised text or in the form of footnotes. Others I rejected, either because I felt that they did not affect substantially what I had to say, or because I was in disagreement with them. Again, I emphasize that while what I have written here obviously could not have been done without the work of my colleagues, the interpretive summary is my own.

2. Important revisions to Culbert's zonation have been made by Hammond. Briefly, Hammond has reduced the area of the Belize Zone considerably by extending the Pasión Zone to the Caribbean Sea and the Central Zone eastward to include much of the western half of Belize (formerly British Honduras). The newly defined Belize Zone is thus essentially the eastern coastal strip and the immediate interior lands of the northern two-thirds of Belize. However, it must be kept in mind that Hammond's discussions in his present paper refer to sites throughout the political domain of present-day Belize.

3. In a postconference commentary M. D. Coe calls special attention to Maya pictorial ceramics as a major cultural trait of the Maya Classic. In his words: "The iconography, ideology, and textual material given on these ceramics, with the strong development of an underworld cult dedicated to the immortality of the elite, is unique to the Maya and entirely confined to the Classic. It is as characteristic of them as the stela cult and, like that cult, disappears with increasing Mexican influence and the Classic collapse. The 'funerary ceramics cult' has no known Olmec roots. It is *sui generis,* appearing at the beginning of the Early Classic, but reaching its full elaboration in Tepeu 2."

4. M. D. Coe, in another postconference commentary, is now inclined to feel that Zoquean was the original Olmec language, but he adds, "I would still bet, however, that La Venta was Maya-speaking—that is, on the Nacaste time level" (ca. 900–750 B.C., or post–San Lorenzo B).

5. There are good soil data for Belize (British Honduras) (see Wright et al. 1959) although these were not used by Sanders, perhaps because they could not be satisfactorily translated into the fertility scale that he was using for the other regions.

6. With reference to Culbert's criticisms and my comments on these and on his statements, Sanders (postconference commentary) writes:

> I believe both of you are still confusing origins with process. The process I describe of a population colonizing an area, increasing in number, and ultimately saturating the area is a universal and, environmental conditions permitting, should always lead to a large, dense population, agricultural intensification, and social differentiation. What will vary is the date of inception of colonization, and my model does not attempt to explain that—yours of spatial periphery is as good as any.
>
> Assuming sufficient time for the entire Maya Lowlands to achieve population saturation, a second characteristic that will vary is population density—and, I believe, derivatively, locations of centers of political power. This is because the region is not uniform in its capacity to sustain a process of agricultural intensification. The fact that the Copan-Quirigua area is a productive one hence is not an argument contrary to my views—in fact, it supports them since two major Maya centers were located there. Whether the region is as productive as the core is unknown since we have no data one way or the other, but I think that the difference in agricultural potential (in Maya terms) will relate to differences in population density and number of centers (the core clearly has a greater overall population density and more major centers than the Copan area).

References

ADAMS, RICHARD E. W.
1971 *The Ceramics of Altar de Sacrificios, Guatemala,* Papers of the Peabody Museum of Archaeology and Ethnology, vol. 63, no. 1 (Cambridge, Mass.: Harvard University).

1973a "The Collapse of Maya Civilization: A Review of Previous Theories," in *The Classic Maya Collapse,* ed. T. Patrick Culbert (Albuquerque: University of New Mexico Press, School of American Research Advanced Seminar Series).

1973b "Maya Collapse: Transformation and Termination in the Ceramic Sequence at Altar de Sacrificios," in *The Classic Maya Collapse,* ed. T. Patrick Culbert (Albuquerque: University of New Mexico Press, School of American Research Advanced Seminar Series).

1974 "Preliminary Reports on Archaeological Investigations in the Rio Bec Area,
(ed.) Campeche, Mexico," in *Middle American Research Institute Publication 31* (New Orleans: Tulane University).

ADAMS, ROBERT McC.
1966 *The Evolution of Urban Society* (Chicago: Aldine Publishing Co.).

1972 *The Uruk Countryside* (Chicago: University of Chicago Press).

AGRINIER, PIERRE
1960 *The Carved Human Femurs from Tomb 1, Chiapa de Corzo, Chiapas, Mexico,* Papers of the New World Archaeological Foundation, no. 5 (Orinda, Calif.).

1964 *The Archaeological Burials at Chiapa de Corzo and Their Furniture,* Papers of the New World Archaeological Foundation, no. 16 (Provo, U.: Brigham Young University Press).

1969 "Dos tumbas tardías y otros descubrimientos en Chinkultic," *Boletín INAH,* no. 36, pp. 21–28.

1970 *Mound 20, Mirador, Chiapas, Mexico,* Papers of the New World Archaeological Foundation, no. 28 (Provo, U.: Brigham Young University).

1973 "Un complejo cerámico, tipo Olmeca, del preclásico temprano el en El Mirador, Chiapas," paper presented at the Thirteenth Mesa Redonda de la Sociedad Mexicana de Antropología, Jalapa, Veracruz.

1974 "Desarrollo del zoque clásico y el problema del estilo Teotihuacano en el occidente de Chiapas," paper presented at the Forty-First International Congress of Americanists, Mexico City.

1975 _Mounds 9 and 10 at Mirador, Chiapas, Mexico,_ Papers of the New World Archaeological Foundation, no. 39 (Provo, U.: Brigham Young University).

ANDERSON, A. H., AND H. J. COOK

1944 "Archaeological Finds near Douglas, British Honduras," in _Carnegie Institution of Washington Notes on Middle American Archaeology and Ethnology,_ no. 40.

ANDREWS, E. WYLLYS, IV

1965a "Dzibilchaltun Program," in _Middle American Research Institute Publication 31_ (New Orleans: Tulane University).

1965b "Archaeology and Prehistory in the Northern Lowlands: An Introduction," in _Archaeology of Southern Mesoamerica, Handbook of Middle American Indians,_ vol. 2, ed. Gordon R. Willey (Austin: University of Texas Press).

1965c "Explorations in the Gruta de Chac, Yucatan, Mexico," in _Middle American Research Institute Publication 31_ (New Orleans: Tulane University).

1968 "Dzibilchaltun, a Northern Maya Metropolis," _Archaeology_ 21:36–47.

1973 "The Development of Maya Civilization after Abandonment of the Southern Cities," in _The Classic Maya Collapse,_ ed. T. Patrick Culbert (Albuquerque: University of New Mexico Press, School of American Research Advanced Seminar Series).

ANDREWS, E. WYLLYS, V

1970 "Excavations at Quelepa, Eastern El Salvador," _Cerámica de Cultura Maya,_ no. 6, pp. 21–40.

1974 "Some Architectural Similarities between Dzibilchaltun and Palenque," in _Primera Mesa Redonda de Palenque,_ ed. M. Greene (Pebble Beach, Calif.: Robert Louis Stevenson School).

BÁEZ-JORGE, FELIX

1973 _Los Zoque-Popolucas: estructura social_ (Mexico City: Instituto Nacional Indigenista).

BALL, JOHN M.

1970 _Introducing New Concepts of Geography in the Social Studies Curriculum Project,_ Geography Curriculum Project occasional paper, no. 1 (Athens: University of Georgia).

BALL, JOSEPH W.

1973 "Ceramic Sequence at Becan, Campeche, Mexico," Ph.D. dissertation, University of Wisconsin, Madison.

1974a "A Co-ordinate Approach to Northern Maya Prehistory: A.D. 700–1200," _American Antiquity_ 39:85–93.

1974b "A Teotihuacan-Style Cache from the Maya Lowlands," _Archaeology_ 27:2–9.

References

1975 "The Ceramics of Chinkultic, Chiapas, Mexico: Progress Report No. 1," manuscript with the New World Archaeological Foundation, Comitán, Chiapas.

BALL, JOSEPH W., AND E. WYLLYS ANDREWS V
1975 "The Polychrome Pottery of Dzibilchaltun, Mexico: Typology and Archaeological Context," in *Middle American Research Institute Publication 31* (New Orleans: Tulane University).

BALL, JOSEPH W., AND JACK D. EATON
1972 "Marine Resources and the Prehistoric Lowland Maya: A Comment," *American Anthropologist* 74:772–76.

BALL, JOSEPH W., AND DAVID F. POTTER
1974 "Preclassic Architecture at Becan, Campeche, Mexico," unpublished manuscript.

BARTH, FREDRIK
1969 "Introduction," in *Ethnic Groups and Boundaries; The Social Organization of Culture Difference,* ed. F. Barth (Boston: Little, Brown and Co.).

BARTHEL, T. S.
1963 "Die Stele 31 von Tikal," *Tribus* 12:159–214.
1968 "Historisches in den klassischen Mayainschriften," *Zeitschrift für Ethnologie* 93:119–56.

BAUDEZ, CLAUDE F., AND PIERRE BECQUELIN
1973 *Archéologie de los Naranjos, Honduras* (Mexico City: Mission Archéologique Française au Mexique).

BEALS, RALPH L.
1945 *Ethnology of the Western Mixe,* University of California Publications in American Archaeology and Ethnology, no. 42 (Berkeley).

BENNYHOFF, JAMES A.
1970 "The Emergence of Civilization in Central Mexico," paper presented at the Wenner-Gren Foundation for Anthropological Research Symposium, Burg Wartenstein.

BERLIN, HEINRICH
1942 "Un templo olvidado en Palenque," *Revista Mexicana de Estudios Antropológicos* 6:62–90.
1953 *Archaeological Reconnaissance in Tabasco,* Carnegie Institution of Washington Current Reports, no. 7 (Cambridge, Mass.).
1955 *Selected Pottery from Tabasco,* Carnegie Institution of Washington Notes on Middle American Archaeology and Ethnology, no. 126 (Cambridge, Mass.).
1956 *Late Pottery Horizons of Tabasco, Mexico,* Carnegie Institution of Washington Contributions to American Anthropology and History, no. 59 (Washington, D.C.).
1970 "The Tablet of the 96 Glyphs at Palenque, Chiapas, Mexico," in *Middle American Research Institute Publication 26* (New Orleans: Tulane University).

BERNAL, IGNACIO
1969   *The Olmec World* (Berkeley: University of California Press).
BERTALANFFY, L. VON
1968   *General Systems Theory* (New York: George Braziller).
BINFORD, LEWIS R.
1968   "Post Pleistocene Adaptations," in *New Perspectives in Archaeology,* ed. L. Binford and S. Binford (Chicago: Aldine Publishing Co.).
BLANTON, R. E.
1972   "Prehistoric Adaptation in the Ixtapalapa Region, Mexico," *Science* 175:1317–26.
BLOM, FRANS
1950   "A Polychrome Maya Plate from Quintana Roo," in *Carnègie Institution of Washington Notes on Middle American Archaeology and Ethnology,* no. 98 (Washington, D.C.).
BLOM, FRANS, AND OLIVER LA FARGE
1926–27 *Tribes and Temples,* Middle American Research Series, no. 1 (New Orleans: Tulane University).
BOGGS, STANLEY H.
1950   *Olmec Pictographs in the Las Victorias Group, Chalchupa Archaeological Zone, El Salvador,* Carnegie Institution of Washington Notes on Middle American Archaeology and Ethnology, no. 99 (Cambridge, Mass.).
BOHANNAN, PAUL
1954   "The Migration and Expansion of the Tiv," *Africa* 2:3.
BOMHARD, M. L.
1945   "Palm Oils and Waxes," in *New Crops for the New World,* ed. C. M. Wilson (New York: Macmillan Co.).
BORHEGYI, STEPHAN F.
1971   "Pre-Columbian Contacts—The Dryland Approach: The Impact and Influence of Teotihuacan Culture on the Pre-Columbian Civilizations of Mesoamerica," in *Man Across the Sea,* ed. C. L. Riley, J. C. Kelley, C. W. Pennington, and R. L. Rands (Austin: University of Texas Press).
BOSERUP, E.
1965   *The Conditions of Agricultural Growth: The Economics of Agrarian Change under Population Pressure* (Chicago: Aldine Publishing Co.).
BRAINERD, GEORGE W.
1951   "Early Ceramic Horizons in Yucatan," in *The Civilization of Ancient America,* ed. S. Tax, Selected Papers of the Nineteenth International Congress of Americanists, vol. 1.
1958   *The Archaeological Ceramics of Yucatan,* University of California Anthropological Records, vol. 19 (Berkeley and Los Angeles: University of California Press).
BROCKINGTON, DONALD L.
1967   *The Ceramic History of Santa Rosa, Chiapas, Mexico,* Papers of the New World Archaeological Foundation, no. 23 (Provo, U.: Brigham Young University Press).

References

BRONSON, BENNET
1966   "Roots and the Subsistence of the Ancient Maya," *Southwestern Journal of Anthropology* 22:251–79.

BUCHANAN, K. M., AND J. C. PUGH
1955   *Land and People In Nigeria* (London: University of London Press).

BULLARD, WILLIAM R., JR.
1960   "Maya Settlement Patterns in Northeastern Peten, Guatemala," *American Antiquity* 25:355–72.
1965   *Stratigraphic Excavations at San Estevan, Northern British Honduras,* Occasional Papers of the Royal Ontario Museum of Art and Archaeology, no. 9 (Toronto).

CAMPBELL, LYLE R.
1975   "The Linguistic Prehistory of the Southern Mesoamerican Periphery," paper presented at the Fourteenth Mesa Redonda de la Sociedad Mexicana de Antropología, Tegucigalpa, Honduras.

CAMPBELL, LYLE R., AND TERRENCE KAUFMAN
1976   "A Linguistic Look at the Olmecs," *American Antiquity* 41:80–89.

CARNEIRO, ROBERT L.
1960   "Slash and Burn Agriculture: A Closer Look at Its Implications," in *Men and Cultures,* ed. Anthony F. C. Wallace (Philadelphia: University of Pennsylvania Press).
1961   "Slash and Burn Cultivation among the Kuikuru and Its Implications for Cultural Development in the Amazon Basin," in *The Evolution of Horticultural Systems in Native South America: Causes and Consequences'* ed. J. Wilbert (Caracas: Sociedad de Ciencias Natural La Salle).
1970   "A Theory of the Origin of the State," *Science* 169:733–38.
1974   "A Reappraisal of the Role of Technology and Organization in the Origin of Civilization," *American Antiquity* 39:179–86.

CASO, A.
1938   *Exploraciones en Oaxaca, Quinta y Sexta Temporadas, 1936–37,* Instituto Panamericano de Geografía e Historia, publication 34 (Mexico).

CASO, A., AND I. BERNAL
1952   *Urnas de Oaxaca* (Mexico).

CEJA, JORGE FAUSTO
1974   "Coatán, una provincia preclásica temprana en el Soconusco de Chiapas," paper presented at the Forty-First International Congress of Americanists, Mexico City.

CHAGNON, NAPOLEON
1967   "Yanomamö Social Organization and Warfare," in *War: The Anthropology of Armed Conflict and Aggression,* ed. M. Fried et al. (New York: Natural History Press).

CHANG, K. C.
1968   *The Archaeology of Ancient China* (New Haven: Yale University Press).

CHILDE, V. GORDON
1950   "The Urban Revolution," *Town Planning Review* 21:3–17.

CHUBB, L.
1961   *Ibo Land Tenure* (Ibadan: Ibadan University Press).

COE, MICHAEL D.
1957a   "The Khmer Settlement Pattern: A Possible Analogy with That of the Maya," *American Antiquity* 22:409–10.
1957b   "Cycle 7 Monuments in Middle America: A Reconstruction," *American Anthropologist* 59:597–611.
1960   "Archaeological Linkages with North and South America at La Victoria, Guatemala," *American Anthropologist* 62:363–93.
1961   *La Victoria: An Early Site on the Pacific Coast of Guatemala,* Papers of the Peabody Museum of Archaeology and Ethnology, vol. 53 (Cambridge, Mass.: Harvard University).
1962   *Mexico,* Ancient Peoples and Places, no. 29, ed. G. Daniel (London: Thames and Hudson).
1965a   *The Jaguar's Children: Pre-Classic Central Mexico* (New York: Museum of Primitive Art).
1965b   "The Olmec Style and Its Distribution," in *Handbook of Middle American Indians,* vol. 3, ed. Robert Wauchope and Gordon R. Willey (Austin: University of Texas Press).
1966   *The Maya* (New York: Frederick A. Praeger).
1968   "San Lorenzo and the Olmec Civilization," in *Dumbarton Oaks Conference on the Olmec,* ed. Elizabeth P. Benson (Washington, D.C.: Dumbarton Oaks).
1970   "The Archaeological Sequence at San Lorenzo, Tenochtitlan, Veracruz, Mexico," in *Contributions of the University of California Archaeological Research Facility,* no. 8 (Berkeley).
1972   "Olmec Jaguars and Olmec Kings," in *The Cult of the Feline,* ed. Elizabeth P. Benson (Washington, D.C.: Dumbarton Oaks).
1973a   "The Iconology of Olmec Art," in *The Iconography of Middle American Sculpture,* ed. Ignacio Bernal (New York: Metropolitan Museum of Art).
1973b   *The Maya Scribe and His World* (New York: Grolier Club).

COE, MICHAEL D., AND KENT V. FLANNERY
1964   "Microenvironments and Mesoamerican Prehistory," *Science* 143:650–54.
1967   *Early Cultures and Human Ecology in South Coastal Guatemala,* Smithsonian Institution Contributions to Anthropology, vol. 3 (Washington, D.C.).

COE, WILLIAM R.
1959   *Piedras Negras Archaeology: Artifacts, Caches, and Burials* (Philadelphia: University of Pennsylvania, Museum Monographs).
1962   "A Summary of Excavation and Research at Tikal, Guatemala: 1956–61," *American Antiquity* 27:479–507.
1965a   "Tikal: Ten Years of Study of a Maya Ruin in the Lowlands of Guatemala," *Expedition* 8:5–56.
1965b   "Tikal, Guatemala, and Emergent Maya Civilization," *Science* 147: 1401–19.
1967   *Tikal: A Handbook of the Ancient Maya Ruins* (Philadelphia: University Museum).

References

COE, WILLIAM R., AND MICHAEL D. COE
1956   "Excavations at Nohoch Ek, British Honduras," *American Antiquity* 21:370–82.

COLLIER, GEORGE A.
1975   *Fields of the Tzotzil: The Ecological Bases of Tradition in Highland Chiapas* (Austin: University of Texas Press).

CONKLIN, H. C.
1954   "An Ethnoecological Approach to Shifting Cultivation," *Transactions of the New York Academy of Science,* 2d series, 17:133–42.

COOK, O. F.
1935   "The Maya Breadnut in Southern Florida," *Science* 85:615–16.

COOK, S. F.
1972   *Prehistoric Demography,* Addison-Wesley Modular Publications, no. 16.

COVARRUBIAS, M.
1946   "El arte 'Olmeca' o de La Venta," *Cuadernos Americanos* 4:153–79.
1961   *Arte indigena de México y Centroamérica* (Mexico City: Universidad Nacional Autónoma de México).

COWGILL, URSULA M.
1961   "Soil Fertility and the Ancient Maya," *Transactions of the Connecticut Academy of Arts and Sciences* 42:1–56.
1962   "An Agricultural Study of the Southern Maya Lowlands," *American Anthropologist* 64:273–96.
1971   "Some Comments on Manihot Subsistence and the Ancient Maya," *Southwestern Journal of Anthropology* 27:51–64.

COWGILL, URSULA, G. GOULDEN, E. HUTCHINSON, R. PATRICK, A. PACEC, AND M. TSUKADA
1966   *The History of Laguna de Peténxil,* Memoirs of the Connecticut Academy of Arts and Sciences, vol. 17.

CULBERT, T. PATRICK
1973a   *The Classic Maya Collapse* (Albuquerque: University of New Mexico Press,
(ed.)   School of American Research Advanced Seminar Series).
1973b   "Introduction: A Prologue to Classic Maya Culture and the Problem of Its Collapse," in *The Classic Maya Collapse,* ed. T. Patrick Culbert (Albuquerque: University of New Mexico Press, School of American Research Advanced Seminar Series).
1973c   "The Maya Downfall at Tikal," in *The Classic Maya Collapse,* ed. T. Patrick Culbert (Albuquerque: University of New Mexico Press, School of American Research Advanced Seminar Series).
1974   *The Lost Civilization: The Story of the Classic Maya* (New York: Harper and Row).

CULBERT, T. PATRICK, P. MAGERS, AND M. SPENCER
1974   "Slash-and-Burn Agriculture in the Maya Lowlands," mimeographed, University of Arizona, Department of Anthropology (Tucson).

DAHLIN, B. H.
1974   "Preliminary Findings of the Albion Island Settlement Pattern Survey,"
        paper presented at the Seventy-Third Annual Meeting of the American
        Anthropological Association, Mexico City.

DELGADO, AGUSTÍN
1965   *Excavations at Santa Rosa, Chiapas, Mexico,* Papers of the New World
        Archaeological Foundation, no. 5 (Provo, U.: Brigham Young University
        Press).

DENEVAN, W. M.
1970   "Aboriginal Drained-Field Cultivation in the Americas," *Science*
        169:647–54.

DÍAZ DEL CASTILLO, BERNAL
1955   *Historia verdadera de la conquista de la Nueva España* (Buenos Aires:
        Espasa-Calpe Argentina).

DIXON, KEITH A.
1959   *Ceramics from Two Preclassic Periods at Chiapa de Corzo, Chiapas,
        Mexico,* Papers of the New World Archaeological Foundation, no. 5
        (Orinda, Calif.).

DRUCKER, PHILIP
1952   *La Venta, Tabasco: A Study of Olmec Ceramics and Art,* Smithsonian
        Institution Bureau of American Ethnology, Bulletin 153 (Washington,
        D.C.).

DRUCKER, PHILIP, AND EDUARDO CONTRERAS
1953   "Site Pat5erns in t..e Eastern Part of Olmec Territory," *Journal of the
        Washington Academy of Sciences* 43:389–96.

DUMOND, D.
1961   "Swidden Agriculture and the Rise of Maya Civilization," *Southwestern
        Journal of Anthropology* 17:301–16.
1972   "Population Growth and Political Centralization," in *Population Growth:
        Anthropological Implications,* ed. B. Spooner (Cambridge, Mass.: M.I.T.
        Press).

DURÁN, FRAY DIEGO
1964   *The Histories of the Indies of New Spain* (New York: Orion Press).

EASBY, ELIZABETH K., AND JOHN F. SCOTT
1970   *Before Cortez: Sculpture of Middle America* (New York: Metropolitan
        Museum of Art).

EATON, JACK D.
1972   "A Report on Excagations at Chicanna, Campeche, Mexico," *Cerámica de
        Cultura Maya,* no. 8, pp. 42–61.
1974   "Chicanna: An Elite Center in the Rio Bec Region," in *Middle American
        Research Institute Publication 31* (New Orleans: Tulane University).
1976   "Ancient Agricultural Farmsteads in the Rio Bec Region of Yucatan,"

mimeographed, University of Texas at San Antonio, Department of Anthropology.

EKHOLM, SUSANNA M.

1969   *Mound 30a and the Early Preclassic Ceramic Sequence at Izapa, Chiapas, Mexico,* Papers of the New World Archaeological Foundation, no. 25 (Provo, U.: Brigham Young University Press).

n.d.   "The Olmec Presence in Chiapas: A Review," in *Prehispanic Cultural Ecology and Human Geography in Southern Chiapas: A Symposium,* ed. S. M. Ekholm and G. W. Lowe, Papers of the New World Archaeological Foundation, no. 42 (Provo, U.: Brigham Young University), in press.

EKHOLM-MILLER, SUSANNA

1973   *The Olmec Rock Carving at Xoc, Chiapas, Mexico,* Papers of the New World Archaeological Foundation, no. 32 (Provo, U.: Brigham Young University Press).

ERASMUS, CHARLES

1968   "Thoughts on Upward Collapse: An Essay on Explanation in Archaeology," *Southwestern Journal of Anthropology* 24:170–94.

FAO

1970   *Amino-Acid Content of Foods,* FAO Nutritional Studies, no. 24 (Rome: Food and Agriculture Association of the United Nations).

FELDMAN, LAWRENCE H.

1973   "Languages of the Chiapas Coast and Interior in the Colonial Period, 1525–1820," in *Studies in Ancient Mesoamerica,* ed. J. Graham, Contributions of the University of California Archaeological Research Facility, no. 18 (Berkeley).

FERDON, EDWIN N., JR.

1959   "Agricultural Potential and the Development of Cultures," *Southwestern Journal of Anthropology* 15:1–19.

FERNÁNDEZ DE MIRANDA, MARÍA TERESA

1967   "Inventory of Classificatory Materials," in *Linguistics, Handbook of Middle American Indians,* vol. 5, ed. Norman A. McQuown (Austin: University of Texas Press).

FLANNERY, KENT V.

1968a   "The Olmec and the Valley of Oaxaca: A Model for Interregional Interaction in Formative Times," in *Dumbarton Oaks Conference on the Olmec,* ed. Elizabeth P. Benson (Washington, D.C.: Dumbarton Oaks).

1968b   "Archaeological Systems Theory and Early Mesoamerica," in *Anthropological Archeology in the Americas* (Washington, D.C.: Anthropological Society).

1970   "Preliminary Archeological Investigations in the Valley of Oaxaca, Mexico,
(ed.)   1966–1969," mimeographed, University of Michigan Museum of Anthropology (Ann Arbor).

1972a   "The Cultural Evolution of Civilizations," in *Annual Review of Ecology and Systematics* (Palo Alto, Calif.: Annual Reviews), 3:399–426.

1972b   "The Origins of the Village as a Settlement Type in Mesoamerica and the Near East: A Comparative Study," in *Man, Settlement and Urbanism*, ed. P. J. Ucko, R. Tringham, and G. W. Dimbleby (London: Duckworth and Co.).

FLANNERY, KENT V., ANNE V. T. KIRKBY, MICHAEL J. KIRKBY, AND AUBREY W. WILLIAMS, JR.
1967   "Farming Systems and Political Growth in Ancient Oaxaca," *Science* 158:445–54.

FLANNERY, KENT V., M. WINTER, S. LEES, J. NEELY, J. SCHOENWETTER, S. KITCHEN, AND J. C. WHEELER
1970   "Preliminary Archaeological Investigations in the Valley of Oaxaca, Mexico, 1966–69," mimeographed report, University of Michigan (Ann Arbor).

FLOYD, B.
1965   "Terrace Agriculture in Eastern Nigeria: The Case of Maku," *Journal of the Geographical Association of Nigeria* 7:91–108.
1969   *Eastern Nigeria* (New York: Frederick A. Praeger).

FOLAN, WILLIAM J.
1972   "Un betellón monopodio del centro de Yucatan, Mexico," in *Estudios de Cultura Maya*, vol. 8, ed. Alberto Ruz Lhuillier (Mexico City: Universidad Nacional Autónoma de México).

FOSTER, GEORGE M.
1969   "The Mixe, Zoque, and Popoluca," in *Ethnology, Handbook of Middle American Indians*, vol. 7, ed. Evon Z. Vogt (Austin: University of Texas Press).

FREEMAN, J. D.
1955   *Iban Agriculture*, Colonial Research Studies, no. 18 (London: Colonial Office).

FRIED, MORTON H.
1952   "Land Tenure, Geography and Ecology in the Contact of Cultures," *American Journal of Economics and Sociology* 11:391–412.
1961   "Warfare, Military Organization, and the Evolution of Society," *Anthropologica* 3:134–47.
1967   *The Evolution of Political Society* (New York: Random House).

FRY, ROBERT E.
1969   "Ceramics and Settlement in the Periphery of Tikal, Guatemala," Ph.D. dissertation, University of Arizona (Tucson).

FURST, PETER T.
1968   "The Olmec Were-Jaguar Motif in the Light of Ethnographic Reality," in *Dumbarton Oaks Conference on the Olmec*, ed. Elizabeth P. Benson (Washington, D.C.: Dumbarton Oaks).

GANN, THOMAS W. F.
1897   "On the Contents of Some Ancient Mounds in Central America," *Proceedings of the Society of Antiquaries of London*, 2d series, 16:308–17.
1900   "Mounds in Northern Honduras," in *Smithsonian Institution Bureau of American Ethnology Nineteenth Annual Report, 1897–98*, part 2.

References

1905   "The Ancient Monuments of Northern Honduras and the Adjacent Parts of Yucatan and Guatemala, the Former Civilization in These Parts and the Chief Characteristics of the Races Now Inhabiting Them, with an Account of a Visit to the Rio Grande Ruins," *Journal of the Anthropological Institute* 35:103–12.

1911   "Explorations Carried on in British Honduras in 1908–09," *Liverpool Annals of Archaeology and Anthropology* 4:72–87.

1914–16 "Report on Some Excavations in British Honduras," *Liverpool Annals of Archaeology and Anthropology* 7:28–42.

1918   *The Maya Indians of Southern Yucatan and Northern British Honduras,* Bureau of American Ethnology Bulletin 64 (Washington, D.C.).

1927   *Maya Cities* (London: Duckworth and Co.).

1938   "Finds in Maya Mounds: New Discoveries in British Honduras," *Illustrated London News* 192:122–24.

1939   *Glories of the Maya* (London: Duckworth and Co.).

1943   "Painted Stucco Heads from Louisville, British Honduras," *Middle American Research Records* 1:13–16.

GANN, THOMAS W. F., AND M. GANN

1939   *Archaeological Investigations in the Corozal District of British Honduras,* Bureau of American Ethnology Bulletin 123 (Washington, D.C.).

GARCÍA DE LEÓN G., ANTONIO

1969   "Pajapan. Una variante del Náhuatl del Este," thesis, Escuela Nacional de Antropología e Historia (Mexico City).

GARCIA PAYÓN, JOSÉ

1966   *Prehistoria de Mesoamérica. Excavaciones en Trapiche y Chalahuite, Veracruz, México, 1942, 1951, y 1959,* Cuadernos de la Facultad de Filosofía, Letras y Ciencias, vol. 31 (Xalapa).

GAY, CARLO T. E.

1967   "Oldest Paintings of the New World," *Natural History* 76:28–35.

GEERTZ, CLIFFORD

1963   *Agricultural Involution* (Berkeley and Los Angeles: University of California Press).

GIFFORD, JAMES C.

1974   "Recent Thought Concerning the Interpretation of Maya Prehistory," in *Mesoamerican Archaeology: New Approaches,* ed. Norman Hammond (London: Duckworth and Co.; Austin: University of Texas Press).

GRAHAM, JOHN

1971   "Sobre la escritura Maya," in *Desarrollo cultural de los Mayas,* ed. Evon Z. Vogt and Alberto Ruz Lhuillier (Mexico City: Universidad Nacional Autónoma de México).

1972   *The Hieroglyphic Inscriptions and Monumental Art of Altar de Sacrificios,* Papers of the Peabody Museum, vol. 64, no. 2 (Cambridge, Mass.: Harvard University).

435

GREEN, DEE F., AND GARETH W. LOWE
1967   *Altamira and Padre Piedra, Early Preclassic Sites in Chiapas, Mexico,*
        Papers of the New World Archaeological Foundation, no. 20 (Provo, U.:
        Brigham Young University Press).

GREEN, E. L.
1973   "Location Analysis of Prehistoric Maya Sites in Northern British
        Honduras," *American Antiquity* 38:279–93.

GREENE, M.
1967   Illustration in *Ancient Maya Relief Sculpture,* ed. J. Eric S. Thompson (New
        York: Museum of Primitive Art).

GROVE, A. T.
1951   "Soil Erosion and Population Problems in South-East Nigeria,"
        Geographical Journal 117:291–306.
1967   *Africa South of the Sahara* (London: Oxford University Press).

GROVE, D. C.
1970   *The Olmec Painting of Oxtotitlan Cave, Guerrero, Mexico,* Studies in
        Pre-Columbian Art and Archeology, no. 6 (Washington, D.C.: Dumbarton
        Oaks).
1973   "Olmec Altars and Myths," *Archaeology* 26:128–35.

GUSSINYER, JORDI
1971   "Primera temporada de salvamento arqueológico en la presa de La
        Angostura," *ICACH* (Tuxtla Gutiérrez), no. 4, pp. 35–52.
1972   "Rescate arqueológico en la presa de 'La Angostura,' Chiapas," *Boletín
        INAH,* no. 1.

HABERLAND, W.
1958   "An Early Mound at Louisville, British Honduras," *Man* 58:128–29.

HAMMOND, NORMAN
1972   "Obsidian Trade Routes in the Mayan Area," *Science* 178:1092–93.
1973   *British Museum–Cambridge University Corozal Project, 1973 Interim Re-*
(ed.) port (Cambridge: Cambridge University, Centre of Latin American Studies).
1974a   "Preclassic to Postclassic in Northern Belize," *Antiquity* 48:177–89.
1974b   "The Distribution of Late Classic Maya Major Ceremonial Centres in the
        Central Area," in *Mesoamerican Archaeology: New Approaches,* ed.
        Norman Hammond (London: Duckworth and Co.; Austin: University of
        Texas Press).
1975a   *British Museum–Cambridge University Corozal Project, 1974–75 Interim*
(ed.)   *Report* (Cambridge: Cambridge University, Centre of Latin American
        Studies).
1975b   "Maya Settlement Hierarchy in Northern Belize," in *Contributions of the
        University of California Archaeological Research Facility,* no. 27
        (Berkeley).
1976   "Introduction," in *Archaeology in Northern Belize: 1974–75 Interim Report
        of the British Museum–Cambridge University Corozal Project,* ed. Norman
        Hammond (Cambridge: Cambridge University, Centre of Latin American
        Studies).

436

References

HARLAN, F. R.
1971   "Agricultural Origins: Centers and Noncenters," *Science* 174:468–74.

HARRIS, D. R.
1972a   "Swidden Systems and Settlement," in *Man, Settlement and Urbanism*, ed. P. J. Ucko, R. Tringham, G. W. Dimbleby (London: Duckworth and Co.).
1972b   "The Origins of Agriculture in the Tropics," *American Scientist* 60:180–93.

HARRISON, PETER D.
1975   "Intensive Agriculture in Southern Quintana Roo, Mexico: Some New Lines of Evidence and Implications for Maya Prehistory," paper presented at the Fortieth Annual Meeting, Society for American Archaeology, Dallas.

HASLER, J. A.
1958   "Situación y tareas de la investigación lingüística en Veracruz," *La Palabra y el Hombre* (Jalapa), no. 5, pp. 43–49.

HASSAN, F.
1973   "On Mechanisms of Population Growth During the Neolithic," *Current Anthropology* 14:535–43.

HAVILAND, WILLIAM A.
1965   "Prehistoric Settlement at Tikal, Guatemala," *Expedition* 7:14–23.
1966   "Maya Settlement Patterns: A Critical Review," in *Middle American Research Institution Publication 26* (New Orleans: Tulane University).
1967   "Stature at Tikal, Guatemala: Implications for Ancient Maya Demography and Social Organization," *American Antiquity* 32:316–25.
1969   "A New Population Estimate for Tikal, Guatemala," *American Antiquity* 34:429–33.
1970   "Tikal, Guatemala, and Mesoamerican Urbanism," *World Archaeology* 2:186–97.
1972   "Family Size, Prehistoric Population Estimates, and the Ancient Maya," *American Antiquity* 37:135–39.

HAYS, CLARENCE L., S. K. LOTHROP, R. L. LINTON, H. L. SHAPIRO, AND G. C. VAILLANT
1940   *The Maya and Their Neighbors* (New York: Appleton-Century-Crofts).

HEIDER, KARL
1970   *The Dugum Dani*, Viking Fund Publications in Anthropology, no. 49 (New York: Wenner-Gren Foundation).

HENDERSON, RICHARD N.
1972   *The King in Every Man* (New Haven: Yale University Press).

IGBOZURIKE, M. U.
1971   "Against Monoculture," *Professional Geographer* 23:113–17.

JOESINK-MANDEVILLE, LE ROY V.
1972   "Concerning Olmec-Maya Relationships: A Correlation of Linguistical Evidence with Archaeological Ceramics," paper presented at the Thirty-Seventh Annual Meeting of the Society for American Archaeology, Miami Beach.

437

JOESINK-MANDEVILLE, L., AND SYLVIA MELUZIN
1976 "Olmec-Maya Relationships: Olmec Influence in Yucatan," in *Origins of Religious Art and Iconography in Preclassic Mesoamerica*, ed. H. B. Nicholson (Los Angeles: UCLA Latin American Center).

JONES, G. I.
1949 "Ibo Land Tenure," *Africa* 19:309–23.

JORALEMON, P. D.
1971 *A Study of Olmec Iconography*, Studies in Pre-Columbian Art and Archaeology, no. 7 (Washington, D.C.: Dumbarton Oaks).

JOSSERAND, JUDY KATHRYN
1975 "Archaeological and Linguistic Correlations for Mayan Prehistory," in *Actas del XLI Congreso Internacional de Americanistas*, vol. 1 (Mexico City).

KAUFMAN, TERENCE
1969 *Some Recent Hypotheses on Maya Diversification*, Language Behavior Laboratory Working Papers, no. 26 (Berkeley: University of California).
1971 "Materiales lingüísticos para el estudio de las relaciones internas y externas de la familia de idiomas mayanos," in *Desarrollo Cultural de Los Mayas*, ed. Evon Z. Vogt and Alberto Ruz Lhuillier (Mexico City: Universidad Nacional Autónoma de México).

KEEBLE, D. E.
1967 "Models of Economic Development," in *Models in Geography*, ed. R. J. Chorley and P. Haggett (London: Methuen & Co.).

KELEMEN, P.
1946 *Medieval American Art* (New York: Macmillan Co.).

KELLY, ISABEL, AND ANGEL PALERM
1952 *The Tajin Totonac*, Smithsonian Institution of Social Anthropology Publication 13.

KIDDER, A. V.
1940 "Archaeological Problems of the Highland Maya," in *The Maya and Their Neighbors* (Hays et al. 1940) (New York: Appleton-Century-Crofts).
1946 *Excavations at Kaminaljuyu, Guatemala*, Carnegie Institution of Washington Publication 561.
1950 "Introduction," in *Uaxactun, Guatemala: Excavation of 1931–1937*, Carnegie Institution of Washington Publication 588.

KIDDER, A. V., AND G. F. EKHOLM
1951 "Some Archaeological Specimens from Pomona, British Honduras," in *Carnegie Institution of Washington Notes on Middle American Archaeology and Ethnology*, no. 102.

KROEBER, A. L.
1944 *Configurations of Culture Growth* (Berkeley and Los Angeles: University of California Press).
1948 *Anthropology* (New York: Harcourt, Brace and Co.).

References

KUBLER, GEORGE
1972   "The Paired Attendants of the Temple Tablets at Palenque," *Twelfth Mesa Redonda de la Sociedad Mexicana de Antropología,* pp. 317–28 (Mexico).

LARSON, L.
1972   "Functional Considerations of Warfare in the Southeast during the Mississippian Period," *American Antiquity* 37:383–92.

LATHRAP, DONALD W.
1972   "The Moist Tropics, the Arid Lands, and the Appearance of Great Art Styles in the New World," paper presented at El Primer Symposio de Correlaciones Antropológicas Andino-Mesoamericano, Salinas, Ecuador.

LEE, RICHARD, AND IRVEN DEVORE
1968   *Man the Hunter* (Chicago: Aldine Publishing Co.).

LEE, THOMAS A., JR.
1969   *The Artifacts of Chiapa de Corzo, Chiapas, Mexico,* Papers of the New World Archaeological Foundation, no. 26 (Provo, U.: Brigham Young University Press).
1973   "Secuencia de fases postformativas en Izapa, Chiapas, Mexico," *Estudios de Cultura Maya* 9:75–84.
1974   "The Middle Grijalva Regional Chronology and Ceramic Relations: A Preliminary Report," in *Mesoamerican Archaeology: New Approaches,* ed. Norman Hammond (London: Duckworth and Co.).
1975   "The Uppermost Grijalva Basin: A Preliminary Report of a New Maya Archaeological Project," *Arqueología II,* papers presented at the Thirteenth Mesa Redonda de la Sociedad Mexicana de Antropología (Mexico City).

LEIGH, H.
1958   *An Identification of Zapotec Day Names,* Boletín de Estudios Oaxaquenos, no. 6 (Mexico City: Mexico City College).
1966   "The Evolution of the Zapotec Glyph C," in *Ancient Oaxaca,* ed. John Paddock (Stanford: Stanford University Press).

LINNE, SIGVALD
1934   *Archaeological Researches at Teotihuacan, Mexico,* Ethnographical Museum of Sweden, publication 1 (Stockholm).

LONGACRE, ROBERT
1967   "Systemic Comparison and Reconstruction," *Linguistics, Handbook of Middle American Indians,* vol. 5, ed. Norman McQuown (Austin: University of Texas Press).

LOUNSBURY, FLOYD G.
1974   "The Inscription of the Sarcophagus Lid at Palenque," in *Primera Mesa Redonda de Palenque,* part II, ed. M. G. Robertson (Pebble Beach, Calif.: Robert Louis Stevenson School).

LOWE, GARETH W.
1959   *Archaeological Exploration of the Upper Grijalva River, Chiapas, Mexico,* Papers of the New World Archaeological Foundation, no. 2 (Orinda, Calif.).
1962   *Mound 5 and Minor Excavations, Chiapa de Corzo, Chiapas, Mexico,*

Papers of the New World Archaeological Foundation, no. 12 (Provo, U.: Brigham Young University).

1965   "Desarrollo y función del incensario en Izapa," *Estudios de Cultura Maya* 5:53–64.

1969   "The Olmec Horizon Occupation of Mound 20 at San Isidro in the Middle Grijalva Region of Chiapas," thesis, University of the Americas, Mexico City.

1971   "The Civilizational Consequences of Varying Degrees of Agricultural and Ceramic Dependency within the Basic Ecosystems of Mesoamerica," in *Contributions of the University of California Archaeological Research Facility,* no. 11 (Berkeley).

1973a   "Archaeological Chronology of Eastern Mesoamerica," paper prepared for volume on New World Chronologies, ed. R. E. Taylor and C. W. Meighan.

1973b   "La cultura barra de la costa del Pacífico de Chiapas: un resumen y nuevos datos," paper presented at the Thirteenth Mesa Redonda de la Sociedad Mexicana de Antropología, Jalapa, Veracruz.

1974   "The Complex Early Preclassic Society of Southern Chiapas," paper presented at the Forty-First International Congress of Americanists, Mexico City.

1975   *The Early Preclassic Barra Phase of Altamira, Chiapas: A Review with New Data,* Papers of the New World Archaeological Foundation, no. 38 (Provo, U.: Brigham Young University).

LOWE, GARETH W., AND PIERRE AGRINIER

1960   *Mound 1, Chiapa de Corzo, Chiapas, Mexico,* Papers of the New World Archaeological Foundation, no. 8 (Provo, U.: Brigham Young University).

LOWE, GARETH W., THOMAS A. LEE, JR.; AND EDUARDO MARTÍNEZ E.

1976   *Izapa: An Introduction to the Ruins and Monuments,* Papers of the New World Archaeological Foundation, no. 31 (Provo, U.: Brigham Young University Press).

LOWE, GARETH W., AND J. ALDEN MASON

1965   "Archaeological Survey of the Chiapas Coast, Highlands, and Upper Grijalva Basin," in *Archaeology of Southern Mesoamerica, Handbook of Middle American Indians,* vol. 2, ed. Robert Wauchope and Gordon R. Willey (Austin: University of Texas Press).

LUNDELL, C. L.

1933   "The Agriculture of the Maya," *Southwest Review* 19:65–77.

1938   "Plants Probably Utilized by the Old Empire Maya of Peten and Adjacent Lowlands," *Papers of the Michigan Academy of Sciences, Arts, and Letters* 24:37–56.

McBRYDE, F. W.

1947   *Cultural and Historical Geography of Southwest Guatemala,* Smithsonian Institution of Social Anthropology Publication 4.

McDONALD, ANDREW J.

1974a   "Two Engraved Monuments Flanking a Central Stairway of a Middle Preclassic Pyramidal Platform at Tzutzuculi on the Chiapas Coast." mimeographed, University of Texas at Austin, Department of Anthropology.

References

1974b   "Middle Preclassic Ceremonial Centers in Southern Chiapas," paper presented at the Forty-First International Congress of Americanists, Mexico City.

McELRATH, DALE

1973   "Report of Preliminary Investigations at the Site of Perseverancia, Chiapas, Mexico," unpublished report, New World Archaeological Foundation (Comitán, Chiapas, Mexico).

MacLEOD, MURDO J.

1973   *Spanish Central America: A Socioeconomic History 1520–1720* (Berkeley and Los Angeles: University of California Press).

MacNEISH, RICHARD S., AND FREDERICK A. PETERSON

1962   *The Santa Marta Rock Shelter, Ocozocoautla, Chiapas, Mexico,* Papers of the New World Archaeological Foundation, no. 14 (Provo, U.: Brigham Young University Press).

MacNEISH, RICHARD S., FREDERICK A. PETERSON, AND KENT V. FLANNERY

1970   *Ceramics. The Prehistory of the Tehuacan Valley,* vol. 3 (Austin: University of Texas Press).

McQUOWN, NORMAN

1971   "Los orígenes y la diferenciación de los Mayas según se infiere del estudio comparativo de las lenguas mayanas," in *Desarrollo Cultural de Los Mayas,* ed. Evon Z. Vogt and Alberto Ruz Lhuillier (Mexico City: Universidad Nacional Autónoma de México).

MALER, TEOBERT

1908   *Explorations in the Department of Peten, Guatemala and Adjacent Regions,* Memoirs of the Peabody Museum vol. 4, no. 2 (Cambridge, Mass.: Harvard University).

MARCUS, JOYCE

1973   "Territorial Organization of the Lowland Classic Maya," *Science* 180:911–16.

1974   "The Iconography of Power among the Classic Maya," *World Archaeology* 6:83–94.

MATHENY, RAY T.

1970   *The Ceramics of Aguacatal, Campeche, Mexico,* Papers of the New World Archaeological Foundation, no. 27 (Provo, U.: Brigham Young University).

1973   "The Hydraulic System of Edzna, Campeche: Preliminary Investigations," paper presented at the Thirteenth Mesa Redonda de la Sociedad Mexicana de Antropología, Jalapa, Veracruz.

MATHEWS, PETER, AND LINDA SCHELE

1974   "Lords of Palenque—The Glyphic Evidence," in *Primera Mesa Redonda de Palenque,* part 1, ed. M. G. Robertson (Pebble Beach, Calif.: Robert Louis Stevenson School).

MEDINA HERNÁNDEZ, ANDRÉS

1973   "Sobre los Mames de Chiapas: notas etnográficas," *ICACH* (Tuxtla Gutiérrez) nos. 7–8, pp. 89–170. See same in *Anales de Antropología* (UNAM) vol. 10.

MEGGERS, BETTY J.
1954   "Environmental Limitation on the Growth of Culture," *American Anthropologist* 56:801–24.

MERWIN, R. E., AND G. C. VAILLANT
1932   *The Ruins of Holmul, Guatemala*, Memoirs of the Peabody Museum of Archaeology and Ethnology, vol. 3, no. 2 (Cambridge, Mass.: Harvard University).

MILES, SUZANNE W.
1965   "Sculpture of the Guatemala-Chiapas Highlands and Pacific Slopes and Associated Hieroglyphs," in *Archaeology of Southern Mesoamerica, Handbook of Middle American Indians*, vol. 2, ed. Robert Wauchope and Gordon R. Willey (Austin: University of Texas Press).

MILLON, RENÉ
1955   "Trade, Tree Cultivation and the Development of Private Property in Land," *American Anthropologist* 52:698–712.

MORGAN, W. B.
1955   "Farming Practice, Settlement Pattern and Population Density in Southeastern Nigeria," *Geographical Journal* 212:320–33.
1959   "The Influence of European Contacts on the Landscape of Southern Nigeria," *Geographical Journal* 125:48–64.
1969a   "The Zoning of Land Use around Rural Settlements in Tropical Africa," in *Environment and Land Use in Africa*, ed. M. F. Thomas and G. W. Whittington (London: Methuen).
1969b   "Peasant Agriculture in Tropical Africa," in *Environment and Land Use in Africa*, ed. M. F. Thomas and G. W. Whittington (London: Methuen).

MORLEY, SYLVANUS G.
1946   *The Ancient Maya*, 1st ed. (Stanford: Stanford University Press).

NARROLL, R.
1964   "Ethnic Unit Classification, *Current Anthropology* 5:283–91.

NAVARRETE, CARLOS
1959   *A Brief Reconnaissance of the Tonala Region, Chiapas, Mexico*, Papers of the New World Archaeological Foundation (Orinda, Calif.).
1960   *Archaeological Exploration of the Frailesca, Chiapas, Mexico*, Papers of the New World Archaeological Foundation, no. 7 (Orinda, Calif.).
1969a   "Los relieves Olmecas de Pijijiapan, Chiapas," *Anales de Antropología* 6:183–95.
1969b   *Evidencias de la lengua Quiche en el Soconusco*, Boletín Escritura Maya, no. 11 (Mexico: Seminario de Cultura Maya).
1973   "El sistema prehispánico de comunicaciones entre Chiapas y Tabasco," *Anales de Antropología* 10:33–92.
1974a   *The Olmec Rock Carvings at Pijijiapan, Chiapas, and Some Olmec Objects from Chiapas and Guatemala*, Papers of the New World Archaeological Foundation, no. 35 (Provo, U.: Brigham Young University Press).
1974b   "Tradiciones esculturales en la Costa Pacífico de Chiapas," paper presented at the Forty-First International Congress of Americanists, Mexico City.

References

NELSON, FRED W., JR.

1973   *Archaeological Investigations at Dzibilnocac, Campeche, Mexico,* Papers of the New World Archaeological Foundation, no. 33 (Provo, U.: Brigham Young University).

NETTING, ROBERT McC.

1965   "Household Organization and Intensive Agriculture: the Kofyar Case," *Africa* 35:422–29.

1969   "Ecosystems in Process: A Comparative Study of Change in Two West African Societies," in *Ecological Essays,* ed. D. Damas, National Museum of Canada Bulletin no. 230.

1972   "Sacred Power and Centralization: Aspects of Political Adaptation in Africa," in *Population Growth: Anthropological Implications,* ed. B. Spooner (Cambridge, Mass.: M.I.T. Press).

1974   "Agrarian Ecology," in *Annual Reviews in Anthropology,* ed. B. Siegel (Palo Alto: Annual Reviews).

NORMAN, V. GARTH

1973   *Izapa Sculpture; Part 1, Album,* Papers of the New World Archaeological Foundation, no. 30 (Provo, U.: Brigham Young University Press).

in press   *Izapa Sculpture; Part 2, Text,* Papers of the New World Archaeological Foundation no. 30 (Provo, U.: Brigham Young University).

OTTENBERG, SIMON

1958   "Ibo Oracles and Intergroup Relations," *Southwestern Journal of Anthropology* 14:295–317.

OYENUGA, V. A.

1959   *Nigeria's Feeding-Stuffs* (Ibadan: Ibadan University Press).

1967   *Agriculture in Nigeria: An Introduction* (Rome: Food and Agriculture Organization of the United Nations).

PADDEN, R.

1967   *The Hummingbird and the Hawk* (New York: Harper and Row).

PADDOCK, J.

1966   *Ancient Oaxaca,* part 2 (Stanford: Stanford University Press).

PAILLES, MARÍA DE LA CRUZ

1974   "Informe preliminar de Pajón, un sitio del preclásico Medio-inferior en la Costa de Chiapas," paper presented at the Forty-First International Congress of Americanists, Mexico City.

1976   "Pampa El Pajón, un Sitio del Preclásico Temprano-medio en la Costa de Chiapas, México," master's thesis, Escuela Nacional de Antropología e Historia.

PARSONS, L. A.

1967   "An Early Maya Stela on the Pacific Coast of Guatemala," *Estudios de Cultura Maya* 6:171–98.

1969   *Bilbao, Guatemala,* vol. 2, Milwaukee Public Museum Publications in Anthropology, no. 12.

1972   "Iconographic Notes on a New Izapan Stela From Abaj Takalik,

Guatemala," in *Atti del XL Congresso Internazionale degli Americanisti,* (Rome and Genoa).

PARSONS, LEE A., AND BARBARA J. PRICE
1971   "Mesoamerican Trade and Its Role in the Emergence of Civilization," in *Observations on the Emergence of Civilization in Mesoamerica,* ed. R. F. Heizer and J. A. Graham, Contributions of the University of California Archaeological Research Facility, no. 11 (Berkeley).

PENDERGAST, D. M.
1971   "Evidence of Early Teotihuacan–Lowland Maya Contact at Altun Ha," *American Antiquity* 36:455–60.

PENICHE RIVERO, PIEDAD
1973   "Comalcalco, Tabasco: su cerámica, artefactos y enterramientos," M.A. thesis, Universidad de Yucatan (Merida).

PETERSON, FREDRICK A.
1963   *Some Ceramics from Mirador, Chiapas, Mexico,* Papers of the New World Archaeological Foundation, no. 15 (Provo, U.: Brigham Young University Press).

PIGGOTT, STUART
1965   *Ancient Europe* (Chicago: Aldine Publishing Co.).

PIJOAN AND SOTERAS, J.
1946   "Arte pre-colombino: Mexicano y Maya," in *Summa Artis, Historia General del Arte,* vol. 10 (Madrid).

PIÑA CHAN, ROMAN, AND CARLOS NAVARRETE
1967   *Archaeological Research in the Lower Grijalva River Region, Tabasco and Chiapas,* Papers of the New World Archaeological Foundation, no. 22 (Provo, U.: Brigham Young University Press).

PLOG, FRED
1973   "Laws, Systems of Law, and the Explanation of Observed Variation," in *The Explanation of Culture Change: Models in Prehistory,* ed. Colin Renfrew (Pittsburgh: University of Pittsburgh Press).

POLLOCK, H. E. D., RALPH L. ROYS, T. PROSKOURIAKOFF, AND A. LEDYARD SMITH
1962   *Mayapan, Yucatan, Mexico,* Carnegie Institution of Washington Publication 619 (Washington, D.C.).

PORTER, MURIEL NOË
1953   *Tlatilco and the Preclassic Cultures of the New World,* Viking Fund Publications in Anthropology, no. 19 (New York: Wenner-Gren Foundation).

POTTER, DAVID F.
1973   "Maya Architectural Style in Central Yucatan," Ph.D. dissertation, Tulane University (New Orleans).

PRING, D. C.
1974   *Type Descriptions of the Freshwater Floral Park Ceramic Complex in*

Northern Belize (Cambridge: Cambridge University, Centre of Latin American Studies).

PROSKOURIAKOFF, TATIANA

1950   *A Study of Classic Maya Sculpture,* Carnegie Institution of Washington Publication 593 (Washington, D.C.).

1951   "Some Nonclassic Traits in the Sculpture of Yucatan," in *Selected Papers of the Twenty-Ninth International Congress of Americanists,* vol. 1, (Chicago: University of Chicago Press).

1961   "The Lords of the Maya Realm," *Expedition* 4:14–21.

1962   "The Artifacts of Mayapan," in *Mayapan, Yucatan, Mexico,* Carnegie Institution of Washington Publication 619. (Washington, D.C.).

1963–64 "Historical Data in the Inscriptions of Yaxchilan," parts 1 and 2, *Estudios Cultura Maya,* vols. 3 and 4 (Mexico City: Universidad Nacional de México).

1968   "Olmec and Maya Art: Problems of Their Stylistic Relation," in *Dumbarton Oaks Conference on the Olmec,* ed. Elizabeth P. Benson (Washington, D.C.: Dumbarton Oaks).

1974   *Jades from the Cenote of Sacrifice, Chichen Itza, Yucatan,* Memoirs of the Peabody Museum, vol. 10., no. 1 (Cambridge, Mass.: Harvard University).

PROTHERO, R. M.

1972   "Toward a Model of Population-Land Relationships," in *People and Land in Africa South of the Sahara,* ed. R. M. Prothero (New York: Oxford University Press).

PULESTON, DENNIS E.

1968   "Brosimum Alicastrum as a Subsistence Alternative for the Classic Maya of the Central Southern Lowlands," M.A. thesis, University of Pennsylvania.

1974   "Early Man in the Maya Lowlands?" paper presented at the Thirty-Ninth Annual Meeting of the Society for American Archaeology, Washington, D.C.

PULESTON, DENNIS E., AND DONALD W. CALLENDER, JR.

1967   "Defensive Earthworks at Tikal," *Expedition* 9:40–48.

PULESTON, DENNIS E., AND OLGA S. PULESTON

1971   "An Ecological Approach to the Origins of Maya Civilization," *Archaeology* 24:330–37.

PULESTON, OLGA S., AND DENNIS E. PULESTON

1974   "A Processual Model for the Rise of Classic Maya Civilization in the Southern Lowlands," in *Atti del XL Congresso Internazionale degli Americanisti,* vol. 2 (Rome and Genoa).

QUIRARTE, JACINTO

1973a   *Izapan-Style Art: A Study of Its Form and Meaning,* Studies in Pre-Columbian Art and Archaeology, no. 10 (Washington, D.C.: Dumbarton Oaks).

1973b   *El estilo artistico de Izapa: estudio de su forma y significado,* Instituto de Investigaciones Estéticas Cuadernos de História del Arte, no. 3, (Mexico City: Universidad Nacional Autónoma de México).

1973c   "Izapan Style Antecedents for the Maya Serpent in Celestial Dragon and Serpent Bar Contexts," paper presented at the Twenty-Third International Congress of the History of Art, Granada.

1973d   "The Representation of Earth and Sky in Izapan Style and Early Classic Maya Art," paper presented at the Meeting of the Mid-America College Art Association, Albuquerque.

1973e   "Izapan and Mayan Traits in Teotihuacan III Pottery," in *Contributions of the University of California Archaeological Research Facility,* no. 18 (Berkeley).

1974   "Terrestrial/Celestial Polymorphs as Narrative Frames in the Art of Izapa and Palenque," in *Primera Mesa Redonda de Palenque,* part 1, ed. Merle Greene Robertson (Pebble Beach, Calif.: Robert Louis Stevenson School).

1976   "The Relationship of Izapan Style Art to Olmec and Maya Art: A Review," in *Origins of Religious Art and Iconography in Preclassic Mesoamerica,* ed. H. B. Nicholson (Los Angeles: UCLA Latin American Center).

RANDS, ROBERT L.

1969   *Mayan Ecology and Trade: 1967–1968,* Mesoamerican Studies (Carbondale: Southern Illinois University Museum).

1973a   "The Classic Collapse in the Southern Maya Lowlands: Chronology," in *The Classic Maya Collapse,* ed. T. P. Culbert (Albuquerque: University of New Mexico Press, School of American Research Advanced Seminar Series).

1973b   "The Classic Maya Collapse: Usumacinta Zone and the Northwestern Periphery," in *The Classic Maya Collapse,* ed. T. P. Culbert (Albuquerque: University of New Mexico Press, School of American Research Advanced Seminar Series).

1974   "Notes on the Ceramic Sequence at Palenque, Chiapas," in *Mesoamerican Archaeology: New Approaches,* ed. Norman Hammond (London: Duckworth and Co.).

RANDS, ROBERT L., AND BARBARA C. RANDS

1957   "The Ceramic Position of Palenque, Chiapas," *American Antiquity* 23:140–50.

1965   "Pottery Figurines of the Maya Lowlands," in *Archaeology of Southern Mesoamerica, Handbook of Middle American Indians,* vol. 2, ed. Robert Wauchope and Gordon R. Willey (Austin: University of Texas Press).

RANDS, ROBERT L., AND ROBERT E. SMITH

1965   "Pottery of the Guatemalan Highlands," in *Archaeology of Southern Mesoamerica, Handbook of Middle American Indians,* vol. 2, ed. Robert Wauchope and Gordon R. Willey (Austin: University of Texas Press).

RATHJE, WILLIAM L.

1970   "Socio-Political Implications of Lowland Maya Burials," *World Archaeology* 1:359–74.

1971   "The Origins and Development of Lowland Classic Maya Civilization," *American Antiquity* 36:275–85.

1972   "Praise the Gods and Pass the Metates: A Hypothesis of the Development of

Lowland Rainforest Civilizations in Middle America," in *Contemporary Archaeology,* ed. M. P. Leone (Carbondale: Southern Illinois University Press).

1973   "Classic Maya Development and Denouement: A Research Design," in *The Classic Maya Collapse,* ed. T. P. Culbert (Albuquerque: University of New Mexico Press, School of American Research Advanced Seminar Series).

1975   "Last Tango in Mayapan: A Tentative Trajectory of Production-Distribution Systems," in *Ancient Civilization and Trade,* ed. Jeremy A. Sabloff and C. C. Lamberg-Karlovsky (Albuquerque: University of New Mexico Press, School of American Research Advanced Seminar Series).

REED, N.
1964   *The Caste War of Yucatan* (Stanford: Stanford University Press).

REICHEL-DOLMATOFF, GIRARD
1975   *The Shaman and the Jaguar: A Study of Narcotic Drugs among Colombian Indians* (Philadelphia: Temple University Press).

REINA, RUBEN E.
1967   "Milpas and Milperos: Implications for Prehistoric Times," *American Anthropologist* 69:1–20.

RENFREW, A. C.
1969   "Trade and Culture Process in European Prehistory," *Current Anthropology* 10:151–69.

RICE, D.
1976   "The Historical Ecology of Lakes Yazha and Sacnab, El Peten, Guatemala," Ph.D. dissertation, Pennsylvania State University (University Park).

RICKETSON, O. G., JR., AND E. B. RICKETSON
1937   *Uaxactun, Guatemala Group E—1926–1931,* Carnegie Institution of Washington Publication 477 (Washington, D.C.).

ROVNER, IRWIN
1974   "Implications of the Lithic Analysis at Becan," in *Preliminary Reports on Archaeological Investigations in the Rio Bec Area, Campeche, Mexico,* comp. R. E. W. Adams, Middle American Research Institute Publication 31 (New Orleans: Tulane University).

ROWE, J. H.
1960   "Cultural Unity and Diversification in Peruvian Archaeology," in *Men and Cultures,* ed. A. F. C. Wallace, Selected Papers of the Fifth International Congress of Anthropological Sciences (Philadelphia: University of Pennsylvania Press).

ROYS, RALPH L.
1943   *The Indian Background of Colonial Yucatan,* Carnegie Institution of Washington Publication 548 (Washington, D.C.).

1957   *The Political Geography of the Yucatan Maya,* Carnegie Institution of Washington Publication 613 (Washington, D.C.).

RUPPERT, KARL, AND J. H. DENISON
1943   *Archaeological Reconnaissance in Campeche, Quintana Roo, and Peten,* Carnegie Institution of Washington Publication 543 (Washington, D.C.).

RUZ LHUILLIER, ALBERTO

1943 "Exploraciones arqueológicas en Palenque: 1957." *Anales del Instituto Nacional de Antropolgía e Historia* 14:35–90.

1973 *El templo de las inscripciones, Palenque,* Instituto Nacional de Antropología e Historia, Colección Científica, Arqueologia, no. 7.

SABLOFF, JEREMY A.

1973 "Continuity and Disruption during Terminal Late Classic Times at Seibal: Ceramic and Other Evidence," in *The Classic Maya Collapse,* ed. T. P. Culbert (Albuquerque: University of New Mexico Press, School of American Research Advanced Seminar Series).

1975 *Excavations at Seibal: Ceramics,* Memoirs of the Peabody Museum of Archaeology and Ethnology, vol. 13, no. 2 (Cambridge, Mass.: Harvard University).

SABLOFF, JEREMY A., AND GORDON R. WILLEY

1967 "The Collapse of Maya Civilization in the Southern Lowlands: A Consideration of History and Process," *Southwestern Journal of Anthropology* 23:311–36.

SAHLINS, MARSHALL D.

1961 "The Segmentary Lineage: An Organization of Predatory Expansion," *American Anthropologist* 63:322–45.

1963 "Poor Man, Rich Man, Big-Man, Chief: Political Types in Melanesia and Polynesia," *Comparative Studies in Society and History* 5:285–303.

1968 *Tribesmen* (Englewood Cliffs, N.J.: Prentice-Hall).

SANDERS, WILLIAM T.

1961 *Ceramic Stratigraphy at Santa Cruz, Chiapas, Mexico,* Papers of the New World Archaeological Foundation no. 13 (Provo, U.: Brigham Young University).

1972 "Population, Agricultural History, and Societal Evolution in Mesoamerica," in *Population Growth: Anthropological Implications,* ed. B. Spooner (Cambridge, Mass.: M.I.T. Press).

1973 "The Cultural Ecology of the Lowland Maya: A Reevaluation," in *The Classic Maya Collapse,* ed. T. P. Culbert (Albuquerque: University of New Mexico Press, School of American Research Advanced Seminar Series).

SANDERS, WILLIAM T., AND BARBARA J. PRICE

1968 *Mesoamerica: The Evolution of a Civilization* (New York: Random House).

SATTERTHWAITE, LINTON

1941 "Some Central Peten Maya Architectural Traits at Piedras Negras," in *Los Mayas Antiquos* (Mexico).

SAUER, CARL

1958 "Man in the Ecology of Tropical America," *Proceedings of the Ninth Pacific Science Congress, 1957,* 20:105–10.

SCHELE, LINDA

n.d. "The Attribution of Monumental Architecture to Specific Rulers at Palenque," Forty-First International Congress of Americanists, Mexico City, 1974 (in press).

References

SCHOLES, FRANCE V., AND RALPH L. ROYS

1968   *The Maya Chontal Indians of Acalan-Tixchel,* 2d ed. (Norman: University of Oklahoma Press).

SEDAT, DAVID W., AND ROBERT J. SHARER

1972   "Archaeological Investigations in the Northern Maya Highlands: New Data on the Maya Preclassic," in *Studies in the Archaeology of Mexico and Guatemala,* ed. John A. Graham, Contributions of the University of California Archaeological Research Facility, no. 16 (Berkeley).

1973   "Preclassic Populations and Writing Systems in the Salama Valley, Guatemala," paper presented at the Seventy-Second Annual Meeting of the American Anthropological Association, New Orleans.

SERVICE, ELMAN R.

1955   "Indo-European Relations in Colonial Latin América," *American Anthropologist* 57:411–25.

1960   "The Law of Evolutionary Potential," in *Evolution and Culture,* ed. Marshall D. Sahlins and Elman R. Service (Ann Arbor: University of Michigan Press).

1962   *Primitive Social Organization* (New York: Random House).

1967   "War and Our Contemporary Ancestors," in *War: The Anthropology of Armed Conflict and Aggression,* ed. M. Fried et al. (New York: Natural History Press).

1970   *Cultural Evolution: Theory in Practice* (New York: Holt, Rinehart and Winston).

SHARER, ROBERT J.

1974   "The Prehistory of the Southeastern Maya Periphery," *Current Anthropology* 15:165–87.

SHARER, ROBERT J., AND JAMES C. GIFFORD

1970   "Preclassic Ceramics from Chalchuapa, El Salvador, and Their Relationships with the Maya Lowlands," *American Antiquity* 35:441–62.

SHARER, ROBERT J., AND DAVID W. SEDAT

1973   "Monument 1, El Porton, Guatemala, and the Development of Maya Calendrical and Writing Systems," in *Contributions of the University of California Archaeological Research Facility,* no. 18 (Berkeley).

SHAW, THURSTON

1970   *Igbo-Ukwu* (Evanston: Northwestern University Press).

SHEETS, P. D.

1971   "An Ancient Natural Disaster," *Expedition* 14:25–31.

SHIMKIN, DEMITRI B.

1973   "Models for the Downfall: Some Ecological and Culture-Historical Considerations," in *The Classic Maya Collapse,* ed. T. P. Culbert (Albuquerque: University of New Mexico Press, School of American Research Advanced Seminar Series).

SHOOK, EDWIN M.

1940   "Exploration in the Ruins of Oxkintok, Yucatan," *Revista Mexicana de Estudios Antropológicos* 4:165–71.

1955   "Yucatan and Chiapas," in *Carnegie Institution of Washington Year Book 54,* (Washington, D.C.).

1958   *Field Director's Report: The 1956 and 1957 Seasons,* Tikal Reports no. 1, Museum Monographs (Philadelphia: University of Pennsylvania, the University Museum).

1960   "Tikal Stela 29," *Expedition* 2:28–35.

SHOOK, EDWIN M., AND R. E. SMITH

1950   "Descubrimientos arqueológicos en Poptún," *Antropología e Historia de Guatemala* 2:3–15.

SIEMENS, A. H., AND D. E. PULESTON

1972   "Ridged Fields and Associated Features in Southern Campeche: New Perspectives on the Lowland Maya," *American Antiquity* 37:228–39.

SIMMONS, C., S. TARANO, AND J. PINTO

1959   *Clasificación de reconocimiento de los suelos de la república de Guatemala,* (Guatemala: Ministerio de Agricultura, Instituto Agro-Pecuaria).

SISSON, EDWARD B.

1970   "Settlement Patterns and Land Use in the Northwestern Chontalpa, Tabasco, Mexico: A Progress Report," *Cerámica de Cultura Maya,* no. 6, pp. 41–54.

SIVERTS, HENNING

1971   "On Politics and Leadership in Highland Chiapas," in *Desarrollo cultural de los Mayas,* ed. Evon Z. Vogt and Alberto Ruz Lhuillier (Mexico City: Universidad Nacional Autónoma de México).

SMITH, A. L.

1950   *Uaxactun, Guatemala: Excavations of 1931–1937,* Carnegie Institution of Washington Publication 588 (Washington, D.C.).

1972   *Excavations at Altar de Sacrificios: Architecture, Settlement, Burials, and Caches,* Papers of the Peabody Museum of Archaeology and Ethnography, vol. 62, no. 2 (Cambridge, Mass.: Harvard University).

SMITH, A. L., AND G. R. WILLEY

1969   "Seibal, Guatemala in 1968: A Brief Summary of Archaeological Results," *Thirty-Eighth International Congress of Americanists* 1:151–59 (Stuttgart-Munich).

SMITH, ROBERT E.

1955   *Ceramic Sequence at Uaxactun, Guatemala,* 2 vols., Middle American Research Institute Publication 20 (New Orleans: Tulane University).

1971   *The Pottery of Mayapan,* Papers of the Peabody Museum of Archaeology and Ethnology, vol. 66 (Cambridge, Mass.: Harvard University).

SMITH, ROBERT E., AND JAMES C. GIFFORD

1965   "Pottery of the Maya Lowlands," *Archaeology of Southern Mesoamerica, Handbook of Middle American Indians,* vol. 2., ed. Robert Wauchope and Gordon R. Willey (Austin: University of Texas Press).

SMITH, T.

1963   "The Main Themes of the 'Olmec' Art Tradition," *Kroeber Anthropological Society,* no. 28, pp. 121–213.

References

SPENCER, J. E.

1966   *Shifting Cultivation in Southwestern Asia,* University of California Publications in Geography, vol. 19 (Berkeley and Los Angeles: University of California Press).

STEGGERDA, M.

1941   *Maya Indians of Yucatan,* Carnegie Institution of Washington Publication 531 (Washington, D.C.).

STEVENS, R. L.

1964   "The Soils of Middle America and their Relation to Indian Peoples and Cultures," in *Natural Environment and Early Cultures, Handbook of Middle American Indians,* vol. 1, ed. Robert C. West (Austin: University of Texas Press).

STEWARD, JULIAN

1955   *Theory of Culture Change* (Urbana: University of Illinois Press).

STIRLING, M.

1943   *Stone Monuments of Southern Mexico,* Smithsonian Institution Bureau of American Ethnology Bulletin 138 (Washington, D.C.).

1957   "An Archaeological Reconnaissance in Southeastern Mexico," in *Smithsonian Institution Bureau of American Ethnology Bulletin 164* (Washington, D.C.).

1965   "Monumental Sculpture of Southern Veracruz and Tabasco," in *Handbook of Middle American Indians,* vol. 3, ed. Robert Wauchope and Gordon R. Willey (Austin: University of Texas Press).

SWADESH, MORRIS

1960   "Interrelaciones de las lenguas mayas," *Anales del Instituto Nacional de Antropología e Historia,* no. 11, pp. 231–67.

1969   "Lexicostatistic Classification," *Linguistics, Handbook of Middle American Indians,* vol. 5, ed. Norman McQuown (Austin: University of Texas Press).

THOMAS, NORMAN D.

1974   *The Linguistic, Geographic, and Demographic Position of the Zoque of Southern Mexico,* Papers of the New World Archaeological Foundation, no. 36 (Provo, U.: Brigham Young University).

THOMAS, PRENTICE M., JR.

1974   "Prehistoric Settlement at Becan: A Preliminary Report," in *Middle American Research Institute Publication 31* (New Orleans: Tulane University).

THOMPSON, J. ERIC S.

1931   *Archaeological Investigations in the Southern Cayo District, British Honduras,* Field Museum of Natural History Anthropological Series, vol. 17, no. 3

1943   "A Trial Survey of the Southern Maya Area," *American Antiquity* 9:106–34.

1945   "A Survey of the Northern Maya Area," *American Antiquity* 11:2–24,

1950   *Maya Hieroglyphic Writing,* 2d ed., Carnegie Institution of Washington Publication 589 (Norman: University of Oklahoma Press).

451

1954   *The Rise and Fall of Maya Civilization* (Norman: University of Oklahoma Press).

1962   *A Catalogue of Maya Hieroglyphics* (Norman: University of Oklahoma Press).

1966   *The Rise and Fall of Maya Civilization,* 2d ed. (Norman: University of Oklahoma Press).

1970   *Maya History and Religion* (Norman: University of Oklahoma Press).

1971   "Estimates of Maya Population: Deranging Factors," *American Antiquity* 36:214–16.

1973a   "Maya Rulers of the Classic Period and the Divine Right of Kings," in *The Iconography of Middle American Sculpture,* ed. Ignacio Bernal (New York: Metropolitan Museum of Art).

1973b   "The Maya Glyph for Capture or Conquest and an Iconographic Representation of Itzam Na on Yucatecan Facades," in *Contributions of the University of California Archaeological Research Facility,* no. 18 (Berkeley).

1974   " 'Canals' of the Rio Candelaria Basin, Campeche, Mexico," in *Mesoamerican Archaeology: New Approaches,* ed. Norman Hammond (London: Duckworth and Co.; Austin: University of Texas Press).

TOLSTOY, PAUL, AND LOUISE I. PARADIS
1970   "Early and Middle Preclassic Culture in the Basin of Mexico," *Science* 167:344–51.

TOURTELLOT, GAIR
1970   "The Peripheries of Seibal: An Interim Report," in *Monographs and Papers in Maya Archaeology,* ed. William R. Bullard, Papers of the Peabody Museum of Archaeology and Ethnology, vol. 61 (Cambridge, Mass.: Harvard University).

TOWNSEND, W. H.
1969   "Stone and Steel Tool Use in a New Guinea Society," *Ethnology* 8:199–205.

TOZZER, ALFRED M.
1941   *Landa's Relación de las Cosas de Yucatán,* Papers of the Peabody Museum
(ed.)   of Archaeology and Ethnology, vol. 18 (Cambridge, Mass.: Harvard University).

1957   *Chichen Itza and Its Cenote of Sacrifice: A Comparative Study of Contemporaneous Maya and Toltec,* Memoirs of the Peabody Museum of Archaeology and Ethnology, vols. 11 and 12 (Cambridge, Mass.: Harvard University).

TREAT, RAYMOND C.
1974   "Submound Domestic Refuse Deposits at Vistahermosa, Chiapas," paper presented at the Forty-First International Congress of Americanists, Mexico City.

TRIGGER, B. G.
1974   "The Archaeology of Government," *World Archaeology* 6:95–106.

References

TURNER, B. L., II
1974   "Prehistoric Intensive Agriculture in the Maya Lowlands," *Science* 185:118–24.

UDO, R. K.
1964   "The Migrant Tenant Farmer of Eastern Nigeria," *Africa* 34:326–39.
1965   "Disintegration of Nucleated Settlement in East Nigeria," *Geographic Review* 55:53–67.

VANCE, J.
1971   *The Merchants' World* (Englewood Cliffs, N.J.: Prentice-Hall).

VAYDA, ANDREW P.
1961   "Expansion and Warfare among Swidden Agriculturists," *American Anthropologist* 63:346–58.

VITA-FINZI, C., AND E. S. HIGGS
1970   "Prehistory Economy in the Mount Carmel Area of Palestine: Site Catchment Analysis," *Proceedings of the Prehistoric Society* 36:1–37.

VIVO ESCOTO, JORGE A.
1949   *Geografía de México* (Mexico: Fondo de Cultura Economica).
1964   "Weather and Climate of Mexico and Central America," *Natural Environment and Early Cultures, Handbook of Middle American Indians,* vol. 1, ed. R. C. West (Austin: University of Texas Press).

VOGELER, I.
n.d.   "Frontier Settlements in Southeastern Campeche," mimeographed, University of Minnesota (Minneapolis).

VOGT, EVON Z.
1963   "Some Implications of Zinacantan Social Structure for the Study of the Ancient Maya," *XXXV Congresso Internacional de Americanistas: Actas Y Memorias,* 1:307–19 (Mexico City).
1969   "The Maya: Introduction," in *Ethnology, Handbook of Middle American Indians,* vol. 7, ed. Evon Z. Vogt (Austin: University of Texas Press).
1971   "Summary and Appraisal," in *Desarrollo Cultural de los Mayas,* ed. Evon Z. Vogt and Alberto Ruz Lhuillier (Mexico City: Universidad Nacional Autónoma de México).

VOORHIES, BARBARA
1974   "Paleoecology of Early Coastal Settlements, Chiapas, Mexico," paper presented at the Forty-First International Congress of Americanists, Mexico City.
1976   *The Chantuto People: An Archaic Society of the Chiapas Littoral, Mexico,* Papers of the New World Archaeological Foundation, no. 41 (Provo, U.: Brigham Young University).

WAGNER, PHILIP L.
1958   "Nicoya: A Cultural Geography," *University of California Publications in Geography* 12:195–250.
1964   "Natural Vegetation of Middle America," in *Natural Environment and Early Cultures, Handbook of Middle American Indians,* vol. 1, ed. R. C. West (Austin: University of Texas Press).

WALLACE, J. W.
1941   "Agriculture in Abakaliki and Afikpo," *Farm and Forest* 2:89–93.

WEBB, MALCOLM C.
1973   "The Peten Maya Decline Viewed in the Perspective of State Formation," in *The Classic Maya Collapse*, ed. T. P. Culbert (Albuquerque: University of New Mexico Press, School of American Research Advanced Seminar Series).

WEBSTER, DAVID L.
1972   "The Fortifications of Becan, Campeche, Mexico," Ph.D. dissertation University of Minnesota (Minneapolis).

1974   "The Fortifications of Becan, Campeche, Mexico," in *Middle American Research Institute Publication 31* (New Orleans: Tulane University).

1975   "Warfare and the Origin of the State: A Reconsideration," *American Antiquity* 40:464–70.

in press "On Theocracias," *American Anthropologist*.

WEST, R. C.
1948   *Cultural Geography of the Modern Taracan Area,* Smithsonian Institution Institute of Social Anthropology Publication no. 7 (Washington, D.C.).

WETHERINGTON, RONALD K.
1974   "Comments on 'The Prehistory of the Southeastern Maya Periphery' by Robert J. Sharer," *Current Anthropology* 15:165–87.

WILKEN, GENE C.
1971   "Food-Producing Systems Available to the Ancient Maya," *American Antiquity* 36:432–48.

WILKERSON, S. JEFFREY K.
1973   "An Archaeological Sequence from Santa Luisa, Veracruz, Mexico," in *Contributions of the University of California Archaeological Research Facility,* no. 18 (Berkeley).

WILKINSON, P. F.
1974   "The Relevance of Musk Ox Exploitation to the Study of Prehistoric Animal Economics," in *Palaeoeconomy,* ed. E. S. Higgs (London and New York: Cambridge University Press).

WILLEY, GORDON R.
1962   "The Early Great Styles and the Rise of the Pre-Columbian Civilizations," *American Anthropologist* 64:1–14.

1970   "The Real Xe Ceramics of Seibal, Peten, Guatemala," in *Monographs and Papers in Maya Archaeology,* ed. William R. Bullard, Papers of the Peabody Museum of Archaeology and Ethnology, vol. 61 (Cambridge, Mass.: Harvard University).

1971a   "Commentary on 'The Emergence of Civilization in the Maya Lowlands' in *Observations on the Emergence of Civilization in Mesoamerica,* ed. R. F. Heizer and J. A. Graham," in *Contributions of the University of California Archaeological Research Facility,* no. 11 (Berkeley).

1971b   "An Archaeological Frame of Reference for Maya Culture History," in

Desarrollo cultural de los Mayas, ed. Evon Z. Vogt and Alberto Ruz Lhuillier (Mexico City: Universidad Nacional Autónoma de México).

1972   *The Artifacts of Altar de Sacrificios,* Papers of the Peabody Museum of Archaeology and Ethnology, vol. 64 (Cambridge, Mass.: Harvard University).

1973   *The Altar de Sacrificios Excavations: General Summary and Conclusions,* Papers of the Peabody Museum of Archaeology and Ethnology, vol. 64, no. 3 (Cambridge, Mass.: Harvard University).

1974   "The Classic Maya Hiatus: A 'Rehearsal' for the Collapse?" in *Mesoamerican Archaeology: New Approaches,* ed. Norman Hammond (London: Duckworth and Co.).

WILLEY, GORDON R., WILLIAM R. BULLARD, JR., JOHN B. GLASS, AND JAMES C. GIFFORD

1965   *Prehistoric Maya Settlement Patterns in the Belize Valley,* Papers of the Peabody Museum of Archaeology and Ethnology, vol. 54 (Cambridge, Mass.: Harvard University).

WILLEY, GORDON R., T. PATRICK CULBERT, AND RICHARD E. W. ADAMS

1967   "Maya Lowland Ceramics: A Report from the 1965 Guatemala City Conference," *American Antiquity* 32:289–315.

WILLEY, GORDON R., AND JAMES C. GIFFORD

1961   "Pottery of the Holmul I Style from Barton Ramie, British Honduras," in *Essays in Pre-Columbian Art and Archaeology,* ed. S. K. Lothrop et al. (Cambridge, Mass.: Harvard University Press).

WILLEY, GORDON R., AND PHILLIP PHILLIPS

1958   *Method and Theory in American Archaeology* (Chicago: University of Chicago Press).

WILLEY, GORDON R., AND DEMITRI B. SHIMKIN

1973   "The Maya Collapse: A Summary View," in *The Classic Maya Collapse,* ed. T. P. Culbert (Albuquerque: University of New Mexico Press, School of American Research Advanced Seminar Series).

WILLEY, GORDON R., AND A. L. SMITH

1963   "New Discoveries at Altar de Sacrificios, Guatemala," *Archaeology* 16:83–89.

1967   "A Temple at Seibal, Guatemala," *Archaeology* 20:290–98.

1969   *The Ruins of Altar de Sacrificios, Department of Peten, Guatemala, An Introduction,* Papers of the Peabody Museum of Archaeology and Ethnology, vol. 62, no. 1 (Cambridge, Mass.: Harvard University).

WILLEY, GORDON R., A. L. SMITH, GAIR TOURTELLOT III, AND IAN GRAHAM

1965   *Excavations at Seibal: Introduction. The Site and Its Setting,* Memoirs of the Peabody Museum of Archaeology and Ethnography, vol. 13, no. 1 (Cambridge, Mass.: Harvard University).

WILLEY, GORDON R., A. L. SMITH, GAIR TOURTELLOT III, AND J. A. SABLOFF

1968   "Seibal 1968: Fifth and Terminal Preliminary Report," mimeographed,

Peabody Museum of Archaeology and Ethnology. (Cambridge, Mass.: Harvard University).

WINTER, MARCUS C.

1972   "Tierras Largas: A Formative Community in the Valley of Oaxaca, Mexico," Ph.D. dissertation, University of Arizona (Tucson).

WISDOM, CHARLES

1940   *The Chorti Indians of Guatemala* (Chicago: University of Chicago Press).

WISEMAN, F. M.

1975   "The Earliest Maya," paper presented at the Fortieth Annual Meeting of the Society for American Archaeology, Dallas.

WITTFOGEL, KARL

1957   *Oriental Despotism: A Comparative Study of Total Power* (New Haven: Yale University Press).

WOODBURY, RICHARD B., AND AUBREY S. TRIK

1953   *The Ruins of Zaculeu, Guatemala* (New York: United Fruit Co.).

WRIGHT, A. C. S., D. H. ROMNEY, R. H. ARBUCKLE, AND V. E. VIAL

1959   *Land in British Honduras,* Colonial Research Publication 23 (London: Her Majesty's Stationery Office).

Index

Index

Index